Lifetime Guide to
BUSINESS WRITING & SPEAKING

JACK GRIFFIN

Author of HOW TO SAY IT BEST

PRENTICE HALL
Englewood Cliffs, New Jersey 07632

Library of Congress Cataloging-in-Publication Data

Griffin, Jack.
    Lifetime guide to business writing and speaking / by Jack Griffin.
          p. cm.
       Includes index
       ISBN 0-13-311606-9 (case)
       1. Business communication. 2. Business writing. I. Title.
    HF5718.G75 1996   96-11434
    808'.06665—dc20   CIP

Printed in the United States of America

10 9 8 7 6 5 4 3 2 1

ISBN 0-13-311606-9

ATTENTION: CORPORATIONS AND SCHOOLS

Prentice Hall books are available at quantity discounts with bulk purchase for educational, business, or sales promotional use. For information, please write to: Prentice Hall Career & Personal Development Special Sales, 113 Sylvan Avenue, Englewood Cliffs, NJ 07632. Please supply: title of book, ISBN number, quantity, how the book will be used, date needed.

PRENTICE HALL
Career & Personal Development
Englewood Cliffs, NJ 07632
A Simon & Schuster Company

On the World Wide Web at http://www.phdirect.com

Prentice-Hall International (UK) Limited, *London*
Prentice-Hall of Australia Pty. Limited, *Sydney*
Prentice-Hall Canada Inc., *Toronto*
Prentice-Hall Hispanoamericana, S.A., *Mexico*
Prentice-Hall of India Private Limited, *New Delhi*
Prentice-Hall of Japan, Inc., *Tokyo*
Simon & Schuster Asia Pte. Ltd., *Singapore*
Editora Prentice-Hall do Brasil, Ltda., *Rio de Janeiro*

CONTENTS

PART TWO: MEMOS

PART FIVE: TELEPHONE

PART SIX: INTERVIEWS AND CONFERENCES

APPENDICES

Author to Reader:
What the Business
Communicator *Really*
Needs to Know

Let's start with a stupid question. *How is business like an automobile?*

Don't waste your time thinking of an answer. It's *my* stupid question, so I'll give you *my* answer.

Both need fuel to get going and keep going.

A car requires gasoline, but business needs two fuels: revenue—cash, money, capital—of course, but also *information.* In fact, it is information that produces the capital (and capital that makes it possible to produce more information in order to produce yet more capital).

Ask any manager what she most needs to do her job, and she will most likely answer: *information.* "In the industrial age, when the strategic resource was capital, the goal of the corporation could only have been profits," John Naisbitt and Patricia Aburdene say in *Reinventing the Corporation.* "In the information era, however, the strategic resource is information, knowledge, creativity."

But, believe it or not, there is also a down side to information. As often as we're starved for it, we're awash in it, drowned by it, smothered in it, rendered deaf, dumb, and blind by it.

It is not just that business requires information. It requires the *right* information, the *useful* information, intelligently, clearly, and forcefully presented. This is precisely the essence of business communication. And *Lifetime Guide to Business Writing and Speaking* is your guidebook to the essence of that essence. Effective business communication is the art of discovering, selecting, expressing, and conveying the information your associate, colleague, supervisor, subordinate, supplier, customer, or client needs to know. And *Lifetime Guide to Business Writing and Speaking* will tell you what you need to know about the art of business communication.

WHO ARE THE BUSINESS COMMUNICATORS?

Like most fields of endeavor, the world of business has become increasingly specialized. But, whether you are director of customer service, a field representative, an executive secretary, a mailroom intern, or chairman of the board, you need to be an effective business communicator.

You need to:

◆ Respond to a customer complaint

◆ Write a winning proposal

◆ Write a cover letter for a job application

◆ Write a letter of congratulations

◆ Write a letter of reprimand

◆ Write a memo changing a schedule

◆ Write a memo clarifying company policy

◆ Create a new employment application form

◆ Create a customer satisfaction questionnaire

◆ Draw up a bulletproof lease agreement

◆ Make the most of your firm's e-mail network

◆ Get somebody to read all those faxes you send

◆ Generate business with effective "cold calls"

◆ Revive an inactive client with a timely call

◆ Talk to collect on a delinquent account

◆ Speak up to your boss

◆ Hold productive meetings with your staff

◆ Speak to customers with confidence

◆ Knock 'em dead with your sales presentation

◆ Write a good speech for a local community organization

◆ Be part of a press conference

If you are active in the business world, and if your business involves contact with any human being other than yourself, you need to be an effective business communicator.

AND WHAT DO THEY NEED TO KNOW?

I happen to be fascinated by personal computers. I like using them, and I like reading about them. But if I'm in the middle of a job—And aren't we all always in the middle of a job?—and I need to know how to change the default margins for my word processing program, I do not want to read a treatise on computer science. I want to find, quickly and simply, the page in the user's manual that explains, quickly and simply, how to do what I need to do.

Communication is a vast and vastly fascinating subject. But, in the middle of a job, when you've just been asked to deliver a status report on Project X, or you need to prepare a quick consignment agreement incorporating a certain set of very specific conditions, or a business associate has passed away and, though you dread it, you need to make a condolence call to the family, you have neither the time nor the inclination to pore through a series of books on communication theory.

What you need is the business communicator's equivalent of the software user's manual: a practical how-to replete with examples and ready-to-use models.

What does a business communicator need to know? Whatever is necessary to do the job at hand. No more, but no less. As recently as two or three decades ago, a book on business communication would have been largely a book on writing business letters. Letters are still important vehicles for business communication. But, today, those of us in business also find ourselves

- Writing critical and sensitive memos
- Creating special forms and questionnaires
- Using fax machines and e-mail systems
- Living on the telephone
- Interviewing and being interviewed
- Organizing and participating in meetings
- Giving speeches and dealing with the media

Some of these varied activities rely on hard-and-fast rules or, at least, time-tested rules of thumb. This book will supply such essential information in comprehensive abundance. However, effective communication, through whatever channel, usually depends on more than mere rules. It is more often a challenge to the skill and judgment born of experience. And, above all else, this book is the product of such experience, which has been distilled into guidelines, tips, and practical examples, as well as timely warnings to help you avoid communication pitfalls.

Part One

LETTERS

1.1. Nuts and Bolts

1.1.1. How to Look Very Good on Paper

To look very good on paper, begin with very good paper. For most business correspondence, $8^{1}/_{2} \times 11$ ("typewriter paper") stock is standard and will fit perfectly into a "number 9" business envelope. Most office supply stores carry a very wide variety of this size of paper—most of it in the 20 lb weight, which is considered standard for general purpose use. However, 20 lb is too flimsy for business correspondence. Choose 24 lb stock instead. It feels more substantial and folds more neatly.

> TIP: 24 lb paper is also an ideal weight for laser and ink jet printers. Lighter-weight papers are more vulnerable to humidity and may cause paper jams. Heavier papers tend to be rather hard on the printer's paper transportation system.

> REVELATION: Words are mighty important for getting your message across. No surprise there. But the feel of crisp 24 lb paper also communicates an important message. The paper is substantial and, therefore, subtly but surely suggests that the person or company using the paper is also substantial. Further, it suggests that what you have to say is valuable. Last but not least, a letter on substantial stock is more difficult to crumple up into a tight little ball and toss in the circular file. Look, you already know the importance of a firm handshake when you are introduced to a new contact or customer. A letter on crisp, firm stock is the written equivalent of a firm handshake.

Color? Proceed with Caution. If you go to an office supply store to buy your paper, you'll also find a dazzling array of colored stock—pinks, blues, greens, yellows, grays, tans, and variations on off-white. Before you get carried away, think about men's business shirts. The 1960s and 1970s saw a phenomenon called the "peacock revolution." A lot of men balled up their plain white shirts in a corner of the closet and wore a variety of brightly colored and patterned shirts to work. It was perfectly acceptable.

That was then. This is now.

Today, the rule of thumb for shirts is plain white. (If you're feeling especially adventurous, perhaps you'll risk pale blue.) For better or worse, the conservatism that dictates taste in men's business shirts should govern your choice of business paper. Usually, plain white is best.

> TIP: Color often looks best in combination with subtly textured paper stock, especially "laid" paper. (This is stationery traditionally made on wire molds, which give it a characteristic watermark of close, thin lines.) Color used on plain paper is a bit suggestive of an advertisement rather than a professional communication.

Let me put it another way. Unless you have given *special* and *deliberate* thought to a *specific* image you want to convey using color, always choose white. But here's some thoughts on color:

♦ Blue: A pale shade of blue can convey dignity and authority. If you want to veer toward a conservative image, choose a slate blue. More conservative? Go with a very light shade of gray. A warmer, sky blue can be used to convey a spirit of imagination. Beware: brighter blues strike many people as infantile ("Little Boy Blue"). Some folks find darker shades depressing.

♦ Gray: Very pale gray can convey dignity and conservatism. It is always best to use this color on laid paper or paper subtly textured with inlaid fibers. To some people, gray on smooth, plain paper just looks dirty. Also, beware: Some correspondents will find gray a "downer," more suggestive of funerals than the realm of business.

♦ Green: A muted ledger-paper shade of green is not only easy on the eyes, it suggests money. Using such paper might send a useful subliminal message if you are in the business of making or saving money for clients—for example, if you are an investment advisor. However, if you are in the business of coaxing people to spend money—say you are a building contractor—the color green may well work against you, subliminally suggesting to your correspondent that you will cost her a lot of dough. Also be aware that many people find green a relaxing color. Depending on your business, this may be an advantage. However, for many people, "relaxing" all too readily translates into boring.

♦ Pink: Except in very special cases—let's say that you run a beauty parlor or a lady's boutique—pink stationery should be avoided. The same holds true for other pastel shades: lavender, lilac, primrose, mint green, and so on. These may be fine for personal stationery, but they are rarely appropriate for business.

◆ Tan: For better or worse, this tint conveys masculinity. It also tends to look old fashioned, even rustic—earthy. Use this color only if you are very certain that you want to produce such an impression.

◆ Yellow: This is another color that is usually best avoided. Many people name yellow as their least favorite color. It is also associated with more negatives than positives: caution, cowardice, and even disease.

◆ Variations on white: These are the most popular alternatives to white for stationery. Cream or ivory tints convey more warmth and richness than plain white. They work especially well with textured and laid stocks. Make certain that the envelope you choose is an exact match with the sheet. Be aware that the deeper the ivory or cream shade, the more traditional or even old fashioned you are making yourself look. If that's the effect what you want, go with it. Parchment effects are rarely appropriate in business correspondence. Parchment-style paper may be useful for certain kinds of advertising leaflets, but, as stationery stock, parchment suggests phoniness, cheapness, and even childishness ("Hey! Let's play pirate! Here's a treasure map!").

PITFALL: The envelope and the paper should always match. Never put colored paper in a plain white envelope or white paper in a colored one. Who cares? You should, because the person who receives your letter will care. He'll open the blue envelope, pull out a white letter, and a little voice will whisper into his ear: *This fella just can't quite get it together.* A makeshift combination of paper and envelope suggests that you are careless or thoughtless or—here's a word I like—feckless. Why sabotage yourself with a message like this?

Stationery: To Buy or Not to Buy?

Does your business need stationery? I'd rather answer that question by telling you what your business does *not* need. It does not need bad, cheap-looking, vulgar stationery.

Tasteful, somewhat conservative, well-designed, and well-manufactured stationery is an asset to any business. It conveys a sense of pride in your enterprise, as well as an image of permanence and professionalism. It also suggests that you value details. Stationery design varies widely. You might look through office supply and job printer's catalogs to find designs, or you might consider hiring a professional graphic designer to create a custom design. The initial cost for this will be somewhat higher, but you will have much greater control over the results, and the results will be more distinctive.

Letterhead

However you purchase it, your stationery should include the following elements in the letterhead:

1. Company name. This is usually designed as the most distinctive feature of the letterhead. It may be designed as a logotype—that is, with the typeface so distinctive as to look like a corporate logo. The familiar signatures of the Coca-Cola company or the Ford Motor Company are famous logotypes, as is the distinctive "double-x" of Exxon.

2. Optionally, the letterhead may incorporate a trademark, service mark, company logo, or other distinctive symbol. You have to tread carefully here. Whimsically and thoughtlessly pulling a symbol out of the air to use as a logo is a very risky move. First, the symbol simply may be inappropriate for your business. You may grow tired of it, or it may become an embarrassment—like an indelible tattoo of an old flame's name. Once established, however, so that the logo is identified with your company, the symbol or device may not be that easy to change. Second, you may end up choosing a symbol that has negative connotations or even offends some people. For example, you may think that Indian head that is part of your logo is very striking, but some Native Americans may find it objectionable. Similarly, use of religious or quasi-religious symbols are likely to turn off as many potential customers as they attract.

   CASE IN POINT: No one is entirely safe. Some years ago, home products giant Procter and Gamble fell under attack by certain extremist groups who identified their venerable logo (a quarter-moon and starry sky) as a Satanic image. Although P & G had used the logo for over a century, the company endured so much pressure that it suppressed its proud emblem.

   The third and most serious consequence of carelessly choosing a logo is violation of some other company's trademark. This can have legal consequences costly enough to put any small business out of business. Fortunately, it is easy to prevent by consulting a trademark attorney. To find one, consult your Yellow Pages or you may look under "Intellectual Property Law" in Steven Naifeh and Gregory White Smith's *The Best Lawyers in America* (Woodward/White, updated every two years).

3. The letterhead must include your address and telephone number. These days, a fax number is usually present, and, with increasing frequency, an e-mail address or two. Depending on the design of the letterhead, all of this information may be at the top or bottom of the sheet.

4. Depending on the size of your company and the size of your stationery budget, you may want to supply personalized stationery for yourself and key staff members. In addition to the other letterhead information, you might supply your vice president with stationery that says "Jane Hanson, Vice President, "your manager with "Edward Hicks, Plant Manager," and so on. If these individuals have their own direct-line phone numbers or extension numbers, include this information as well.

5. Optionally, letterhead can also include a listing of corporate partners, key consultants, board members, and the like. If lengthy, this is often run down the left side of the page.

6. Optionally, letterhead can include a company slogan or concise description of services. Slogans strike most people as corny these days—although your business might call for a deliberately tongue-in-cheek, "fun" approach—but a descriptive phrase such as "Serving the widget industry since 1957" or "Makers of Fine Widgets" is always acceptable.

Letterhead Printing in Color

There is nothing wrong with a black-type letterhead. It is dignified and conservative. Color adds a touch of flair to the letterhead. If you specify a single color, the letterhead should cost no more to print than plain black. However, if you want to use more than one color, printing prices will rise. Consider this alternative if you have a colorful logo or if you want to convey the special vibrancy and creativity of your firm.

> TIP: With color, it is a good idea to heed the famous advice of modern architect Mies van der Rohe, who said "Less is more." A splash or two of vibrant color worked into a simple design will really "pop" and call welcome attention to itself.

Raised or Engraved Type

A lot of people think that letterhead must have engraved type (or type that looks engraved) or raised type. In fact, well-designed letterhead does not need these extras—although, if handled skillfully, they do add an unmistakable touch of class to your stationery. Be aware, however, that genuine engraving is expensive. While the look and feel of print physically pressed into fine paper conveys a very positive message, you will pay a premium for it.

It is possible to get stationery featuring *raised* type quite inexpensively. However, the cheap raised printing really does look cheap: shiny, bumpy, thick, and crude. If you want the look of raised type, go to a professional engraver, look carefully at a full range of samples, and select a style that is crisp, sharp, and smooth, with a matte rather than a shiny, plastic-looking surface. You'll pay a good deal more for this kind of work, but saving money on cheap raised printing will, indeed, make you *look* cheap. Remember, the point of using stationery in the first place is to convey an image of quality and permanence.

A Uniform Look

The decision to purchase custom stationery might prompt you to think about designing or redesigning your whole range of mailing supplies: your large envelopes, shipping labels, billing and invoice forms, even your business cards. Creating a uniform look among all these items achieves 3 objectives:

1. It conveys orderliness, organization, and coordination.

2. It conveys a sense of "official" confidence.

3. It creates brand awareness for your company. The more you use a good logo, logotype, or even a letterhead design adapted to envelopes, shipping labels, invoices, and business cards in addition to your letterhead stationery, the more closely and thoroughly your firm will be identified with a certain graphic image. Pretty soon, you will develop a brand identity, and that can be a powerful asset.

PITFALL: Brand identification and brand awareness are indeed powerful. For that very reason, be certain that you are thoroughly satisfied with the letterhead look you create. You want to be identified with a positive image, not one that makes you look less than terrific, let alone silly or slipshod.

Roll Your Own

You might not have to go to an outside designer or even an outside printer to create attractive stationery. Many high-end word processing software programs for IBM-compatible or Macintosh-compatible computers offer predesigned templates for a variety of letterhead designs. If you are feeling creative, you can go well beyond the templates to create your own designs, too. You will need a personal computer, a word-processing program that offers the ability to create letterhead, a selection of software "fonts" (typefaces), and a graphics-quality printer, preferably a laser or LED printer—although ink-jet and "bubble jet" models may produce satisfactory results as well.

Sample Letterheads

111 Industrial Way, West Des Moines, Iowa 50266 • (515)555-5555

120 KEENE AVE., SECAUCUS, N.J. 07094 ◯ (201)555-5555

Dewey, Billem & Howe
1170 Broadway, New York, New York 10010
(212)555-5555

DESIGN ORIGINAL GRAPHICS • 24 W 57th Street • N.Y., N.Y. • (212) 555-5550

1.1.2. Letter and Envelope Formats

There need be no mystery about laying out business correspondence. Let's begin with some general rules.

1. Be concise. If possible, limit business letters to a single page. Of course, allow common sense to rule. If what you have to say requires more than a single page, use another page.

    TIP: If what you have to say will take more than two pages, consider putting it in the form of a multipage memo or a short report, *accompanied by* a very brief cover letter.

2. Business letters should be single-spaced, with double spacing between paragraphs.

3. Try to keep the first paragraph short. Chapter 1.1. explains why this is important for effective persuasion. A short first paragraph is also important visually. Sir Isaac Newton could have applied his First Law of Motion to human behavior just as readily as he applied it to inanimate objects. A body at rest, Newton said, remains at rest and a body in motion remains in motion at a constant velocity as long as outside forces are not involved. He called this property of matter *inertia.* Something very like inertia is at work on the recipient of your letter. Your hardest task is to get her moving, into and beyond that first paragraph. If, at first glance, the reader beholds a big block of a paragraph, her inertia will intensify and, proportionately, her receptive enthusiasm for whatever it is you have to tell her will die. In contrast, the appearance of a brief opening paragraph may provide just the kick your reader needs to get over the hump of the opening paragraph, overcome inertia, plow through the letter, and respond as you want her to.

4. Fold the letter carefully. Your first fold should bring the top of the letter about two-thirds of the way down the page. Your second fold should be made along the line formed by the folded-down top of the letter. This will allow you to fit the letter neatly into a standard #9 envelope. Sounds pretty trivial, huh? Not if you consider that a crooked fold conveys a sloppiness that sabotages whatever message you are sending, or that the "oops fold" (multiple creases that say let's-try-it-one-more-time) conveys carelessness and/or indecision.

The physical layout of business letters falls into four categories, any of which is acceptable. All use standard $8^1/_2 \times 11$-inch stationery.

Block Style

This style features text that, without exception, begins flush with the left-hand margin. Assuming that you are using letterhead stationery, begin two spaces below the bottom of the letterhead. Provide a one-inch margin on the left and right, and end the letter a minimum of one inch from the bottom of the page.

Begin with the date, skip two spaces, type the inside address (explained in 1.1.3.), skip two spaces, type the salutation punctuated with a colon (explained in 1.1.3.), skip two spaces, and type your first paragraph. All elements begin flush with the lefthand margin. Do not indent paragraphs, but do separate them with double spaces. After the last paragraph, skip two spaces and type the complimentary close (explained in 1.1.4.), leaving a four spaces for your signature, followed by your typed name. Optionally, on the line below your typed name, include your title. Three to four spaces below your typed name or title, type reference initials, if applicable (explained in 1.1.4.), and, on the line below this, indicate any enclosures (explained in 1.1.4.).

When to Use the Block Style

This is a general-purpose format, which is quick and simple to type. Because each element falls into line flush left, it conveys a formal sense of order, and it is therefore especially well suited to conveying a thoroughly professional image.

Modified Block Style

The margins are the same as for the Block Style letter. All elements begin flush with the lefthand margin *except* for the date—at the top—and the complimentary close, signature, and typed name below the signature at the bottom of the letter. The left side of these elements should be flush with the center of the page. Note that any elements below the signature and typed name should be flush with the lefthand margin. This includes reference initials and the indication of any enclosures.

When to Use the Modified Block Style

The Modified Block Style may be used in any business situation. However, be aware that it conveys a lesser degree of formality than the Block Style. Note that, while the Block Style works well with letterhead that is either centered or justified flush left or flush right, the Modified Block Style *may* conflict with letterhead that is not centered. You be the judge.

Indented Style

Margins are the same as for the other styles. Here the entire date is centered—not just the lefthand side of the date. Skip two spaces under the date and type the inside address flush with the lefthand margin. Skip another two spaces and type the salutation, again flush with the lefthand margin. Two lines below the salutation, begin the first paragraph, indenting its first line one-half inch (a standard tab setting). Skip two lines between paragraphs, and indent the first line of each paragraph. After the last paragraph, skip two lines and insert your complimentary close, with its lefthand side flush with the center of the page. Leave four spaces for your signature, then type your name. If you wish to include your title, type it directly below this. Skip three or four lines and type reference initials and enclosure references (if applicable) flush with the lefthand margin.

When to Use the Indented Style

Although this style is quite acceptable for all business applications, it is less formal than either the Block or Modified Block styles. It looks friendlier, and if "friendly" is the image you want to convey, this format is a good choice for your correspondence. As with the Modified Block Style, the Indented Style *tends* to work best with centered letterhead designs rather than flush left or flush right letterheads.

Simplified Style

Margins are the same as for the other styles, and all elements begin flush with the lefthand margin. However, the Simplified Style includes no salutation. Instead, two spaces below the inside address is a statement of the letter's subject in CAPITAL LETTERS. Two spaces below this, the first paragraph begins, flush left, without indentation. Skip two lines between paragraphs. After the last paragraph, leave four spaces for a signature. There is no complimentary close. Two spaces below the signature, type your name in CAPITAL LETTERS. You may include your title (in capital and lowercase letters) on the line below this.

When to Use the Simplified Style

This is an impersonal format. It should be reserved for notices, bulletins, policy statements, advisories, and the like, which are mass mailed. It is not suitable for more personal correspondence or for business correspondence to specific clients and customers regarding individual issues.

Must I Justify?

In the days before the personal computer and word processing, the chief element that separated the look of typewritten text from book-printed text was the "ragged right" line endings of the former versus the "justified" endings of the latter. Nowadays, word processing software makes it easy for anyone to justify (i.e., vertically align) the right-hand margin of any letter. Precisely because anyone can now right-justify a letter, correspondence featuring a justified right-hand margin is no longer a big deal. If you are using the Block Style, and you want a very formal look, go ahead and turn on your word processor's full justification feature. For most purposes, however, a ragged right margin is the norm for business correspondence.

> **Tip:** Full justification looks good *only* with computer fonts that offer proportional letter spacing—that is, the ability to vary the space between letters, not just between words. If you try to fully justify monospaced fonts— such as Courier, which does not offer letter spacing—you will end up with varying gaps between certain words, making your page ugly, awkward, and difficult to read. Also, some dot matrix and old-fashioned daisy-wheel printers do not permit proportional letter spacing. If you want to use full justification, be sure that you have the requisite fonts and hardware.

A Font of Fonts

During most of the long reign of the typewriter, you could have had any font (that is, typeface) you wanted, as long as it was the one that your typewriter was built around, which was either Elite, or Pica, or Courier (a variation on Pica). Whatever the typeface was called, it *looked* like typewriter type. Then the IBM corporation introduced the Selectric typewriter, which offered changeable "typing elements"—either a metal ball or a plastic "daisy wheel"—and you had a choice among a handful of faces, many of which looked like "book type" instead of "typewriter type." With the rapid evolution of the personal computer and the laser printer, most offices now have access to thousands of typefaces.

> **Definition:** As computer-oriented folk use the terms, *font* and *typeface* are synonyms. Bona fide typesetting professionals make a distinction between the two, however. For them, a *font* is a complete set of type in a single size and face, whereas a *typeface* is the full range of type, of any size, in a particular design.

Available fonts include any number of exotic and grotesque designs, and it is tempting to try to make use of some of them in a letter. In a word, *don't.* Unless you are writing a promotional letter intended to create a certain kind of impact, avoid unusual typefaces in business correspondence. Moreover, avoid using more than a single font in any given letter. Except for the letterhead, you should also avoid varying the size of the font.

Which Size?

Most business letters are printed in 11 point type. If you have a reasonably short letter, you may want to kick this up to 12 point type. Some fonts are quite readable at 8 or 10 points, but it is best to use 11 or 12 point type.

Which Font?

Graphic designers know full well that the choice of typeface can have a profound emotional influence on a reader. Some of this is quite obvious. If you choose to write a business letter in a font that is better suited to a circus poster, you will come across as something between silly and bizarre, regardless of your letter's message. On the other hand, using an appropriate typeface can lend clarity and authority to what you have to say.

First, it is important to distinguish between "text" faces and "display" faces. Text faces are intended primarily for use in the body of a printed piece, whereas display faces are meant to be set large in headlines. While you can use text faces in headlines, it is usually a bad idea to employ display faces in body text. Generally, set in smaller sizes, display text is hard to read. While you might use headlines in certain promotional and advertising letters, you will not use them in general business correspondence, so stick with text fonts.

There are a great many of them, with hundreds more being invented every year. Despite the profusion, however, fonts tend to fall into one of three categories: serif, sans serif, and styles that combine a bit of both of these categories. For all practical purposes, you need distinguish only between serif and sans serif. "Serifs" are the fine lines that finish off the strokes of a letter. Serif fonts consist of letters that are adorned with these ornamental finishing touches. It follows that sans serif fonts lack these ornaments.

Sabon, Times, Century.

Helvetica, Futura, Optima.

Common sense tells you that sans serif typefaces—the simple, clean, modern looking styles bearing such names as Helvetica, Optima, and Arial—should be easier to read than the more traditional and ornate serif faces, such as Times Roman and Century Schoolbook. Oddly enough, common sense is wrong. In running text, traditional serif faces are actually easier to read than sans serif faces.

But ease of reading should not be your primary concern in choosing a typeface for a given business letter. No one should suffer undo fatigue reading a page-long letter, whether it's set in a serif or sans serif face. Instead, consider the subtle emotional impact of the serif versus the sans serif face.

A serif face is a nod toward tradition. This does not mean that it is old-fashioned. Indeed, the tried-and-true serif faces—Times Roman, Century Schoolbook, Caslon, and so on—suggest a kind of timelessness or, at least, an evergreen quality. In contrast, sans serif faces—such as Arial, Optima, and Helvetica—convey a contemporary and informal feeling. They underscore simplicity and clarity (even if, in the long run, they are actually harder to read).

You need to decide which emotional effect best suits your purposes. It's fun to look at a lot of different typefaces and to identify several from each major family—serif or sans serif—that seem to you to convey whatever shade of emotional impact best serves you, your message, and your image.

> **Tip:** You might also think about how the typeface you choose harmonizes with your letterhead. Common sense would suggest that it is best to match a serif-style letterhead with serif text and a sans serif letterhead with sans serif text. It ain't necessarily so. Magazine and book designers often deliberately use sans serif type in headlines and a serif typeface in the body text, or vice versa. If you think of your letterhead as your letter's headline, why not try a body text that contrasts with it?

Is There More to Life Than $8^1/_2 \times 11$?

Most business correspondence should be conducted on $8^1/_2 \times 11$ sheets. However, less formal correspondence—such as invitations, condolence messages, congratulations, and the like—can be typed or handwritten on $6^1/_2 \times 9$-inch note-style stationery. Since word processing has become the norm, however, this smaller stationery has been increasingly relegated to very informal handwritten notes.

Envelope Format

The envelope should include your full return address in the upper left-hand corner. If the envelope is preprinted with this information, you may want to write your last name above or below the preprinted area, in case returned mail needs to find its way through a busy mailroom and back to you. The name, title, company, and full address of your correspondent should be roughly centered left to right, and the name line should begin about halfway down the envelope. You may put any special reader notation (such as "PERSONAL" or "CONFIDENTIAL") in the lower lefthand corner of the envelope.

> TIP: Many word processing programs will "pick up" the name and address from the internal address in your letter and properly position the information when you use your printer to print out an envelope. Some of this software also gives you the option of translating the postal zip code into a computer-readable bar code. If you use the long-form "5+4 digit" zip code, the bar code that is generated should help the post office expedite your letter.

1.1.3. Address and Salutation

"Know thyself," said the Oracle of Delphi. Had he/she given advice to a letter writer it would have been "Know thy correspondent. "That's hardly as simple-minded as it sounds. Think of the volume of letters you receive addressed to your title ("Office Manager") rather than your name. If at all possible, do whatever research is necessary to identify your correspondent by name, then address him or her by name and title. Modern usage dictates that women be addressed as "Ms.," even if you know whether or not the woman is married. However, if your correspondent expresses a preference for "Miss" or Mrs.," do oblige. In any case, for purposes of the internal address you may leave off the "Ms." or "Mr." entirely. Just make certain that you use it in the salutation ("Dear Ms. Smith:"). In the case of medical doctors or holders of the Ph.D. degree, include the degree *after* the addressee's name in the internal address:

Edward P. Schurz, M.D.
546 W. Petersen Place
Topeka, KN 29832

Never use "Dr." before the name if you include the degree designation after the name, and degrees below that of M.D. or Ph.D. are usually not identified.

Etiquette dictates that some professions receive special treatment. Attorneys often enjoy being addressed with the abbreviation "Esq." (for Esquire) following their name. If you use this form of address, do not preface the name with "Mr." Sexist or not, it is fundamentally absurd to address a female attorney as "Jane Doe, Esq." Don't do it. Political office holders, judges, and clergy all require special forms of address. Where the title does not substitute for the name, be certain to include the appropriate title following the name as part of the envelope address as well as the internal address :

Addressee	Envelope/Internal Address	Salutation
U.S president	The President	Dear Mr./Madam President
Former president	The Honorable John Jones	Dear Mr. Jones
U.S. vice president	The Vice President	Dear Mr./Madam Vice President
Cabinet members	The Honorable John Jones	Dear Secretary Jones
Chief Justice	The Chief Justice	Dear Mr./Madam Justice
Associate Justice	Mr./Madam Justice Jones	Dear Mr./Madam Justice
U.S. Senator	The Honorable John Jones	Dear Senator Jones
Speaker of the House	The Honorable John Jones	Dear Mr./Madam Speaker
U.S. Representative	The Honorable John Jones	Dear Mr./Ms. Jones
U.S. Ambassador	The Honorable John Jones	Dear Mr./Madam Ambassador
U.S. Diplomat	The Honorable John Jones	Dear Mr./Ms/ Jones
Foreign ambassador	His/Her Excellency	Excellency
Governor	Honorable John Jones	Dear Governor Jones
State legislator	Honorable John Jones	Dear Mr./Ms. Jones
Judge	Honorable John Jones	Dear Judge Jones
Mayor	Honorable John Jones	Dear Mayor Jones
The Pope	His Holiness, Pope John Paul II	Your Holiness
Cardinal	His Eminence, John Cardinal Jones	Your Eminence
Bishop	The Most Reverend John Jones	Your Excellency
Monsignor	The Right Reverend John Jones	Right Reverend Monsignor

Addressee	Envelope/Internal Address	Salutation
Priest	The Reverend John Jones	Reverend Father
Brother	Brother John Jones	Dear Brother John
Sister	Sister Maria Theresa	Dear Sister Maria Theresa
Protestant clergy	The Reverend John Jones*	Dear Mr./Ms./Dr. Jones
Episcopal bishop	The Right Reverend John Jones*	Dear Bishop Jones
Rabbi Jonas	Rabbi Jonathan Jonas	Dear Rabbi (or Dr.)
Military personnel	Captain John Jones**	Dear Captain Jones

*If the addressee holds a Doctor of Divinity degree, also add D.D. after the name.

**Address military personnel by rank and name—full name in the address, last name only in the salutation. Use the appropriate short form of the rank. For example, in a letter, you would address Master Sergeant John Jones simply as Sergeant John Jones and Dear Sergeant Jones. Brigadier General Jane Jones is addressed as General Jane Jones and Dear General Jones.

One final word regarding the salutation. In business letters, the salutation is always punctuated with a colon—Dear Dr. Perkins:—whereas in personal (or "friendly") letters, a comma is customarily used—Dear Mary, .

First Name Basis?

If you are in doubt whether or not to address your correspondent by his or her first name, use the surname. However, you may indicate that you would like to move on to a first-name basis by signing with your first name only (above your typewritten full name). If you are answering a letter that addresses you by your first name or that closes with a first-name-only signature, it is appropriate for you to address the correspondent's by his or her first name.

1.1.4.   Closing Graciously

The safest "complimentary close" is a simple "Sincerely." If you want to create greater warmth, choose from among "Cordially," "With best wishes," "Best personal regards," and the like. "Yours truly" and "Very truly yours" are generally regarded as outdated.

Reference Initials

These go flush left below your signature and typed name. Often, they give the initials of the author of the letter in upper case, followed by a slash and the initials of the typist in lower case. They may also list a computer file or diskette reference.

> **Tip:** Here's one for your conscience to wrestle with. Should you make yourself look more important by making up reference initials? For example, I might use "JG/bms," knowing full well that the "bms" does not stand for Barbara Marie Smithers but for "By My Self." As sins go, telling this white lie isn't so bad. But in these days of a personal computer on every desk, it's very common even for top executives to type their own letters.

Copy Designations

If you are sending copies of the correspondence to a third party or parties, indicate this fact and the name(s) of the recipient(s) below your signature and typed name and the reference initials (if you've used them). The list should be flush with the lefthand margin. The designation "cc" (for "carbon copy" or "courtesy copy") is customarily used, although "pc" ("photocopy") is also acceptable. It is helpful to your correspondent if you include not only the name(s) of the third party recipient(s), but the relevant job title(s) as well:

cc: John Jones, Vice President, Marketing
Wilma Torrington, Director of Licensing
Edward Smith, Esq., Corporate Counsel

b.c.

No, this doesn't indicate a prehistoric period, but stands for "blind copy." This designation is included on a copy sent to a third party, but not the original. In other words, the original addressee is unaware that a copy has been sent to a third party.

Indicating an Enclosure

If you enclose something with your letter—say, a pamphlet or a report—include the notation "Encl." or "Enclosure" (or "Att." or "Attachments") flush left, following your signature and typed name and following the reference initials and copy designations, if you have used either of these. The "Encl."

notation is a good idea, because it will alert your correspondent if something you had intended to send has been inadvertently left out.

P.S.

Avoid postscripts in business letters. With a word processor, it takes no great effort to add in the body text whatever you forgot to say, then just print the letter out again. The P.S. suggests poor planning and laziness.

1.2. A MATTER OF STYLE

1.2.1. Formal or Informal?

REVELATION: A business letter is the communication of one human being to another. I've put this "revelation" up front because, looking at most business letters, you'd never know it was the case. Put a bunch of business letters in a time capsule, let someone dig up and read them a thousand years hence, and that person of the future will likely conclude that we were a different species. While it is true that most business is by its nature fundamentally conservative, it does not follow that business correspondence must, therefore, be stuffy, stilted, bleached out, pompous, and dead. When you sit down to write a letter, remember that you are not the embodiment of Acme Widgets writing to the embodiment of Smith Framiss, Inc., but that you are a human being writing to another human being. True, when you write a business letter, you are representing your company. But don't try to *impersonate* the company. Be a person.

Let's say you've got a very demanding client who has just placed a major order for 10,000 widgets. You're thrilled about the order, but you're also worried about the million things that can go wrong—and that always seem to go wrong—precisely at the most critical time. You decide to alert one of your principal suppliers to the importance of the demands you are about to place on him. You could write company-to-company:

Dear Mr. Harris:

This is to inform your firm that our company has recently contracted with the Jerkins Company to supply said firm with a substantial quantity of widgets. Accordingly, in fulfillment of this order, our firm will be placing a substantial order for widget blanks with your firm. It would be appreciated by this company if your company would take whatever steps are necessary to insure that delivery of the said widget blanks is expedited.

Very truly yours,
[Full signature]
Helen Wheeler
General Manager

Or you could write human being to human being:

> Dear Jim:
>
> I'd like to ask a special favor of you. We've just landed a major piece of business from Bert Wainwright at Spencer-Wainwright for 10,000 widgets. This is good news for you, too, since I've just ordered 10,000 widget blanks from you. But, Jim, I've got to tell you: Bert is a very demanding client, and I can use all the special help you can give me.
>
> I know you folks will come through for me, but I'm asking you to supervise our order personally, to ride herd on it, troubleshoot it, and see that it gets to me by the May 7 deadline.
>
> This one means a lot to us.
>
> Best personal regards,
> [First-name signature]
> Helen Wheeler
> General Manager

I suppose I have to ask the question, even though it's quite rhetorical: Which letter do *you* think is more likely to get results?

The point is not that the first is stiffer and more stilted than the second, or that it is more formal, but that it is less *human.* Want a rule of thumb? Here it is: When formality threatens to replace humanity, try being informal.

Being Human Without Crossing the Line

Don't get me wrong. It certainly is possible to be too informal in business correspondence. It is also possible to be over-familiar, impolite, and downright rude:

> Hey, Jim—
>
> Spencer-Wainwright just ordered 10,000 widgets from us. We're ordering 10,000 widget blanks from you. Listen: I can't afford for you guys to screw up on this one. Get with the program. Jim, I'm holding you personally responsible for making sure I get every last blank and get them on time.
>
> I mean it!
>
> [First-name signature]

Just by reading and comparing these three letters, it is easy to come up with a list of rules for effectively balancing the formal with the informal, the human with the courteous, and the caring with the forceful. Here's the list:

Rule #1: Be a Person. Okay, but *which* person? I've got an answer that's as glib as it is true: Just be yourself—a person interested in doing the best job possible. Don't try to impersonate the Voice of Business.

Rule #2 Know Your Correspondent. Successful writers share one characteristic in common: they know their audience. The same is true of any successful salesperson: they know their customer. When you write, you are selling. You are selling an idea, a point of view—in the case of Helen Wheeler and her letter to Jim Harris, the product being sold is a request for a favor, for special handling and an extra-high degree of service.

Know your correspondent. Make an effort to be sensitive to his needs and interests, and tailor the tone of your letter (its relative informality versus formality) to suit the nature of your relationship. In the case of Helen Wheeler and Jim Harris, we're assuming that the two have done business on various occasions and know each other as familiar business contacts. The most effective of the three letters is pitched at the level of such a relationship: friendly, but polite, neither artificially stiff nor aggressively over-familiar.

Rule #3: Use the Right Words and the Real Words. Take the time to consider just exactly what you need to communicate, then select the *right* words to convey that message most effectively. Invariably, the *right* words will be *real* words. We'll talk more about this in the very next section (1.2.2. Plain Talk, Persuasive Talk), but, right now, consider an example.

Put yourself in Helen Wheeler's place. Jim Harris has just proposed assigning production and delivery of your 10,000 widget blanks to his assistant, who joined his firm a few months ago. You don't like this. You could respond, "Jim, this makes me feel funny" or "I don't feel quite right about doing that" or "Absolutely unacceptable! I won't stand for it!" or "That seems a potentially counterproductive strategy with a substantial downside." In all four cases, the language is undeniably English, the words are correctly spelled, and the grammar and syntax are just fine. The problem is, none of these responses communicate effectively. "Jim, what you propose makes me nervous because you and I have worked so effectively as a team in the past, that I don't want to choose this very critical deal as the occasion for forging—or trying to forge—a new team. Can we—you and I—work together on this one? I really do need 110 percent, and I know that you, personally, will give no less."

Finding the right words does not mean groping for beautiful and exotic adjectives. It means finding the *real* words that get to the heart of the matter. "Real" words are words most closely and immediately connected to the *real* world—that is, nouns and verbs, the words that describe things, events, ideas, and actions. Connect your letters to the real world by means of object and action words rather than vague abstractions (such as: "That seems a potentially counterproductive strategy with a substantial downside.").

Rule #4: Create a Team. Keep the Helen Wheeler–Jim Harris examples in mind for a few moments more. The fifth example is most effective as communication, in part, because it creates a team, a sense of common interest and joint goals. Ineffective communication uses language to divide and oppose: "Absolutely unacceptable! I won't stand for it!" There is a stated or implied "I" set up in opposition to a stated or implied "you." In contrast, effective communication tends to synthesize the "I" and the "you" into "we."

Rule #5: Keep It Positive. Psychologists call it "positive reinforcement" and have been telling us for years that employing it is far more effective than using punishment or reprimand ("negative reinforcement") to produce whatever behavioral results you want. Even before there was such a thing called "behavioral psychology," generations of kindly grandmothers have been wagging fingers and reminding us that "You get more flies with honey than with vinegar."

To the greatest degree possible, focus your communication on positive issues. That's easy, of course, when you're writing a letter of thanks or congratulating a subordinate on having done a great job. But what happens when Jim Harris tells Helen Wheeler that he wants to put his assistant on her crucially important job? Compare "Absolutely unacceptable! I won't stand for it!" with "Jim, what you propose makes me nervous because you and I have worked so effectively as a team in the past, that I don't want to choose this very critical deal as the occasion for forging—or trying to forge—a new team. Can we—you and I—work together on this one? I really do need 110 percent, and I know that you, personally, will give no less." It is not that the latter response sugarcoats or glosses over the problem presented by Jim Harris's proposal, but it does identify the *positive* reasons why Jim should instead do what Helen wants him to.

The worst aspect of emphasizing the negative is that it confuses your *correspondent* with the *problem*. The idea is to identify and address the problem, while using language that makes clear your assumption that you and your correspondent can resolve the problem—because you and your correspondent are good, talented, competent people who, together, make a great team.

1.2.2. Plain Talk, Persuasive Talk

Take a good long look at Rule #3: "Use the Right Words and the Real Words." A lot of nervous letter writers make the mistake of thinking that eloquence requires flowery language and ornate syntax. Nothing could be farther from the truth.

The best language is the simplest language capable of conveying your meaning. Now, I ask you to read that sentence carefully. Both the first and second parts of it are important. "Simple" does not mean simple-minded. Do not oversimplify what you have to say, leaving out important information or details. But don't obscure your message with overblown words and convoluted syntax.

The Right Words

Let's look for a moment at a famous piece of eloquence. Abraham Lincoln used this expression to describe the necessity for loyalty and consistency in a crisis: *Don't change horses in midstream.* It is a memorable phrase, but there is absolutely nothing flowery about it. Only two of the words in it have more than a single syllable. Anyone with a third-grade education could read it. The phrase defines abstract concepts—loyalty and consistency—but it uses *concrete, real* words to do it. Each of the words in the phrase describes an action or an object in the real world. And, if you were a nineteenth-century American listening to Lincoln when he spoke these words, they would be even more vivid and real, because you would be very well aware of the consequence of trying to get off one horse and on to another in the middle of a flowing—perhaps rapidly flowing—stream. In Lincoln's day, people forded streams on horseback everyday. Had Lincoln said, "It is critically important that one does not alter one's loyalties and commitments when one is in the midst of a crisis," we would not remember his words.

In general, minimize the use of adjectives and other qualifiers, while emphasizing solid verbs and nouns. Moreover, the more precise you can be, the better.

Straightarrow Syntax

Now, a word on syntax. Perhaps you haven't heard the term since grade school. It refers to sentence structure, and, quite frankly, most business writers get it all wrong. That's the bad news.

The good news is that the error most business writers make is very easy to correct—really, a no-brainer. Here is a typical sentence that might be found in a typical business letter: "The report was reviewed by this department and found to be generally correct."

Nothing unusual here. It's English, and you can understand it. But I ask you to look more deeply into the sentence. You see, it comes from an alien world, an unreal world apparently devoid of human life. For there is no evidence of human beings in this sentence. There is a "report" and a "department." But where have the people gone?

Perhaps your grade school teacher told you what is wrong with a sentence like this. It is in the passive voice. Technically speaking, the roles of object and subject are reversed. But there is no need to get technical. Just look at this sentence:"This department reviewed the report and found it to be generally correct." Already, we see an improvement. The sentence is easier to understand at a glance. It is written in the active voice—that is, with the subject ("this department") and the object ("the report") in their proper, most logical order.

The beauty of all this is that active-voice sentences are not only more effective communication, they are less complicated and, therefore, *easier* to write!

A Step Further

While"This department reviewed the report and found it to be generally correct" is much better than "The report was reviewed by this department and found to be generally correct," it is still pretty dull and certainly not as informative as it could be. Whenever possible, take the next step. After making sure that subject and object are in their proper places, think about how you can sharpen that subject and that object. For example:"Pete Williams in our department reviewed the October sales report and takes exception to only one figure. He shows 2,500 Type A widgets sold, not 2,450."

Sharpen, define, and—whenever possible—quantify subject and object.

PITFALL: Why are so many business writers so in love with the passive voice? Two reasons: They think it makes them sound like God, and it gives them the opportunity to pass the buck. The absence of a human actor in an event suggests that the event"just happened," and that no particular human being is responsible for it. Remember: the passive voice is essentially phony and unreal.

1.3. APOLOGIES AND ADJUSTMENTS

1.3.1. How to Make the Best Out of a Bad Situation

Damage control. Nobody likes to do it, but we all know it's sometimes necessary. Think about when you've been on the receiving end of somebody's error. That Plaque Master electric toothbrush you bought slows down and stops the moment it comes into contact with your teeth. You were so excited about your Plaque Master that you've rounded up all the "old-fashioned" hand-operated toothbrushes and tossed them in the trash—with old fish heads, the rotten fruit. You aren't about to root around in the trash. So here you are, teeth unbrushed. You're steamed. You do not feel very good about Plaque Master, Inc.

But that's only half the story. If you call the folks at Plaque Master, and somebody in charge apologizes and assures you that the company will stand behind the product and will ship you out a new Plaque Master right away, well, you may still be annoyed with the product—at this time—but at least you'll feel pretty good about the Plaque Master company. They haven't abandoned you. They've taken responsibility. They are determined to help you.

I'm not here to tell you that errors, failures, and disappointments are good things. But an effective letter of apology or adjustment can take these disasters and turn them into opportunities for creating a positive relationship between customer and company.

> REVELATION: No matter what your business, you don't just sell a product, you also sell yourself and your firm. If a particular product should happen to fail, you still have an opportunity to sell yourself and your firm by sending the message that you will make things right. You can turn damage control into relationship building.

1.3.2. Responding to Complaints and Claims

The principal objective of a response to a complaint is to communicate a willingness to help the client or customer. This builds a positive relationship between you and the customer. Let's take it step by step:

1. Acknowledge that you have received the complaint or the returned product.

2. Express sympathy for the customer and concern for his situation and his feelings.

3. If possible, provide a solution to the customer's problem. For example: "Please take the widget to the nearest authorized dealer, who will repair it at no cost to you." If you require additional information or some other action on the part of the customer, explain it here: "So that I can get this problem corrected as quickly as possible, I need to know . . ."

An Assurance of a Speedy Solution

A personal letter assuring prompt action can turn a bad experience with a product into a positive impression of the company overall. If you can give your customer choices, do so. It gives her a sense of empowerment, which makes her feel less like a victim—less like *your* victim.

Dear Ms. Quinn:

I was very sorry to learn that the bearing unit on your Hacker Weed Trimmer is defective. I can work with you in two ways to resolve the problem:

1. While the your bearing unit certainly failed prematurely, it is a "wear part" that must be replaced from time to time. It is designed to be replaced by the customer. Therefore, I can send you a new bearing unit, with instructions on how to replace it.

2. Alternatively, you may return the entire unit to us, and we will replace the part and return the unit to you, together with reimbursement of your shipping costs.

The first alternative is faster, but if you really don't like to use a screwdriver, just pack the unit in its original carton and return it to us. Just follow the warranty return instructions in your Owner's Manual.

Be assured that, whatever option you choose, we will make every effort to get you up and running with a minimum of delay. If you would like us to send a replacement bearing unit, just call me at 555-555-5555. You may leave a message on my voice answering system.

On behalf of Hacker, I apologize for the inconvenience and disappointment, and I thank you for your patience and understanding.

Sincerely,

TIP: Do not fail to thank your customer for patience and understanding. Not only is this courteous, it strengthens the bond between you and the customer by reminding her that she has made an emotional investment in you. She's given you her patience and understanding.

Here's a shorter version of the speedy action letter:

Dear Mr. Clemens:

I've received your comments concerning your Hacker Weed Trimmer. I am very sorry that the unit is not performing to your expectations, and I am eager to resolve the problem as quickly as possible. For this reason, I ask that you bring the unit to your nearest authorized Hacker service center, which is located at 2345 West Harrison Street in Hammond. The technician there will examine the unit and take whatever steps are necessary to insure that it will operate to its optimum specifications. If the service center is unable to repair the problem within twenty-four hours, I have authorized that you be given a replacement unit.

We want you to be 100 percent satisfied.

Sincerely,

1.3.3. Getting the Facts

Often, you lack sufficient information to respond to a customer with an assurance of prompt action. Until you have the facts, you cannot propose a course of action. It is even quite possible that your product or service has not failed, but that your customer is mistaken or is using the product incorrectly. Nevertheless, the request for information should be written in the same helpful spirit as the promise of a speedy solution. It should never strike your customer as an attempt to stall or to evade responsibility, and the requests the letter makes should be defined carefully in order to avoid burdening an already annoyed customer with unnecessary paperwork. Here's an example:

Dear Ms. Delacort:

I am very sorry to learn that you have experienced a problem with your Hacker Weed Trimmer. I am very eager to work with you to resolve the problem, and, in order to do so most quickly and accurately, I need some more information from you. Please take a few moments to answer the following questions. You don't need to write me a letter. Just give me a call at 555-555-5555.

1. Does the rear of the unit become hot?

2. Do you have difficulty starting the unit after it has been turned off for less than a few seconds?

3. Does the unit make any unusual noise?

I greatly appreciate your taking the time to help me help you. Your answers will enable me to resolve the problem more quickly and more accurately—and, I believe, to your complete satisfaction.

Sincerely,

Securing complete information about customer complaints is, if anything, even more important when the complaint involves the actions or attitudes of your personnel. In order to correct a problem or a misunderstanding, you need the facts. Documenting the complaint in writing is also critically important if you must take disciplinary steps against an employee. Not only is such documentation necessary to insure fairness both to the customer and to the employee, it is also essential to protect you and your firm in the event of legal action by a disgruntled employee or even a very unhappy customer.

The documentary function of the information letter aside, you should frame the communication just as you do other adjustment-related correspondence: in the spirit of helping the customer and building a relationship with him. For example:

Dear Mr. Young:

I was very concerned to receive your letter of September 12, 19XX, in which you mention that you were significantly dissatisfied with the work of one of our sales representatives, Alice Hargrove.

I have discussed the matter with Ms. Hargrove, but before I meet with her again to discuss an appropriate course of action, I would like to have as much information from you regarding the difficulty you experienced. Your comments on the following questions will help me, as well as Ms. Hargrove, understand the situation more fully and resolve it to your satisfaction:

1. In what way(s) was Ms. Hargrove "rude" to you?

2. Your impression was that Ms. Hargrove "deliberately delayed" action on your order. Can you explain what created that impression?

Mr. Young, you need not trouble yourself to write down formal responses to these questions. You might just jot down a few points and call me at 555-555-5555 with your comments.

We at Norton-Muller, Inc., are proud of the level of service we offer. You can understand, then, how concerned I am that you were dissatisfied. Both Ms. Hargrove and I are eager to turn this situation around and create your complete satisfaction.

Sincerely,

Tip: There should be no secrets in employee performance matters. Provide both the employee and the customer with all correspondence related to the matter. Use a "cc:" notification at the bottom of the letter to note that a copy has been sent.

1.3.4. Rejecting a Claim

Many customer complaints and adjustment claims are invalid and without basis. Sometimes, in the interest of creating customer satisfaction, it is both expedient and cost effective to honor the claim nevertheless. If a customer is dissatisfied with a perfectly good widget and wants a new one, it may be both cheapest and most useful—depending on the cost of the widget—simply to replace the widget. Chances are that doing so will have what physicians call a "placebo effect" on the customer. No physical cure is achieved (in this case, because nothing was wrong with the product in the first place), but the customer feels better about the product. Many firms operate under an essentially no-questions-asked return policy. They consider it not just a cost of doing business, but an investment in customer satisfaction.

However, on various occasions it will be necessary to dispute or reject a claim. Your goal is to do so without alienating the customer. You must also preserve your rights, yet express concern for—and continued commitment to—the customer. The key is to help the customer by educating him, explaining the reasons for disputing or rejecting the claim without, however, lecturing or admonishing. Remember, this is not a contest. You may be in the right, but you do not *win* by proving that you are right if, to do so, you alienate the customer. Here are the steps to follow:

1. Clearly state the subject of your letter: "I am replying to your letter . . .")

2. Clearly state the rejection or dispute. Do not beat around the bush or attempt to soften the blow by burying the rejection in the body of the letter.

3. Give full reasons for the rejection or the dispute. Provide as much information as possible.

4. Now, this is important: If at all possible, offer an alternative in order to generate—or preserve—goodwill. Avoid compelling the customer to accept a no-win ultimatum: "Like it or lump it."

5. Do not apologize. After all, your point is that you and your product are not at fault. However, do express your regret that the customer has experienced a problem.

6. Close by expressing the hope that whatever alternative you offer will be of assistance to the customer and will create satisfaction.

Customer Error

Let's begin with the most difficult claims-rejection situation, the customer error. Nobody likes to be told that they've made a mistake. Therefore, you must break the news with sensitivity to the customer's feelings. You want neither to alienate—and, therefore, lose—the customer, nor to provoke stubborn resistance.

Dear Ms. Thompson:

I am replying to your letter of January 3, 19XX, in which you described damage to your set of Elite Deluxe dishware caused by your automatic dishwasher.

I am very sorry to hear about the damage. Unfortunately, the Elite company cannot comply with your request for a refund. Warnings against washing your Elite Deluxe dishware are prominently displayed on the interior as well as exterior shipping cartons. A loose sheet within each box also bears this warning.

In short, Elite makes no claim to dishwasher safety and clearly warns against putting the dishware in a dishwasher.

Elite wants you to be satisfied with our product. While we cannot make a full refund, I can offer you the opportunity to replace your damaged pieces at cost. I've enclosed a cost-price list. Please use the list to determine your cost and enclose a check for that amount, along with the damaged pieces you are returning. Although we ask that you assume responsibility for the cost of shipping the pieces to us, we will pay the freight for the replacement shipment.

On behalf of Elite, Inc., I hope this offer will be of help to you.

Sincerely,

PITFALL: Avoid references to "company policy." Nothing is more infuriating to a customer to have a claim rejected because "company policy" forbids this or that. If necessary, explain the reasons behind whatever policy is applicable—without, however, using the phrase *company policy.* Your "policy" is irrelevant to the customer's needs.

Just Following Customer's Orders

One of the most frequent—and frustrating—sources of customer claims is the order filled according to erroneous customer instructions. Either the customer has made an error in specifying the order—or has simply changed her mind. It is always best to respond with documentation of the original order. If at all possible, even though the customer is clearly mistaken, do accommodate her wishes:

Dear Ms. Reynolds:

I am responding to your letter of June 4, 19XX, in which you state that you ordered our model 1234, but were shipped model 1235 instead. I understand that you are requesting an exchange.

I have enclosed a photocopy of your original order specifying model 1235. The error, as you can see, was not ours.

The matter is complicated a bit by the fact that model 1235 is a special-order item we custom make only in response to an order. I cannot, therefore, simply exchange it for model 1234. Let me suggest an alternative: Return your model 1235, and we will give you $45 credit toward purchase of model 1234.

There is yet another alternative. Why not keep your model 1235? It should serve your needs as well as our model 1234 would.

I hope these suggestions are helpful to you.

Sincerely,

It's *Supposed* to Be That Way

Finally, customer complaints and claims arise from a perception that the product (or service) has not performed as anticipated or as promised. Sometimes, this is a legitimate claim. For whatever reason or reasons, a product does fail to perform to specifications. But, often, the claim is the result of a mismatch between the customer's expectations and what the product (or service) is actually designed to do. Your primary aim in responding to claims of the latter type should not be to defend your product or your firm, but to provide help and instruction to your customer. Educate him so that his expectations will be brought into line with what the product (or service) can actually deliver. If necessary, suggest a different product, which may be better suited to his application.

Here is a response to a simple problem:

Dear Mr. Williams:

Your letter of March 30, 19XX was referred to me for response.

The "problem" you describe at start-up of Mark XIV is not a symptom of faulty operation. It is a normal product safety feature, designed to prevent circuit overload. Please refer to page 54 of your Owner's Manual for a full explanation.

I am happy to tell you that your unit is operating correctly and that no replacement, repair, or adjustment is required.

Please contact me at 555-555-5555 if you have any further questions about your Mark XIV. I'm here to help.

Sincerely,

The issue becomes more complicated when a product disappoints a customer, yet operates as it should. In these cases, you may want to seek information from the customer to determine if he is using the product incorrectly or for an inappropriate application. Here is a letter to a customer who complained that his cordless electric screwdriver did not function well as a drill.

Dear Mr. Smith:

Thank you for your letter of June 4, 19XX, explaining that your Model 65-43 does not perform adequately as a drill.

The Model 65-43 was designed primarily as a moderately priced electric screwdriver. As such, it has a high-torque, relatively low RPM electric motor. This is the ideal design for an electric screwdriver, and, in many cases, also functions adequately for drilling relatively soft materials. The drill bits supplied with your Model 65-43 are intended to extend the usefulness of your tool for occasional "convenience" drilling applications only. The Model 65-43 is not intended as a substitute for an electric drill—just as an electric drill is no substitute for an electric screwdriver.

Please be assured that your Model 65-43 is operating as designed. I am enclosing a catalog that features our full line of electric drills, all of which are fully guaranteed to do the job you want them to do.

Sincerely,

1.3.5. Our Action Will Be Fair

It is not always possible to act on a complaint or claim instantly and definitively. Depending on circumstances that include cost of replacement/repair, warranty issues, and even liability issues, time may be necessary to investigate the merits of the claim. In these cases, you should respond to your customer as soon as possible with an assurance of fair action. Stress your pledge of efficiency, accuracy, and fairness. It is often helpful to make reference to your firm's upper management in order to convey the impression that the claim is being taken with utmost seriousness and is being given high priority.

> Dear Ms. Lawrence:
>
> Frank Wilson, president of Acme Rug Company, asked that I reply to your letter of May 4, 19XX, in which you describe a wear problem with one of our Excellence rugs.
>
> Of course, you are anxious for immediate action. We feel the same way, and we want to resolve your problem as quickly as possible. However, in order to insure an informed and fair assessment of the damage to your rug, we need to send one of our field representatives to your house. You may expect to hear from the representative within two weeks.
>
> Please be assured that we will resolve this matter as quickly as prudence and fairness will permit.
>
> Sincerely,

1.3.6. We're Sorry

Nobody likes to be wrong, and, certainly, nobody wants to be put a position where apology is required. Paradoxically, however, most people welcome the opportunity to forgive. "To err is human," the old saying goes, but "to forgive, divine." Your apology can make your correspondent feel good by giving him the opportunity to perform a divine act: forgiveness. After all, who wouldn't enjoy feeling like a saint—even for a moment or two?

Here are the steps basic to any letter of apology:

1. Begin by expressing concern and sympathy.

2. Emphasize that the problem or error is an *exceptional* circumstance. You value quality, you make vigorous efforts to ensure quality, and you *usually* achieve quality.

3. Own up to the error, and apologize straightforwardly for it.

4. If appropriate, state the corrective action you will take. Otherwise, close the letter by assuring your correspondent that the error will not be repeated.

5. Always end by thanking your correspondent for understanding and patience.

The Widget Broke

If a product fails, and you agree that the product has failed, you may want to write a letter of apology rather than an adjustment letter. This can be a very positive relationship builder, especially if the letter accompanies a replacement product or is sent as a follow-up *after* the adjustment has been made.

Dear Mr. Kane:

I was very sorry to hear that the Ram Master computer you recently purchased from us was defective. I realize that it comforts you little to learn that such problems are very rare. We make every effort to insure that our products are free from defects. But, sometimes, even the best efforts are not always adequate.

George Meyer, one of our Customer Service representatives, tells me that a replacement unit has been sent to you. I am confident that it will give you years of trouble-free service.

Mr. Kane, I apologize for the inconvenience you were caused, and I sincerely thank you for your patience and understanding. I invite you to call me at 555-555-5555 if you have any questions concerning your Ram Master.

Sincerely yours,

We Didn't Fix It

Bad as it is when your product fails, it does at least give you the opportunity to build a positive relationship by quickly and efficiently fixing the problem. But what do you do when the fix fails? You write a strong, positive letter, owning up to the error and apologizing for the inconvenience.

Dear Ms. Torrington:

We don't like to hear that one of our products has failed to perform as expected. But on the rare occasions when we fail to service the product adequately the first time we're called out, we are painfully aware that we have really let you down. That's why I was concerned when I learned that the service we provided on April 15 didn't take care of the problem, and it is why I sent our service supervisor to your plant to insure that our fix would work once and for all.

Ms. Torrington, I am very sorry for any inconvenience the problems with the unit and with the subsequent servicing may have created. I am sincerely grateful for the patience and understanding you have shown. I hope that you will believe me when I assure you that such problems—both with the product and with the service—are rare indeed.

If you have any questions at all, please phone me directly at 555-555-5555.

Sincerely yours,

Wrong Place, Wrong Time, Wrong Everything

Unfortunately, billing and shipping errors are not uncommon occurrences. Since they involve time and money—your *customer's* time and money—they can be particularly aggravating. Go the extra mile to soothe the irritation and to assure your customer that the error will not be repeated.

Dear Mr. Taskly:

We were half right. On March 5, 19XX you ordered 25 Mark V 24-inch shelf units. On March 6, we shipped 25 Mark VI wall units. Right quantity, wrong merchandise.

When you called about the error, you had every right to be irritated. But you were gracious, patient, and understanding. For that, I thank you. You are a valued customer, and your understanding is greatly appreciated.

For the error, I apologize, and I assure you that we will make every effort to insure that your patience and understanding are not tested again.

Sincerely,

Dear Mr. Hassler:

I am very sorry that you had to go to the trouble of helping us to resolve an error we made in billing your account. I understand that the problem is now resolved, and that your account has been properly and fully credited.

Mr. Hassler, I sincerely regret the problem, and I assure you that we will make every effort to prevent such an occurrence in the future. I appreciate your patience and understanding in this matter.

Sincerely,

Damage Control

In all good faith, you embark on a project for a client. Something goes wrong. A deadline is missed—

Dear Mr. Nutley:

When we agreed on a deadline for completion of our project, we made a promise to you. We promised to complete the work by February 15, 19XX. As you are very well aware, we are unable to keep that promise.

I don't take a promise lightly, Mr. Nutley, and, for that reason, this is a very difficult letter for me to write. Even though it was inclement weather that made it impossible to complete the work as quickly as we had planned, we accept full responsibility for having missed the deadline—and, more importantly, we are committed to making up for lost time. We are devoting all available resources to completion of construction on or before April 15.

You have been very understanding in this matter. I value you greatly as a client, and I appreciate your patience and continued confidence.

Sincerely,

Sometimes a project simply fails—

Dear Ms. Moran:

Without doubt, it's a heartbreaker. After we—you and I and our staffs—have worked so intensively on a project, it is a difficult thing to admit that the proposal just won't fly.

I know that our companies gave this proposal everything we had to give. I'm sorry it wasn't enough to put us over the top. However, I have no regrets about having worked with your firm, and I look forward to further collaborations—which, I sincerely believe, will be more successful.

Please give me a call at 555-555-5555 when you are prepared to set up a review of the project. Working together, I'm sure we can learn something from what happened, as well as what failed to happen.

Sincerely,

The Check Is in the Mail

A special apology is helpful in cases where you have been unable to render timely payment for merchandise or services. Enclosing a letter with a check mends a lot of fences. It is best if you can include an explanation—not an excuse, but an explanation—for the slow payment.

Dear Ms. Kelly:

Herewith a check for $4,200 in full payment of your invoice number 1234, dated October 3, 19XX.

Along with the check, I hope that you will accept my apologies for the late payment. We have had some internal difficulties here, which are now fully resolved, and I can assure you that future invoices will be paid promptly.

I am very grateful for your patience and understanding in this matter.

Sincerely,

1.3.7.   A Letter or a Phone Call?

Why write? After all, many claims, adjustments, and apologies can be handled quickly over the phone.

Or can they?

Phone calls—especially in these busy days, with two-income families predominating—often meet with answering machines and voice mail. A hearty game of telephone tag can take a good deal more time and effort than a simple letter.

More importantly, letters document problems and their resolution. They provide a paper trail, which is very useful in the event of further claims or even legal action. And, finally, writing a letter about a problem sends the message that you consider the issue an important one—important enough to take the time to write a letter. In and of itself, a letter is a positive act of communication.

1.4. BIDS

1.4.1. Getting the Lowball

Businesses don't only sell goods and services to others, they also buy. But, the fact is, a good "buy" letter is really a good "sales" letter. When you make a purchase, you need to *sell* your supplier on the concept of serving you well, giving you the best deal and the best value possible, and supplying you with the highest-quality product. Your sales pitch must begin with the very first inquiry you make seeking information or with your letter inviting the supplier to bid. Begin by describing your business, emphasizing your reputation, special needs, and so on. In a polite, businesslike, but no-nonsense way, *challenge* the supplier to measure up to your requirements. Finally, and most important, be as specific as possible about the kind of information you are requesting. It is often best to put this material in the form of a list.

If you solicit a bid *after* you have solicited information, include a cover letter with the spec sheet you send. Begin by complimenting the vendor on his product and presentation; let him know that he has persuaded you to expect great things from him. Use the cover letter to highlight any points you may wish to emphasize in your spec sheet, or to ask for information that may have been omitted from the spec sheet (for example, "What is your customer-support policy?"). Be certain to let the supplier know that you have solicited bids from other *excellent* companies. Close by inviting questions and establishing a firm deadline for submission of the bid.

Information, Please

If you decide to gather general information about suppliers before soliciting specific bids, you might send a very simple letter:

Dear Ms. Marsh:

We are in the market for superfine-quality widgets, which we plan to purchase in a quantity exceeding four gross. Please send us as soon as possible spec sheets and price information for your line. We would also appreciate a statement of your credit policy.

Sincerely yours,

Nothing wrong with this approach—as far as it goes. But it doesn't go very far. If you are taking the time and effort to write, why not also take the time and effort to *sell* your company—and *sell* the supplier on giving you his best shot:

Dear Mr. Jenkins:

We are a custom software developer, known for the high quality of our work and the efficiency with which we carry out assignments. We are in need of a supplier who can live up to our reputation. We are interested in the following products:

Individual diskette mailers
CD-ROM jewel cases
Colorful diskette label stock

Please send us a catalog and spec sheets for the above, including a quantity-purchase price list.

Sincerely yours,

Here's another:

Dear Mr. Blankenship:

We are a small manufacturer of specialty electric motors in a highly competitive market. What sets us apart from the crowd is our reputation for top-quality customer support. To provide that level of service, we need dependable support from our own suppliers.

Can you promise to be there for us when need you?

Please send us your latest price list, together with a statement of your customer support policy.

Sincerely,

May I Have Your Bid?

Here is a letter you might write to a supplier from whom you've solicited and received information and from whom you have decided to solicit a bid:

Dear Ms. Reichsman:

We were all highly impressed by your presentation on April 20th, and we believe that you can furnish the products and service we require. Therefore, we ask that you bid on the project we have discussed, per the specification sheet enclosed.

We have solicited bids from a number of excellent suppliers, and since we intend to review them all carefully, we must ask that you submit your bid no later than June 30, 19XX. We cannot grant any extensions.

Please call if you have any questions concerning the specifications. We look forward to receiving your bid.

Sincerely,

Here is a more general letter, which might be used as a follow-up to a presentation or other information, but which can also stand on its own as bid solicitation without any prior communication:

Dear Ms. Maxwell:

Enclosed please find specifications for assorted widgets, which we wish to purchase in gross quantities. We anticipate an initial combined order of approximately eighteen gross. We hereby solicit your bid on supplying these quantities. Kindly include a statement of your credit and customer support policies with your bid.

As we have solicited bids from a number of excellent suppliers, we ask that you submit your bid no later than March 14, 19XX, so that we can fully evaluate all proposals. We cannot grant extensions.

Please call if you have any questions regarding the specifications.

Sincerely,

Here is letter that is effective for mass solicitation—that is, soliciting bids from a number of suppliers at once:

Dear Mr. Yardley:

Vortex Drain Plugs, a small specialty plumbing wholesaler serving the Warrenville area, is soliciting bids for plumbing work to be supplied for a major new hotel. A full specification sheet is enclosed, and we direct your particular attention to the following three critical areas:

◆ Quality of product
◆ Quality of service
◆ Price

Your bid will be evaluated in terms of all three areas of concern to us.

We have solicited bids from a number of excellent suppliers, and since we intend to review them all carefully, we must ask that you submit your bid no later than January 4, 19XX. We cannot grant any extensions.

Please call me at 555-555-5555 if you have any questions concerning the specifications.

We look forward to evaluating your proposal.

Sincerely yours,

Suppliers are often selected on the basis of recommendation from colleagues and even friendly competitors. In soliciting bids from suppliers recommended to you, always stress that they have a lot to live up to:

Dear Ms. Walters:

Walter Bernard of Ajax, Bernard, and Company has recommended you to us as a fine supplier of widget retainers. We've worked with Mr. Bernard for more than eight years and have learned to value his opinion. Based on his recommendation, we've come to you and ask that you bid on the items specified on the enclosed spec sheet. Please provide prices on the quantities indicated, plus run-on prices for additional 1,000s.

If you have any questions concerning the specifications, please call me at 555-555- 5555. As mentioned on the spec sheet, we go into production on August 25, 19XX, so we need to have your bid no later than May 30, which will give us sufficient time to evaluate it.

Sincerely,

1.4.2. Pitching the Fastball

Here is an elementary truth that some of us forget all of the time and all of us forget some of the time: A good value is not the same as a low price. The price of an item or service is a fixed amount, a figure in isolation. The value of an item or service is the ratio of price to benefit. We've all had experiences with so-called bargain products that perform poorly or break down quickly. Their price may be low, but their cost—in terms of time, aggravation, inconvenience—is outrageous. A cover letter to accompany a bid should educate your customer by pointing out the value you offer. You cannot control the prices others may charge, but you can exercise a substantial degree of control over the value you offer. Therefore, emphasize the component you can regulate.

In addition, use the cover letter to remind the customer just what it is that you are bidding on, and take the opportunity to point out any special product or service features or any assumptions you have made. For example, if the customer has asked you to bid on bolts and has failed to specify the matching nuts, you probably will want to bid on the bolts alone and on the bolt-and-nut package. Point out in your letter that you have done so.

Here are three brief examples:

Dear Ms. Donaldson:

It is a pleasure to send you the enclosed bid on your project number 657/89. You have made your specifications and requirements very clear indeed, and our figures reflect strict adherence to them. In short, you can act on our bid with complete confidence.

Do call if you have any questions. I look forward to hearing from you.

Sincerely,

Dear Mr. Edwards:

Many thanks for your phone call of April 8. It is my pleasure to send the enclosed estimate. I know you will find our prices competitive, but what the numbers can't show you is the special quality of our service. That, too, will make a big difference in your bottom line and represents true value.

Please give me a call if you have any questions. I look forward to hearing from you.

Sincerely,

Dear Mr. Watson:

I'm pleased to enclose our estimate for the Youngstown project. We take pride in our competitive edge—when it comes to numbers and when it comes to the high quality of our service. We go the extra mile for each and every customer.

I'll call you at the end of the week to answer any questions you may have, unless, of course, I hear from you before then.

Sincerely,

1.5. COLLECTIONS

1.5.1. The Fine Art of Getting What's Yours

You against a deadbeat: If ever there was an adversarial relation in business, *this* is it.

No question, right?

Wrong!

There is a remarkable secret to collections that all smart business communicators need to know. You and your delinquent account are *not* enemies. In fact, you have something very much in common: a problem with money. You need to be paid, and he can't pay you. This situation does not make you enemies, but allies, whose mutual best interest will be served once he is enabled to pay you and you are paid.

Don't make the mistake of confusing the natural desire to avoid forking out cash with the equally natural desire to discharge a debt. True, few people like paying, but virtually no one likes owing.

> **REVELATION:** He *Wants* to Pay You. In writing collection letters, the business communicator should work from the assumption that—whether he knows it or not—your delinquent account *wants* to pay you. He may not be able to pay at the moment, or he may believe that he is unable to pay, but, if he's a normal human being, he has no desire to owe you money.

> **TIP:** To Get What You Want, Give *Him* What *He* Wants. You want to be paid, so give your account the opportunity to pay you. Here's how:

1. These days, it seems that businesses routinely hold invoices for thirty days before paying. Sixty or even ninety days is not unusual. Do you really want to wait that long to get paid? Stop taking the thirty-day (let alone sixty- or ninety-day) payment cycle for granted.

2. Don't wait for thirty days to pass before writing your first collection letter.

3. Send a *positive* reminder at ten or fifteen days.

4. Offer an incentive to prompt payment.

5. Send a *helpful note* at thirty days, reminding the account of any incentives you offer or advising him that he can still avoid finance charges. Include a duplicate invoice.

6. At sixty days, appeal to the account for his *help* and *cooperation.* Include a duplicate invoice. Invite communication.

7. At ninety days, reintroduce an incentive. Invite communication.

8. Past ninety days, warn of credit suspension or legal action. This should not be issued as a threat—something that *you* will do to *him*—but as a dangerously impending action *you* (and your account) very much want to avoid.

How to Practice Preventive Medicine

The best way to deal with collections is to avoid having to make them in the first place. Send a cover note or insert with your invoice, reminding the account that your low prices are based on ten-day (or whatever) net terms. For example:

Dear Ms. Firkins:

At Foxworth, we take pride in giving our clients the best service at the lowest prices. You can help us control costs—ours and yours—by noting our ten-day terms and making payment no later than October 4.

It is a pleasure to serve you.

Sincerely,

How to Administer Stronger Medicine

You'll be pleasantly surprised by the power of good communication—a simple note, like the one above, included with an invoice. But, truth to tell, nothing speaks louder or more convincingly than money or extra value.

RECOMMENDATION: Offer a positive, tangible incentive to prompt payment. Usually, this will be a very modest discount on the cost of goods or services (say 2 or 3 percent), but it might also be a coupon discounting future goods or services (this is also an incentive to continue doing business with you), or some other consideration (free delivery, say, or a baker's dozen for the price of twelve). Include a cover note with the invoice clearly explaining the incentive:

Dear Ms. Brookes:

The enclosed invoice says you owe us $575. Do you *really* want to pay that much?

I invite you to subtract $11.50 from the invoice total for rendering payment before September 5. That's a 2 percent discount from our already low price—just for paying promptly.

Sincerely,

RECOMMENDATION: Intervene Even Earlier. Why hold off announcing an incentive until you submit your invoice? If you send the customer a bid or proposal, include with *it* a cover note explaining your incentive program:

Dear Mr. Thoth:

I am pleased to enclose our bid on the complete computer system you have specified. I am confident that you will be gratified not only by the system, but the value it represents. At Aegis, we take special pride in giving our clients something extra—and that begins right now. I invite you to take a 2-percent discount on the low price of our Vectrex 560 when you pay within ten days of our invoice date.

It's our way of thanking you for helping us control costs and continue to give you the very best value in computer equipment.

Sincerely yours,

How Incentives Give You Leverage in Collections

Ideally, the incentive you offer will not only avert delay and delinquency, but will promote exceptionally prompt payment. Even if your customer or client does not avail himself of the initial incentive offer, you can use the incentive as a negotiating tool in a subsequent reminder letter. Let's say an account has just slipped past the thirty-day mark:

Dear Mr. Francis:

You are about to pay us more than was really necessary.

No kidding.

No, it's not a mistake, and we're not out to cheat you. It's just that you've chosen not to take advantage of the 2-percent discount we offer on accounts paid within fifteen days of our invoice date.

So why am I telling you this now that *thirty* days have passed?

Because we're willing to extend those terms. But just a little bit.

Send payment in full by April 5, and take that 2 percent off the total. If you've already sent us the payment, we'll credit that 2 percent toward your next order with us.

Sincerely yours,

Of course, you can vary the incentive from the original, if you wish. At thirty days, you might offer a 2 percent discount on the next order only. Or you might offer, say a 1.5 percent discount for payment received by a certain date.

How to Use Negative Incentives

Another incentive strategy is based on telling your account that, by paying promptly, he can avoid a finance, service, or administrative charge. Since you are waiving a charge rather than offering a discount, this incentive is "negative." It is important that you clearly and fully inform your client or customer about your policy regarding finance or administrative charges. Your invoice should say something like: "Payments received more than thirty days after invoice date are subject to a 1.5 percent administrative fee." But to make the administrative fee really effective as a negative incentive, include a cover letter or insert with your invoice:

Dear Customer:

Please remember—Avoid the 1.5 percent administrative fee by remitting payment in full no later than March 15.

Let's say your policy is to charge a $6 administrative fee on accounts unpaid after thirty days. At fifteen days, send your customer a friendly reminder:

Dear Customer:

Thanks for your recent order!

We appreciate prompt payment and will therefore waive our $6 adminis-
trative fee if we receive your check by April 4.

Why not save money and send your payment today?

Sincerely,

Such reminders can be framed as helpful, money-saving advice rather than
issued as an annoying collection notice.

SPECIAL CASE: *The New Customer.*

Customer service experts caution against using such phrases as "company policy" because they convey an inflexible adherence to rules and procedure at the expense of the individual customer or client. In short, they
suggest that you think more of the company manual than of the human
beings you are supposed to serve. On the other hand, it is possible to
administer a policy with so much flexibility that it becomes completely
meaningless and ineffectual. Strike a happy medium. Let's say you allow a 2
percent discount on accounts paid within fifteen days. After two weeks,
account number 1234 remains unpaid and you want to send a reminder.
What's the incentive? If she's a new customer, why not cut her a break?

> Dear Ms. Hacker:
>
> Thanks for your recent order. Our policy is to assess a $5 administrative fee
> on accounts unpaid after thirty days. Your account has now gone past that
> point, but, because you are a brand-new customer, we will be pleased to
> waive the administrative fee if we receive your payment by September 30.
>
> Why not put your check into the mail today?
>
> Sincerely,

How to Write a Collection Series

Preventive medicine and incentives are effective, but, let's face it, the
time will come—and come repeatedly—when you will need not one, but a
series of collection letters. Don't wait until the days, weeks, and months pass
by to compose the necessary document. And don't reinvent the wheel each
time you need a letter. Plan a series of letters, beginning with a reminder at
fifteen days and going through thirty, sixty, ninety days and beyond. Here is a
generic series you can modify to suit:

Fifteen Days

Dear _____:

Just a friendly reminder that, after **date**, finance charges of **percent amount** will begin to accrue on the payment due for your recent order with us.

Why not avoid unnecessary finance charges by sending your payment today?

Sincerely yours,

Thirty Days

Dear _____:

It's so easy to forget.

Your account with us is now past 30 days and is, therefore, subject to a finance charge of **percent amount** percent.

But, as I said, it *is* easy to forget, and you *are* a brand new customer, with whom I look forward to doing a lot more business. So why don't you send us a check today for **$ amount**, and I will waive the finance charge.

I look forward to hearing from you.

Sincerely yours,

Or:

Dear _____:

I'm not worried. Place another order with us, and we'll fill it just as quickly and efficiently as we always do.

But it does take cash to keep us going, and I'm writing to remind you that your account with us is now beyond our thirty-day net terms.

Please help us out by sending your check today.

Sincerely,

WARNING: Threats may or may not get action. But, as often as not, the action they get is not the action you want. Maybe a threat will get you your money, but it will probably lose you a customer as well. Better than threatening your tardy account is appealing to him for *help* and *cooperation*. A threat takes away choice. In contrast, an appeal for help empowers your customer or client by giving him the opportunity to choose to help you.

Sixty Days

Dear _____:

As you know, the price we quoted for your recent order was based on 30-day net terms. Now that your unpaid account is 60 days old, we need your help.

We want to continue to provide you—and our other clients—with the personal, high-value service you've come to expect from us. To do this, however, we need to adhere to 30-day terms in order to keep carrying costs at a level we can manage.

Won't you help us by mailing your check in the amount of **$ amount** today?

Please give me a call at **555-5555** if you have any questions.

Sincerely yours,

TIP: Try adding to your appeal for help an appeal to fairness. The reasonable price you quoted was based on certain terms, which your account, in all fairness, must now live up to. Point this out—but without preaching.

Ninety Days

Dear _____:

I'm puzzled. Your account has just gone past 90 days and is therefore subject to **$ amount** in administrative fees. I know that you aren't eager to throw money away, so there must be a good reason why this bill has gone unpaid.

Why not tell me about it? Please give me a call at **555-5555** so that we can work together to keep you from incurring any additional charges.

Better yet, put a check for **$ amount** into the mail today, and I will waive the 90-day administrative fee.

Sincerely yours,

Or:

Dear _____:

When a great customer like you lets an invoice go ninety days unpaid, there's always a good reason: illness, cash-flow problem—something.

Maybe I can help. Certainly, it would be to our mutual advantage to work together to settle your account.

But I can't do anything until you let me know what's going on. Why not give me a call at **555-5555**, so that I can be of assistance?

Sincerely yours,

TIP: The concepts of *helping* and *fairness* are powerful collections tools. Even more important is the idea of *working together* to solve what is, after all, a problem you and your account share. You may resent and feel angry toward a delinquent account; that's normal. But you literally cannot afford to alienate him. Like it or not, you're in this thing together.

Lack of Response. Many accounts that go past ninety days simply clam up. You stop hearing from them. And you get angrier and angrier and increasingly frustrated. Maybe the account is in serious financial difficulty and is being dunned left and right. When an account is wholly unresponsive, try addressing the issue of communication rather than the issue of money. Get him talking first; then you can begin to work out a financial solution. In the absence of communication, however, neither of you has a chance.

Dear _____:

They say silence is golden.

But after three months, it begins to tarnish. And soon I will be left with no choice other than to compel communication—by means of our attorneys.

Why should we let things get that far?

Please, give me a call today at **555-5555** so that we can discuss your account and, together, work out a reasonable plan for settling it—a plan that will let you pay it and keep us in business together.

I look forward to hearing from you.

Sincerely,

Warning of Credit Suspension. At some point (for many businesses, the time limit is 90-120 days), something more than a letter or request is appropriate. Suspension of credit not only protects you from incurring additional bad debt, it sends a strong message to your account. After all, a business deprived of credit is soon gripped by a financial paralysis that may well prove fatal. Unfortunately, credit suspension is also a double-edged sword. Suspend a client's credit, and, sure enough, he can't do business—with you. Therefore, it is important to communicate fully and convincingly before you actually suspend credit. An effective warning letter can make this necessary evil a potent negative incentive.

Dear _____:

This is not a letter I enjoy writing. Your unpaid account with us is now approaching 120 days. We have earnestly and repeatedly offered to work with you to help settle the account, but we have made no progress.

I must now advise you that we will be forced to suspend your credit privileges with **Name of company** if we do not receive a payment of **$ amount** by **date**.

It is in our mutual best interest to avoid this step. And it is within your power to avoid it. Send your payment by **date**, and your credit account will remain active and your credit standing unblemished.

Why not send a check today?

Please call me at **555-5555** if you have any questions.

Sincerely,

The letter above pulls no punches, but it still invites positive action and cooperation. Another strategy that communicates the urgency of the situation without pitting you against your account is a letter that separates you from the impending action. It is not that *you* will suspend your customer's credit, but that your *credit manager* or *accounts supervisor* will. A letter like the one that follows teams you and your account against this menacing third party:

Dear _____:

My accounts supervisor is on my back. When your unpaid account slipped past ninety days, she suggested a credit suspension. Now that it's about to go past 120 days, she's screaming for me to stop credit and turn the account over to a collection agency.

I don't want to do this.

What I want is to get your account back on track and to continue doing business with you.

But I need your help and cooperation. Sending a payment of **$ amount** today will hold off my accounts supervisor and give you and me time to work out, together, a plan for settling your account in full.

Please let me hear from you today.

Sincerely yours,

Warning of Collection or Legal Action. If you have had the misfortune of writing (or, worse, receiving) letters warning of impending collection agency action, you know that these are calculated to make the delinquent account feel like an outcast, a financial pariah. *You are a deadbeat,* such letters say, *and we wash our hands of you.* Most collection warnings are designed to make the recipient feel bad. *You owe. You haven't paid. You should feel terrible.*
What's the point of that?

> **TIP:** The purpose of a collection letter is *not* to make the delinquent account feel bad. The sole purpose of a collection letter is to collect the debt owed to you.

A good way to avoid merely making your correspondent feel bad—and, instead, to get him working on a way to settle the account—is to use the warning of agency or legal action much as you use the warning of credit suspension: not as a cudgel, but as a potent negative incentive to payment.
It's hard to find anybody who likes lawyers or bill collectors. And this is a fact you can use to your advantage:

Dear _____:

Our attorneys have advised us to act immediately to collect the balance due on your account.

I am not eager to resort to legal action, but, since we have received no response to our letters and phone calls, I may have no choice.

You, however, still have choices. Either send us your payment in full immediately, a partial payment with a note of explanation and a proposal for settling the account, or telephone me at **555-5555** so that we can discuss your account.

Alternatively, you can continue to ignore our attempts to communicate and deal instead with our attorneys. But, I think you will agree that it would be far more productive to work *together* to settle your account rather than wait for our legal people to work *against* you.

Sincerely yours,

Tested Strategies for Dealing with Repeat Offenders

There are some firms and individuals—and, these days, the number seems to be growing—who routinely pay their bills late. One surefire way to deal with these folks is to stop doing credit business with them, and, indeed, in some cases, this may be the only workable solution. But, if you don't wish to cut such accounts off, you need to find a way to break the cycle of repeated delinquencies. The best strategy in these cases is to let your account know that you take your billing cycle seriously and that prompt payment is part and parcel of the terms of sale of goods or services. Make it clear that you are aware of the pattern of delinquencies, and that such a habit of business is unacceptable. If possible, offer to discuss alternative payment terms that may better accommodate the client or customer's own cycle of payables and receivables.

Dear _____:

I don't want to stop—but I soon may have no other choice.

Your account with us is now more than ninety days past due for the **third, fourth, and so forth** time this year.

We are very grateful for your business, but, as you know, it is extremely difficult to manage cash flow without a stable and reliable pattern of payment from all customers.

Cash flow is a critical subject at our firm, and we try to be sensitive to the cash flow needs of our customers. Your pattern of repeated late payments suggests that our billing cycle may be inconvenient for you. Please call to discuss your account so that we can establish a payment plan we both can live with.

Sincerely,

What to Write When the Check Bounces

Few payment situations are more aggravating than getting hit with a rubber check. You have a choice of responses:

1. Simply redeposit the check. It is your right—though, depending on your relationship with your bank, you may be assessed additional fees if the check is returned again.

2. Telephone the client or his bookkeeper or controller to advise her that you are redepositing. Or request a cashier's check as a replacement.

3. Write to the bookkeeper or controller.

In addition, you need to decide on the appropriate tone of the letter. Avoid angrily scrawled notes. In most cases, a cool, businesslike letter sufficiently conveys displeasure and should promote a prompt remedy. Keep it simple:

Dear _____:

Your check number **123** in the amount of **$ amount** and dated **date** was returned to us because of insufficient funds **or other reason**. At your option, we will redeposit the check (in which case, please send us an additional check for **$ amount** to cover bank charges and our handling costs) or, on receipt of a new check in the amount of **$ amount** (this includes bank charges and handling costs), we will return the dishonored check.

Or:

Please send us a cashier's check, certified check, or bank money order for the balance due plus **$ amount** to cover bank charges and our handling costs. We will return the dishonored check on receipt of payment.

Sincerely,

In cases where you have a longstanding and friendly business relationship with an account, you may want to use a lighter touch aimed at letting your correspondent know that you realize "accidents will happen":

Dear _____:

It happens to the best of us. And you certainly qualify as one of the best.

Your check number **123** in the amount of **$ amount** was just returned to us because of insufficient funds **or other reason**.

Would you like me to redeposit the check? (If so, please send me an additional check for **$ amount** to cover bank charges and handling.) Or would you rather send a new check for **$ amount**, which includes bank fees and handling costs?

Please let me know—and I appreciate your prompt attention to this matter.

Sincerely,

How to Respond to Partial Payments

Sometimes a customer will send you partial payment on an invoice. When this is the result of mutual agreement, there is no problem. But the matter is more delicate when something less than expected arrives unannounced. It is best to acknowledge the payment with more than a receipt or a statement. Send a note that balances thanks with a gentle but firm admonition for the future:

Dear _____:

Thank you for your payment of **$ amount** on your account **number**. Please note that the total due at this time is **$ amount**, which leaves an open balance of **$ amount**.

At **Name of company**, we believe in being sufficiently flexible to accommodate our customers' needs. Should you find it necessary to modify payment terms in the future, please call me in advance to set up a mutually agreeable schedule. In the meantime, please call me at **555-5555** to let me know when to expect the balance due on the current invoice.

Sincerely yours,

SPECIAL CASE: How to Mend Broken Vows. As movie mogul Samuel Goldwyn once said, "A verbal contract ain't worth the paper it's printed on." Whenever you agree to modify payment terms, send a reminder/memorandum confirming your understanding of the agreement:

Dear _____:

To confirm this morning's telephone conversation: Regarding invoice number **1234**, you agree to make **number** payments of **$ amount** each on **dates**.

Sincerely,

But what happens if the promised payment doesn't arrive?

You have a right to be angry, but that won't help you get your money. The more effective approach is to send a reminder that makes prominent use of the powerful word *promise:*

Dear _____:

Please note that we have yet to receive the **$ amount** you promised by **date** in our **date** agreement. I'd appreciate your sending the check today. Please give me a call at **555-5555** if there is any problem.

Sincerely yours,

If you prefer, you might make a phone call first, secure a new promise date, then drop a confirmation note in the mail:

Dear _____:

Just to confirm our phone conversation this afternoon: On invoice number **number**, you now will send **$ amount** immediately and **number** payments of **$ amount** each on **dates**.

Since this is a revision of what you originally promised, I trust this payment schedule will remain firm.

Sincerely,

Is all of this back-and-forth too much writing? Well, it is annoying, and maybe a few simple phone calls would do. Maybe. But, where money is concerned, *written* communication is most powerful, and the time and trouble you take to send notes and reminders is likely to produce surer results than a telephone call alone.

What if, after phone calls and written reminders, the promised payments still do not show up? You could justifiably resort to the final stages of the collection process, perhaps beginning with a warning of credit suspension and/or legal action. However, you might first try a letter that addresses the breach of promise as a crisis in communication, understanding, and trust.

Dear _____:

I am very concerned about the outstanding balance on your account with us.

It is not just the sum owed, but the fact that you and I have repeatedly made payment arrangements that have failed to materialize. As you know, communication, understanding, and trust are as important in business as cash. And, right now, I can only conclude that we are facing a crisis of communication, understanding, and trust.

Please, **Name**, let's work together to settle this account once and for all. Let's work out a payment schedule we both can live with and we both will honor.

Please give me a call at **555-5555** to discuss this matter while we still have a variety of options for settling it.

Sincerely yours,

TIP: The object is not to threaten, but to make your correspondent aware of present and future consequences. Communicate frankly, but never deprive your correspondent of choices. Instead, empower your correspondent. Make him responsible for the next move. Make it clear that he has it within his power to choose to honor the agreement(s) he made. The goal is not to trap and contain, but to liberate and motivate—to *move* your correspondent in the direction you want him to go.

Checklist for Effective Collection Letters

1. Approach the task positively by assuming that your correspondent actually *wants* to pay you.

2. Remember that, like it or not, you and your correspondent are financial partners, not enemies.

3. Don't wait for an account to become delinquent before reacting. Take a proactive approach by making incentives to prompt payment part of your bid, proposal, or invoice.

4. Use incentives for negotiating leverage.

5. Develop and use negative incentives.

6. Think of collection letters as a series of correspondence spanning the entire payment cycle.

7. Do not make threats, but do make your correspondent aware of consequences.

8. Empower your correspondent by making it clear that it is within his power to *choose* to settle the account.

9. Develop the powerful concepts of *helping* and *fairness*.

10. Make every effort to establish and maintain lines of communication.

11. When strong measures are required—credit suspension, legal action—distance yourself from the impending step: Credit suspension is imminent, but it is a step you as well as your correspondent want to avert. Make it clear to your correspondent that it is not too late for her to take action to avert it.

12. Angry as you are, remember that you literally *cannot afford* to alienate a customer or client who owes you money.

The Bottom Line

The bottom line? Collection letters are really sales letters. Their job is to sell your correspondent on the idea of paying you. Selling, of course, is based on an appeal to a need and/or a desire. A good collection letter shows your correspondent how she can satisfy her *need* to pay you as well as her *desire* not to owe you. Stop thinking of collection letters as attempts to *get* something. Start thinking of them as efforts to *sell.* The "products" you offer are freedom from a particular debt, peace of mind, credit in good standing, and the feeling that comes with paying what is owed.

1.5.2. How to Respond to Collection Letters—When It's in the Mail (and When It's Not)

Few business situations are more annoying than having to respond to an erroneous or unjustified collection demand. And few business situations are more painful than having to respond to a demand that is justified. Let's begin with the first situation.

False or Erroneous Collection Claims

There are two distinct approaches available for responding to unwarranted collection attempts. You can be friendly, enlisting the agency's help in clearing up a vexing matter, or you can be stern, demanding that the collection agency immediately cease and desist collection action. The first approach is appropriate for fairly minor problems, but the second approach packs more legal power. In the case of an erroneous or unjustified claim, it is important to get on record a demand that the agency cease and desist attempts to contact you. Keep the demand businesslike. Remember, collection agencies are made up of human beings, and it will not serve your purposes to antagonize anyone. However, you don't have to be particularly pleasant. If the claim against you is unwarranted, there may be little point in building a relationship with the agency.

Here is an example of the friendly, "help me" approach:

Dear **name of agency representative**:

Maybe you can help me out.

I received your notification that my account with **name of creditor**, account number 1234, has been turned over to your agency. On September 5, 19XX, I refused to take delivery of the merchandise for which I am being charged. The reason for my refusal was that I had not ordered the merchandise. **Name of creditor** acknowledged the return of their goods on September 12, and a photocopy of that acknowledgment is enclosed.

Since October 24, 19XX, when **name of creditor** first notified me of their mistaken assertion that I owe them money, I have communicated with them by telephone and letter, advising them of the error.

Now they've turned the account over to you.

I ask that you help me by speaking with your client. Perhaps you can convince **name of creditor** to stop harassing me.

In any event, I will expect a prompt response from either you or **name of creditor** finally and absolutely acknowledging that the charges asserted here are in error and that I do not, in fact, owe this amount or any other to **name of creditor** or your agency.

Sincerely,

Here is a generic form of the "stern" letter:

Dear **name of agency representative**:

I received your notification that our account with **name of creditor**, account number 1234, has been turned over to your agency. On **date** I advised **name of creditor** by letter (photocopy enclosed) that financial difficulties made it impossible for us to render full payment on our account. I proposed alternative payment terms, which **name of creditor** accepted in a letter dated **date** (photocopy enclosed). Our firm has kept faithfully to those alternative terms, and **name of creditor** has not advised me of any dissatisfaction, let alone default. Therefore, I must advise you that the account was turned over to your agency in error. Please inform your client.

I expect a timely response either from you or from **name of creditor** acknowledging that our agreement of **date** is in force and has thus far been satisfied. I also expect **name of client** to recall the account from your agency, and I am sending him a letter to that effect, together with a copy of this letter.

Inasmuch as your attempt to collect on this account is without basis, I demand that you cease and desist all further attempts to collect from me.

Sincerely yours,

Special Circumstance: The Bankruptcy Rebuttal

A judgment of bankruptcy generally gives you immunity from the assaults of creditors and their agents. Use this letter form to make a bankruptcy rebuttal:

Dear **name of lawyer or manager of collection agency**:

I have received your letter, dated **date**, demanding payment of **$ amount** on behalf of **name of creditor**.

On **date, name of creditor** was notified of a petition of business bankruptcy filed on behalf of **name of business**, in **city and state**, on **date**, under docket number **123456**.

Please be advised that all creditors, once advised of such a petition, are barred from pursuing collection of a debt through their own efforts or those of a second party. There are serious penalties for violating this provision of the bankruptcy code.

All future correspondence on this matter should be directed to my attorney, **name and address**.

Sincerely,

When You Owe

So much for *their* mistakes. What happens when *you* make one? Cash flow problems and simple errors sometimes put you on the receiving end of a collection letter. Your first impulse may be to hang your head in shame—and then bury that head in the sand. Your second impulse? To avoid your creditor or creditors by whatever means necessary.

Fight both impulses. Unfortunately, cash flow problems and errors are part of doing business. They happen, they aren't pleasant, but they're nothing to be ashamed of. It is critical not only that you do not avoid your creditors, but that you establish and maintain communication with them. If you have payment problems and then play hard-to-get, your creditor will assume that you are, in effect, a thief. If, on the other hand, you approach the creditor as what he is—in effect, a business partner—you have a good shot at maintaining a viable relationship, and you will most likely be able to work out payment terms you can live with.

This is a time to take a proactive stance. If possible, don't wait until you actually become delinquent and need to reply to a letter from your creditor or from a collection agency. It is better to write in advance of delinquency when you know that you are going to have a payment problem.

> **TIP:** Believe it or not, advising a creditor of a payment problem can actually help build a positive relationship. Asking for help empowers your business "partner." Make the best of a difficult situation. Transform it into an opportunity.

Here are letters advising a vendor of a payment problem:

Dear Mr. Kelton:

I am writing to advise you that our payment for order number 1234 will be made on October 5, which is 20 days beyond your thirty-day terms.

I hope this will cause you no undue inconvenience, and please rest assured that all future payments will be on time.

Kindly call me if you have any questions.

Sincerely yours,

If feasible, it is helpful to explain the nature of the problem you are experiencing. Make certain that your explanation comes across as an explanation and not as an excuse. Also stress that the problem is a temporary one, will be resolved, and will not be repeated:

Dear Ms. Gorham:

Because of a temporary cash flow problem, it will be necessary for us to split the payment due to you on March 6. We will pay $850 on the due date, and the balance, $1,200, on April 5.

I will call before February 15 to confirm that this arrangement is satisfactory with you. Please be assured that all future payments will be made in full and on time.

I greatly appreciate your understanding in this matter.

Sincerely yours,

Tip: It is better to propose a specific plan of action than it is simply to tell your creditor that you have a problem and "something needs to be figured out." It's bad enough that you are causing your creditor inconvenience and, possibly, anxiety. Don't force him also to do a lot of thinking. Of course, you must invite the creditor's approval of and agreement to your proposal.

Asking for help does not put you in a subservient or weak position. Quite the contrary, it empowers you by giving you the opportunity to empower your creditor. Asking for help also prompts the creditor to make, in effect, an additional investment in you instead of writing you off:

Dear Ms. Frances:

Can you help me? I have just been confronted with a group of emergency expenses. It would greatly help me to manage next month's cash flow if you would allow me to defer $1,500 of the payment due on August 20 until October 1. The balance of the payment, $1,000, will be paid on the August 20 due date.

Unless I hear otherwise from you, I will call on July 15 to confirm that this arrangement is acceptable. It would be a terrific help in the present situation.

Sincerely,

An especially embarrassing and potentially destructive situation occurs when you experience a payment problem with a brand-new vendor. A proactive message can save the day—and save a relationship:

Dear Mr. Nesbitt:

I regret beginning our relationship this way, but funding for the Johnson project is being delayed until the end of March, which means that we will have to defer payment on the order we placed with you until March 20. I realize that this falls 15 after our 30-day terms, but I ask that you waive any interest penalty because the problem is beyond our control.

Ms. Gloria Wrentham of Johnson and Wrentham, our client, assures me that, after this initial glitch, all subsequent funding will be timely and that we need anticipate no further problems.

Unless I hear from you before then, I will call before the end of this month to confirm your agreement to defer the first payment without penalty.

I appreciate your understanding in this matter, and I look forward to working together to make this project a success.

Sincerely yours,

When It Hits the Fan

One of the big problems with a cash crunch is that you can't always see it coming. When it does, you need to fight the impulse to panic. Channel the energy that would otherwise be wasted in panic into getting the help and cooperation of your creditors.

The adage "Let sleeping dogs lie" is especially destructive in business. When a payment problem occurs, apologize—not with a simple "I'm sorry," but with an explanation of how you propose to deal with the problem and, equally important, how your creditor can help. If possible, the communication should be accompanied by some portion of the money owed.

Here are some sample letters to accompany partial payment of accounts payable:

> Dear Mr. Turkington:
>
> Enclosed is our check for $800, which I am sending in partial payment of the invoice due on June 3. I will send a check for the balance on August 3, which, I realize, puts us past thirty days on the invoice.
>
> We are experiencing a cash flow crunch because of some emergency expenses. Rather than hand you a lot of excuses, I thought it better to mail you a check instead—even though it is less than the total due.
>
> I hope this does not cause you any inconvenience. If you have any questions, please call me at 555-5555. I thank you for your patience and understanding.
>
> Sincerely,

A more familiar approach—useful if you are well acquainted with the creditor:

> Dear Joe:
>
> Enclosed please find half a loaf, which, as you know, is better than none.
>
> We've run up against a raft of emergency expenses, which has left us, frankly, strapped. Cash flow should be back to normal by the middle of September, and I will send you a check for the balance of the invoice total before the end of that month.
>
> I'm sorry to do this to you, but I am, in a word, stuck. You can, however, count on getting the balance before September 30. For now, please accept half, along with my sincere thanks for your understanding.
>
> Best regards,

Apologizing for Late Payment

Begin by realizing that the mere fact of formally apologizing for a late payment or a missed payment or other financial glitch goes a long way toward defusing a potentially rancorous situation. An apology need not be elaborate and should not be abject. Simply do the following:

1. Make it clear that you are apologizing. Use such phrases as "I hope you will accept my apology," "I'm sorry," and the like.

2. Include with your apology some positive steps toward remedying the problem. Enclose a check, if possible, for the full amount due or, at the very least, propose a definite plan for settling your account or rectifying the error.

3. Include a brief and direct explanation of whatever has caused the problem.

Depending on your relationship with your correspondent, it might be appropriate to keep the tone light-hearted, even humorous—especially at your own expense. Honesty is disarming. If you tell your correspondent that you made a "dumb" mistake, she will respect your hard-nosed self-assessment and admire your willingness to cut through any pretense of corporate bureaucracy by taking responsibility for your actions. A good, direct apology is personal and human. Your customer is made to feel that he is dealing with the person in charge.

Here is an assortment of damage-control letters:

Dear Mr. Bronson:

I hope you will accept my apology for having let this invoice go over thirty days. More to the point, please accept the enclosed check for payment in full.

We've had a very hectic month, including some internal glitches, which are now fully resolved. Be assured that future invoices will be paid promptly.

Thanks for your patience and understanding.

Sincerely yours,

Dear Ms. Roderick:

We're in a squeeze. This has been a very rough quarter for us, and we are just easing out of a cash flow bind. I am writing to apologize for paying your December 3 invoice late. You will receive my check for payment in full by February 15. I hope this will pose no problem for you. Your patience and understanding at this time will certainly help us out.

Do call me at 555-555-5555 if what I propose is not agreeable to you.

Sincerely,

Dear Fred:

Don't cuss and don't break up laughing. The truth is that I really did file your invoice of September 20, forgot about, and only now resurrected it.

The check, as they say, is in the mail.

I hope my delay has not caused you any inconvenience.

Sincerely yours,

Dear Mr. Mason:

The enclosed check is a few days late because we experienced delays with checks from our clients. I apologize for the delay, which, you may be assured, will not be repeated. We have set up this project account to insure timely payment—even if our clients hiccup again.

Sincerely yours,

If possible—and appropriate—give a very specific reason for delayed payment:

Dear Ms. Calloway:

You may have heard about the fire we had in our offices on April 14. Fortunately, no one was injured, but our records took a beating—more from water than flame. Our first order of business was to sort through our payables in order to expedite funds due to folks like you.

Enclosed is a check for $2,321.98, which represents payment for your invoice number 1234. I apologize for the delay in paying. We are now back up to speed, and you will experience no further delays.

We at Acme Widget greatly appreciate your patience and understanding in this crisis.

Sincerely yours,

Dear Mr. Thomas :

Enclosed please find our check for $497, and please accept our apology for its late arrival.

Our bookkeeper of very long standing left us suddenly, and, frankly, in the scramble to keep money going in and out while we broke in another bookkeeper, we stumbled.

Rest assured that we're back on track, and you will not have to endure any further delays.

Sincerely yours,

What if you just paid late and have no excuse? Try this approach:

Dear Ms. Larson:

It's embarrassing for us both, and I should not have put you in the position of having to call about our late payment. I'm sorry.

My check in the amount of $650 is enclosed. Again, I apologize.

Sincerely yours,

Checklist for Responding to Collection Requests

1. The best alternative is to be proactive. Advise creditors of problems before they occur. Propose a solution to the problem.

2. Do not evade or ignore your creditors. Go out of your way to build a partnership with her.

3. If possible, include at least partial payment with all explanations for late payment.

4. Provide a payment schedule. Be specific about what you propose to do in order to resolve payment problems.

5. Stress that your current financial problem is temporary and that your policy is prompt payment.

1.6.   COMMUNITY RELATIONS

1.6.1.   How Good Letters Make Good Neighbors

To its employees and to other firms, a business is a business. To the community in which the business resides, however, it is a neighbor and a citizen. Thoughtfully produced letters can enhance your firm's image within the community and, indeed, can even enhance the life of the community itself.

Businesses often participate in community affairs by working to raise funds for charitable and community-oriented causes. You may, therefore, be called on from time to time to write effective fundraising appeals. Just as you may originate charitable campaigns, you will likely be asked by others to contribute to various causes. You may be unable or unwilling to contribute to some of these. An effective letter will prevent your alienating members of the community.

The activities of business sometimes cause conflict with neighbors. Letters can be instrumental in resolving such conflict. Yet why wait for a complaint to foster a stronger relationship with your community? You may write a variety of goodwill letters to address various common concerns of the community to which you belong.

1.6.2.   For Charity

Nothing can substitute for sincerity when you appeal for funds. Solicitation letters are much easier to write if they are written from the heart. Do not hesitate to make your appeal personal, especially if you are passionate about the cause. Here are the steps to creating a letter to raise funds on behalf of a charitable organization:

1. Present the need or the problem the charitable organization proposes to address.

2. Explain the solution the organization offers.

3. Discuss your personal or corporate relation to the community and to the organization. You may want to begin your letter this way. It personalizes the appeal.

4. Answer the question: How can your correspondent help?

5. Ask a rhetorical question: Wouldn't it be wonderful to resolve the problem, address the need, help the community?

6. End by inviting specific action. Tell the reader not only what to do, but how to go about doing it.

Here's a letter beginning with a need:

Dear Walt:

A lot of us have been talking for a long time about how Smallville needs a new supervised city park—a place not only to enhance the lives of our children, but to nurture those lives and to protect those lives from the dangers of the street.

We've talked a lot.

Now I'd like to tell you about an opportunity to stop talking and start doing.

I am proud that the Smallville Coalition for Snodly Park has asked me to direct its fundraising efforts. Let me get right to the point: Three hundred thousand dollars will build a park, furnish it with a suite of recreational equipment, and provide six months' salary for a qualified recreational counselor.

I am appealing to 120 businesses in this community. I'm asking for $300 from each of you—more, if you can spare it. And I'm asking that you contribute right now so that we'll have the entire funding no later than the end of February.

I've made it easy for you. Just write out a check to SCSP Development Fund and send it to me at the address on this letterhead.

I've enclosed a brochure that details what we propose for Snodly Park. If you have any questions, I'd like nothing more than to talk about this project with you. Just call my direct line: 555-5555.

Sincerely yours,

WARNING: Your good name is a valuable asset. Make certain that you are thoroughly familiar with the cause of the organization for whom you are soliciting funds. Also be certain that you clear all of your communications with the organization before sending them. It is all too easy to make mistaken claims the organization cannot honor.

Another approach is more personal and trades on your good standing in the business community:

Dear Bert:

Hadleyville has given me much since I first opened my hardware store here in 1979. And it's about time I gave something back.

My business is pledging $1,500 for sports and recreational equipment at Parker High School.

Why am I telling you this, Bert?

The reason is that I believe your relationship to Hadleyville has been very much like mine. It's a great place, and it's done a lot for us all. I believe that, like me, you want to give something back to the community by helping it buy much-needed equipment and supplies for our youngsters.

It's easy to make a difference. I ask that you write a check for whatever amount you feel is appropriate. Of course, the more you can spare, the more equipment we can buy.

Bert, thanks. I've enclosed a return envelope for your convenience.

Best personal regards,

To Neighbors (Your Customers)

Not all of your letters will be to business associates or even to others in the business community. You may be called upon, or feel moved, to generate a mailing to your neighbors in the community. Communicating with the community on behalf of a worthwhile cause is a winning proposition for everyone involved. A worthy organization receives help, your community becomes a better place, and you have the opportunity to play a role in this—while also creating goodwill among neighbors who are also your customers and potential customers. This is a valuable opportunity for contact.

If possible, obtain or create a mailing list so that you can personalize the appeal. Your present customer list is a great place to start, but if you want to appeal to more of your neighbors—and to potential customers—you might want to contact a commercial mailing list house and purchase a local list. The best-case scenario is working with a charitable organization that maintains its own lists. It is unethical to exploit such a list for strictly commercial purposes, and you should not keep a copy of the list unless you have explicit permission from the organization. However, using such a list for the purpose of the charitable appeal will not only enhance the effectiveness of the appeal, but will broadcast your name to a new group of people.

Writing on behalf of an organization involves an "I" (you, the writer), a "they" or "it" (the organization), and a "you" (your correspondent). The most effective solicitation strategy is to transform those three pronouns into a single "we." Here's a generic example:

Dear _____:

I am grateful and proud that **Name of organization** has called on me to help direct its fundraising efforts this year to create a new **name of project** for **Name of community.**

We have all known for long time that **Name of community** desperately needs a new **name of project.** Well, now we have an organization that stands ready to convert those words into action. All it needs is our help.

We need a grand total of **$ amount** to finance construction and the first year's operating costs. A lot of money? If half of us in this community gave just **$ amount,** we'd have enough. We'd reach our goal. Give even more, and we'll reach our goal sooner—while also getting a headstart on funding for next year.

I've enclosed a brochure that explains the project in detail: what it will cost and what it will do for us. If you have any questions, give **Name of organization representative** a call at 555-5555. Or you can speak to me, at 444-4444.

Let's help each other.

Sincerely,

Keeping the Fire Lit

Charities often complain that it is difficult to sustain giving from year to year. It's true: Keeping the fire lit requires attention, requires work. Here's a letter that builds on an existing commitment:

Dear Ms. Donaldosn:

It's hard to ask for more . . . unless you're asking on behalf of the Woodton Recreation Fund. No one knows better than you, a woman who gave so generously last year, how important this organization is to our young people. This year their program is more ambitious than ever:

- ♦ Extending Garfield Park to the creek
- ♦ Repairing the pool at Summerdale Park
- ♦ Hiring a full-time assistant recreation director

Such ambition takes money, of course. It takes even more money than we raised last year. So I'm coming to you. My suggestion is that you commit $750, which is $250 more than your fine contribution last year. Of course, we will be grateful for whatever contribution you choose to make.

Why not write out a check today and return it in the enclosed envelope?

Sincerely yours,

In appealing to businesses, the resistance you most likely will encounter is a plea of hard times. If you have reason to expect such a response, try anticipating it in your renewal letter:

Dear Mr. Henderson:

I know times are tough. Maybe you had more last year than this year. That, quite frankly, is the case with us. We're doing just fine; but, like almost everybody else, we were doing better last year.

So that makes it hard for me to ask you to give even more to the Woodton Recreation Fund than you did last year. But it is very important for me to ask, and it is even more crucial that you find the funds to make the largest donation you possibly can.

As hard as times are for business people like you and me, they are devastating for children whose recreational opportunities are limited. It is a hard fact: Tough times are toughest on those who have the least.

Last year you were generous enough to give $350. This year, I hope you can find an additional $100, making a total contribution of $450. Of course, we are grateful for anything you can give.

Why not send a check in the enclosed return envelope today?

Sincerely yours,

1.6.3.   Declining Charitable Requests—Without Alienating Anyone

Life would be a lot easier if being a good citizen meant simply contributing to whatever charity happened to solicit you. Life would be simpler—in part because you'd soon have no more money and would be out of business. Not only do limited funds require that you turn down charitable requests from time to time, it is also very dangerous to contribute haphazardly. You owe it to yourself, your company, and your community to get to know the organization that is asking for your support. Determine if its aims and policies are consonant with your own. Decide if supporting the organization will enhance your image and improve your community. If not, turn the request down.

> **WARNING:** Being in business is in itself a public statement. You and your firm are "out there." As such, you may be solicited by various organizations whose aims and policies not only differ from your beliefs, but which offend you. In this case, resist the urge to reply in anger. Either firmly decline the invitation to contribute, stating without passion that the aims of the organization are not consonant with yours, or ignore the appeal and hope that it goes away.

Here's a step-by-step guide to declining a charitable request gracefully:

1. Acknowledge receiving the request. Optionally, thank the sender for thinking of you.

2. Decline the request. As a rule, you want to do this with an expression of regret.

3. Give a reason for declining the request. Be succinct.

4. If you wish to, suggest that your correspondent solicit you again at an appropriate time.

5. Thank your correspondent for his/her understanding.

Here are some generic forms to help you decline gracefully. Use this one if you are overcommitted to charitable causes:

> Dear _____:
>
> I regret that **Name of company** cannot contribute to **Name of charity** this year.
>
> We are committed to several charities, including some that address the same needs as your organization. I know that your work is important and your needs very real, but our funds are limited, and I am forced to make difficult choices.
>
> I wish you well in your program.
>
> Sincerely yours,

You may genuinely regret being unable to make the requested contribution. If possible, suggest a future time when you might be able to act positively on the request. Here is a generic reply for such a case:

Dear _____:

Your organization's efforts to fund **type of program** are commendable and, certainly, you are addressing a vital community need. I only wish that you had contacted us earlier in the year. Our budget for community giving has already been allocated, and, particularly in these difficult times, I am sure you can appreciate the importance of remaining within the limits of a budget.

We allocate our charitable budget early in **month**. I invite you to contact us next **month**, when we will be able to give your program serious consideration.

Sincerely,

Dear _____:

I agree that **Name of cause** is worthwhile, but, in all candor, I cannot say that I agree with the policies of your organization, namely **specify.**

For this reason, I believe that it would be hypocritical of me to make the donation you ask for.

Sincerely yours,

1.6.4. Responding Positively to Complaints

WARNING: Apparently minor complaints can grow into major headaches—for you—including lawsuits, injunctions, regulatory action—the whole nine yards. Take complaints from your neighbors seriously. If the issue cannot be easily addressed in a simple communication, seek the advice of appropriate counsel, including legal counsel, if necessary.

The letters that follow deal with everyday issues in relations between your business and the community. The idea is to take a potentially negative situation and turn it into a positive demonstration of your company's willingness to be a good neighbor and a good citizen. Responding positively to a complaint can earn your firm a substantial quantity of goodwill. Your response should embody five or six elements:

1. Express your concern about the complaint.

2. State any relevant policies or practices bearing upon the complaint.

3. Propose action. If action has already been taken, explain the action and the effect you hope it will produce. If, however, you dispute the complaint, state the dispute here.

4. Invite comment. Invite dialogue. Suggest a community meeting or a meeting with community leaders or other concerned parties.

5. Thank your correspondent for bringing the matter to your attention. Thank him or her for exercising patience and understanding.

6. If appropriate, express the hope that you can work with the community cooperatively to correct the problem.

The following examples not only suggest strategies for responding to complaints, but also provide an idea of the kinds of complaints you can safely address in an informal letter. More serious matters require the advice of professionals.

Dear Mr. Thompson:

I very much regret that you and your neighbors—*our* neighbors—have been disturbed by the noise of our recent construction activity. Our policy is to be a good neighbor and that means, in part, keeping noise levels to a minimum—even though we are well within the legal noise limits established for the commercial zone in which we operate.

Mr. Thompson, I have spoken to our construction crews, who tell me that the heavy work is now completed and that the noise level will drop dramatically. Nevertheless, the crews promise to work as quietly as the nature of their jobs will permit.

I thank you for your patience and understanding—and for bringing this important matter to my attention.

Sincerely yours,

Increasingly, in cities and suburbs alike, the volume of traffic and the number of parked vehicles associated with a business is becoming a problem. These are touchy areas, because they can make your neighbors feel "invaded." Here are two generic responses to such problems. First, excessive traffic:

Dear _____:

Thank you for your letter of **date,** in which you call attention to the neighborhood's feelings about the impact of our truck activity on local traffic conditions.

As your neighbors, we are concerned about traffic congestion in our community. As business people, traffic congestion is also a concern. After all, we want to attract customers and move goods in and out of the area as efficiently as possible. Traffic, therefore, is not just *your* problem, or the *neighborhood's* problem, but *our* problem as well.

I am currently working with my shipping and receiving department to study our trucking operations with the aim of creating a plan to alleviate peak-hour congestion. I expect to have this plan in place within **number** months.

Sincerely,

Anyone who doubts that human beings are territorial animals does not live in a community with tight parking. This can become a heated issue:

Dear **Name:**

Thanks for your letter concerning the parking situation in our community.

What you point out is true. Our employees park their cars on neighborhood streets—just as almost everyone else in our area does. And you are certainly right: more cars means fewer available parking spaces. Finally, I absolutely agree that parking in our community is tight.

But, **Name,** I cannot agree with everything that you say in your letter. I don't see how you can determine which of the cars parked on the street belong to our employees. I also must observe that a great many of our employees take public transportation to work. Only **number** regularly drive their cars into the neighborhood. Really, I don't believe that number makes a significant impact on parking here.

Nevertheless, **Name,** I agree that we—you, my company, our community—have a problem, and I would like to suggest that we all work together to persuade the city to provide more parking in the neighborhood. I invite you to give me a call at your convenience to discuss who, where, and when we might set up a community meeting devoted to this subject.

Sincerely yours,

Hire Locally

A special—and especially sensitive—area in community relations is the actual or perceived economic impact of your business on the community. Your neighbors may naturally feel that you should hire locally. Depending on the nature of your business, this may or may not be possible. At the very least, strive to maximize the perception that you are responsive to the community and that you make an effort to hire locally:

Dear Mr. Ansley:

I greatly appreciate your letter of September 14, because, like you, the people of Acme Widgets are concerned about the welfare of our neighborhood. This is, after all, where we work. And, Mr. Ansley, it is also where many of us live. I understand your desire that Acme "hire more neighborhood people." I understand it, and I agree with it. In fact, it reflects our company's policy. At present, 57 percent of our employees live within five miles of this plant.

This is a significant percentage.

Obviously, it would be unfair and illegal for us to discriminate against any job applicant because he or she does not live in the neighborhood. But the law does not prevent us from encouraging local folks to apply, and this is exactly what we do by posting openings in the neighborhood newspaper and on our signboard facing McCarthy Street. By the legal and fair means at our disposal, we give maximum *local* notice of all openings.

I hope this addresses your concerns. If you would like to discuss the matter further, please give me a call at 555-5555. I would be pleased to hear any ideas you may have for improving our local recruitment efforts.

Sincerely,

1.6.5. Creating Goodwill

Have you ever thought of writing a letter to your neighbors? Not in response to a complaint—but as a proactive gesture on behalf of the community. Remember, you and your company are citizens and neighbors. Consider taking a leadership role in the community by addressing issues of common concern, such as security, the need for more parking, the need for better recreation facilities, the need for better street lighting, the need for pothole repair—whatever. Consider opening your facility to a community meeting:

> Dear _____:
>
> All of us in **Name of community** are concerned about **issue/problem.** Many of us here at **Name of company** have heard talk about the subject in this neighborhood, and we thought it might be useful to concentrate that talk in one place and at one time.
>
> We thought that a community discussion would help us all air our concerns.
>
> **Name of company** would like to help.
>
> On **date** at **time** at **location, Name of company** invites you to attend an open meeting on **issue/problem.** We think—we hope—that this meeting will be a first significant step in effectively addressing **issue.** Please attend, and please invite your neighbors.
>
> Sincerely,

Checklist for Effective Community Communications

1. Love thy neighbor.

2. Communicate your love for your neighbor.

3. Use good judgment in determining what issues can be handled by friendly, timely communication, and what issues require professional help (for example, legal counsel).

4. Treat neighborhood complaints as opportunities to build positive relations.

5. Remember that your key strategy is to transform *I* and *you* into *we.* Structure your communications accordingly.

1.7. COMPLAINTS

1.7.1. Making Waves without Mouthing Off

It doesn't take a rocket scientist to tell you that you do not complain when you are happy. The emotion that motivates a complaint is anger or, at the very least, irritation and displeasure. Now, if your goal in complaining is to let off steam—to give expression to your rage—why write a letter? Why not just get on the phone and yell?

Giving vent to a primitive impulse may make you feel better temporarily, but it will not address the problems and issues that underlie the emotions.

Before you sit down to write a complaint, think about your goals and aims. The object of an *effective* letter of complaint is not to shame your correspondent or to make him feel bad. It is to improve a flawed situation or to correct an error. In the process, the letter should also serve to strengthen—not threaten or erode—the relationship between you and your correspondent.

> **TIP:** Try to address the *problem* rather than focus on people and personalities. Emphasize facts—things and events—rather than emotions.

Complaining effectively is easier if you follow these clear steps:

1. Succinctly state the problem. Stress facts. Make no accusations. Do not refer to motive. List such details as the duration or frequency of the problem or error, as well as the material effect of the problem or error. Whenever possible, quantify the consequences: "Late shipments this month have cost us upwards of $1,300."

2. Propose a solution.

3. Close by converting "I" and "you" into "we." Affirm that you want to work *with*—not against—your correspondent to improve the situation, correct the problem, rectify the error.

Here is a bouquet of generic complaint letters. Simply add your problem:

Dear _____:

We ordered **items** from you on **date** and paid with the order a deposit of **$ amount.** You have deposited our check, but, after **amount of time,** we have yet to receive the merchandise.

Unless we receive delivery by **date,** we will cancel the order and secure return of the deposit.

This is not something we *want* to do. What we want is the merchandise we ordered. Please work with us now to avoid something neither of us wants.

Kindly call me to confirm delivery by **date** or to confirm that you have canceled delivery and have mailed me a check for **$ amount.**

Sincerely,

Dear _____:

Delivery of order number was received yesterday. Of the **number** items shipped, **number** were damaged in shipment.

Accidents, of course, will happen. But this is the **ordinal number** of **number** deliveries we have received from you in which goods arrived damaged.

I am very pleased with the quality and pricing of your merchandise, and I am gratified by the prompt attention with which you have made adjustments for damaged goods in the past. However, prompt as you are, the repeated delays caused by the almost routine arrival of damaged goods costs us significantly in cash and time. Certainly, it must cost you even more heavily.

I would appreciate a call or a note from you within the next week or two outlining what you propose to do to prevent shipping damage in future deliveries. I have a few suggestions that I am more than willing to share.

Sincerely yours,

Dear _____:

We received delivery today of order number _____, but we were disappointed to discover that you had substituted, either erroneously or intentionally, model number _____ for what we had specified, model number _____.

Your driver may pick up the goods we received when he delivers the goods we actually ordered.

If you cannot supply the goods ordered, notify us immediately, and we will release the rejected goods to you upon return of our payment of **$ amount,** which was made on **date** by check number _____ and cashed by you.

As this error has caused us great inconvenience, we ask for your prompt action on this matter.

Very truly yours,

Canceling and Repudiating an Order

When all else fails, be emphatic and absolute about canceling an order:

Dear _____:

"Better late than never," goes the old saying.

Unfortunately, it doesn't apply this time.

We ordered **item(s)** from you on **date** . At the time of our order, we paid in full by check, which you have deposited. When we failed to receive the goods by **date,** we sent a letter demanding immediate delivery or return of our money.

We have received neither.

Therefore, we cancel and repudiate the order on the grounds of unreasonable delay of delivery and demand the return of our money within ten days from the date of this letter. Please be advised that we will take all necessary legal action to compel the return of our money without further notice to you.

Sincerely,

Checklist for Effective Complaining

1. Set goals: What result do you want your complaint to produce?

2. Address the problems, not the personalities involved.

3. Whenever possible, create a team, transforming "I" and "you" into "we."

4. If possible, quantify the impact of the problem about which you are complaining.

5. Be clear about the remedy you seek.

1.8. CREDIT

1.8.1. How to Tip the Balance Sheet in Your Favor

The bad news is that no letter is going to convince a bank to lend you money if you don't have a reasonably clean credit record and some believable prospects for a bright future—or any future at all, for that matter. The good news is that an effective cover letter will go a long way toward *helping* to launch any loan.

With the Application

Including a good cover letter with the application papers personalizes your application. But while the cover letter is valuable as a courtesy, it is more than that. The cover letter is your opportunity to make the officer in charge of your loan aware of the flesh and blood and personality behind the account number.

> TIP: Applying for a loan can be one of life's hat-in-hand experiences. You feel like you're *asking*—maybe pleading—for something. Be aware that this is nothing more (or less) than a feeling. The fact is that securing a loan is, like any other business transaction, a two-way street. Lending funds keeps both you *and* the bank in business. A loan is a product. You are the customer. Go into the negotiation with that in mind.

K*I*S*S

The cover letter is no place to get complicated. Make it as easy as possible to allow the bank officer to approve your loan. (That's really what she wants to do, after all.) Follow the K*I*S*S formula: *Keep it simple, stupid.* Plead the particulars of your case in the application form, not in the cover letter. However, take the opportunity to direct attention to the highlights of the application or such accompanying documentation as financial statements, quarterly reports, and so on.

1. Begin by thanking the loan officer for meeting with you or talking with you by telephone. Be sure to convey that the meeting was a pleasant experience.

85

TIP: Loan officers are like dentists; they are subject to professional depression because they feel nobody really *enjoys* doing business with them. A kind word or compliment will go a long way.

2. Assert your belief that the accompanying loan application materials are accurate and complete.

3. Invite the loan officer to telephone with any questions.

4. Deliver the message that you are in a position to work with the loan officer.

The goal of the cover letter is to promote your application by selling the loan officer on the idea of, in effect, taking you on as a business partner. You are not a bashful petitioner, passively leaving everything to him or her, but a partner in a joint venture.

Here are generic forms to help you write effective cover letters to accompany the initial application. If the loan officer has assigned a number to your loan, include that number on all correspondence.

Re: Business Loan Application Number _____

Dear **Name of bank loan officer:**

It was a pleasure meeting with you last week. I have completed the loan application forms you gave me and have enclosed them, together with the required documentation.

If you need additional information, call me directly at 555-5555, and please accept my appreciation for your prompt attention to this matter.

Sincerely,

The letter is apparently neutral—no pleading, no sales pitch. But, really, it is far from neutral. It uses a word—"pleasure"—rarely associated with applying for a loan, suggesting to the loan officer that he has done an exceptional job and conveying as well your confidence that you will indeed secure the loan. By inviting further inquiry, the letter conveys your openness and eagerness to cooperate. Finally, without pressing, the letter asks for prompt action.

Here is a letter that includes highlights from the material found in the application:

Re: Business Loan Application Number 123456

Dear Ms. Ruxton:

Thank you for a great meeting last week. I have completed the loan application forms you gave me and have enclosed them, together with the required documentation, including our latest annual report (of which I am particularly proud).

As you review the enclosed material, I ask that you bear in mind the following about my business and myself:

◆ Book Pushers, Inc., has a client base of 623, up from 540 just last quarter.
◆ We are backed by a broad base of individual investors, as outlined in the loan application.
◆ I have been in the book-distribution business for more than twenty years.

As I explained during our discussion, our expansion is so rapid that it threatens to outrun immediately available capital. The rapid pace of our expansion makes me particularly eager to secure your prompt attention to this application.

Sincerely yours,

In general, it is best to limit the information you supply in connection with a loan application to what is actually requested in the application form. However, if you feel that you have important information to convey beyond what the application form requests, use the cover letter to address the additional issues:

Re: Business Loan Application Number 123456

Dear Ms. Ruxton:

Enclosed please find the loan application forms you sent me. Even though the forms ask for a reasonably thorough amount of information, I would like to make two points you will not find on the application forms:

1. I have been in the book distribution business for twenty years, most recently as general manager of Acme Books before I left to run Book Pushers full time.

2. Although the loan form has a space to list the total amount of investment capital we control, it does not provide space for me to mention that the capital derives from nine individual investors. The contribution of each of these individuals is compelling testimony to the company's strength and promise, both actual and perceived.

We are a fast-growing company in need of cash to cover immediate expansion. I would, therefore, greatly appreciate your prompt attention to my application. Please call if you have any questions.

Sincerely,

With a Line of Credit

Opening up a line of credit, in contrast to a lump-sum loan, is usually a less formal process.

Nevertheless, a good cover letter can expedite processing of the application:

Re: Line of Credit Application Number _____

Dear **Name of bank loan officer:**

It was a pleasure speaking with you on **Day of week** about establishing a line of credit for **Name of company.** The completed loan forms are enclosed, together with the documentation you requested.

If you have any questions, please call me directly at 555-5555. I am grateful for your prompt attention to this matter.

Sincerely,

Re: Line of Credit Application Number _____

Dear **Name of bank loan officer:**

Thank you for being so helpful during our discussion on **Day of week.** I have completed the application forms and have enclosed them with the required documentation. I have also included letters from **Name,** president of **Name of company,** and **Name,** CEO of **Name of company,** who have done business with me for **number** years.

As I mentioned during our discussion, we are in a period of expansion, which, while very encouraging, makes often unpredictable demands on our cash flow. A flexible line of credit will be invaluable in managing our prospering company. I am counting on (and very grateful for) your prompt attention to my application.

Sincerely,

As with lump-sum loans, include a cover letter when you are asked to send additional documentation. Here is an example:

Re: Line of Credit Application Number _____

Dear **Name of bank loan officer:**

Thank you for your phone call this morning requesting additional documentation. The material requested is enclosed, except for **document,** which is coming to you under separate cover directly from **Name of company.** I will telephone on **Day of week** to confirm that you have received all of the material you need to process our application.

I am very grateful for your efforts to expedite the application.

Sincerely,

Upping Your Line of Credit

The principal factor influencing whether or not you are able to secure a bigger line of credit is your history with the lender. Use a cover letter to highlight that history:

Re: Credit Account Number _____

Dear **Name of bank loan officer:**

We have maintained a line of credit with **Name of bank** for more than **number** years. Our current needs have outgrown the present line's $ **amount** limit, and we request a new limit of $ **amount** at the current terms.

I enclose a copy of our latest financial statement. In return, please send me any necessary forms. Do call, of course, if you have any questions.

I greatly appreciate your prompt attention to this matter.

Sincerely,

Re: Credit Account Number _____

Dear **Name of bank loan officer:**

I enjoyed our meeting regarding my application for an increased line of credit. The completed application forms are enclosed, along with the documentation you requested. I realize that an increase from **$ amount** to **$ amount** is substantial, but we have expanded substantially since we originally secured the line back in 19XX. Perhaps it will expedite the decision process if you bear in mind the length of our exclusive association with you and the steady rate at which we have expanded.

Please give me a call if you need any further information.

Sincerely,

With Your Answer to a Request for Financial Information

Often, the loan process does not end with your application. You may be asked to submit additional or supplementary financial information. The main purposes of cover letters in response to such requests include:

1. Acknowledging the lender's request

2. Inventorying the materials being sent

3. Explaining any omissions

4. Alerting the loan officer to expect a document or documents to arrive under separate cover.

Here are generic forms to help you respond to requests for financial information:

Dear **Name of loan officer:**

I am pleased to enclose the following documents you requested on date pursuant to our loan application 1234:

◆ Document 1
◆ Document 2
◆ Document 3

Name of document, which you also requested, is coming to you under separate cover directly from **Name of company.**

I will call early next week to confirm that you have received all of the documents you need.

Sincerely,

Re: Loan Application Number: _____

Dear **Name of bank loan officer:**

Enclosed are the financial statements you requested on **date.**

The documents speak for themselves—and, as you can see, they tell a story of healthy expansion. The single losing quarter, **date–date,** was due solely to the purchase of new equipment at that time.

Please call me if you have any questions or need additional documents.

Sincerely,

Re: Loan Application Number _____

Dear **Name of bank loan officer:**

Please be advised that **number** of the documents you requested, **list unavailable documents,** are unavailable. **Document** was destroyed in a fire on **date,** and **documents** are missing.

I enclose **documents,** which contain substantially the same information as the documents you requested.

I trust these will suffice; however, if you have any questions concerning them, please telephone me directly at 555-5555.

Sincerely yours,

Re: Loan Application Number _____

Dear **Name of bank loan officer:**

I have received your request for **documents.** I am gathering them now and will send them out to you, via **method of delivery,** on **date.** I will call on **date** to confirm their safe arrival.

Sincerely,

1.8.2. Applying the Spurs

The wonderful thing about clichés is that you can use them to cancel one another out. "A watched pot never boils," but "The squeaky wheel gets the grease." Somewhere between these two extremes lies the most effective strategy for following up on your loan application. Banks are notorious for crawling just when you need them to sprint, and *judicious* note can help speed up the process.

1. Begin by acknowledging that the loan officer is busy. You realize and understand that.

2. However, you have a problem, and you are asking for help.

3. Explain the problem, stressing the reason why you need a prompt answer.

4. Thank the bank officer for her cooperation.

> **TIP:** Address the bank officer as an individual, a human being. Keep the language of the letter simple. Appeal on a human level. It is amazing to discover that business people welcome the opportunity to be helpful.

Here is a generic follow-up:

Re: Loan Application Number _____

Dear **Name of bank loan officer:**

It has been **number** days since I submitted my application for this business loan. I telephoned on **date(s),** but you were unable to take my call.

I realize that processing a business loan can be painstaking and time-consuming, and I understand that you must be very busy, but I am confidant that you appreciate the impossibility of maintaining responsible financial management in the absence of financial information. I would greatly appreciate your calling me at 555-5555 with an update on the status of my loan application.

Sincerely yours,

You might also take a simpler, even less formal approach:

Re: Loan Application Number _____

Dear **Name of bank loan officer:**

Having filed my loan application **number** days ago, on **date,** I thought it time to monitor progress. Please give me a call today to update me on the status of my application. A decision date will greatly help me manage my immediate cash flow.

I look forward to your call.

Sincerely,

A stronger motivator is to ask, point-blank, if there is a problem. It takes some positive effort on the part of the loan officer to ignore a follow-up that uses this strategy:

Re: Loan Application Number _____

Dear **Name of bank loan officer:**

Silence, they say, is golden. But this is taking the virtue a bit far. I first met with you on **date** and filed my loan application on **date.** Since that time, I have had no substantive word on the status of my application.

Is there a problem? If so, let me know what it is so that we can work on it together. If not, please give me a call at 555-5555 to update me on the progress of my application.

Sincerely yours,

It is particularly helpful if you can bring up a particular issue that makes it imperative for you to get an update on the loan *now.* Here is an example:

Re: Loan Application Number 12345

Dear Ms. Inwood:

In less than ten days I face the quarterly chore of advising my backers of the financial state of my company. Right now there is a disturbingly large question mark looming over "funds available." You can remove it by advising me of the status of my loan application as soon as possible.

Is there any additional information you need? Please call—even if it is only to update me. This will be a tremendous help to me.

Sincerely,

1.8.3.   What to Do When Your Bank Says No

Bankers used to enjoy feeling that they were somehow above the fray—financial guardians, as it were. A bank was a formidable institution, which one approached humbly and in trepidation.

Those days are past. Like just about every other sector of business, banking is now highly competitive and consumer oriented. Nevertheless, loan officers are torn by opposing objectives. They want your business. Nowadays, banks refer to their various loan programs as "products," a term that reveals the way they think about the loan. It is a product to be sold. Yet the loan officer also has the obligation to protect his company from undue risk. Your object is to appeal to the side of the loan officer who wants to sell you a product. If the other side—the conservative side—interferes, you need to address the needs of that side.

What are these needs? The chief need in almost all cases is for an explanation of any questionable episodes in your credit history. Indeed, such letters are often specifically requested by the bank in order to satisfy its obligation to practice "due diligence," that is, the lender's duty to follow up and investigate any glitches in an applicant's credit record.

1.   Begin by letting the reader know that you are responding to his request.

2.   Provide a concise explanation of the problem, emphasizing all mitigating circumstances.

3.   Put the glitch into perspective by emphasizing the positive. This is, after all, a small blot on an otherwise exemplary credit history.

WARNING: The effectiveness of your letter is limited by the gravity of the financial or credit problem in question. If your business is broke or you make it a habit not to pay your bills, no letter, regardless of how convincing, is likely to get you a loan.

Here are some examples of letters that address gaffes, glitches, and gulfs in one's credit history:

Re: Loan Application Number _____

Dear Mr. Thwaite:

This is a response to your request for an explanation of a late payment on our corporate Passport Card, due on April 15, 19XX, and made on May 5.

From April 9 to May 1, both principals of our company were out of the country. The simple explanation for this single tardy payment is that neither my partner nor I was present when the bill arrived, and in the backlog of work that had accumulated on our return, this bill was shuffled to the bottom of the heap.

Please note the following:

1. The payment was made only 20 days beyond the thirty-day limit.

2. In the five years we have held the Passport credit card, this is the single instance of a late payment.

3. In the three years since this single instance, we have consistently maintained the account in a current status and are cardholders in good standing.

Please call me directly if you have any questions or need further information.

Sincerely,

Re: Loan Application Number 123456

Dear Ms. Younger:

This is to explain the two late payments to two creditors you noted in the credit report you secured pursuant to this loan application.

Please note that both of the late payments occurred in the period March 19XX to July 19XX. During that time, we lost two of our major clients: Acme Widget failed to secure anticipated funding for a project contracted with us, and Dewey Decimal System petitioned for Chapter 11 bankruptcy on June 23, 19XX. Consequently, our available cash was unexpectedly low for the period. We contacted Mr. Karl Wilhemstrasse, credit manager of Gorgo Products, and Ms. Mary Moll, credit director of Unicycle Limited, to arrange deferred payment of accounts due them. If you wish, you may contact them at 555-5555 and 444-4444, respectively, to confirm the arrangements we made at that time.

Both of these accounts are currently up to date and in good standing. We continue to do business with these firms on a regular basis.

I direct your attention to our otherwise exemplary credit history, as well as to our most recent financial statements (enclosed with our loan documentation), which indicate that we have long since recovered from any past difficulties.

Please call if you have any questions.

Sincerely,

Correcting Erroneous Information on Credit Reports

Believe it or not, the job of credit reporting agencies is to help you. The information they provide can quickly give a lender the confidence required to make the loan you want. However, accidents happen, and misinformation or outdated information can certainly crop up to cause you trouble. This is a generic form to help you respond in cases of error:

Re: Loan Application Number: _____

Dear **Name of bank loan officer:**

I was surprised and distressed to hear that **Name of credit reporting agency** reported late payments to **Name of firm.** This report is in error. I have contacted **Name of credit reporting agency** to advise them of their error and to demand that they correct it. I have also contacted **Name** at **Name of firm,** who has agreed to send you directly a letter confirming that the credit report is indeed in error and affirming our good payment record with them.

I will call early next week to confirm that you have received **Name**'s letter.

I trust that this "glitch" will not delay processing our application, and I thank you for your continued timely attention.

Sincerely,

Frank Statement of Significant Problems

Serious credit problems in the past should be addressed forthrightly and without seeming to offer an excuse. Try this form:

Re: Loan Application Number _____

Dear **Name of bank loan officer:**

We have made no secret of the financial problems we experienced during **date** to **date.** The delinquent accounts to which you refer, however, have been settled, as the enclosed documents attest.

As is evident from our most recent financial statements, our difficulties are well behind us, and we are in a period of growth and increased profitability. Since **date,** our credit record—with banks as well as vendors—has been without blemish.

With all confidence, I can assure you that we are not only a "good risk," but we are a good investment.

Please call if you have any further questions.

Sincerely,

Checklist for Credit-Application Cover Letters

1. An effective cover letter is a courtesy, but take the steps that follow to make it work even harder for you.

2. Point out highlights of your application.

3. Explain any circumstances that place apparent problems in context. For example, a dip into the red during the third quarter was due to necessary equipment purchases.

4. Emphasize your need for quick action.

5. Invite communication.

6. Transform "I" and "you" into "we."

1.8.4. Helping Your Customers Do Business with You

Extending credit is risk. But it is also a favor—a favor you do your customer and yourself. For credit makes it possible for many of your customers to do business with you. Most business relationships may be viewed as alliances or even partnerships. This is particularly true of credit relationships. When you extend credit to a customer, you are, in effect, taking him on as a partner. Effective correspondence relating to credit embodies this partnership concept. Respond to credit applications with the following five steps:

1. Thank the applicant.

2. Acknowledge the good value of credit with your firm.

3. Assure the applicant of prompt, careful, and fair consideration. If at all possible, tell the applicant how long the process will take.

4. This is a good time to request any additional information you may need.

5. Close with thanks.

Here are effective generic responses to credit applications:

Dear _____:

Many thanks for your order of **date.** We have processed it and are shipping it on **date.** We enjoy doing business—especially with a new customer.

Now I would like to ask you a favor. Please send me copies of your financial statements for **period required** so that, as you requested, I can set up a line of credit here that will facilitate our filling what I hope will be many more orders. For your convenience, I am enclosing a return envelope.

Sincerely,

Dear _____:

Thank you for your letter of **date,** requesting a line of credit with us. Before we can oblige you, we need copies of your financial statements for **period required,** which you may send directly to me in the return envelope enclosed.

All of us at **Name of your firm** look forward to doing business with you.

Sincerely,

A Welcome with *Semi*-Open Arms

Extending credit is not a simple yes or no proposition. Not only do you have to decide whether or not to extend credit, but also what limits and terms to set. A series of generic forms for responding graciously while setting sane limits follows:

Dear _____:

I am delighted to respond to your application for credit. At this time, we are prepared to extend to you a **$ amount** line. Your financial statements indicate a healthy business with a great future, but we do have to weigh this against the fact that you have been in business less than two years. Once you have crossed that two-year mark, let's review your updated statements and see if we can do better for you. Based on your current statements, I expect that we can!

We thank you for your business and look forward to your next order.

Sincerely,

Dear _____:

I am pleased to set up for you **$ amount** credit (subject to **terms**), which should make doing business with us more convenient. If you like, send us your next quarter's financial statement, and, based on this (together with your payment record, of course), we will review your credit line with an eye toward increasing it.

I look forward to a long and mutually profitable relationship.

Sincerely,

If you are aware that the amount of credit you have extended is significantly less than what the applicant had requested, you might want to address the issue even more directly:

Dear _____:

Thank you for your application for a credit line of **$ amount.** I'm happy to set up for you a line of **lesser $ amount** and only wish that we could oblige with the full amount you requested. However, the recent financial statements you sent show that you are presently too heavily obligated for us to add to that burden beyond **$ amount.** If you like, send us your next quarter's financial statement, and, based on this (together with your payment record, of course), we will review your credit line with an eye toward increasing it as much as we possibly can.

We appreciate your continued business.

Sincerely,

Dear _____:

Thank you for your application for a credit line of **$ amount.** I'm happy to set up for you a line of **lesser $ amount** and only wish that we could oblige with the full amount you requested. However, since you have only been in business since **date,** we feel that, until we have had a bit more experience with you, the **$ amount** is a prudent beginning. Let's review financial statements for your next two quarters and see if we can get closer at that time to the amount you requested.

I appreciate your interest in us and look forward to doing business with you.

Sincerely,

1.8.5. How to Turn Them Down Without Turning Them Off

It is difficult to be positive when you reject an application for credit. About the best you can do—and you should do this only in cases where it is appropriate—is to offer hope of reconsideration at some later time. When you do this, either state a definite time for reapplication or a specific set of conditions under which a new application would be considered.

What if there is no hope? Strike a tone of apology, but remember that the rejection is not your fault—and you should not place any blame on yourself or your firm. Furthermore, make it clear that you are turning down a credit application, not a customer. Emphasize that you that you look forward to serving the customer—or continuing to serve the customer—on a cash-with-order basis.

> **TIP:** Avoid references to"company policy"as a reason for rejecting a credit application. Give a specific reason for rejecting the application rather than an anonymous appeal to"policy."

Here is an outline to follow:

1. Thank the customer for his application.

2. State the rejection clearly.

3. If possible and appropriate in this particular case, offer the opportunity for reapplication either at a specific time or when specific conditions have been met.

4. Assure your customer of his value to you. Make it clear that you are looking forward to doing business on a cash-with-order basis. Make it clear that he will be treated as a first-class customer.

5. Close with thanks for the customer's understanding.

> **WARNING:** It becomes second nature for many of us to close letters with an invitation to call if there are further questions. Do not do that in the case of a letter rejecting credit. It will only invite possibly argumentative class and therefore promote further disappointment and frustration.

The following are generic forms for letting down the credit applicant gracefully. Here is one to an applicant who has been in business only a short time:

Dear _____:

Thank you for your interest in **Name of your company** and your application for credit with us. We cannot help noticing that you have just established your business here. The limitations on our own resources suggest that we need a little more experience with you as a "pay-as-you-go" customer before we can set up a line of credit.

I urge you to reapply in three months, after we've worked together for a while. In the meantime, rest assured that **Name of your company** will give you the very best prices and service possible. We appreciate your business and do look forward to helping you establish yourself in our community.

Sincerely,

Sometimes, an examination of the applicant's financial statements gives you pause:

Dear _____:

Thanks for your recent order, which we will ship on **date.**

We are eager to work with you in setting up a line of credit, but, based on the financial statements you furnished at our request, you appear to be undercapitalized, which, we believe, would make it difficult for you to meet payments on our terms.

We would be happy to reconsider your application now if you can find a person or firm to guarantee your open account with us. Perhaps that would get you over the hump by allowing us to serve you as you become established. Alternatively, we invite you to reapply in three months.

In the meantime, we are delighted to continue serving you on a pay-as-you-go basis.

Sincerely,

Perhaps a credit-reporting service or a check with the applicant's credit references has suggested a history of problems:

Dear _____:

Thanks for applying for credit with **Name of your company.** At present, your credit record shows a history of slow payment, and we feel, given your current obligations, that it is necessary to postpone acting on your request for six months, which should give you time to catch up on your open accounts.

For now, we are delighted to serve you on a cash-with-order basis. We invite your reapplication for credit in **Month.**

Sincerely,

If an applicant's financial statements show a massive obligation, you may decide to steer clear. Show some understanding:

Dear _____:

I've got a problem. You have asked me for credit, but, try as I might, I can't find a way to add you to our list of credit customers at the present time. Your financial statement and your credit record for the past year won't allow me to oblige you. It will help neither of us if we add to your outstanding debts.

Why is this my problem? I have to turn you down, but I don't want to lose you as a customer. It's been a hard year for all of us, and as soon as your financial situation turns around, I invite you to reapply for credit. In the meantime, let me assure you that your business is valuable to us, and I encourage you to continue to consider us as a supplier on a cash-with-order basis.

Sincerely,

Then there are those who have stiffed you in the past, but come back to haunt you. You can turn on your heel indignantly, or you can exercise discretion. Here is one way to do the latter:

Dear _____:

It was great to receive your order of **date** and to find that you are still interested in working with us. As you may recall, the last time you purchased merchandise from us, we had a difficult time collecting payment and even called on an outside agency for assistance.

That, however, was **number** years ago, and conditions certainly do change. We're willing to give it another try—though we ask that you send us a copy of your most recent financial statement and that you provide three current credit references.

In the meantime, we would appreciate your payment in full, by check, for the current order. We shall ship it promptly on receipt of payment.

Sincerely yours,

Checklist for Responding Effectively to Credit Applications

1. Remember that, by extending credit, you are helping customers do business with you.

2. Regard each credit relationship as a business partnership for mutual benefit.

3. Make your applicant feel welcome.

4. In cases where you must give less credit that applied for, emphasize the positive.

5. Be specific about instructions for reapplication.

6. In case of rejection, attempt to salvage as much of the relationship as possible.

1.9. FAVORS

1.9.1. Turning a Request into an Opportunity to Help

Few people look forward to asking for a favor. It's hard to request something for nothing. That's why you should rethink the definition of *favor.* Think of your request not as a bid to get something for nothing, but as providing your correspondent with an opportunity to help you. The fact is that most people enjoy helping others. Being asked to help empowers the helper. It is a compliment and a vote of confidence. It is an opportunity to feel good about oneself. Moreover, difficult as it may be to believe, the business community operates according to a kind of unspoken notion of karma—the belief that what goes around comes around. Doing a colleague a favor creates goodwill. Most of your colleagues recognize that.

The most difficult step in asking for a favor is broaching the subject. Here is step 1:

1. Provide a basis for the request—"We've worked together for so long that I feel comfortable asking you for a favor."

Then go on:

2. Be clear about what you want.

3. Explain how the favor will benefit you. This gives your correspondent a way to gauge just how much he can help.

4. Express gratitude.

> WARNING: Make your gratitude known, but do not use such phrases as "thanking you in advance." This implies that you take your correspondent's compliance for granted. It is offensive, and it may be embarrassing for both of you.

Dear Joe:

We've had such a great working relationship that I actually look forward to asking you for a favor.

I need a brief letter of recommendation to the Regency Company to help us secure a major contract with them.

We've been asked to bid on supplying them with widgets and widget-maintenance services. I don't have to tell you that this represents major business for us. It would be very, very helpful if, in addition to whatever else you feel inclined to comment on, you could make the following points about your experience with us as a supplier:

♦ We supply high value
♦ We furnish a high level of client support
♦ We offer three-hour emergency response

Joe, we're working on a tight schedule to make Regency's tight schedule, so I would appreciate your sending out the letter before June 15. You'll be writing to:

Ms. Karen Sendhouse
Vice President
Regency, Inc.
1313 45th Drive
West Haven, NY 02345

Please call me if you have any questions, and, as always, I appreciate your time and attention.

Sincerely,

Here is a more generic form you might follow:

Dear **Name:**

I need help!

We're currently being considered by **Name of company** as a contractor for **describe project.** As you know, your firm and mine have just worked successfully on a similar project, and it would be very helpful if I could use that experience as a reference.

It would be very helpful if you could call or write **Name** at **Name of company** to discuss with him our experience working together. You might review the following points:

List points.

Name's phone number is 555-5555, and the address is **address.**

As you can well imagine, this contract would mean a great deal to us, and I would be very grateful for whatever kind words you can spare. Please call me at 444-4444 if you have any questions.

Sincerely,

The classic favor one neighbor asks of another is to borrow something. This is a situation that also arises from time to time in business. Depending on the nature of what you are asking, you will probably want to include in your letter something more than an appeal to goodwill—perhaps outright compensation for the favor or perhaps the promise of a return favor. Here is an example:

VIA FAX

Dear Mr. Gould:

We're in a jam.

One of our most important clients, John Kelly and Company, needs a rush series of flyers for a special project. We usually design, print, and bind right here, in house. But our binding machine has gone down. I can't get emergency repair in time, and I can't get a local firm to do the binding for us.

I understand that you have a Mark VII binding machine, and I wanted to ask you if I could buy four hours of time on the machine. We are willing to come in after hours or at your convenience.

Mr. Gould, you and I know that there are some clients you can put on hold and some you cannot. Kelly is one of the "cannots." Please give me a call at 555-5555 to discuss this. I'd need to get on the machine no later than Monday. I appreciate your consideration.

Sincerely,

Then there is the kind of favor that is particularly uncomfortable to ask—the kind that sets up, or gives the appearance of setting up, an embarrassing situation for everyone involved. How do you ask a business associate to grant an employment interview for a relative? Here's a generic form. Anticipate objections in your letter, and acknowledge that such requests are often a royal pain—*but* not in this case:

Dear _____:

We can't choose our families, and you and I, I'm sure, have at least some relatives we wish would—well, let's just say go away. But sometimes we get lucky, and that is the case with my niece, **Name.** She is extraordinary.

Name is about to graduate from **University** with a degree in **subject** and a grade-point average that has made us all very proud. She has already interned at **Name of company** and **Name of company.** I expect at least one of them to offer her a job. But I'd like you to have the benefit of meeting her—whether it's to talk about a position you may have open now or in the future—and I would most definitely love for her to have the benefit of talking with you.

Would you be willing to set something up? **Name** can be reached at 555-5555.

You know, I wouldn't waste your time. It's too valuable to you, and your friendship is too valuable to me. I am confident that the two of you will enjoy talking.

Sincerely,

Checklist for Requesting a Favor

1. Think of the request as an *opportunity* for your correspondent to help.

2. Do not apologize for asking the favor.

3. Express yourself in positive terms.

4. Be clear about what you want.

5. Be clear about the benefit you will receive.

6. If you can offer a quid pro quo, do so.

7. Do not thank your correspondent in advance; it suggests that you take his/her help for granted.

1.9.2. How to Say No Without Being a Scrooge

In a perfect world, you would be able to grant all favors requested of you. On the other hand, in a perfect world, no one would ask you for a favor. In any case, ours is far from a perfect world, and there will be any number of requests that you will have to turn down. The object is to do so clearly, unmistakably, but always gently. Be certain to provide a reason for your being unable—or unwilling—to meet the request. Take these steps in your correspondence:

1. Begin by citing the request.

2. Express regret that you cannot satisfy the request.

3. Explain why you cannot.

4. Express your wish that this will cause no inconvenience.

5. If possible and appropriate, suggest an alternative.

    WARNING: In suggesting an alternative, beware of "volunteering" others to fulfill the request.

6. Thank your reader for his/her understanding.

    A generic turn-down letter:

    Dear _____:

    I have received your request for **favor.** Unfortunately, I am not able to do what you ask because **state reason.** Might I suggest that you try **alternative?**

    I hope **alternative** will suit your needs.

    Sincerely,

Sometimes a favor is simply unrealistic. For example, a customer asks for a product modification that cannot be made cost effectively:

Dear Mr. Thomason:

Thank you for your inquiry about the availability of the Super 66 in a modified form.

Unfortunately, the cost of modifying the Super 66 is prohibitive in orders under a gross. Allow me to suggest two alternatives. You could, of course, increase the amount of your order to 144 units, a quantity that will make the retooling required for modification cost effective. Or you might consider upgrading your order to the Super 77, which offers all the benefits of the 66 if we were to modify it, except for the automatic reverberation feature. The cost of the upgrade is $45 per unit as compared with $35 per unit for the Super 66.

Why not give me a call at 555-5555 to discuss these options?

Sincerely,

Particularly difficult to refuse is a request for beating an impossible deadline. Often, your correspondent is in a state of panic that is impervious to reason:

Dear _____:

I really wish I could accommodate your request for early delivery of **product,** but, alas, I cannot. Believe me, it isn't for lack of trying.

The minute you asked me to push up the delivery date, I called our principal suppliers. Only one was able to accommodate the accelerated schedule. The other three could not. Obviously, if we can't get what we need earlier, we can't deliver what you need earlier.

The news isn't all bad. I can—and will—push the delivery date from **date** to **date.** That will save you **number** days, and I hope that will help.

Please call me at 555-5555 if you have any questions or if you have any other suggestions.

Sincerely,

Checklist for Declining Favors

1. While you may apologize for declining the request, do not emphasize the apology. Instead:

2. Explain why you cannot honor the request.

3. Express concern over any inconvenience your declining the request may cause.

4. If at all possible, suggest alternatives.

TIP: Suggesting alternatives is the most positive step you can take when you decline a request for a favor or special service. It empowers your correspondent. The worst situation is to be faced with no alternatives.

1.10. GOODWILL

1.10.1. How to Write Healing Condolences

It is not always easy to believe, but the world of business is a community. You may be competitive, you may insist on keeping your business associates separate from your friends and family, but, nevertheless, you and the people you work with, both inside and outside your company, are a community. It is up to you to help make the community as civilized and human to live in as possible. It will not only help make daily life more pleasant and rewarding, it is, ultimately, good for business.

One of the hallmarks of a viable community is that its members respond with appropriate sympathy and kindness in times of stress and sorrow. Yet even the most intelligent and articulate people sometimes find it hard to say the right things on occasions of death, serious illness, or other loss.

TIP: Be yourself. Sit down to write, and be yourself.

Knowing the right thing to say in a sad or traumatic situation requires a leap of imagination. Put yourself in your correspondent's position. Under these circumstances, what would *you* like to hear? What would help *you* most? The form of the typical condolence letter consists of five parts:

1. Express your sorrow at hearing of the death or loss.

2. Sympathize by acknowledging the emotional pain of loss.

   TIP: Avoid vivid adjectives and nouns that may even magnify the loss: "your *terrible* loss," "your *horrible tragedy*," and so on. Your correspondent does not need help feeling bad.

3. Say something good about the deceased. If possible, share a memory.

4. It is often helpful gently to remind your correspondent of the healing power of time.

   TIP: Be careful to avoid minimizing the loss. Acknowledge it simply, with sympathy and understanding.

5. To the extent possible and appropriate, offer your help and support.

Strike the emotional tone appropriate to your correspondent. You may be writing to a business associate on the death of one of her valued employees or you may be writing to that person about the death of a mutual business friend. Another circumstance involves writing a letter of condolence to the decedent's family.

On the Death of a Business Associate

Create a simple and dignified tone, straightforward, but not perfunctory. Here is an example:

Dear John:

I was very sorry to learn of the passing of your president, Arthur Benjamin. As you know, I've done business with Art for the past five or six years, and it was always a great pleasure. You know even better than I that Art was a brilliant, generous, and honorable man. You'll miss him, I know, not just as a leader, but as a friend. I feel for your loss.

John, if there is anything I can do to help during what will be a difficult time for you, please don't hesitate to call.

Sincerely,

On the Passing of a Business Friend

Dear Mary:

You know all too well that Henry Wohlman was more to me than a business associate. He was a great friend, and I miss him very much. Believe me, I feel for your grief—because I feel your grief as well. For you, the loss is double: a good friend is gone, and so is a valued member of your management team.

But, Mary, you have to believe that Henry will live on. For he has left a legacy of leadership, entrusted to people like you, and he has also left us great memories of personal friendship.

If there is anything you need from me—any service I can render—please don't hesitate to call.

Sincerely,

If appropriate, you may want to express more strongly your confidence in your correspondent's capacity to carry on after her loss.

Dear Susan:

Karl was such a good friend to us both that I am painfully aware of how deeply you feel his loss. I also know that, hard as his passing is on me, it's even more of a trial for you, who has lost not only a dear friend, but a key member of your management team.

Well, Susan, nothing can replace Karl, our friend, but I know how much confidence and trust he placed in you. He always spoke of you as a full partner. He relied on you. He shared his knowledge and judgment with you. Karl was savvy about people. He knew how well you could manage the company, and we all believe you will do just that, not only *carry* on, but *move* on—to even greater success.

Susan, please know that I am here to help in any way I can. Don't hesitate to call.

Sincerely,

To the Family of a Business Associate

Dear Mrs. Howard:

I was saddened to hear of the death of your husband, Morris. As a business associate, it was impossible not to respect him and not to like him. He was a strong person. I can only imagine how wonderful a husband and father he must have been. I'm truly sorry for your loss.

Mrs. Howard, you don't need many words from someone who's almost a stranger to you. Take heart in the knowledge that time will at least soothe your pain. And, please, if I can be of any assistance to you, don't hesitate to call me.

Sincerely,

To the Family of a Business Friend

Dear Gary:

Betty's passing was a shock to me. I can only imagine what a blow it was to you and your family. I will miss the good times we had with you and Betty, and I will miss her wise counsel in business. But while I have lost a friend and a key business associate, you have lost, I know, far more. Gary, there is nothing I can say to you that will diminish that loss. Know that time will ease your pain and will leave you rich with memories.

If there is anything I can do for you, my friend, please call.

Sincerely,

Belated Condolences

There is no excuse for failing promptly to send condolences, unless, for whatever reason, you did not receive the news of the passing in a timely fashion. In such cases, the adage "better late than never" applies. Be certain to explain—concisely—the reason for your delayed response. Here are two generic notes:

Dear _____:

I just returned from my vacation to the very sad news that **Name** had left us. I hope that you will accept my belated condolences on the loss to yourself and to your firm. **Name** was a person with whom it was a pleasure and a privilege to do business.

Sincerely,

Dear _____:

I just returned from abroad and was told this morning that **Name** had passed on. Please accept my sincere condolences, belated as they are. I know that this is a personal loss as well as a loss to your business. Indeed, it is a loss to our community.

Sincerely,

Illness

Death is not the only loss your business friends and associates may suffer. Serious illness is also an occasion for an understanding letter.

Dear _____:

Name tells me that you are laid up. I can't begin to imagine how a mover and shaker like you puts up with it. My advice is that you get better fast before you make life impossible for everyone in that hospital.

Get well!

Best personal regards,

Dear _____:

I was very sorry to learn that you are in the hospital, and I trust that your recovery will be swift. I miss hearing your voice on the other end of the line when I call **Name of company.** Get well soon.

All the best,

Catastrophic Property Loss

It is not flesh alone that, in the words of Shakespeare's Hamlet, is subject to a "thousand natural shocks." Flood, fire, earthquake, storms—you name it, property is at jeopardy. For even well insured businesses, property damage can be a severe, painful, and disruptive blow. A letter offering understanding and assistance is highly welcome at a time like this.

Dear _____:

I was very sorry to learn of the **disaster** that hit your offices. I'm sure it was a blow to you, but I'm just as sure that you are mentally and emotionally more than a match for any **disaster. Name,** you'll come out of this stronger than ever before.

That is the kind of person you are.

I'd like to help you in any way I can. Please, give me a call.

Best personal regards,

The End

Another kind of death is that of a business. When the doors close, the consequences can be devastating, not just economically, but emotionally as well. If this circumstance is not the loss of a life, it is the next worst thing, the loss of a way of life. However, the object in these cases—usually—is to keep your tone as upbeat as *reasonably* possible. Help out with a letter:

> Dear Bob:
>
> I read in *Modern Wire Works* that Youngblood Wire and Cable is closing its doors. I know that Youngblood has been one of your major clients, and I can imagine that their calling it quits comes as anything but welcome news to you.
>
> As my football coach used to say to us, *shake it off.* You have an awfully strong organization there, and I am confident that you'll weather this loss, coming out of it stronger than ever.
>
> Maybe you'd like to get together to discuss some strategies for the future. Why don't you give me a call? I'd enjoy talking with you.
>
> Sincerely,

Condolence Checklist

1. Your job is to help heal.

2. The most powerful healing instrument you possess is your imagination. Use it. Put yourself in the place of your correspondent. What would *you* want to hear at a time like this?

3. Offer sympathy, but not pity.

4. Be careful not to aggravate feelings of despair and hopelessness.

5. Offer help.

1.10.2. Congratulations—and other Epistolary Pats on the Back

Congratulations are fun to write. Just as important, they can serve as a way to acquire new business while building goodwill. Make it a habit to keep your ear to the ground in order to learn of promotions and appointments in your industry. Write letters of congratulations to promotees and new appointees. Before long, you'll find yourself with a full-fledged network.

TIP: Congratulating an individual on a promotion or new position gives you an opportunity to introduce yourself, your product or service, and your firm.

The letter of congratulations is straightforward.

1. Begin with the congratulation itself.

2. Emphasize your business relationship to your correspondent—or introduce yourself to him or her.

3. Offer help and advice as appropriate. If you are introducing a product, service, or firm, briefly suggest how you can be of assistance in your correspondent's new position.

4. Express the desire to continue or annotated a successful business alliance.

5. You may close by repeating the congratulations. This is especially important if you are introducing yourself, lest the letter seem wholly self-serving.

Dear Eunice:

Congratulations on your promotion to regional sales director. I'm not going to tell you that you don't deserve all the credit for your great success—but, well, I'd like to think that we at Acme Widgets helped by supplying prompt, personal service and terrific value.

I wish you all the best in your new position, and I look forward to continuing our partnership and raising it to even greater heights.

Sincerely,

Dear Tom:

What a year for you! You've really redefined the state of the art.

I have to tell you, it's a lot of fun working with a winner, and I look forward to many more years of continued success as your supplier of high-quality peat moss. Congratulations!

Best personal regards,

Strictly Personal

The folks you work with are not two-dimensional cardboard cutouts, but real people, with lives inside and outside of the office. Offer congratulations on life's major happy events, marriage and birth.

Dear Ted:

Word is that you're about to leave the bachelor ranks and the join the rest of us. I extend my hand in welcome. Well done!

You know, marriage changes everything. For the better. And, Ted, you'll find that includes your professional life as well as your personal life. It gives you added focus and motivation.

I'm happy for you. Congratulations.

Best regards,

Dear Roberta:

Ed told me the great news. An addition to your family! Wow!

Please accept the congratulations and very best wishes of all of us here at Acme Widgets.

All our best,

Congratulations Checklist

1. Be generous. Never qualify your congratulations.

2. Take the opportunity to reinforce existing business relationships and to establish new ones.

3. Make it a habit to keep abreast of promotions and appointments in your industry. congratulating a new appointee is an opportunity to enlarge your network and your customer base.

1.10.3. Surefire Ways to Make Invitations Special

Depending on the nature of the occasion, you may write a stand-alone letter of invitation, or you may want to insert a cover note with a printed invitation. The basic process is very simple;

1. State the occasion or event.

2. Briefly describe the occasion or event, if necessary.

3. Sincerely express your wish that the correspondent will attend.

4. State the response due date, making certain that you've furnished a name and address or telephone number for response.

> **TIP:** If spouse or family is included in the invitation, be certain to specify this.

A generic invitation to a corporate dinner:

Dear _____:

We at **Name of your company** would be delighted to have the pleasure of your company, as well as that of your **wife/husband,** at our annual dinner. It is an evening everyone enjoys.

Kindly respond by **date** to **Name** at 555-5555.

Sincerely,

Speaking Engagement

It is an honor to be asked to speak, albeit an honor that many would just as soon pass up. Praise is in order for such invitations. You should also provide as much information about the event and relevant speaking subjects as possible.

> **TIP:** No matter how convincing an invitation you write, expect some turn downs. Therefore, plan well in advance, and be certain to state a reply deadline, so that you can invite alternative speakers.

> **WARNING:** Resist the temptation to cover yourself by *simultaneously* inviting more than one person to make the same speech. What if they all accept? Allow enough time to invite alternates *serially.*

Dear Mr. Burke:

I cherish the recollection of your speech last year at the Baldwin Club. Your talk was eminently lucid and thoroughly riveting. I'm still quoting you to my colleagues. So, when I met with the Speakers' Committee Wednesday to plan our annual fund raiser, I instinctively brought your name up.

The mention of it met with instant and unanimous approval.

Mr. Burke, you would be doing our organization a great service if I could succeed in persuading you to speak. The event raises money for such community services as Baldwin Park, the Baldwin Recreation Center, and the Baldwin Free Clinic. I've enclosed a flier that describes the event, with particular emphasis on this year's theme of volunteerism. It would be great if you could relate the subject of your talk to that theme.

I know what you bring to the dais. As for us, we can offer a great meal, convivial companionship, and an honorarium in the amount of $250.

Take time—a short time, I hope—to think it over, and please give me a call no later than August 3. You can reach me at the office, at 555-5555 or at home, 444-4444.

Another common situation is the invitation to join a club or organization. Strike a balance between expressing the privilege and exclusivity of membership on the one hand and, on the other hand, your desire to have your correspondent as a member. For example:

Dear _____:

It was a pleasure to speak with you the other day about our organization, the **Name of organization.** I've never been a "joiner" myself, but this organization is a great group of people, who have made a positive difference in our **industry/community.** You can imagine, then, how delighted I was to learn of your interest in the organization.

I discussed the matter of your membership with the roster committee, and they agreed enthusiastically to extend an invitation to you.

Won't you please attend our next meeting at **time** at **location?** At that time, you will be given full information on membership, and you will be given the opportunity to make a formal application.

I look forward to seeing you then.

Sincerely,

Finally, you may be called upon to invite a prominent person in your community or industry to accept an honorary position in some worthwhile organization or in relation to some charitable cause. Flattery is the order of the day, since that is what establishes the grounds for the nominee's selection:

> Dear _____:
>
> Those of us in **Name of organization** have long greatly admired your key work in **charity, cause, and so forth** You are one of the **community's/industry's** most influential and forceful voices, and we would be deeply gratified if you would accept our invitation to become honorary chairman of **Name of organization.**
>
> I know that you are familiar with our work. However, I'm sure that you have questions about the duties and responsibilities of the position of honorary chairman, and I will call on you next week to learn if we can get together for a lunch meeting at which I can discuss the details.
>
> Until then, I ask that you give thought to our invitation.
>
> Sincerely,

Checklist for Effective Invitations

1. Write in a tone—ranging from informal to formal—appropriate to the occasion and appropriate to your relationship with the invitee.

2. Never apologize for an invitation.

3. Be certain to communicate the sincerity of the invitation as well as its value.

4. Be certain to supply the essential information: where and when.

1.10.4. Giving Thoughtful Thanks

For too many of us, writing a thank you letter brings back uncomfortable memories of our mothers or fathers goading us into writing to thank Auntie Alice for those "very nice" socks she sent us. A thank you letter should not be written out of a sense of burdensome obligation. Be aware that everyone appreciates *timely* and *sincere* thanks and that, therefore, a thank you letter is an occasion to build and develop and affirm a relationship.

Tip: In business situations especially, avoid greeting card thank you notes. Write a letter.

The dominant tone here is warmth. You can avoid the impression of a perfunctory thanks by making certain that you explain just how valuable the service, favor, and so forth has been to you: "Your recommendation was a key factor in our landing this contract."

1. Begin with thanks.

2. Explain the beneficial effect of the favor, service, and so forth for which you are thanking your correspondent.

3. Close by reiterating your appreciation.

4. State your feeling of good fortune to associated with the correspondent.

5. If appropriate, state your desire to return the favor, to help out in the future, and so forth.

Dear _____:

Thanks so very much for the letter of recommendation you sent **Name** at **Name of company.** It was timely, and it was highly convincing. We got the contract.

You really came through, **Name,** and I appreciate it. I hope that you will not hesitate to call on me so that I can return the favor.

Best personal regards,

Dear _____:

When I asked you if I could come by your office to chat about **subject,** I had no idea that you would give me so generous and thorough a tutorial. Your generosity with expertise and time was extraordinary—and extraordinarily helpful. I was able to make the decisions that were hanging over my head.

Please accept the accompanying **gift** as a small token of my thanks.

Sincerely,

TIP: You don't have to write a thank you letter only in response to some specific favor or service. How about thanking a longtime customer for being so loyal? Or a supplier for giving you special service?

Dear _____:

You've been such a great customer for so long that it would be easy to start taking you for granted—and that is one thing I do not want to happen. So, I just wanted to take this opportunity to thank you for your many years of business, loyalty, and congeniality.

I am delighted that you have entrusted your **product/service** needs to us, and please be assured that we will continue to earn your confidence with each and every order we fill.

Best personal regards,

Thank You Checklist

1. The key is to be specific. Avoid generic thanks. Give the particulars.

2. Use thanks to build or affirm relationships.

1.10.5.   Warming Up a Letter of Welcome

A letter of welcome is a good idea when you acquire a new client or customer. It goes beyond the particular sale or service and lays the foundation of an ongoing relationship.

1. Begin by expressing your pleasure in welcoming the client/customer.

2. Express appreciation for confidence demonstrated.

3. Assure the client/customer that his/her confidence has been well placed.

4. Invite communication.

Dear _____:

What a pleasure to welcome you to your family of customers!

We at **Name of company** are well aware of the range of choice you have in choosing a supplier of **product,** and we promise that we will do everything possible to make you happy with us for a long time to come.

If you have any questions or special needs, you can always reach me directly at 555-5555.

Welcome to a new level of quality and service!

Sincerely,

Tip: Write welcome letters to inactive customers who suddenly revive.

Dear _____:

We missed you! We're delighted to see you back, and we intend to do our very best to make certain that you don't go away again.

Name, we want you to be satisfied, so if you have any questions or special needs, comments—whatever—please call me directly at 555-5555. I'm here to help.

Welcome back.

Sincerely,

Welcome Checklist

1. A welcome letter lays the foundation of a an ongoing relationship.

2. Use the welcome letter to promise special service and high quality.

3. Establish the principle of communication. Allow the customer feel that he has a "friend" in the business.

1.11. GOVERNMENT

1.11.1. Writing Effective Applications—For Goodies and for Necessities

You might not think it when you try to call them and get tangled up in an end-less voice mail loop more complicated than an L.A. freeway interchange, but government agencies are made up of human beings. And since human beings respond to courtesy and, more often than you might think, are actually willing and eager to offer help, there is a place for something more than forms and form letters when you write to the government. This doesn't mean that you should strike an inappropriately personal tone or waste your correspondent's time with irrelevant happy talk. The clerk or official who receives your letter does not want to dwell on what is probably a routine request. Do get to the point quickly, then, but also pause long enough to drop a kind word along the way. This lets him know you are a human being and that you know *he* is a human being, too.

Licences and Permits

Expedite your applications for local business licenses, permits, state occupational licenses, and sales tax and seller's permits with a cover letter. You will first need to get the necessary information:

Licensing Agency, and so forth
Appropriate Division
Address

Re: Small business licensing information

Dear Sir or Madam:

I am planning to open a **type of business,** employing **number** persons, in **Name of community.** Please send me official information on which licenses and permits are required, the procedures for obtaining them, and all necessary forms for obtaining them.

Please send the material to:

Name and address

I can be reached at 555-5555 if you have any questions.

As I am planning to begin operating within **number** weeks, I would be very grateful for your prompt attention to this matter.

Sincerely,

You could just send in the completed forms. However, a brief cover letter will set your application apart from the crowd and may be just the boost you need for prompt attention:

Licensing Agency, etc.
Appropriate Division
Address

Re: Application for **license or permit type**

Dear Sir or Madam:

Enclosed please find the completed **form(s) number(s)** required to apply for **type of license, permit, and so forth,** together with all necessary documentation requested and my check for **$ amount** to cover application and license **or permit** fee.

I believe that all of the materials are complete and in order; however, if you have any questions, please do not hesitate to call me at 555-5555.

As I hope to begin operating within **number** weeks, I would be very grateful for your prompt attention to this matter.

Sincerely,

Inevitably, someone, somewhere will determine that your application is "incomplete," and more information is required. Flag it with a cover letter.

Tip: Send responses via certified mail and request a return receipt.

Licensing Agency, etc.
Appropriate Division
Address

VIA CERTIFIED MAIL, RETURN RECEIPT REQUESTED

Re: Additional Material Requested Pursuant to **type of** Application **number**

Dear Sir or Madam:

Enclosed please find **material requested,** which you requested on **date** in order to complete the processing of my application for **type of license or permit.**

I trust that this material does complete my application; however, if you have any questions, please call me at 555-5555. I am still hoping to begin operating by **date,** so I am very grateful for your efforts to expedite issuance of the **license or permit.**

Sincerely,

Getting Money

Various federal and local-government agencies are prepared to lend money to smaller businesses. Here are some letters to help you probe the possibilities:

Small Business Administration
1441 L Street, NW
Washington, DC 20416

Dear Sir or Madam:

Please send me "Business Loans from the SBA," "Your Business and the SBA," and "Business Development Pamphlets" (Form 115A).

As I operate a small business in need of financing, I would be grateful for your prompt attention to this request.

Please send the pamphlets to **Name and address.**

Sincerely,

Superintendent of Documents
Government Printing Office
Washington, DC 20402

Dear Sir or Madam:

Please send Form 115B, "Business Development Booklets," to the following address: **Name and address**

Sincerely,

Local office
U.S. Small Business Administration
address

Dear Sir or Madam:

Please send me the forms and documentation necessary to apply for SBA-guaranteed bank financing **or direct financing.** I am sole owner of my firm, which produces annual revenues below **$ amount,** and employs **number** in addition to myself.

Kindly forward the material to: **Name and address**

Sincerely,

Local office
U.S. Small Business Administration
address

Dear Sir or Madam:

Enclosed are the completed forms, together with the necessary documents from my bank, pursuant to my application for SBA-guaranteed financing.

I have completed the forms as fully as possible. However, if you have any questions, please call me at 555-5555. The loan officer responsible for my account at **Name of bank** is **Name,** whose direct line is 555-5555.

I am grateful for your prompt attention to my application.

Sincerely,

Local Development Agency

Dear Sir or Madam:

I own and operate a **type of business** in **Community,** with gross revenues under **$ amount** and **number** employees. We have been operating in **Community** since 19XX.

Please send me any information available on small business development programs that may be applicable to my case. If you have any questions, please call me at 555-5555.

I am grateful for your prompt response.

Sincerely,

Local Development Agency

Dear Sir or Madam:

Your bulletin **title or number** mentions the availability of **name of program** for small businesses like mine. Please send me form **number,** which is mentioned in the bulletin, and any other information or documents necessary to apply for **name of program.**

I am grateful for your prompt attention to this matter.

Sincerely yours,

Local Development Agency

Dear Sir or Madam:

Enclosed is the completed form **number** pursuant to my application for **type of loan, name of program.** I believe the information I have provided is quite complete, but do not hesitate to call me at 555-5555 if you have any questions.

As we are committed to doing business in this community and are eager to expand, I would greatly appreciate your prompt attention to the enclosed application.

Sincerely yours,

1.11.2. Surefire Answers for the Taxman

The object of the cover letter is to prompt the anonymous bureaucrat who is processing your request or application to see you as a person, not just a form. A brief but effective cover letter will not work miracles, but it can give you a valuable edge by getting your request or application processed a bit faster and maybe a little more attentively. Nowhere is this strategy more valuable than in communicating with the IRS or tax agencies at the state and local level. The people who work for such agencies expect you to resent, hate, or fear them. Anticipating such negative feelings, they may tend to feel tension themselves. A good letter to a taxation department may help to preempt bad feelings on both sides. Show yourself to be polite and cooperative.

Warning: In all but routine tax issues, consider seeking professional counsel before responding to such matters as audits, disputed deductions, and so on.

In simple tax disputes, a letter may suffice. For example:

Dear Sir or Madam:

I have just received correspondence from you indicating that my company owes **$ amount** on our 19XX tax return. Please be advised that we dispute your claim that we owe this amount.

Your claim is in error because **state reason for dispute.**

I enclose a copy of the **appropriate tax form** that refutes your claim, together with the bottom half of the notice you sent.

Please note that our taxpayer identification number is **number.**

Please make the necessary corrections to your records **and mail the refund due** as promptly as possible.

Sincerely,

Dear Sir or Madam:

I have received notification from you that our firm's 19XX **tax return** is being audited.

As you requested, I enclose the following items for your examination and review: **list**

I trust that these items will answer your questions concerning our return. If you do have further questions, however, please call me at 555-555-5555.

Our taxpayer identification number is **number.**

Sincerely,

Government Communications Checklist

1. Do not communicate with agencies and bureaucracies. Communicate with people.

2. Create a friendly, polite, businesslike tone.

3. Do not waste time. State your business clearly.

4. Do not use letters as a substitute for required official forms, but as communications to expedite handling of the forms.

5. Seek professional counsel when appropriate.

1.12. INFORMATION

1.12.1. A Guide to Giving More than Just the Facts

Business correspondence addresses problems, crises, complaints, sales, and myriad other issues, but the overwhelming majority of business letters do nothing more—and nothing less—than convey information.

Seems simple enough—and it is, as long as you are able to maintain focus and create clarity and economy of expression. In these letters, you want to keep your language transparent. That is, you don't want your correspondent to mull over your words or to guess at any hidden meanings, but rather to get from point A to point B, to find out what he needs to know.

But let's think about how you get from A to B. A letter conveying information is like an automobile. It's transportation. Yet most of us think of the car we drive as more than basic transportation. We have feelings about the vehicle: pride and even affection, perhaps, or contempt and even anger—as the body rusts away, the engine refuses to start when the temperature drops below forty degrees, and the repair bills mount. Clearly, the automobile is a vehicle of motion as well as emotion.

The same is true of letters conveying information. Utilitarian, no-nonsense vehicles, they nevertheless convey feelings in addition to information. This means that informational letters provide a valuable opportunity for creating positive feelings in your correspondent and for projecting a positive image of yourself and your organization.

When you write a letter providing information, take these steps:

1. State the subject of the letter clearly. If the letter is a response to a request for information, announce it as such and repeat or briefly summarize the request.

2. Provide the information.

3. Conclude by thanking your correspondent for her interest in doing business with you or your firm. If appropriate, offer your cooperation or further assistance.

TIP: Customers typically ask for the same basic types of information. You may want to prepare boilerplate letters on your personal computer, modifying them as appropriate for each response. Much basic information can be conveyed effectively in a brochure or pamphlet. When you send such corporate literature, personalize the correspondence by including a cover letter.

A typical instructional letter follows. Note the use of a bulleted list. This is often the most efficient means of conveying simple information.

Dear _____:

Thanks for your recent inquiry about **Name of company.** It's easy to order from us. Just use our toll-free ordering number, 1-800-555-5555 and have the following information on hand:

◆ The item number
◆ The quantity of each item you wish to order
◆ Your major credit card number
◆ Your shipping and billing address

I've enclosed our latest catalog.

If you have any additional questions, please call me directly at 555-555-5555.

Sincerely,

TIP: Include a phone number the customer can call for more information and answers.

Here's another situation. You're setting up a series of meetings or seminars. Convey the information straightforwardly, but add a touch of the right attitude:

Dear Ms. Ferris:

I am very happy that you will be attending our series of sales seminars during March. Here is the schedule:

Sales Essentials	3/5	10 A.M.–2 P.M.	Main office
Always Be Closing	3/6	11 A.M.–4 P.M.	Auditorium
Upselling	3/7	11 A.M.–2 P.M.	Main office
Ethics	3/8	10 A.M.–1 P.M.	Main office

Please give me a phone call at 555-555-5555 if you have any questions.

Sincerely,

You can handle the announcement of a change of address with plain old postcards mailed to your clients and customers, or you can take the opportunity to say something extra:

Dear Friend:

Acme Widget is a company on the move. We *mean* it!

After June 4, our new address will be:

> 1234 West Rodney Road
> Sinkhole, IL 23455

Telephone numbers will remain the same, with Customer Service at 555-5555, Shipping at 444-4444, and Billing at 333-3333.

Sincerely,

Or try this as an expression of pride:

Dear Friend:

Acme Widgets has moved! We're now at 1234 West Rodney Road, Sinkhole, IL 23455.

Why don't you drop by and see our new state-of-the-art facility? The doughnuts and coffee are on us during our official Open House, from October 4 through October 24—but you're welcome to come by any time.

All the best,

Checklist for Providing Information

1. Above all, be clear, but do not hesitate to flavor your letter with personality.

2. Use the letter to enhance your image and that of your firm.

3. Build a relationship with offers of assistance or further information.

4. Invite calls.

1.12.2.   What to Say to Get What You Need

It is no surprise that the principal requirement of a letter requesting informa-tion is that it clearly and fully state your request. Just what do you need to know? However, the letter should also serve to motivate a full, accurate, and prompt response. Use an "if . . . then" structure": "*If* you tell me what I need to know, *then* I can serve you better, or do business with you, or buy your product, or correct your problem."

1. Begin by stating what you need and why you need it.

2. If the request is for information pursuant to doing something for your correspondent—for example, you need information in order to process a credit request—begin by thanking your correspondent for his interest, order, application, and so forth, then motivate your request: "In order to process your order, we need to know . . ."

3. If appropriate, ask your correspondent for any additional information she thinks relevant. You may also ask for advice.

4. If necessary, request a rapid response. Explain why time is of the essence.

5. Thank your correspondent for cooperation or for doing business with you. You may also close with thanks for "prompt attention."

Some fill-in examples:

Dear _____:

Please send us your most recent catalog of **products.**

We are a small **type of company** and regularly order **products.** We've heard good things about your company, but, apparently, we are not on your catalog mailing list.

We'll be placing our next order by **date,** and we would like to consider you as a supplier. Therefore, please get the catalog to us right away. Address it to: **address.**

Sincerely,

Here is a letter to a firm that has made an inquiry of you:

Dear Ms. Ronalds:

We would be delighted to bid on your overhaul project. It is the kind of work in which we specialize and excel.

Please note that your RFP did not specify the following information, which we need in order to prepare a bid in a format most useful to you:

Is a narrative proposal required?
Do costs include delivery?
Do you want us to handle subsidiary suppliers?
Please mail or fax this information. Our fax number is 555-555-5555.

Sincerely,

Another:

Dear Mr. Kroy:

I am highly interested in attending the seminar series you and I discussed. But before I can give you a definite yes, I need to see the seminar schedule. Please mail or fax me a complete schedule, including subjects, times, and places. Let me check my calendar, and I'll give you a call.

Sincerely,

Checklist for Requesting Information

1. State fully and clearly what you want.

2. Motivate a full, accurate, and prompt reply by suggesting how the reply will benefit your correspondent as well as yourself.

3. Explain why you need the information.

1.13. PERSONNEL

1.13.1. Put It in Writing

In many cases, there is no substitute for face-to-face, person-to-person contact to resolve personnel issues and to build an effective team. However, the most momentous personnel issues—including salary, evaluation reprimand, hiring, and termination—require documentation.

Let's say you've got a two-room office. You are in one room. Your assistant is in the other. You feel foolish writing a letter. Why do it?

Like it or not, even *single*-employee businesses are regulated by state and federal governments. Protect yourself by documenting all employment agreements and transactions. Note, too, that the human memory shrivels in proportion to the emotional intensity of an immediate situation. In a crisis, you may demand something of an employee to which she never agreed, or she may ask you for something that you never intended to be part of the deal. It is best for all parties involved if there is a document to which you can refer.

1.13.2. Creatively Coping with Complaints

A letter is an excellent medium for responding to employee complaints because it clearly and dispassionately states circumstances, positions, policies, and remedies for the record. Oftentimes, the letter will be used as a supplement to a verbal exchange.

> TIP: Depending on the nature of the complaint, it may be most effective to respond verbally—in a meeting—and to follow up that meeting with a letter. Again, depending on circumstances, some employees may find a written response, in the absence of a face-to-face meeting, arbitrarily authoritative and cold.

Letters avoid the emotional fireworks that may erupt in a face-to-face confrontation. A written response also shows that you take the complaint seriously. Moreover, a letter should provide the following documentation:

1. The nature of the complaint

2. Your understanding of the complaint

3. Your responsiveness to the complaint

4. The action you propose.

In responding to a complaint, take the following steps:

1. Acknowledge receipt of the complaint, or acknowledge discussion/meeting with the employee regarding the complaint.

2. If possible and appropriate, thank your correspondent for bringing the matter to your attention.

3. Express your responsiveness.

4. Propose an action.

   TIP: "Action" does not necessarily mean doing what the employee asks for. An action may include a remedy or solution, or it may be a further discussion, a meeting, or a mediation.

5. If the substance of the complaint cannot be resolved, explain why. If at all possible, propose alternatives.

6. If you cannot propose an immediate solution, affirm your commitment to work together to address and resolve the issue. If the issue cannot be resolved, assert your willingness to find a way to "work around" the issue.

Of course, a certain proportion of complaints will be unfounded or inappropriate. The key here is to respond to the issues, the facts, rather than the personalities, and to avoid criticizing the employee for making an inappropriate request. The key is to explain the basis of your decision rather than throw your weight around.

When an employee complains that his work load is too heavy, you must listen carefully. Perhaps the employee requires counseling. Perhaps it's time to consider transferring him to a different position. But, most often these days, the fact is that the work load *is* too heavy:

Dear Roy:

Thanks for meeting with me yesterday and being so frank about the workload in your department. I certainly am convinced that your workload is heavy, and I appreciate the maximum effort you always put forth.

As you know, we operate under a variety of economic pressures. We just won't have the funds to hire additional personnel soon. I know that's not what you want to hear, and it does not mean that I intend to ignore your complaint. Here's what I suggest for the present: Let's work out some interim solutions by getting together with supervisors from other departments to discuss strategies for immediate relief—something to hold us over until we're in a position to make more hires.

I will notify you within a few days of the time and place of the meeting.

Sincerely,

Two other areas are the subject of frequent complaints: the actions or attitudes of fellow employees and those of supervisors. Responses in these situations require very careful thought and consideration. Sometimes, they require the wisdom of Solomon.

> **Warning:** Sometimes your response requires the benefit of legal counsel. Make certain that you are thoroughly aware of your legal rights and obligations in responding to disputes among employees or between subordinates and supervisors. Beyond your rights and obligations, you may need a professional assessment of your "exposure"—the likelihood that an issue will involve you in expensive litigation.

Usually, the most prudent course is to respond by proposing a meeting, with you, of the parties involved. If your firm has a Human Resources department with prescribed procedures for addressing these kinds of complaints, you should involve that department.

> Dear _____:
>
> I am pleased that you came to me on **day** to discuss your differences with **Name.** It suggests to me your willingness to resolve these differences rationally and to the benefit of yourself, **Name,** and the entire team.
>
> I value both of you greatly, and I am confident that we can arrive at a resolution of the issues you discussed with me.
>
> I would like for you and **Name** to meet with me in my office on **day** at **time.** Let's all talk this out—without accusation and with an eye toward resolving the situation.
>
> Please confirm that you will be available for the meeting.
>
> Sincerely,

Rightly or wrongly, employees often complain about facilities. Sometimes you can fix the problem. Sometimes you cannot. Here's a memo:

To: _____
From: _____
Re: Breakroom facilities

Your memo regarding the break room was very helpful. It is useful for me to know just what the issues are and what features of the facility you would like to see improved.

There are some things I can do and others that I cannot.

Our physical plant is far too limited to make all the changes that you enumerate in your memo to me. This does not mean that I will, therefore, ignore the problem. Instead, I suggest that you select a delegation of three representatives to meet with me and with **Name,** our operations manager, to determine, first, which items on your list are most important to you and, second, which items can be addressed immediately, which ones can be addressed in the longer term, and which ones cannot be resolved.

If you agree, please have a designated representative call me so that we can set up the meeting.

One employee complaint you must take very seriously is a complaint of unsafe—or potentially unsafe—conditions. Respond quickly. Respond in writing, for the record. Then do not delay in taking action.

To: _____
From: _____
Re: Unsafe condition in _____

I have received and thoroughly reviewed your report of an unsafe condition in **location, operation, and so forth.** In response, I have ordered the following action:

   provide a numbered list

I have also asked **Name** to investigate the situation thoroughly and to submit her detailed evaluation by **date.** Based on that report, I expect to formulate long-term remedies for the situation.

Checklist for responding to Complaints

1. Avoid emotion.

2. Address issues rather than personalities.

3. Demonstrate that you take the complaints seriously.

4. Use your response to strengthen your relationship with employees.

1.13.3.   Improving Performance with Effective Evaluations

Many larger firms evaluate employees with prescribed evaluation forms. Even if your organization does not do this, you should regularly evaluate employee performance, and you should put it writing. Not only will such a written evaluation document reasons for making or not making promotions, raising or not raising salaries, and so on, it will serve as a powerful communication to the employee.

The general rule is, to whatever degree legitimately possible, emphasize the positive. Only after developing the positive aspects of the employee's performance should you enumerate any areas that need improvement. Here are some other steps to take:

1. Put the emphasis on teamwork. Wherever you can, use "we" rather than "I" or "you."

2. Be as positive *as possible.* Express the positive before launching into any negatives.

3. In listing areas of deficiency, try to use positive rather than negative terms. For example, instead of "not successful in such and such," say "could use improvement in such and such."

    PITFALL: Being unrelentingly negative will make an employee feel hopeless and will drive him away. However, if significant problems exist, be certain to address these fully and clearly. Do not sugarcoat them. It is your responsibility to the company and to the employee to provide a clear and explicit evaluation. You need an unequivocal basis for salary-related and status-related actions, including demotion, disciplinary action, and even termination.

4. Thank the employee for contributing to the team.

The year-end letter is a routine evaluation:

Dear _____:

We've worked together for another year, and I thought you would find it useful to receive my assessment of that year.

In general, your work has been of a very high caliber, especially in **areas and/or specific projects.**

No one is perfect, of course, and I believe you'll appreciate a comment on **number** areas in which your performance might be improved: **list and explain.**

Name, you are a valuable member of the team. I rely on you with confidence. It's been a great year. Together, we can make next year even better. Thanks for your cooperation, your effort, your inventiveness, and your hard work.

Sincerely,

Checklist for Employee Evaluation

1. Stress the positive and stress it first.

2. Avoid opposing "I" against "you." Use "we" to develop a feeling of team.

3. To the degree possible—and without sugarcoating—express negatives in terms of positives. Talk about a need for improvement rather than simply blasting the employee for deficiency.

4. Treat the evaluation letter as documentation—the basis for important actions with regard to the employee's compensation and status.

1.13.4. How to Reprimand Fairly, Forthrightly, and Firmly

The object of a reprimand letter is twofold: First and foremost, the letter should provide creative and constructive criticism in order to correct or improve a negative situation and to promote the positive development of an employee. Secondly, the letter serves as documentary evidence of an employee's performance. This is important for purposes of evaluation and, if worse comes to worst, in backing up a decision to terminate the employee.

In most cases, the reprimand should be expressed in as positive terms as the situation permits—without, however, obscuring or sugarcoating the facts in the matter. In some cases, of course, it will be difficult, impossible, or simply undesirable to find any positive material. However, even in the most serious cases, avoid personal assaults. Focus on issues. Make no threats—although you may clearly outline the possible consequences of an unremedied situation.

> **WARNING:** Make no accusations based on hearsay or rumor. The truth is a strong defense against libel. Be certain of your facts before issuing a reprimand.

1. Begin the letter of reprimand, if possible, by acknowledging a context of generally positive performance. Set the infraction in a positive context, if possible. If the context is, in fact, generally negative, do not disguise that fact.

2. State the problem or issue. Be clear. Stick to the facts. Avoid personalities. Avoid imputation of motive.

3. Explain how the employee's action(s) impact on the organization.

4. Suggest a remedy to the situation.

5. Advise the employee of the consequences of uncorrected performance or a repetition of the infraction.

6. Advise the employee of your willingness to work with him to help correct the problem.

Generic forms for a variety of reprimand situations follow.

Dear _____:

For the __nth time this month, you reported late to work on **date.**

Name, I am well aware that occasions arise when being late is unavoidable. Traffic may be exceptionally bad, you may have an emergency at home, and so on. But, I believe you will have to agree, your lateness has become a habit—the rule rather than the exception.

We depend on you. And one of the things we depend on is your keeping regular hours. You are needed here. You are a highly valued asset to our operations.

I must insist that you make whatever adjustments are necessary in your morning routine to insure that you arrive at the office on time. If there is some problem or issue that I should know about, please talk to me. Together, we can resolve the issue.

Sincerely,

Dear _____:

I received a highly disturbing phone call yesterday, **date,** from a very unhappy customer—a customer angry enough to become an ex-customer.

She claims that you treated her rudely and even exchanged harsh words with her. **Name,** this is not the first time I have had such a report.

We need to talk. We need to talk about your performance and your attitude. We need to talk about how ours is a service-oriented company, which is pledged to treat each customer as a special person and a valued asset.

The consequences of rudeness are loss of business for the company. For you, the consequences could include disciplinary action—even dismissal.

Let's resolve this issue before it gets that far. Please see me in my office at **time** on **date.**

Sincerely,

Dear _____:

On **date, Name,** your supervisor, reported to me that you had refused to take direction from her and had declined an assignment because, in your judgment, it was "not worth doing."

It has always been our policy to consider carefully the judgment and opinions of our staff. However, when you joined the team, you agreed to take direction from your designated supervisors. In view of this, I would consider what happened on **date** to be an instance of insubordination.

We don't want a troop of unthinking robots. However, simply refusing to do a legitimate assignment is not acceptable professional performance.

I would be happy to discuss this incident with you. Just give me a call for an appointment. However, please consider this letter a formal reprimand

and warning: If you are unwilling or unable to live up to your agreement with us, we cannot retain your services.

Name assures me that she harbors no hard feelings toward you. If you are willing, this incident may be put behind us. If not, I suggest you rethink your professional priorities.

Sincerely,

Checklist for Effective Reprimands

1. The rule of thumb is to frame the reprimand in terms that are as positive as circumstances will permit.

2. Do not sugarcoat or downplay the problem.

3. Avoid attacking personalities.

4. Avoid accusation. Stick to documented fact.

5. Avoid idle threats, but do not hesitate to spell out the consequences of an uncorrected situation.

How to Respond to Requests

It's easy to comply with employee requests and usually requires no documentation. Responding negatively, however, or responding with something less than an employee asks for is more difficult. A letter is often useful to defuse emotion, to explain a position, and to document reasons for rejecting a request.

Common requests include changes in work hours, additional break time, increase in salary, new equipment, new office space, and so on. While your object is to express and explain the refusal clearly, it is also to avoid alienating the employee and to maintain—if possible, even reinforce—the sense of community and teamwork.

Let's take it step by step:

1. Acknowledge receiving and reviewing the request.

2. State the rejection. Do so neutrally or with an expression of regret, such as "Unfortunately, . . ."

3. Explain the reasons for refusal, emphasizing the context of the team.

4. Whenever possible, propose an alternative, a compromise, or a later date at which the request might be made again.

5. Thank the employee for his understanding, cooperation, and team spirit.

There are many reasons to decline a request for a raise or promotion. Some reasons relate to the employee's performance, and some relate to external circumstances. Be certain to distinguish between these.

> **TIP:** Resist the temptation to offer an excuse for not giving a raise. Explain the real reason, whatever it may be. If you believe the employee's performance does not merit a raise or promotion, try to explain how that performance could be improved. Do not avoid the negative, but try to emphasize the positive.

Dear _____:

I have reviewed your request for a salary increase, and that review has required me to look at your job performance.

I have to tell you that your present level of performance does not merit a raise at this time. Here is why:

♦ Reason
♦ Reason
♦ Reason

Perhaps you would find it useful to sit down with me and review these items. I believe that, together, we can work out a plan to bring your performance to a level that will permit me to consider a salary increase at a later time. Please call to arrange an appointment, if you wish.

Sincerely,

External pressures may also prevent your granting a request for a salary increase:

Dear _____:

I would like nothing more than to give you the raise you have requested and that you deserve. Unfortunately, we have not achieved the level of revenue this quarter necessary to make such a raise possible. In short, I don't have the money available at this time.

I need you to know that I greatly value your contribution to the team, and I feel confident that, with your continued imaginative hard work, we will achieve the revenue levels necessary to give you the increase you most certainly merit.

Let's review the situation next quarter.

Sincerely,

In responding to any request, including one for a salary increase, consider compromise and alternative:

Dear _____:

I have reviewed your request for a salary increase. **Name,** after careful consideration, I have determined that the level of your compensation is quite appropriate to your position at this time.

I can offer two alternatives to a raise.

First, I am willing to reconsider the matter at the end of the next quarter, which is a more appropriate time for considering an increase.

Second, for the present, I am willing to increase the number of vacation days to which you are entitled, from **number** to **number.** This is effective immediately.

If you have any questions, please drop by my office.

Sincerely,

Checklist for Responding to Requests

1. Positive responses rarely require a written response, unless you desire to document the response.

2. Avoid alienating the employee by explaining reasons for rejection. You owe her that much.

3. Suggest alternatives or compromises whenever possible and appropriate.

1.13.5. Terminating: Closing the Door—Gently, or with a Slam

Legally, morally, and emotionally, the most sensitive area of employer-employee relations is termination. At minimum, the dismissal letter should announce the action and should state the effective date of the dismissal. It should clearly list reasons for the action. Finally, the letter should include information regarding the disposition of the employee's final check and also address any applicable issues of vacation pay or severance pay due.

Many employers will want to do more than this, especially if the employee is being terminated through no fault of his own—for example, as a result of corporate restructuring, loss of revenue, and so on. In these cases:

1. Express your regrets, explain what circumstances have made the termination necessary

2. Provide the basic information:
   a. Effective date of termination
   b. Disposition of final check
   c. Vacation pay and severance due

3. Express satisfaction with the employee's performance.

4. If possible and appropriate, offer assistance in finding the employee another position (perhaps simply by encouraging him to use you as a referral).

5. Conclude by wishing the employee well and expressing confidence in his ability to find suitable employment speedily.

Even in cases where the termination is due to employee performance, avoid accusations, especially of a personal or subjective nature. When an employee is being terminated "for cause"—failing to do a job, doing it poorly, or for having violated company rules—enumerate the instances of failure, the duties that have not been performed, the goals that have not been reached. Do not evaluate the person or the personality.

> **PITFALL:** Making personal attacks is not only counterproductive—for you as well as for the employee—but doing so leaves you vulnerable to legal action. Moreover, with highly charged emotions involved, making dismissal a personal matter may provoke an employee response ranging from sabotage, to verbal abuse, and even to physical threat.

The following may be adapted to suit particular circumstances:

Dear _____:

I regret to inform you that your employment with **Name of company** is terminated effective immediately for the following reasons: **list**

Please vacate the premises immediately with your personal possessions. Your salary earned to date will be forwarded to you at your home address by **date,** together with any vacation pay to which you are entitled.

Sincerely,

Dear _____:

I regret having to tell you this, but due to a sharp decrease in orders I am compelled to terminate your services effective two weeks from the date of this letter.

I have greatly enjoyed having you work here, and you have made a valuable contribution to the company. Please be assured that you will be the first person I call if the volume of orders returns to its previous level. In the meantime, do not hesitate to call on me for personal recommendations to other employers.

Your final check, which will be issued on **date** will include any vacation pay to which you may be entitled.

I wish you all the best, and I am confident that a person with your ability will quickly find suitable employment.

Sincerely,

Dear _____:

We have been friends for as long as you have worked here, which makes this a very painful task. After lengthy consideration, I have concluded that it would be best for **Name of company** and for you to terminate your employment here effective two weeks from the date of this letter.

Based on your years of service here, you will draw full salary for **time period,** which should give you ample time to secure another position. I will be glad to help in your search in any way that I can.

Sincerely,

Checklist for Terminations

1. If your firm has a Human Resources department, refer terminations to that department.

2. Follow your firm's policies in regard to terminations.

3. Avoid making personal attacks.

4. Address issues rather than personalities.

5. Provide all necessary basic information.

6. Express regret, if appropriate, but do not express doubt or hesitation in regard to the action.

1.14. RECOMMENDATIONS

1.14.1. Using Your Judgment to Best Advantage

Recommendations can be a pleasure to write. They not only present an opportunity to help a deserving associate or employee, they are also in your interest. It pays to extend your influence and judgment throughout the business community. Populate your world with people who know and respect you.

> **TIP:** The key to writing effective recommendations is to be as specific as possible. Avoid reliance on vague adjectives. Instead, enumerate specific events, projects, and accomplishments relating to the person whom you are recommending.

> **PITFALL:** Do not write a recommendation unless you can do so without reservation. If you have any doubts about the employee, decline the request for a recommendation. *Never write a negative recommendation.* Not only is it inappropriate, it exposes you to serious legal liability. If you cannot be 100 percent positive, decline the request for a recommendation.

The most effective way to begin a recommendation is to express your pleasure at making the recommendation, then:

1. Detail your working relationship to the job candidate. Include:

    a. Most recent position she has held

    b. Years on the job

    c. Specific projects and accomplishments

> **PITFALL:** Avoid mentioning salary figures. This is a matter between you and the subject of your recommendation, on the one hand, and between the subject and the new potential employer, on the other. You can easily sabotage salary negotiations by mentioning a figure.

2. Assure your correspondent that he will find working with the candidate a rewarding experience.

3. Express your willingness to discuss the candidate further.

TIP: Call on the candidate to help you write a letter containing specifics. Ask her to list for you what she considers her most significant accomplishments, the most successful projects she has completed, and so on. Use these in your letter.

Making Sure Your Opinion Counts

Some successful letters of recommendation:

Dear Mr. Thompson:

I have mixed emotions about recommending Sarah Garfield to you for the position of sales manager.

No, I don't mean I have any doubts about her ability to excel in the position, to increase your sales, and to provide innovation, and leadership. My emotions are mixed because I am not in a position to offer Sarah the kind of promotion she deserves, and I must, therefore, recommend her services to another firm.

The position of sales manager presents a valuable opportunity for both of you. Sarah was instrumental in developing a highly successful special promotion program for us, which resulted in a 15 percent increase in revenue last year. When illness forced our sales manager to take an extended leave, Sarah stepped up to the plate and hit one home run after another. She is capable of taking on a wide variety of assignments, mastering each of them quickly.

Sad as I am to see her go, I recommend her to you without hesitation. Please call me if you have any questions.

Sincerely,

You may, from time to time, be called on to recommend the services of a freelance employee:

Dear _____:

I am delighted to recommend **Name** for **position.** We have engaged his services on **number** occasions during **time period** and have found him to be an outstanding professional. **Name** completes jobs quickly and efficiently. He worked with us on the following projects—**list**—each of which was highly successful.

Name has the ability to enter a situation and get up to speed almost immediately. He works very effectively with your permanent staff.

I invite you to call me at 555-5555 if you need any further information.

Sincerely,

Checklist for Recommendations

1. Be 100 percent positive. If you have any reservations regarding a candidate, decline his request for a recommendation.

2. Include as many specifics as possible.

3. Call on the candidate to help you. He may supply the specifics, which you can work into the letter.

1.15. SALES

1.15.1. A Prospector's Backpack

There are almost as many how-to books on the subject of selling as there are products and services to sell. All of these books promise to provide formulas for prospecting new sales opportunities. Unfortunately, no formula can control all four of the variables involved in a sales situation:

1. The perceived character of the seller

2. The skill of the seller

3. The needs and desires of the buyer

4. The intrinsic desirability—quality and value—of the product or service

Most sales books will tell you that you do not sell a product; you sell yourself. There is truth in this. Part of selling is creating confidence in yourself. However, you cannot ignore the underlying product. It is certainly easier to sell a product of obvious value than it is to sell junk.

So much for what you can't do. A good sales letter *can* help to build a positive image of the seller's character. Properly structured, the sales letter also enhances the skill of the seller. Finally, the letter can do much to create desire in the buyer.

There is no hard-and-fast outline for a sales letter, but there are time-tested structures. The most basic and most flexible is known as AIDA—attention, Interest, Desire, Action:

A. Begin by capturing your correspondent's attention. Make a short, provocative statement, or ask a rhetorical question: "Could you use free cash right now?"

I. Having gotten your correspondent's attention, develop his interest. Explain the deal. You must emphasize that the deal represents opportunity.

D. Express your correspondent's desire in your own words. Let him know that he is not alone. "Everybody will want to take advantage of this opportunity." Or: "You do not want to be locked out." Or: "A chance like this comes along once every ten years."

A. Tell your correspondent what to do next. Provide instructions that will prompt him to act. Push him over the hump of inertia with a special offer.

Let's jump in with a few "cold letters." These are sales appeals that, in effect, come out of nowhere. They are probes—attempts to interest new prospects in what you have to sell.

TIP: Depending on the product or service you have to offer, you may send cold letters at random—perhaps to names selected from the local telephone directory—or you may develop a mailing list based on research. Perhaps you have a list of current customers. Your current customers are your best prospects for additional sales. To expand your customer base, you may want to rent mailing lists from various companies, especially special interest publications. For example, if you sell specialized audio equipment, you may want to rent a mailing list from a publication for high-end stereo enthusiasts. The point is that cold letters may be warmed up a bit by targeting your prospects.

Dear Mr. Hemhaw:

Do you share your chair with somebody else? How about your pens and pencils? And your computer?

No?

Then why are you sharing your copy of *Office Politics?*

I don't have to tell you how valuable *Office Politics* can be to your business and to your personal advancement? It's the only magazine of its kind, and we pride ourselves on being the first to get you the news that really matters. Matters in a direct and personal way. To you. Matters in a way that means money. Money for you.

Can you afford to be number two, three, four, or more in line to get this kind of news?

How many people see *Office Politics* before it reaches your desk?

Why not use the enclosed card to subscribe today. Get your own copy of *Office Politics.*

It's about time.

Sincerely,

Here is a specialized appeal. You would send such a letter to a selected list of potential customers:

Dear Mr. Younger:

Fall in and take command! Charge! Because our prices are in retreat.

Warbooks, America's leading military book club, is holding its biggest sale in years. We're discounting everything—new releases as well as bargain titles and old standbys, including hard-to-find classics. Yes: every single title is available at a reduced price.

Why are we doing this?

We want to recruit you into the ranks of the most exciting book club you'll ever join. Now, this muster-in won't last forever. These very special prices will end on July 5, and, after that, all prices will return to their regular club discount levels.

Don't go AWOL on us, soldier. Take command—and take advantage of this very special offer.

It's easy. Just look through the accompanying catalog, select any three books at our limited-time-only super discount, fill out the order form, and then PAY ONLY FOR TWO.

You've heard us right. Not only will you benefit from a special-price offer, we'll send you one book absolutely free.

Sound off today.

Sincerely,

1.15.2. Surefire Follow-Ups

Here's a chilling statistic about cold letters. You can expect the best of them to produce a sale 3 percent of the time. That is correct. For every hundred letters you send out, expect three sales—and that's if you're writing *effective* letters. The more precisely you target your cold letters, the higher that slim hit rate will be. Now, the most precisely targeted kind of letter is not a cold letter, but a follow-up. You write these after you've made some sort of contact with a prospect. Perhaps your correspondent has responded to a survey or has made a call to you, inquiring about a product or service. Follow-ups don't necessarily close a sale, but they bring you closer. Always begin such letters by defining your relationship to the correspondent, then proceed through the last three stages of AIDA: develop interest, stir desire, and prompt action.

> **TIP:** In defining your relationship to your correspondent, try to focus on something you agree on: "I agree: health insurance is expensive." Then develop your pitch from this point of agreement: "That's why it is so vital to make certain that you are getting the best value for your money."

Dear Mrs. Robertson:

I appreciate your inviting me into your home to discuss the health insurance options available from SecureComp. You know, I couldn't agree with you more: Health insurance is *very* expensive these days. And that is precisely why it is so important to make certain that you are getting the very best value for your money.

Because if there is one thing that's far more expensive than health insurance, it's health *care.* Hospitals in our area charge $ amount per day. A "simple" operation—an appendectomy—will set you back $ amount, And that's if nothing goes wrong. Major cardiac surgery: $ amount. Why, an aspirin dispensed by the hospital will cost you at least $ amount per pill.

Health insurance serves two purposes: To make certain that you can afford the very best care. And to protect your assets and loved ones in case of major need. Let's add a third purpose. High-value health insurance helps *keep* you healthy by giving you peace of mind, 24 hours a day, 365 days a year.

All of this is hard to put a price tag on.

I've enclosed copies of the plans we discussed. If you have any additional questions about them, please give me a call on my direct line, 555-5555.

Sincerely,

Dear Mr. Johnston:

We've been working like dogs. Folks like you have been responding to our special Home Tune-Up offer, and we've been doing our best to answer each call promptly.

Well, we don't want anyone to be left out. So here's some exciting news: We're extending the special Home Tune-Up offer for another month.

That's right! There's still time to order the entire tune-up package at a very special price. This includes:

◆ Siding inspection and spot repair
◆ Detailing inspection and spot repair
◆ Roof inspection and spot repair
◆ Gutter "new up"

—all for one low package price.

And our estimate? That will cost you absolutely nothing.

Give us a call at 555-5555, and we'll do the rest.

Sincerely,

1.15.3.   CPR for Inactive Customers

Remember, your best *prospective* customers are your current customers. Perhaps surprisingly, that includes inactive customers—folks who haven't done business with you for a protracted period of time. Even though your inclination may be to give up on the inactive customer—perhaps assuming that she is dissatisfied and has taken her business elsewhere—the fact that you have had dealings with her makes her a better prospect than a total stranger. Customers, even inactive customers, are valuable assets. Don't squander them. An example:

Dear Ms. Pailson:

It's been an entire year since you rented a video from Technocrats. Where have you been? We'd like to see you back.

Like a lot of companies, we used to give our sales staff bonuses for bringing back wayward customers. Well, we thought about it, and we've got a better idea. We're going to give the bonus to you.

Here's how it works: Come on in and rent two videos from Technocrats, and you will receive a third rental absolutely free.

With rental prices as low as ours, that's a deal you won't be able to beat anywhere else.

Come on, Ms. Pailson, give an old friend a visit. We'd love to see you again.

Sincerely,

Some customers become inactive by deliberately canceling a service. Don't give up on them, either:

Dear Mr. Kenyon:

Pete Wilson, our agent in Hargrove, tells me that you are not planning to renew your homeowner's policy with us. I'm sorry to hear that.

I respect your decision, and I certainly won't pester you with a phone call. But I would like to ask you to call me at 555-5555 to hear why you've decided to move your coverage to another carrier. Perhaps I can even offer you some money-saving options that will persuade you to reconsider.

I won't call you. But I would sure like to hear from you.

Sincerely,

Even after a customer stops buying a particular service, you might take steps to continue the relationship, at least for a time:

Dear Mr. Patrick:

This letter confirms that, per your instructions, we have closed your account (number 123456) with us. A closing statement and check in the amount of $2345.67 are enclosed.

We have enjoyed serving you, and we hope that you will consider us in the future for your investment needs.

Unless you instruct us otherwise, we will continue to send you our monthly newsletter, which will keep you informed of the many investment opportunities we offer.

Sincerely,

Checklist for Sales Letters

1. Use the AIDA formula to structure effective sales letters.

2. Command attention with a provocative opener or with a question that has an obvious answer: "Can you use extra cash right now?"

3. Always end the letter with an instruction for specific action. Make it easy for the customer to act.

4. Cultivate customers. Your object should be, *first,* to create customers, and, *second,* to make the sale.

5. Don't give up on inactive customers.

1.16. JOB HUNTING LETTERS

1.16.1. How to Write Your Own Ticket

Chapter 1.17, which is coming up, deals with writing effective résumés. But you should go into that chapter knowing one sad fact: most prospective employers routinely toss unsolicited résumés into the waste basket. They treat unsolicited résumés the way most of us treat "junk mail." They throw them away unread.

Two strategies may prevent this frustrating fate. Either include an effective cover letter with your résumé, or consider sending a letter *instead* of a résumé. The sight of an unsolicited résumé may provoke the throw-away reflex, whereas a letter is more likely to get looked at.

> TIP: If you are sending unsolicited correspondence to a large organization (more than 500 employees) or to an organization you know has a Human Resources Department, send a cold letter without a résumé. It is less likely to get filed away or thrown away. If you send unsolicited correspondence to a smaller organization (under 500 employees), send a résumé accompanied by a great cover letter. It stands a better chance of being read.

Prepare Yourself

An unsolicited job-hunt letter is a cold letter, and, if you've looked at 1.16. Sales, you know that even the best cold letters generate sales only about 3 percent of the time. From the point of view of your correspondent, a cold letter is a chance occurrence. What happens in the case of most chance occurrences? They lead to nothing more.

Wouldn't it be wonderful if you had the great luck to send your unsolicited letter to the one person who *really* wanted what you have to offer?

Luck? You can't count on luck like that.

You don't have to. Before you write and send out a job hunting letter, do some homework to identify the needs of your target employer. Then write a letter that addresses these needs.

Homework Resources

But how do get the kind of inside information that tells you what a prospective employer needs? Don't you have to know somebody in the company?

Make no mistake, an inside contact helps, and you should make good use of any that you may have. However, the most effective way of discovering "inside" information is to begin by identifying those employers who interest you. If an employer interests you—*you*, defined as the sum of your abilities, qualifications, and skills—it is a pretty good bet that you will interest the employer.

Check out the following resources:

◆ An official job description (if available)

◆ The target company's annual report

◆ The target company's catalogs, brochures, ads, and other published material

◆ Material supplied by the target company's Public Relations and/or Customer Service departments

◆ Journals and newsletter articles concerning the target company or the industry as a whole

◆ Books (available in the public library) that mention the target company or the industry as a whole

◆ Online sources: Check out the Internet and commercial online providers.

What Do You Need to Know?

Before you even bother to sit down to write a job-hunting letter, learn something about:

◆ The business of the company: What does it do or make?

◆ The scope of the company: How large? Where does it do business?

◆ The competition: Who are they, and what is the target company's standing among them?

Review the available sources in an effort to determine:

◆ Hot company issues—problems and opportunities critical to the firm

◆ Hot industry issues: problems and opportunities critical to the industry as a whole

◆ Relevant current events: What's going on in the world, nation, community, or neighborhood that affects the company or the industry?

1.16.2.   Structuring Your Letters for Success

Five elements go into an effective job-hunt letter:

◆ A strong opening

◆ An appeal to the employer's self-interest

◆ Highlights of your qualifications and accomplishments

◆ Solutions to challenging issues

◆ A bid for an interview

If you include a résumé, add:

◆ An introduction to the résumé

Let's explore these elements in detail.

TIP: The most convincing opening says absolutely nothing about yourself—except as it relates to what you can do for the target employer.

Be Specific

Get rid of as many adjectives and adverbs as possible. Substitute nouns and verbs. Put another way, favor objective fact over subjective assertion. *Not:* "I am a great customer-service manager, who will make a real difference to you." *But:* "As customer service manager at Jones and Company, I have developed techniques for upselling that have increased the Jones bottom line by 15 percent."

TIP: Speak the language of business; that is, whenever possible, express yourself in dollars and cents: money earned for an employer, money saved for an employer.

Appeal to Self-Interest

The target of your letter doesn't care about you. Why should he? He doesn't even know you!

But you can bet that he cares about himself, his well-being, and his success. Appeal to these concerns, rather than to what you need or want. Begin by introducing some valuable aspect of your experience in terms of how it can benefit the target employer. Be specific, but brief.

Qualifications and Accomplishments

Create a powerful statement of qualifications and accomplishments by describing only those qualifications and accomplishments that directly appeal to the self-interest of the target employer.

Create Desire

As with any sales letter, your next-to-last step is to create desire for the product—in this case, *you*. Show how the terrific things you've outlined in the opening paragraphs of the letter are available to the target employer.

Provoke Action

End this "sales" appeal by leading your prospect to act. What do you want your target to do? Make you an offer? Well, ultimately, yes. But your more immediate objective is to secure an interview. But you don't even have to ask your reader for that. Instead, lay the foundation: "I will call you next week to learn when we might get together. If you will not be available during that week, please call me." You've made action about as simple as it can be made.

Job Hunt Letter Checklist

1. Address your letter to a specific individual—preferably one you have identified as a person with the power to hire you.

2. Focus on issues related to the employer's self-interest.

3. Demonstrate that you possess the qualifications and abilities to provide what the employer needs.

4. Use the AIDA formula. (See page 152.)

5. End by bidding for an interview.

1.16.3. Sample Letter

Don't shuffle your feet. Step right up to the plate and take your best shot:

> Dear Mr. Karlson:
>
> As customer service manager at Jones and Company, I developed upselling strategies that were responsible for $24,400 in revenue last quarter. I'd enjoy talking with you about this as well as some other revenue-generating ideas I think you'll find valuable. I discovered that Jones and Company, like many similar firms, was under-utilizing customer service operations, looking at CS as nothing more than a support department rather than as a potential revenue source. I introduced upselling as a major customer service function.
>
> In addition, I supervised the installation of a customer-friendly automated call director and participated in the redesign of the customer service database. I estimate that the quarterly overhead savings of these innovations approach $14,000.
>
> I accomplished all of this during five years. You will find this experience detailed in the enclosed résumé.
>
> I would enjoy sharing some of my ideas with you, and I will call you during the week of June 4 to learn when we might get together. If you will not be available during that week, please call me.
>
> Sincerely,

1.17. RÉSUMÉS

1.17.1. Putting Together a Great Package

Here's a sobering thought: 1 out of every 1,470 unsolicited résumés produces a job offer. If you send an unsolicited résumé, chances are you'll hear nothing. How can you increase your chances?

1. Do your homework. Don't submit résumés at random, but carefully target your prospects.

2. Research your targets and tailor your résumé to suit the needs of each target you contact.

> TIP: Many of us have been taught that the résumé is a kind of sacred document, like the U.S. Constitution or the Ten Commandments. Not so. Revise your résumé as necessary to make yourself most appealing to a particular employer.

> PITFALL: Most résumés describe the candidate's "experience." Now, what's wrong with that? Nothing—unless you want to get a job. Experience is merely what you've done—or what's happened to you—in the past. Instead of experience, try thinking about your "qualifications." These encompass not just what you have done, but what you have *accomplished.* Qualifications also include qualities, skills, and abilities that make (in the words of the third edition of *The American Heritage Dictionary of the English Language)* " a person suitable for a particular position or task."

What Am I Qualified For?

Answer: The job.

That's obvious, right? Yet most résumés fail to address precisely this: the job—that is, the needs of the employer. The fact is that most résumés focus on the needs of the applicant. And that is why so few unsolicited résumés produce job offers. Who cares about the needs of a stranger?

Boldly depart from the old-fashioned résumé form in three big ways:

1. Instead of listing your duties, describe your abilities.

2. Provide some indication of just how well you do your job.

3. Instead of listing your responsibilities, describe your accomplishments.

Objective

Kick off the résumé with a statement of your career purpose, your "objective." This may seem to contradict what I've just said concerning *not* talking about yourself. But there's a trick here. Based on your research covering the needs of the target company, write a statement of objective that "miraculously" coincides with just what the company is looking for.

> **PITFALL:** Most résumés that include statements of objective make these statements either too narrow or too broad. Here's one that is too narrow: *OBJECTIVE: To be an Assistant Quality Assurance Engineer.* Unless the employer has available a position with this precise title, it is not likely that a job offer will be forthcoming. Here's one that is too broad: *OBJECTIVE: Seeking an opportunity to utilize my skills, education, and energy in a working environment that offers advancement.* Reading this, a potential employer will ask: "What's in it for me?" The statement is vague. None of the terms is defined. Just what are the applicant's skills, education, and energy? It is also entirely self-centered, telling the employer something about what the applicant wants ("advancement"), but offering the potential employer nothing.

Be specific in your statement of objective, but avoid specific job titles, Emphasize skills, abilities, and qualifications. For example: *OBJECTIVE: To obtain a position where my ten years of creating innovative and cost-effective systems for material, production, and inventory control will be a strong company asset.*

You can sharpen the statement even more: *OBJECTIVE: To join a team that needs my ten years of experience creating innovative and cost-effective systems for material, production, and inventory control.* Two words—*team* and *needs*—speak to an employer's heart.

> **TIP:** What's the objective of an objective statement? To make the target employer take his feet off his desk and pick up the phone to call you.

1.17.2 Sample Résumés

Let's cut to a pair of examples:

ALICE LEE

433 Leland Avenue • Thorndike, IL 60344 • 555–555–5555

OBJECTIVE

Office assistant, where typing skills, mastery of all major word-processing software, absolute commitment to deadlines, a strong sense of responsibility, detail-orientation, energy, and a positive attitude are required.

EDUCATION

Graduated in top third of my class from Stephen J. Austin High School in June 1996.

My best grades were in English and foreign language (German). I also excelled in general science. I learned to type 50+ wpm—with maximum accuracy. I speak and read German.

SUMMER EMPLOYMENT

Clerk, Best Food Store

During summers from 1993 to 1996, I worked as a checkout clerk and had responsibility for maintaining general stock. I reported to Mr. Chuck Stone, owner of the store, who was always complimentary about the efficiency and accuracy of my work. He relied on me to create small in-store displays of special sales items.

RELATED EXPERIENCE

I was a reporter for the *Austin Crier,* our high school newspaper. I never missed a deadline. I also participated in student government as a Student Council representative. My classmates elected me each time I ran.

AIMS AND ASSETS

I am a fast learner and a self-starter. I enjoy taking on new responsibilities and going the extra mile. I have always made friends, especially among those who have worked with me. I plan on continuing my education in evening school, as work permits.

This résumé is attractive and effective, and it shows what somebody just starting out can do to set himself or herself apart from the crowd. Note that the "Objective" is clear and unmistakable: to satisfy the *employer*.

Here is a résumé for a more experienced job candidate:

FREDERICK TATE

5024 W. Jackson Blvd. • Westerly, NJ 04278 • 555-555-5555
Fax: 555-555-4444

OBJECTIVE

Project/Design Engineer in an organization that requires strong, efficient, cost-effective management of projects from conceptualization through implementation of final design.

EMPLOYMENT

PETERMAN CORPORATION, DENHAVEN, NEW YORK
Manufacturing/Project Engineer, 1987-89
I was responsible for all projects pertaining to assigned customers, which included Westinghouse, Pratt & Whitney, and Lycoming. The scope of work ranged from the production of gas and turbine components to the manufacture of orthopedic implants used in biomedical engineering.

◆ My cost estimates were critical to the company-wide cost-savings initiative. Between 1987 and 1989, I reduced fabrication costs an average of 8 percent.

◆ I initiated and chaired concept meetings for new programs, including our Customer Education program, which (according to Sales Department estimates) increased sales by 5-9 percent in 1988-89.

◆ I acted as liaison between the Engineering Department and our customers.

◆ I performed extensive troubleshooting and completed a Total Quality Assurance Program, which resulted in significant cost reductions for the company.

TARNWOOD, INC., POULSON, NEW JERSEY
Tooling Supervisor, 1985-87
I was in charge of in-house tooling, and I supervised tool room personnel.

◆ I conceived, planned, and organized the total structure of a new department, customizing the shop layout to achieve increased flexibility of production and to save money. My design was credited with reducing product turn-around time by 3-5 percent.

◆ I designed injection molds for an aerospace product line—a task that required familiarity with military specifications and a complete understanding of engineering drawings.

EDUCATION

YOUNGWOOD SCHOOL OF ENGINEERING, NEW PROVIDENCE, CALIFORNIA
B.S., Mechanical Engineering, 1987
I was editor of the *Mechanical Journal* from 1985 to 1987. I graduated with high honors.

SKILLS SUMMARY

◆ Strong technical experience

◆ Absolute understanding of complex engineering drawings

◆ Complete familiarity with manufacturing processes and supporting tool designs

◆ Communicate clearly with customers and subcontractors

This résumé is clean, functional, and specific. All of its elements add up to a single point: *I will create satisfaction.*

1.17.3. Résumé Rules of Thumb

Let's review some of the nuts and bolts of résumé writing.

1. *Length.* Pick up any book on résumé writing and you will encounter what must be the Eleventh Commandment: *Thou shalt not write more than a page.*

This can drive you crazy. Let's look at a saner approach to length. As a *general* rule, be brief—that is. as brief as expressing your experience, abilities, and qualifications allows you to be. Don't ramble. If your qualifications and abilities cannot be contained on a single page, go on to another.

> **TIP:** If you've worked fewer than ten years, you probably can fit your résumé on a single page. Anything beyond ten years will likely require a second page. Extensive relevant educational background may also require a second page.

2. *What to Dump.* Eliminate the following from your résumé:

   a. Detailed descriptions of jobs held more than ten years ago. You should list such positions; just don't explain them.

   b. Reasons for leaving previous jobs. Never stress the negative.

   c. Salary history and/or pay desired.

   > **TIP:** Sending a résumé is often the first step in a negotiation. The subject of salary is like a game of chicken. The first one who mentions a number is in the weaker negotiating position. Try not to be the first to bring up salary. Even if you are answering a want ad that requests "salary history," do not include it in your résumé or cover letter.

   d. Your personal biography: where you grew up, how many kids you have, and so on.

   e. Date of availability. Don't complicate things. Let the employer assume that you are *available,* period. The nitty-gritty of dates can be addressed in the interview.

   f. Social security number

   > **PITFALL:** Fraudsters can wreak havoc with your Social Security number! Guard it. The only reason an employer will need your SSN is to get you on the payroll and that is done after you're hired. Keep it off your résumé.

   g. Names of references. The target employer will assume that you have references available. Let him ask.

   h. Quotations from official job descriptions. The résumé should be in your own words.

   i. A title page or cover sheet

   j. Official documents

3. *Letters of recommendation.* Do not include letters of recommendation with your résumé. These should be sent by the recommender directly to the target employer. They should *not* come from you.

   > **TIP:** Avoid "boilerplate" letters of recommendation addressed "To whom it may concern." Avoid photocopied letters. Your recommender should write an individual letter directly to the prospective employer. If your recommender does not think highly enough of you to write individual letters, find somebody else.

4. *Extras.* If appropriate, feel free to include with your résumé such items as

   a. A bibliography of professional articles you've written or contributed to

   b. A list of special courses you've taken

   c. A listing of technical equipment with which you have competence

   d. An impressive client list.

Design Guide

Usually, it's best to accent the positive. But let's begin by noting three *don'ts:*

♦ Don't be sloppy.

♦ Don't be flashy.

♦ Don't let a "professional" résumé-writing outfit make your résumé look like it's been churned out by a "professional" résumé-writing outfit.

> **Pitfall:** You are usually best off avoiding "professional" résumé preparers. Nobody knows you better than you do.

Design points to remember:

1. Favor a neat, conservative, and functional page layout. Your object is not to make the target employer marvel at the design of your résumé, but to focus on its content.

2. Put information in short paragraphs.

3. Double-space between paragraphs.

4. Provide generous margins: $1^1/_2$ inches, left, right, top, bottom.

5. Make *sparing* use of highlighting devices: marginal descriptions, underlining (or italics, or boldface type—but not all three).

6. Use centered headlines to stress positions held and achievements achieved.

7. For word-processing, use a conservative, readable typeface.

8. In general, use 12-point type for the body text of your résumé. You may want to use 14-point type for centered headings.

TIP: A sans-serif face (such as Helvetica, Optima, or the equivalent) suggests streamlined functionalism; a serif face (such as Times Roman, Schoolbook, and so on) communicates traditional solidity. Don't mix the two type styles. However, you may want to use a sans-serif face for your centered headlines and a serif face for your text. Avoid weird or wild typefaces. Avoid script faces that mimic handwriting.

9. You may include a photograph of yourself. This is strictly optional. If you do include a photo, it should not be a casual snapshot. Be sure that you are wearing appropriate business attire.

PITFALL: Federal law prohibits employers from discriminating on the basis of race, gender, age, or physical disabilities. So much for the law. If you have reason to believe that a photograph will suggest anything about yourself that may discourage an employer, omit the photograph.

1.17.4. Making Your Résumé Computer Friendly

An increasing number of employers are requesting that you submit your résumé via e-mail. Some firms make it a practice to scan paper résumés and file them electronically.

Putting Your Résumé Online

This is not the place to explain the complexities of getting online. There are scores of books that can do this for you. You might want to check out in particular Joyce Lain Kennedy and Thomas J. Morrow's *The Electronic Résumé Revolution* (New York: John Wiley). However, here are important pointers for preparing the résumé to work online:

1. Use ASCII text only—plain, non-document text, free from word-processing formatting codes. Not too pretty, perhaps, but ASCII text will enable anyone with any kind of software to download and read your résumé. Note that, in ASCII, you won't be able to use underlining, boldface, or italics. Substitute paired asterisks (*like this*) to indicate italics, and use a lowercase "o" (letter, not numeral) wherever a graphic "bullet" is called for.

2. Set your margins at 0 for the right-hand and 65 for the left. Your monitor may well display 80 characters across the screen, and your printer is most likely set to print 80 characters across the width of the paper. But the target employer's equipment may not be set up this way. A 0 and 65 setting will ensure that none of your lines will be cut off.

3. One of the reasons employers like to get résumés online is that they can search them for keywords. These keywords should help the employer zero in on applicants with certain qualifications. Give yourself an edge by including at the very top of your online résumé a heading titled "Keywords." Under this heading, list the keywords that you think apply to the target position.

Making Your Résumé Scanner Friendly

Even if you produce a traditional paper résumé, it may well end up in electronic form. Many employers use a digital scanner and optical character recognition (OCR) software to translate paper résumés into electronic form. Once digitized, the résumés can be filed and searched electronically. Give yourself an edge by avoiding the following:

a. Fancy typefaces, graphics, hand lettering, and handwriting

b. Colored or patterned papers

c. A folded résumé (it may jam the scanner).

Always use high-quality $8^1/_2 \times 11$ white paper, preferably 24-pound stock, and be certain to include your e-mail address (if you have one) along with your street address, phone, and fax. If possible, print the résumé with a high-quality laser printer.

Résumé Checklist

1. Emphasize how your qualifications and abilities will satisfy the needs of the prospective employer. Don't just list "experience."

2. Tailor a different résumé for each target employer.

3. Make your résumé computer friendly and scanner friendly.

4. Be brief, but don't arbitrarily limit yourself to a single page.

5. Adopt a conservative design approach.

1.18. RAISES AND PROMOTIONS

1.18.1. What You Need to Say When You Want to Advance

Getting a raise or a promotion *requires* two accomplishing two goals.

1. You must make your supervisor *feel* like complying with your request for a raise or promotion.

2. You must provide an *intellectual* rationale to augment your boss's feeling that you deserve a raise.

   Achieve these goals by:

1. Emphasizing your loyalty and commitment to the firm.

2. Developing your personal regard for your supervisor.

3. Citing your record of performance and length of service.

4. Citing industry standards—what others in comparable positions are earning.

   PITFALL: Base your request on job-related reasons only. Do not plead poverty. Do not cite personal reasons for needing the raise or promotion.

   The letter relating to a salary increase or a promotion is not a substitute for a meeting. However, it can be a highly effective preparation for a meeting. Take the following steps:

1. If the letter is preparatory to a scheduled salary/promotion review, begin the letter as a reminder of the upcoming review.

2. If no regular salary/promotion review is scheduled, begin the letter by forthrightly stating your business: "I would like to set up a meeting to talk about my salary" or "I would like to get together to talk about a promotion to **position.**"

3. Launch into your commitment to the firm.

4. Explain your determination to develop with the firm even as you work to improve it.

5. Inventory the facts that support your request for a raise or promotion.

   TIP: The most convincing facts are numerical. First and foremost, translate your request into terms of money: how much you have added to the bottom line. If you are seeking a promotion, try to demonstrate that, in the new position, you will add even more to that bottom line.

6. Appeal to fairness.

7. Ask for a meeting.

8. Thank your correspondent for his/her consideration.

1.18.2. Sample Letters

Two sample salary-related letters follow. The first emphasizes performance, the second stresses length of employment:

> Dear _____:
>
> I would like to set up a meeting to discuss my salary with you.
>
> This is a highly appropriate time for the meeting, because I recently completed **name of project,** which, as you know, has resulted in **$ amount** revenue for the quarter. It is only the most recent example of the level of performance I have achieved. But, to be frank with you, it is a high note— and I wanted to have this meeting while this accomplishment is fresh in your mind.
>
> Please consider that such performance is the rule for me, rather than the exception. And I would like to bring my compensation to a level more appropriate to the level of my performance and achievement.
>
> I look forward to our meeting.
>
> Sincerely,

TIP: Any of these letters can also be put into the form of an internal memo.

MEMO
TO:
FROM
RE: SALARY REVIEW

As you are aware, my annual salary review is scheduled for **date.** It has been a delight working here at **Name of company** for the past **number** years. My commitment to the firm, I think you'll agree, is obvious. However, since 19XX, my salary has increased only **percent amount.**

I believe that you'll agree that I am substantially overdue for a more equitable salary increase at this time.

I would appreciate your giving careful consideration to an increase now that would be the equivalent of **percent amount** increases averaged over **number of years.**

I look forward to the review.

Promotion may be based primarily on years of service, on performance, or on both:

Dear _____:

I have been **job title** for **number of years.** I was passed over for promotion to **job title** in 19XX. Now this position is about to become available again, and I believe that my promotion is long overdue.

Name, I have the seniority, the experience, and—more importantly—I have the qualifications and skills to achieve excellence in the job.

I would appreciate a meeting with you on **date** to discuss the promotion.

Sincerely,

TO:
FROM:
RE: Promotion from **job title** to **job title**

During the past **number of years** as **job title,** I have achieved major advancements for our firm, including **list accomplishments,** which have resulted in a total of some **$ amount** in revenue.

Needless to say, this has been a very rewarding experience for me. But I believe it is now time for me to bring my skills and accomplishments to a position with even greater responsibility. I think that you'll agree that promotion to **new position** will give me even greater scope for increasing revenue.

I would like to meet with you by **date** to discuss promotion to **new position.**

TIP: What do you do if there's no place to go? If no ready-made position is available, consider suggesting that a new position be created. Be prepared to outline the responsibilities and requirements for the position and to justify it within the structure of the company.

Raise and Promotion Checklist

1. Use letters and memos to set up a meeting. It is generally more effective to discuss raises and promotions rather than deal with them exclusively through written correspondence.

2. Base your appeal on professional or job-related issues.

3. Avoid appeals to personal issues—such as a family to support.

4. Do not plead poverty. Doing so will prompt your employer to question your competence.

1.19. QUITTING

1.19.1. How to Leave Without Slamming the Door

Does this seem like the least of your worries? After all, when you quit, you quit. Why devote much effort to a letter?

Because the world of your business is a relatively small world, and the people and company you leave behind do not vanish from that world. You are likely to deal with them again. Now, when you visit a friend or an acquaintance—or even a total stranger—you do not end the visit by storming out and slamming the door behind you. You say goodbye. You thank your host. You wish your host well. Perhaps you even express regret at having to end the visit.

Give your about-to-be-former employer the same consideration.

Don't slam the door behind you. Close it gently. Better yet, try to leave it ever-so-slightly ajar. One way or another, you may need or want to reenter.

1. Begin the letter of resignation by announcing the fact of your resignation. In many cases, this will be accompanied by some expression of regret.

2. State your reasons for resigning.

   TIP: Try to frame your reasons for resigning in the most positive way possible.

3. Supply key information relating to your resignation:
   a. Effective date
   b. Proposal for handling the transition to a new person
   c. An offer of assistance in making a smooth transition.

4. State or restate regret.

5. Affirm the good feelings created by your experience with the firm.

   Here is a generic resignation "with regret":

Dear _____:

As the old saying goes, all good things must come to an end. I am leaving **Name of company.**

My **spouse** has accepted a position as **job title** with a firm in **Name of city.** It is a wonderful opportunity, and we have decided to relocate.

My resignation is effective as of **date.** I trust this gives you sufficient time to hire a suitable replacement. I believe this will also provide a period in which I can "break in" the new person. Please be assured that I am committed to making this transition as smooth and efficient as possible.

Naturally, I am excited about the move my family is making. However, I am sorry to have to leave **Name of company** and especially you and the other staff. Your are, indeed, my second family.

Sincerely,

Don't be phony. If, as is most often the case, you are leaving one company either to change career or to accept advancement in another firm, say so. Don't gloat. Don't cheer obnoxiously. But don't hide the facts, either. There is nothing wrong with making your about-to-be-former employer fully aware of your value.

Dear ____:

Name of company has offered me the position of **job title.** I have given the matter very careful thought and have decided to accept. I am, therefore, resigning here effective on **date.**

My experience here has been nothing less than delightful and rewarding. It has been a pleasure and honor to work with all of you. However, my responsibility to my family, to myself, and to my career make it necessary for me to move on.

I will do everything within my power, between now and **date,** to make the transition to my replacement as painless and productive as possible.

Sincerely,

Health and age are other reasons for stepping down:

Dear _____:

I'm afraid that you are all too well aware that my health has been poor for some time. You have been patient and understanding during what has been a very difficult period for me and, because of my frequent absences, for the company.

I can no longer afford to put additional strain on my health—and on the well-being of the firm. Therefore, I will resign from **Name of company** effective on **date.**

As far as I am able, I will work with you to locate a suitable replacement for me and to make the transition as smooth as possible.

I've greatly enjoyed working with you, and I truly regret that I must leave.

Sincerely,

Dear _____:

What a ride!

But now it's time to get off. On **date,** I will be retiring.

My work here has been highly rewarding, and I will look back on these years with great pleasure. They were fulfilling.

I am not vanishing from the face of the earth, and I'm not just going fishing. I plan to contribute part of my time as a volunteer for **Name of organization.** I hope that you—and the others in the office—will drop in there from time to say hello. I warn you that I intend to be a frequent visitor here at the office.

Best of luck.

Affectionately,

1.19.2. Quitting Under Difficult Circumstances

If you resign under unfavorable circumstances, resist the temptation to vent your anger and frustration. In general, keep the resignation as neutral as possible:

Dear _____:

My basic differences with the management of **Name of company** have made it necessary for me to resign at this time.

My resignation is effective as of **date.** I believe that this should give you sufficient time to locate a replacement for me. If you wish, I will assist in identifying and evaluating candidates for the position, and I will do all that I can, between now and my departure, to ease the transition.

Sincerely,

Checklist for Quitting

1. Leaving a position does not necessarily terminate human relationships. Keep this in mind when you write your letter.

2. Avoid bitterness.

3. Provide reasons for your resignation.

4. If possible, offer your help in effecting an efficient transition.

5. If appropriate, express your regrets.

Part Two

MEMOS

2.1. OBJECTIVES AND STRATEGY

2.1.1. Office "Junk Mail"

Most offices are awash in memos. The great Eleventh Commandment—"Thou shalt cover your assets"—prompts many of us to put just about everything in writing "for the record." The result is a kind of memo inflation, which threatens to reduce even important inter- and intra-office communication to the equivalent of junk mail. The advent of e-mail communication within many offices has, if anything, caused memos to proliferate even more intensively.

The effective memo invites attention. Where appropriate, the effective memo prompts timely action. By convention, memos generally begin with a simple format:

DATE:
TO:
FROM:
SUBJECT: (or SUBJ: or RE:)

This is generally useful and should not be abandoned. However, give special thought to the "SUBJECT" statement and to the opening line of the memo. Do your best to make these as clear and provocative as possible. Strange as it may seem, you have to *sell* ideas and information to your coworkers and colleagues much as you sell products and services to the outside world. Open with a statement that commands attention and that appeals to your correspondent's needs.

TIP: You might think of the memo in terms of the AIDA formula used in sales letters. Begin by commanding Attention. Next, develop your reader's Interest and Desire (to take action, to agree with you, to consider a matter, and so forth), then conclude by provoking Action. Be certain that you are clear about what action you want your reader to take.

2.2. A Matter of Style

2.2.1. When and How to Be Formal, Official, Informal, and Downright Friendly

Too many business persons believe that there is only one tone appropriate to a memo: the Voice of Authority. Most often, this results not in an authoritative memo, but in a harsh one:

DATE: 10/2/XX
TO: Sales Personnel
FROM: Customer Service/Sales Manager
RE: Salary and hours

Non-exempt employees in this Department are expected to report for work on Saturdays, during the non-holiday season, in rotation. Each employee shall take the rotation per the schedule issued by the Customer Service/Sales Manager.

As commissions will be payable on Saturday sales, no overtime salary will be paid.

Note the scarcity of pronouns and the total absence of "we." The Voice of Authority memo draws a line in the sand, as if deliberately to pit management against labor. Moreover, the scarcity of pronouns makes it sound as if The Company were some godlike entity, far greater than the sum of the human beings who comprise it. The vocabulary is rigid: "are expected," "shall take," "issued by," and the like. The tone is one of command rather than genuine team management.

At the other extreme is the loose memo of a half-hearted manager:

DATE: 2/10/XX
TO: The gang
FROM: Joe
RE: A Big Favor

Okay, you guys. It's time for the please-work-on-Saturday memo. Look, this isn't something any of us enjoys doing, but, please, help me out here. I need volunteers to work Saturdays.

You won't get overtime, which is a bummer. But you do get commissions—just like on any other day. Drop by and see me. Please!

This is a memo from a manager who wants to be a pal instead of a manager. It mistakes lack of direction for friendliness.

Different companies have different personalities. The style and tone of internal memos reflects both the writer's personality and that of the company. All else being equal, the best strategy is to strike a tone somewhere between the ultra-authoritative/impersonal and the friendly/personal:

DATE: 2/9/XX
TO: Sales Department staff
FROM: Sarah Domville, Sales/Customer Service Director
SUBJECT: Saturday schedule

As we have discussed, Saturday work assignments will be made according to the rotation attached to this memo.

I realize that Saturday duty is a hardship, but we're all agreed that the rotation is a fair way to spread the load. While overtime compensation is not available, Saturday does present ample opportunity for impressive commission income.

I appreciate your cooperation and commitment to the sales team.

Checklist for Memo Tone

1. Use personal pronouns and names to make memos less arbitrarily authoritarian.

2. Develop a friendly, but precise vocabulary.

3. Think of memos as team communication rather than directives issued from on high.

2.3. Action Memos

2.3.1. Lessons in Lighting a Fire

Everyone knows the story of The Boy Who Cried Wolf. And many of us have worked in environments where some manager habitually wrote memos threatening this or that dire consequence if this or that task was not accomplished. Let's face facts. It is very possible to motivate action by issuing commands or by inducing panic. For example:

> DATE: 10/5/XX
> TO: Break-room users
> FROM: Housekeeping staff
> RE: Refrigerator danger
>
> THIS IS A FOOD POISONING ALERT!
>
> The refrigerator is often jammed with food that has been neglected. This poses an extreme danger for everyone. It is possible that the old food will contaminate everything kept in the refrigerator, endangering your health.
>
> It is urgently imperative that you remove old food immediately!

How many memos like this can you read before their effect is blunted? Hysteria may motivate action once or twice, but soon it recedes into the background din of annoying noises to be ignored.

The effective action memo accomplishes the following:

1. It realistically states an issue, goal, or problem.

2. It realistically establishes how the issue, goal, or problem relates to the "team."

3. It realistically proposes or directs an action that will address the issue, goal, or problem to the benefit of the team.

DATE: 10/5/XX
TO: Break-room users
FROM: Peter Reynolds, Housekeeping Staff Director
RE: Refrigerator Etiquette

Opening our refrigerator should be a refreshing and appetizing experience. I think that you'll agree that, in our breakroom, this is hardly the case.

The refrigerator is loaded down with food items that have been there for quite some time. The sight is not a pretty one, and the smell is even worse.

You can help make the dining experience more pleasant for all of us by making sure that unused food is removed and taken home each and every Friday.

It is always more effective to motivate action by stressing positive results rather than negative consequences. Your department is faltering, having failed for three consecutive months to meet sales quotas. You can issue a memo warning of layoffs and the like. Maybe your thought is that you have nothing to lose. That may be true. But it is also true that, with most negative approaches, you also have nothing to gain. Take a positive approach:

DATE: 3/4/XX
TO: The Sales Team
FROM: Pete Wilson, Sales Manager
RE: Progress

Let's face it: We've had a rough time this past quarter. But, thanks to all of you, we've come through it—disappointed, perhaps, but also ready to make this next quarter a great success.

In the months to come, I am confident that you will work to improve our bottom line. In fact, we will work together to create strategies for increasing sales and commissions.

With your help, we will not only meet our projections, but exceed them.

Action Memo Checklist

1. Avoid hysteria.

2. Establish the relevance of the action to the "team."

3. Do not gloss over problems, but emphasize positive action.

2.4. CHANGES IN PLAN OR POLICY

2.4.1. How You Can Keep Everyone in Sync

One of the most important reasons for writing memos is to inform individuals or groups about changes in policy, plans, goals, the availability of products, and so on. Such memos demand special attention in order to avoid errors and to prevent your staff from making promises to customers that cannot be kept.

> TIP: Color coding informational and update memos is a good idea. Print the memo on colored paper. For example, red may be reserved for urgent policy updates, yellow for a product availability advisory, green for price changes, and so on.

It is helpful to think of advisory and update memos not as one-shots, to be read, digested, and tossed away, but as parts of an ongoing dialogue. You might instruct staff members to maintain a memo book or a loose-leaf policy and procedures manual, to which update memos are to be added. The point is that, with advisory-type memos, it is not only essential to make certain that the individual memo gets the attention it deserves, but that the information is preserved and can be retrieved when it is needed. In general, a loose-leaf binder is better than a file.

Here is an example advisory:

IMPORTANT BILLING UPDATE
FOR YOUR *POLICIES AND PROCEDURES MANUAL*

DATE: 10/2/XX
TO: Sales Team Members
FROM: Joan
RE: Billing Changes

Beginning tomorrow, instead of billing all credit card customers when we receive the order, we will bill when the order is shipped.

Please advise your customers of this policy in a sales-positive manner: "For your safety, you'll be charged only when we actually ship your order." Then advise the customer of the expected ship date.

Changes Checklist

1. Use color coding or a set of specific headings to draw special attention to update and advisory memos.

2. Create a system for filing—and accessing—updates and advisories on an ongoing basis.

3. If one update replaces another, make this perfectly clear.

4. Keep memos brief and specific.

2.5. COMPLAINTS

2.5.1. Foolproof Moves to Make Yourself Heard

The complaint memo—a memo that advises a colleague, subordinate, or supervisor of a condition that requires remedy—can be a powerful tool. Like most powerful tools, it can also be dangerous. Remember, a memo becomes part of "the record." If it contains accusations or threats, these also, for better or worse, become part of the record.

Before you sit down to write the memo, think about what you want to accomplish. Chances are that you are angry. Maybe you want to embarrass someone, or, at least, place some blame where you believe it belongs. In most cases, however, the personal approach, the attack on a person or personality, is a dangerous and counterproductive course. It is safer and far more effective to focus your complaint on a problem or issue rather than a person or personality. Remedy a situation before you try to change a colleague's character.

> **TIP:** Many problems can be resolved by informal conversation. In many cases, it is more appropriate to try this before committing words to paper.

DATE: 4/6/XX
TO: John Williams, Physical Plant Manager
FROM: Joan Crawford, Credit Department
RE: Burned-out lights

Three weeks ago, I informed you about burned-out or missing fluorescent tubes in our department. After no action was taken to replace the tubes within a week, I spoke to you again. Still, no action.

John, we can't see back here. We can't do our work properly. We cannot serve our customers efficiently. Conditions are gloomy and even dangerous. If there is some problem obtaining fluorescent tubes, please let me know. Maybe I can help. If there is no problem, please expedite replacement of the tubes.

I think you'll agree that we've waited long enough.

DATE: 4/9/XX
TO: Ron Purse, Customer Service Representative
FROM: Paul Roberts, Sales Associate
RE: Customer complaints about telephone hold time

Ron, I thought you should know that my department has received no fewer than ten complaints from customers last month regarding excessively long hold times when they call Customer Service.

It seems clear that this has become an issue, and since one of the chief product benefits we sell is service, I'm sure you'll agree that it is an issue that should be addressed.

I know that you and your staff do a terrific job supporting our products and helping our customers. The problem is the length of time it takes our customers to get through to you. Short of hiring additional staff, is there a way to upgrade your automated telephone answering system—which might take some of the routine load off of your people?

I suggest we get together to discuss this issue. I would like to work with you to help you obtain whatever you need to expedite customer calls. I want Customer Service to remain a strong selling point for us.

I propose meeting on 4/12 over lunch in the cafeteria. Let me know. I'm at ext. 456.

DATE: 5/9/XX
TO: Accounting Team
FROM: Tom Turk, Director of Accounting
SUBJECT: Rumors

Einstein said that nothing can travel faster than the speed of light. He never heard our office grapevine. Most offices have plenty of prophets of doom to go around, but we seem to have a bumper crop this season.

I have heard—we have *all* heard—rumors about impending layoffs in our department. I have two things to say in this regard:

1. No layoffs are planned for this department. That is not a rumor. It is the truth.

2. Rumors are destructive. They are destructive to morale. They are dangerous, especially if they get outside of the department or, even worse,

outside of the company. If enough of our customers start to believe that we are thinking about layoffs, what are those customers going to think about us? What will happen to their confidence? Where will they take their business? My point is: we could generate a self-fulfilling prophecy. When our customers leave us, we will lose staff.

Please, stop the rumors. If you hear something that disturbs you, bring it to me. I'm not asking you to point fingers. I just want us all to have the best and most accurate information we can get.

Complaint Checklist

1. Exhaust informal, usually verbal, complaint channels before resorting to a memo.

2. Avoid accusations and threats.

3. Remember: You are writing "for the record."

4. Avoid dwelling on the negative. Suggest positive actions to remedy the problem.

5. Emphasize cooperation.

6. Always address the problem or issue rather than individuals or personalities.

2.6. CONGRATULATIONS

2.6.1. Making the Most of Achievement

Clichés have a sometimes annoying and sometimes wonderful way of often being true. Here's one to think about: Nothing succeeds like success.

Build an atmosphere of success in your business, office, or department, and it is likely to breed more success. Memos acknowledging achievement build morale, not only for the recipient of the memo, but for everyone who reads it. These memos communicate:

1. The responsiveness and gratitude of management.

2. The caliber of personnel.

3. The expectation, not only of management, but of the entire team.

Finally, while the primary purpose of the congratulatory memo is to make the achiever feel good, these memos also serve to "raise the bar" of achievement for the entire organization. They acknowledge a new standard.

> **PITFALL:** Don't fall into the trap of the left-handed congratulations: "You've done well . . . but you can do even better." Give full credit to present achievement. Do make it clear, however, that the quality of the *present* achievement gives you—and the team—reason to look forward to the future.

DATE: 3/8/XX
TO: Karl
FROM: Pat
RE: Congratulations

Wow!

Your work organizing the recent convention was nothing less than miraculous. You made us look very, very good. The display of the new line was especially effective and sparked a lot of conversation. I have no doubt that it will also bring us a good deal of new business.

I am looking forward to next year's convention. With you organizing the show, it will be another great event.

On behalf of the entire department, I congratulate and thank you.

TIP: Include specifics in your congratulation memo. This is the most effective and convincing way to personalize the message.

Congratulations are not just conveyed to individuals. Timely messages to a group or a department is great for morale and reinforces positive progress:

DATE: 5/4/XX
TO: Quality Assurance Task Force
FROM: Pete Young, Quality Assurance Manager
SUBJECT: Project 99.9

Industry standard: 97.5 percent error-free average. A lofty goal for a healthy industry.

It was not good enough for Healthgood Industries. A lot of industry pundits shook their heads when we said that. It's not practical, not feasible to do any better.

Your Project 99.9 task force proved otherwise. We now enjoy a 98.7 error-free rate. It is the best in the business. Maybe the best in *any* business.

Well done, ladies and gentlemen. You've pushed the envelope and raised the bar.

Congratulations Checklist

1. Congratulatory memos boost morale and reinforce desired levels of performance.

2. Give full credit for the present achievement, but look toward the future.

3. Consider writing congratulatory memos to groups as well as individuals.

2.7. EMERGENCIES

2.7.1. What to Say When It Hits the Fan

In urgent or crisis situations, memos are a means of providing clear instructions. However, perhaps even more important, memos can convey the official voice, carrying it above the din of rumor that characteristically accompanies and aggravates a crisis. The greatest power of memos in a crisis is their power to keep the team together and the actions of individuals coordinated.

The tone of the crisis memo is critically important. Avoid scolding and threats. Avoid the Chicken Little syndrome, predicting imminent doom and a falling sky. On the other hand, attempts to minimize a serious problem are not only misguided, but ineffective. False optimism tends to be transparent. You will lose credibility.

> **TIP:** In theory, honesty is, in fact, the best policy. In practice, the crisis memo should be as honest as possible while still producing a positive result. That is, if the negatives substantially outweigh the positives, do your best to emphasize the positive. Doing so is your chance to turn the situation around.

Here is a memo written to a group:

DATE: 4/6/XX
TO: Production Staff
FROM: Harry Thornton
SUBJECT: Layoff Rumors

I'd have to be in a coma not to be aware of the anxiety over the proposed merger. I issued a memo last week in which I reported what I know: no layoffs are planned.

Result: the rumors continue to fly.

Not only does this situation make life unpleasant for all concerned, it diminishes team cohesiveness, impacts on productivity, and, I'm sure, has sent a number of folks looking for other jobs.

Let's get a grip on this thing before it chokes us.

I ask that we all get together on 4/11 at 3:30 in the third-floor conference room for a frank discussion. I'll share what information I have, and I will invite you to ask whatever questions you have.

Let's get together on this issue, and let's do it now.

You may also write a memo to individuals:

DATE: 5/7/XX
TO: Alice Williams
FROM: Harry Thornton
SUBJECT: Rumor control

Alice, I need your advice on a matter of critical concern to the personnel in my department. The proposed merger has sparked widespread rumors of general layoffs, particularly in Production. Morale is faltering, as is loyalty. I know I've got people submitting applications to other firms.

I want to make an official statement regarding the merger and the likelihood of layoffs. It would be very helpful to me to get your thoughts on just what I should say. I don't want to mislead anybody here, but I do want to stem the panic. Our productivity is suffering—and so is my staff.

Sometimes, emergencies are even more urgent:

DATE: 8/9/XX
TO: Sales Personnel
FROM: Gerry Wilson, Sales Manager
SUBJECT: Customer outreach

I won't kid you: last night's fire was a real blow to us. Sure, insurance will pay for replacing damaged equipment and inventory. But no insurance can adequately compensate for time lost and for the number of disappointed customers.

We are faced with two critical tasks:

1. We need to recover as many of our files as possible.

2. We need to get on the phones to our customers.

The Recovery Team is working on the files, and they are making great progress already. What I need from all of you, is to use *your* personal data files to reach *your* customers *now*. Please do five things:

1. Tell them what has happened.

2. Tell them that we expect a five- to ten-day delay in shipping current orders.

3. Tell them that we will resume accepting orders by 8/15.

4. Ask them what their concerns are.

5. Assure them that we will address their concerns.

Do not minimize the severity of the damage we have suffered. However, emphasize continuity of service. We're down, but we're hardly out.

Emergency Memo Checklist

1. Be clear.

2. Be honest. However, emphasize facts that contribute to positive action. Stressing the negative will only deepen the crisis.

3. Do not minimize the seriousness of a problem, but maintain an authoritative, positive tone.

4. Avoid giving rumor the authority of the printed page.

5. Invite dialogue.

2.8. EMPLOYEE DEPARTURE

2.8.1. Whatever Happened to Whatshisname?

What are the consequences of failing to acknowledge the departure of an employee?

1. Rumors. Other employees will assume that the departure is mysterious, most likely made under unfavorable circumstances.

2. Loss of morale. Employees will get the message that the organization is impersonal and regards staff as just so many disposable parts.

Acknowledging an employee's departure is the right thing to do, the decent thing to do. Moreover, it preempts destructive rumors and potentially bad feelings.

The acknowledgment can be simple and neutral, as this generic form suggests:

DATE:
TO:
FROM:
SUBJECT: Employee departure

I'm sorry to announce that **Name** has resigned as **Job title.**

Name has been with us for more than **number** years. While we are all sad to see him/her leave, he/she will be going on to even greater responsibilities at **Name of company** [or simply in his/her new position].

Name will be with us until **date.** Please join me in thanking him/her for his/her contribution to the team, and join me, too, in wishing him/her all the best.

TIP: If at all possible announce the departure as soon as it becomes official. Usually, this will be a minimum of two weeks before the employee actually leaves.

Is it all right to get personal?

The answer is a qualified yes. However, instead of emphasizing such issues as friendship and affection—which certainly may be mentioned—list some specific accomplishments or contributions the employee has made.

PITFALL: Getting too personal tends to exclude, even alienate other employees.

DATE: 4/7/XX
TO: The Acme Family
FROM: Eunice Owens, President
SUBJECT: Departure of Howard Edwards

As some of you already know, Howard Edwards is stepping down as Production Manager here at Acme. He is establishing his own consulting business.

Proud as we are of Howard—and we know that he will have a great success in his new venture—we can't help being sad over seeing him go. He's been a great friend to me personally and, I know, to many of you. He is the first person a good many of us have turned to for advice. It was under his supervision and leadership that the Production Department has expanded to its present formidable size.

Fortunately, we'll have Howard with us until July. He is assisting me in identifying a new Production Manager and will direct the transition to the new person.

Please join me in thanking Howard and in wishing him all the great good fortune he deserves in his new endeavor.

2.8.2. Departure Under Unfavorable Circumstances

Tread carefully when announcing the departure of an employee under less than ideal circumstances. At the very least, you run the risk of endangering morale, and, at worst, you may foster the gripes of a disgruntled employee, which could result in legal action or in some form of verbal sabotage—or even worse. Keep the announcement brief and as neutral as possible:

DATE:
TO:
FROM:
SUBJECT: Resignation of **Name**

Name has announced his/her resignation as **job title** effective **date.**

Please join me in wishing Name good fortune in his/her next position.

If the employee was dismissed, handle the announcement with this line: "**Name** will be leaving **Name of company,** on **date** and will no longer serve as **Job title.**"

Employee Departure Memo Checklist

1. Do not fail to acknowledge the departure of an employee.

2. Invite the team to wish the employee well.

3. If appropriate, express your personal feelings, but beware of excluding other employees.

4. Cite a few specific achievements or contributions.

5. In the case of departure under unfavorable circumstances, maintain neutrality. Avoid pejoratives. Avoid editorializing. Avoid gratuitous expressions of relief ("Joe Blow is leaving. Thank goodness!").

2.9. INSTRUCTIONS

2.9.1. Getting It Right—the First Time

The purpose of many memos is to provide instructions, directions for doing a particular job or carrying out a procedure. The most important quality in such memos is clarity. Usually, this is achieved by providing *step-by-step* instructions. You can insure that the instructions you give are complete by resorting to the classic mantra of journalists. A good reporter writes stories that include the "Five W's":

Who

What

When

Where

Why

Include these elements in your instructions, and, chances are, you will be understood.

> TIP: Pay attention to your tone. No-frills, no-nonsense instructions convey confidence that your instructions will be carried out. Overly elaborate instructions, loaded down with warnings and *unnecessary* detail, suggests that you lack faith in the intelligence and ability of the memo recipient.

DATE: 8/25/X
TO: Nan Dokely
FROM: George Harris
RE: Processing XYZ Product Recall

As you know, Acme Industries has issued recall notices to customers who purchased our XYZ Super Refinisher. Please follow this procedure in processing recalls:

1. Thank the customer for responding to the recall notice.

2. Obtain the serial number of the customer's product and check it against the recall list.

3. Confirm that this serial number is included among the recall group.

4. If it is not, inform the customer that his product is safe and is not included in the recall.

5. If the serial number is among those recalled, obtain the customer's zip code.

6. Using your Zip Code List, identify the nearest authorized dealer.

7. Instruct the customer to take or ship his unit to the dealer for repair at no charge to the customer.

8. Assign a recall number to the customer and product.

9. Insure that the recall number has been recorded in the system. *PLEASE NOTE:* Federal regulations make this step critical!

10. Thank the customer for his/her understanding and cooperation.

11. Provide the following phone number—1-800-555-5555—and invite the customer to call it if he/she has any additional questions concerning the recall or the XYZ model.

TIP: The world of business moves fast. But, if at all possible, let twenty-four hours pass between the time you write the instructional memo and the time you distribute it. Reread the memo. Make certain that the instructions are clear and unambiguous, and that you have left nothing out.

Instruction Memo Checklist

1. Step-by-step is generally the best structure.

2. Numbering the steps is usually an effective means of presenting the information.

3. Make liberal use of the if . . . then structure: *If such and such happens, then take such and such step.*

4. In the case of the instructional memo, a neutral, no-nonsense tone is best. It conveys confidence in the professionalism and competence of the recipient of the memo.

5. Avoid frivolous comments.

6. Avoid patronizing the recipient through undue repetition and detail.

7. Instruct customer to take the product to the nearest authorized dealer.

2.10. LAYOFFS

2.10.1. How to Communicate a Necessary Evil

Depending on the policy of your firm and the status of the employee involved, a memo may *not* be the most appropriate means of telling an employee that he or she has been laid off. A more formal letter may be more appropriate or a face-to-face meeting. If you decide to use the memo form, however, take the following steps:

1. Announce the layoff.

2. State the effective date.

3. Explain the reason(s) for the layoff.

4. Advise the recipient of the disposition of his/her final check, and address such issues as vacation pay due, severance pay due, removal of personal belongings, and soon.

5. Express regrets and best wishes.

6. If appropriate, offer assistance—such as letters of recommendation, and so forth.

> PITFALL: A layoff is termination through no fault of the employee. Dismissal—firing an employee—is due to faulty performance or even a transgression of company rules. A memo is never an appropriate vehicle for communicating this kind of dismissal. A letter should be used, probably in conjunction with a face-to-face meeting.

DATE: 5/7/XX
TO: Ralph Gorlick
FROM: Sarah Nervi
SUBJECT: Layoff

As you know, you were hired for the duration of the Johnson project. I had hoped that another project would start up before this one ended. However, that is not the case. Therefore, with regret, I must inform you that we will be unable to utilize your services after 6/7/XX.

We have all been greatly pleased with your work, and we will be sorry to see you go.

This thirty-day notice is made in lieu of severance pay, and you may pick up your final check at my office on 6/7.

Please be assured that, as soon as a suitable project comes along again, I will be in touch with you. In the meantime, please accept my gratitude for a job well done, and my best wishes for your future.

Tip: Using a memo to advise an employee of a layoff is best suited to temporary employees or staff whose employment is for the duration of a particular project only.

2.11.   Meetings

2.11.1.   Who, What , Where, When, and Why

If many businesses suffer from memo inflation—a glut of memos, which causes many important memos to be ignored—even more firms are afflicted by an overabundance of meetings. Memos announcing meetings should provide basic information:

1. Time

2. Location

3. Subject

If possible, also provide an agenda. But, in addition to these essentials, it may be necessary for you to "sell" the meeting to your colleagues. Include in the memo a statement of why the meeting is important. This means why the meeting is important *to the recipient or recipients of the memo:* what it will mean to *him/them,* how it will benefit *him/them,* what vital information it will generate relevant to *him/them.* Here is an example:

> DATE: 2/7/XX
> TO: Marketing Managers
> FROM: Anne Friendly, Director of Marketing
> SUBJECT: MarketMaker software meeting

We are currently evaluating a new software system, which, we hope, will allow us all to evaluate more effectively and more quickly the performance of our products in the marketplace.

This software promises to limber up the organization, making us more flexible, more responsive to the market, and, even more important, more capable of making accurate *proactive* decisions.

In short, MarketMaker promises to make your lives easier and more profitable.

If:

1. You know how to use it.

2. It actually works.

On 2/11 at 9 A.M. in the main conference room, you will have an opportunity to explore the software, find out how it works and if it will work for you. A representative from MarketMaker will be here to demonstrate the product and to answer all of your questions.

This could be a very important tool for us. Attending this meeting will be your opportunity to hit the ground running with this new technology.

In addition to "selling" meetings to your subordinates, supervisors, and colleagues, use memos to advise of changes in time, location, subject, attendees, and so on. It is always best to put such changes in writing.

DATE:
TO:
FROM:
RE: Change in meeting time

The **meeting** scheduled for **date** at **time** has been changed. The new meeting day and time will be **date** and **time**. The meeting will be in the **location**.

Sorry for the inconvenience, but the change was necessary because of **reason**.

Meeting Memo Checklist

1. Always provide the essentials: time, location, subject/purpose.

2. If possible, include an agenda.

3. In an environment plagued with a glut of meetings, take the time and effort to "sell" the meeting to the recipient(s) of the memo.

4. Focus on how the meeting will benefit the recipient(s) of the memo.

2.12. MOTIVATION

2.12.1. Using Memos to Tune Up the Team for Maximum Performance

Oh, no! The boss is going to give her Pep Talk again!

Well, it isn't easy to make effective, genuine motivating remarks. Few of us are comfortable doing so. We find ourselves degenerating into generalities and platitudes. We find ourselves sounding like our high school sports coaches or maybe even—help!—our parents.

The reason? Most motivating speeches and memos are written in a vacuum, without reference to specific circumstances. They're the equivalent of a store-bought greeting card on a special occasion—about as "special" as a paper cup.

Want to write an effective motivating memo? Dig into what's happening today. Talk about a real problem or a current triumph or a genuine opportunity—something specific and immediately relevant *to those who will read the memo*—and discuss what it means *to those who will read the memo*.

DATE: 6/9/XX
TO: Sales Team
FROM: Randy
SUBJECT: Motivation

I'm not naming names, but I want to share with you a remark I overheard in the hall yesterday:

"I missed the sale because BLEEPING Joe Blow didn't get me the right BLEEPING numbers until it was too late!"

I mean, the speaker was steamed—and had every right to be, losing a sale. But what he didn't have the right to do is blame someone else for it. When an unfortunate individual starts blaming his own misfires on others, he can usually forget about achieving his goals.

You and I know that *any* sale can be saved, even if we don't always have all the information at our fingertips. It takes extra effort, but it can be done.

You have all shown me that you are not only capable, but also superb salespeople. I am proud of all that you have accomplished. But I don't want you to get the idea that it should always be so easy. Make the sale, if you can. Save the sale, if you must. By all means, lean on the team—but depend on yourself, and take responsibility for what you do and for what you fail to do.

TIP: The best motivators are positive, not threats or warnings of dire consequences.

Miniature success stories are effective motivators. For example:

DATE: 3/9/XX
TO: Customer Service Staff
FROM: Ed Walters
SUBJECT: Extra Mile

We really blew it last week. We shipped one of our best customers, Ajax Supply, a bad 546 circuit board. Ajax called Bert Wheeler, the customer service rep assigned to the account, and Bert moved heaven and earth to get a new board out there.

Guess what? The new board failed.

There was another call to Bert. He scrambled to get yet another 546. No dice. Nothing available.

As I said, we really blew it.

At least, that's what some of us might have said, with a shrug of the shoulders and a sad shake of the head.

But not Bert Wheeler. He got on the phone and called a list of his customers until he was able to find one who was willing to lend a 546 unit to Ajax. We picked up the tab for the loaner, and Bert *personally* ran the board over to Ajax.

That is motivation. Not just doing everything that's expected of you, but more—committing yourself to each and every customer, becoming that customer's partner, and refusing to give up, even when the "normal" options are exhausted.

Well done, Bert. You not only saved an important client, but you taught us all a valuable lesson—and you set the service bar one notch higher.

Motivation Checklist

1. Avoid generalities.

2. Base your motivational memos on specific events, people, and incidents. This will keep them from degenerating into clichés.

3. Tell a good story. Make sure that the story is directly relevant to the people who will read the memo.

4. Avoid negative motivation—warnings of dire consequences, threats, scolding.

5. Foster a sense of team, even when you focus on individual accomplishments.

2.13. NEW EMPLOYEES

2.13.1. How to Welcome Them

Memos welcoming new employees are not addressed to the employee, but to his or her coworkers. Such memos introduce the new employee to the team. Usually, the following elements are included:

1. An invitation to the group to join you in welcoming So-and-so

2. Identification of department, job, and job title

3. The new employee's background, with emphasis on what he or she "brings to the table"

4. Personal background—often with reference to spouse and children; perhaps a hobby or special interest

5. An invitation to the group to drop by and get acquainted with So-and-so.

Here is a sample:

DATE: 4/9/XX
TO: Accounting Department
FROM: Howard
SUBJECT: Welcome Liz Xerxes

Please join me in welcoming Liz Xerxes to our department. She will be serving as assistant controller, working closely with Ben Thompson and his group.

Liz comes to us from Bean & Bean, where she was associate receivables coordinator. She earned her accounting degree from Hobright University and has worked in the field for five years.

Liz lives in Arlington, with her husband, Dirk, a civil attorney, and their son, Jake. She is an avid ski enthusiast and a sky diver—in other words, a typical CPA.

I hope that you will all find the time in the next week or so to drop by Liz's office to say hello. We are very excited to have her with us.

If the new person is replacing someone, you may mention this fact by way of information: "Liz is replacing Dick Smith as assistant controller." However, make no comparison between the two, and do not mention anything negative about the former incumbent, even if he or she left under adverse circumstances.

New Employee Checklist

1. This is your opportunity not only to provide information about a new hire, but to break the ice and ease the new person's entry onto the team.

2. Be certain to clear all personal information with the employee before "publishing" it.

3. Avoid any comparison between the new employee and the previous holder of the position.

2.14. PROBLEMS

2.14.1. How You Can Invite Solutions

Memos are great ways to explain a problem to an individual or a group and to solicit suggestions for a solution. Unlike a phone call, the memo gives you an opportunity to spell out the nature of the problem. It also invites a written response, which you can peruse at your leisure and which can also serve as a record.

Take the following steps:

1. Ask for help.

   TIP: Most colleagues and coworkers are eager to help. The act of helping makes them feel good. Even being asked is flattering. Never be reluctant to ask for advice.

2. Explain the problem as concisely as possible.

3. Ask for thoughts and guidance.

4. Express your gratitude.

DATE: 6/8/XX
TO: Ralph
FROM: Sheila
RE: Advice

I need your help.

Lately, we have been experiencing a problem with small-scale employee pilfering. Nothing big, but the problem is growing. At this point, I don't want to make a major security issue out of the matter. I certainly don't want to point fingers or make accusations.

I would be very grateful for your advice on how I might discreetly handle this problem now and keep it from getting worse. Thanks for your time and consideration.

DATE: 5/8/XX
TO: Larry Wilson, Quality Assurance
FROM: Pat Riley, Production
RE: Quality Assurance bottleneck

Larry, please be assured that I think nothing is more important to customer satisfaction than the quality of our product. However, we've got a problem. We have been consistently delivering late, and this is beginning to impact customer satisfaction. The slow-down occurs in quality assurance.

I am *not* pointing fingers. Your staff does an outstanding job. However, we do need to address the problem and establish some means of expediting quality assurance without in any way compromising quality.

Please give this matter top priority. Let's get together to discuss strategy. I appreciate it, and, even more important, our customers will appreciate it.

Problem Memo Checklist

1. Focus on the problem, not on personalities.

2. Do not solicit agreement, but seek solutions.

   PITFALL: Avoid sending memos that say, in effect, "As far as I'm concerned, the problem is XYZ. I'm sure you'll agree." This kind of statement looks for a rubber stamp, not a solution.

3. Invite advice. Do not demand instant answers.

2.15. PROGRESS REPORTS

2.15.1. Where We Were, Are, and Hope to Be

Ongoing projects often require periodic progress reports. Even in cases where such reports are not absolutely required, a progress memo or series of progress memos can help keep a client satisfied and a project team in sync. Progress memos also help avoid nasty surprises when a project, for one reason or another, bogs down.

> TIP: Provide explanations for any glitches or delays. Avoid pointing fingers and fixing blame. Emphasize positive action that can and will be taken to get the project back on track.

It takes discipline to write optional or voluntary progress memos, especially if you are explaining a delay. Our natural tendency is decidedly *not* to share bad news with others, especially clients and supervisors. But it is usually better to keep these individuals informed rather than to set everyone up for a surprise fall when a project fails to materialize on time. Properly framed, the progress memo—even when a schedule has slipped—can convey the impression that you are in control and on top of the situation.

1. Begin by stating the purpose of the memo, referencing the program or project title, identifying number, and so on.

2. State key mileposts that have been passed.

3. Is the project on schedule, ahead of schedule, behind schedule?

4. If it is ahead of or behind schedule, state reasons. If it is ahead of schedule, state the benefits of this. If it is behind, try to provide a strategy for getting back on track.

5. If possible and appropriate, project a completion date. Provide the context for the date: On target or not?

Here is a generic progress memo form:

DATE:
TO:
FROM:
SUBJECT: Project XYZ Progress Report

As of **date,** we have entered Phase 2 of Project XYZ. The second of four phases, this puts us on track for completion by **date,** as specified in our agreement with you.

We anticipate no delays.

DATE:
TO:
FROM:
SUBJECT: Project XYZ Progress Report

As of **date,** we have entered Phase 2 of Project XYZ. The second of four phases, this puts us **number of days** behind our projected schedule.

Delays were caused by **reason.**

We expect to pick up some time in phases 3 and 4 by **procedure.** This should allow us to complete the project by **date,** which is only **number of days** beyond or projected completion date of **date.**

Tip: How do you keep an explanation from sounding like an excuse? By following it with a feasible solution to the problem: "Delays in securing materials from our suppliers have cost us ten days. However, by expediting shipment of materials for the next phase of the project, and by putting another shift on the job, we will recover at minimum five of those days. In the worst case, we anticipate delivery by 5/6 instead of the projected 5/1 date."

Progress Memo Checklist

1. The basic assumption: information—even unpleasant information—is better than a nasty surprise.

2. Keep progress and delay in perspective by providing the context of original projections.

3. Explain delays.

4. If a delay has occurred, try to provide and explain solutions and workarounds.

2.16. SCHEDULES

2.16.1. Laying It All Out

Scheduling memos can either be formal timetables or informal advisories. Formal schedules should be done in tabular form that, at minimum, lists the event, action, or process, gives a start time/date and a completion/time/date. You may also need to include a listing of personnel or departments involved in each step.

> TIP: Complex scheduling can be greatly simplified by using one of the "project" or "time line" software packages now available for personal computers. With such programs, you can lay out a schedule in tabular or even graphical format. The latter is especially useful in projects that include overlapping and simultaneous phases.

Here is a simple format to follow:

DATE:
TO:
FROM:
SUBJECT: Schedule for **project**

Here is the projected schedule for **project:**

Activity	Start date	End date	Personnel
Activity	Start date	End date	Personnel
Activity	Start date	End date	Personnel
Activity	Start date	End date	Personnel
Activity	Start date	End date	Personnel

Time and timing are critical in this project. The schedule has been established in consultation with all the departments and individuals involved, and keeping to the schedule should be assigned the highest possible priority.

> TIP: To avoid cumbersome repetition and space problems, you might work out a system of initials to indicate the participation of individuals and/or departments in each phase.

Pitfall: Don't get carried away by letting the format of the memo get more complicated than the content. Keep the schedule as simple and straightforward as possible.

Simple projects require an informal memo. For example:

DATE:
TO:
FROM:
SUBJECT: Schedule for **project**

Project will kick off during the first half of **Month.** This makes it necessary for all of us to follow a tight timetable.

On **date 1,** we must finalize **activity 1.** Let's meet in my office on **date** to accomplish this. On **date 2,** we need to present **activity 2. Name** will confirm the order of these presentations and will get this information to you no later than **date 3.**

If you have any questions or comments relating to the schedule, please give me a call right away.

Schedule Checklist

1. Schedules lend themselves to tabular presentation.

2. Stress the importance of adhering to the schedule.

3. Keep the form of the scheduling memo as simple as the nature of the project permits.

2.17. SUGGESTIONS

2.17.1. How to Sell Your Ideas to the People Who Matter

In contrast to requests for promotions and raises and the like, suggestions are made not on your own behalf, but for the good of the organization. Remember this fact. Don't let ego get in the way of the ultimate goal of the suggestion: to improve matters for the team. While the suggestion memo is a piece of salesmanship, it should be devoted more to the rationale for the suggestion than to making an emotional appeal for its adoption. The structure is straightforward:

1. Begin by stating the subject of the suggestion.

2. Explain the problem or situation that the suggestion is intended to address. Emphasize the impact of the problem or situation on the firm.

3. Make your suggestion(s) and explain it/them. Just how will the suggestion(s) work?

4. Invite action. This will most often be a meeting or conference to discuss the proposal further.

TIP: As in a sales letter, the call to action at the conclusion is critical. Invite—induce—action, lest the suggestion remain academic.

Here's a typical suggestion:

DATE: 7/14/XX
TO: R. J. Kent, Manager
FROM: Peter Shilts
SUBJECT: Staggered lunch breaks

I worry that we rely on our voice mail system too heavily during the lunch hour. How many customers do we turn off by failing to have a human being available to answer the phone?

I'm very grateful for voice mail. A recorded answer is better than no answer at all. But from the noon hour to about 1:30, almost all of us are out to lunch, and a disproportionately high volume of calls gets answered mechanically.

I suggest that we consider introducing staggered lunch periods so that at least six people are available to answer calls at all times.

I don't think this would present any great scheduling challenge, and I'm sure that, presented as a way of enhancing revenue, the staggered lunch breaks would meet with a high degree of acceptance.

I suggest that we meet to discuss this matter. I'll call later in the week to set something up.

Another:

DATE: 5/9/XX
TO: Randa Owen, Vice-President, Human Resources
FROM: Ken James, Manager, Shipping
SUBJECT: Flex time

A great many companies these days are introducing flex time schemes that stagger starting and ending times according to employee preference. I believe that we should consider introducing a new time policy here for the following reasons:

1. It empowers employees.

2. It allows employees to integrate their personal and professional time more effectively.

3. It reduced traffic congestion at rush hours. This will go a long way toward relieving employee stress.

4. Flex time maximizes the use of the physical plant.

5. Flex time is perceived as a perk—yet it costs nothing.

6. The flex time option improves employee morale.

Can we discuss introducing flex time here? I suggest a get-together with the departmental managers within the next week or two. I strongly believe that we would benefit by it.

Here's a suggestion memo concerning a more critical situation:

DATE: 2.27/XX
TO: Howard Ross, Quality Assurance Director
FROM: Maria Valdez, Customer Service Coordinator
SUBJECT: Quality Assurance evaluation

Over the past three weeks, Customer Service has fielded a disturbing number of complaint calls concerning defective parts in models 45, 56, 72, and 98. The nature of the complaints—and the fact that they concern four models—suggests that we are not shipping a faulty design, but that too many bad units are slipping past Quality Assurance.

I recommend that you and your staff conduct an audit of your policies and practices where inspection of these particular products is concerned.

I am concerned that the volume of warranty returns will soon impact negatively on revenue. I would be pleased to discuss this situation with you in detail.

Suggestions Checklist

1. Your object is to convince the recipient(s) of your memo that the suggestion is motivated by a concern for the organization and team rather than self-interest.

2. Push toward action.

3. Recognize that, as regards suggestions, the most appropriate "action" may be a meeting or discussion.

2.18. THANKS

2.18.1. Working Wonders with Gratitude

Expressing thanks is not just an act of courtesy—although it certainly is that—but also a means of reinforcing positive action and building a cohesive organization. Behavioral psychologists have long known that positive reinforcement is much more effective than negative reinforcement (threats and the like) in creating desired behavior or action. The memo expressing thanks is a powerful vehicle of positive reinforcement.

What spells the difference between a pro-forma, perfunctory thank you and a meaningful expression of thanks? In a word, specificity. State exactly what you are thanking the recipient of the memo for, and say something about the positive effect that person's suggestion, action, or good deed, has had on the organization. Here are some examples:

DATE:	6/23/XX
TO:	Gary Nash
FROM:	James Madden
RE:	Your suggestion

Your suggestion regarding an upgrade incentive program has stimulated a lot of discussion—lively and beneficial discussion. I believe that we will end up introducing some sort of high-profile program. I also believe that this will significantly improve our bottom line.

Speaking on behalf of the management team, we are very grateful for your stimulating idea and for the initiative you have shown.

TIP: Thanks are great. However, some companies reward useful suggestions with a cash bonus or other concrete incentive. In this case, the memo may accompany the "gift."

DATE: 5/4/XX
TO: Larry Larson
FROM: Sarah T. Lane
SUBJECT: Pulling the fat out

You saved the day when you managed to expedite shipment of the Johnson order. We came very close to losing a major customer, but, thanks to your quick and skillful action, we ended up by strengthening the relationship.

You acted professionally and with great initiative. The entire sales team is proud of you—and grateful as well.

Thanks Checklist

1. Keep it straightforward.

2. Instead of lavishing adjectives upon the recipient, get specific with nouns, verbs, and positive consequences.

3. The sincerity—and effectiveness—of your thanks is directly proportionate to the degree of specificity you include in the memo.

2.19. WARNING AND REPRIMAND

2.19.1. Improve Performance and Protect Yourself

By far the most effective means of shaping employee performance is through guidance, clear instruction, and positive reinforcement. Unfortunately, situations do arise that make positive reinforcement either inappropriate or impossible.

Reprimands serve four purposes:

1. First and foremost, a reprimand should guide the employee, showing him or her what went wrong and why. Most importantly, it should also indicate what can be done to prevent further problems or correct a situation.

2. The reprimand should also discuss the impact of the employee's error or misbehavior on the organization.

3. The reprimand may also explicitly warn the employee of the consequences of repeated problems—up to and including dismissal.

4. Finally, the reprimand provides a "paper trail" leading to disciplinary action, up to and including dismissal. The reprimand becomes part of the employee's record. Ultimately, it may serve as legal justification for dismissing the employee.

As serious, or even grave, as a reprimand can be, you should still endeavor to begin by acknowledging the generally positive nature of the memo recipient's performance—if this is an accurate assessment. From here, go on to:

1. State the problem, error, or issue.

2. Describe the impact of the problem, error, or issue on the company.

3. Suggest remedies or steps to resolve the problem, error, or issue.

4. If appropriate, advise the recipient of the consequences to himself if the problem, error, or issue is repeated or unresolved.

5. End by affirming your willingness to work with the recipient of the memo in order to help him repair the situation.

The most common issues requiring reprimand include:

Absenteeism

Repeated early departure or late arrival

Insubordination

Rudeness or uncooperative attitude with colleagues

Rudeness to customers

Inappropriate appearance (slovenly dress)

Faulty record keeping

Repeated errors

Disclosure of privileged information

PITFALL: Among the most serious areas where disciplinary action is required include sexual harassment and disputes or actions involving possible discrimination on the basis of race, gender, or disability. In such cases, employers are best advised to seek professional legal counsel before acting.

Absenteeism

DATE:
TO:
FROM:
SUBJECT: Too many personal days

Our company has deliberately avoided setting an absolute limit on the number of personal days an employee may take. We have relied instead on the good faith and judgment of the employee and the supervisor alike. The clear understanding is that the employee is to use personal days only when absolutely necessary.

Name, you are a valuable member of our team. We need to be able to rely on you. We need you here. However, since **date** you have taken **number** personal days. Clearly, this is an abuse of the privilege.

Is there some problem I should know about? I invite you to have a discussion with me in strictest confidence.

Otherwise, I must advise you that repeated abuse of personal days will result in disciplinary action up to and including dismissal. We cannot continue to work together this way.

Repeated early departure or late arrival

DATE:
TO:
FROM:
SUBJECT: Repeated late arrival

This month alone you have reported more than fifteen minutes late on **number** occasions. Frankly, **Name,** this is not acceptable.

You are a valuable member of this team. Your work is excellent. We need you—and we need you on time. Business hours begin promptly at **time.** I can't have someone covering for you until you arrive.

If there is a difficult situation I should know about, let's discuss it. Maybe I can help. Otherwise, you must resolve the problem—and it is a problem—immediately.

Name, the next step is formal disciplinary action, which may include suspension and, ultimately, dismissal. Let's remedy the situation right now.

Insubordination

DATE:
TO:
FROM:
SUBJECT: Insubordination

On **date, Name,** your supervisor, assigned you to **perform task.** You refused without giving a reason.

When you started working here, you agreed to take direction from your designated supervisors. Of course, that does not mean mindless obedience. But neither does it permit arbitrary refusal to take perform assigned tasks. This, clearly, is insubordination, and it is not acceptable.

If you wish to discuss this incident with me, either in the presence of your supervisor or alone, my door is open to you.

Otherwise, you must regard this memo as a reprimand and as a warning. If you cannot or are unwilling to abide by your employment agreement with us, **Name of company** cannot continue to employ you.

I have asked **Name,** your supervisor, to report to me at weekly intervals for the next three months. He is to inform me of your performance during this period. Based on these reports, we will determine your continued status here.

Rudeness or uncooperative attitude with colleagues

DATE:
TO:
FROM:
SUBJECT: Rudeness to colleagues

Even on a close-knit team, disputes arise. I worry if things get *too* harmonious. That suggests to me that folks just aren't thinking for themselves.

However, your behavior on **date** and **date** to **Name** was just plain rude. We cannot tolerate the use abusive language at any time.

Name, I direct you to take two actions:

1. Apologize to **Name** and **Name** for your rudeness, and assure them that the incident will not be repeated..

2. Report to my office on **date** at **time** to discuss the incident and issues involved. I will meet separately with the others involved.

This is a serious breach of behavior. Repetition may lead to further disciplinary action, including dismissal.

Rudeness to customers

DATE:
TO:
FROM:
SUBJECT: Rudeness to a customs

On **date,** I received a complaint from a customer who was upset by rude and curt remarks from you. This is the __nth complaint of this nature I have received concerning your behavior.

You must understand that ours is a service-oriented business. We cannot tolerate sales personnel who are rude to customers. If we do, none of us will have jobs for very much longer.

Please be advised that I am putting you on probationary status for the next thirty days. During this period, I intend to examine very carefully any complaints I may receive. You are in peril of dismissal.

Inappropriate appearance (slovenly dress)

DATE:
TO:
FROM:
SUBJECT:

As you know, we have never had a formal dress code at **Name of company.** However, it is assumed that you will dress neatly. That means suits and jackets dry cleaned, shirts laundered and unwrinkled, shoes shined and in good repair. We don't expect spit-and-polish uniforms, but we do expect our sales staff to present an appearance that inspires the confidence of our customers.

Please look to the condition of your clothing, **Name.**

Faulty record keeping

DATE:
TO:
FROM:
SUBJECT: Incomplete records

I am well aware of how hectic the pace can get here. With hardly a moment to take a breath, we are often tempted to cut corners. But there are some corners we cannot afford to cut—and that includes keeping full and accurate records of all transactions immediately upon the conclusion of each transaction.

That is why I was highly distressed on **date** when I requested the file on **Project** and found the following records missing or incomplete: **list.**

We cannot do business this way.

You must begin a file-by-file audit, noting each incomplete file and taking the necessary steps to bring each to the appropriate level of completeness. I expect this work to be completed by **date.**

Repeated errors

DATE:
TO:
FROM:
SUBJECT: Errors

We all make mistakes. That is to be expected, forgiven, and corrected as necessary. However, of greater concern is a pattern of errors, which indicates more than human fallibility. Repeated errors must cause us to review our procedures, and that is precisely what I want you to do at this time.

Submit a Quality Assurance review to me by **date.** I want explanations for:

1. What, exactly, has been going wrong.

2. Why it has been going wrong.

3. What you propose to do to remedy the situation.

Name, you have been productive and successful as **job title.** I am confident that you will be able to turn this very alarming situation around. If there is anything I can do to help you, please call me.

Disclosure of privileged information

DATE:
TO:
FROM:
SUBJECT: Indiscreet conversation

I do not enjoy writing this memo. I do not enjoy finding myself obliged to remind you that you are entrusted with a position of great sensitivity and confidence.

I greatly enjoyed seeing you at the trade convention reception last night. However, I was highly distressed to overhear you talking about our upcoming line of **products.**

True, your remarks were framed in general terms. But, even so expressed, new product development information is strictly privileged.

How seriously do I take confidentiality?

Any repetition of last night's indiscretion will result in your dismissal. *That is how seriously I take confidentiality.*

This memo is your official reprimand and warning. Future indiscretions will not be tolerated. I will, in accordance with company policy, dismiss you if an incident of this nature is repeated.

Reprimand Checklist

1. State the problem, error, or issue clearly.

2. Describe the impact of the problem, error, or issue on the company.

3. Instruct the employee as to steps he should/must take to correct the situation.

4. Offer constructive assistance.

5. If appropriate, advise the recipient of the consequences to himself if the problem, error, or issue is repeated or unresolved.

6. If necessary and appropriate, warn the recipient of possible disciplinary action, including dismissal.

7. Affirm your willingness to work with the recipient of the memo in order to help him repair the situation.

8. Never make idle threats.

9. Avoid attacks on personality or character. Address the situation only.

10. Avoid humor or levity of tone.

Part Three

FORMS

3.1. OBJECTIVES AND STRATEGY

3.1.1. Why People Hate Forms

The problem begins with the word: *form.* Such a simple word. But it implies a world of red tape, hoop jumping, and a generally judgmental attitude. Forms are supposed to expedite action, but most people, faced with filling them out, see them as obstacles to getting what they want. Characteristically, forms combine the taste of a midterm exam (in a subject for which you—some-how—have failed to study) with all the discomfort of a strait jacket.

In fact, there is nothing inherently evil about forms. They are not only necessary, but helpful. In many cases, they make needed action possible. Here's what a form should do:

1. Present necessary information clearly

2. Provide a means for obtaining necessary information efficiently

3. Filter out unnecessary information

4. Make careful decisions easier

5. Enable efficient and appropriate action

6. Convey invitation rather than exclusion.

Here's what it should *not* do:

1. Confuse the person who fills out the form

2. Confuse the person who interprets the form

3. Cause frustration

4. Convey the impression of bureaucratic red tape

5. Convey exclusion.

3.2. Nuts and Bolts

3.2.1. The Ergonomic Form

Beginning during the late 1970s, business and industry became increasingly concerned with ergonomics: the science of making the tools and accouterments of industry, business, and trade comfortable, efficient, and safe to use. The industrial revolution worked toward making one mechanical device work well with another. The ergonomic revolution focused on making nonhuman devices work well with human beings. The object of this is to increase efficiency and productivity in large part through reducing stress and fatigue.

As traditionally conceived, business forms had very little to do with ergonomics—with making the form "comfortable" for its users. Instead, the object was to look "businesslike," which usually equated with institutional; that is, the form functioned to give the impression of an enterprise bigger than any single human being or even the sum of the human beings associate with the enterprise. This tended to produce forms with a lot of fine print; forms that asked for more information than necessary; forms that demanded unnecessarily invasive information; forms that requested repetitious information—often repeating much information from one side of the sheet to the other; forms that provided insufficient space for information; forms that used technical terms and thereby created confusion and bewilderment.

These days, even big business is trying, in some ways, to look small. Small companies are perceived as providing a level of personal service that customers find appealing. Riding this trend, bigger businesses are spending millions of PR dollars to modify their image, to project a customer-centered image rather than an institutional orientation. As high technology, even cutting-edge technology, becomes almost instantly available to any organization, business has come to recognize that the true competitive edge is in serving the customer better. Accordingly, business has increasingly addressed the human side of the equation. And that extends to all customer contact, including through the medium of forms.

3.2.2. Titles, Numbers, or Both?

"Please take a seat and fill out a three-forty-three-slash-four." Or: "I can't do a thing for you until you fill out a five-sixty, a three-twenty, and a five-one-oh."

Not very inviting, is it?

Identifying forms with numbers used to be highly fashionable in business. It sounded so *official,* so *businesslike.* Never mind that it alienated and turned off customers. Everybody used numbers, and that's the way it was done.

This exclusionary approach doesn't cut it anymore. Numbers are inherently cryptic. Their meaning is not inherent and descriptive, but arbitrary. Numbered forms discourage your customers and other people you work with. It is far better to title your forms—and to title them as descriptively as possible. If your business uses many forms, you may want to use a title and a number, but, when dealing with customers, be certain to refer to the form by its title rather than its number.

3.2.3. Room Enough

The single biggest complaint leveled against forms is that they provide insufficient space for supplying the requested information. Cramped forms are not only frustrating, they are rude. How would you feel if you were asked a question and started to answer it, only to be cut off in mid sentence? Well, that's exactly how the user of a stingy, cramped form feels. Forms with insufficient space discourage and turn away business. "There's no *room* for me here."

> TIP: Design forms that provide ample space for the responses you request. Try to provide the space directly after each question. Avoid "continuation sheets" or advising the user to "use back of form if necessary." This makes it hard on both the filler and interpreter of the form.

3.2.4. Multiple Choices

Providing multiple choice responses—usually by means of check boxes—greatly expedites filling out any form. Just make certain that:

1. The multiple choices you provide cover *all* the bases—the full range of possible responses.

2. The multiple choices are clear and unambiguous. Each response should be distinct. There should be no confusion or overlap.

TIP: Wherever appropriate, make one of the choices "Other: _____." You don't want the filler of the form to feel constrained by *your* choices.

3.2.5. Instructions

To whatever extent possible, forms should be self-explanatory. That is, the information solicited and the questions asked should be clear and unambiguous. However, if you need to include additional instructions, keep them as short as possible. Usually, the most effective means of providing instructions is to give examples. Remember: you want to make all of this quick and easy.

3.2.6. Computers, Word Processors, Forms Software, and Laser Printers

As in so many other areas of business, the personal computer has revolutionized the world of forms. It used to be that a business had three choices for creating forms:

1. Buy preprinted forms

2. Have a job printer custom create forms

3. Design and duplicate forms itself.

The number 1 option had—and still has—the advantage of being relatively hassle free and relatively inexpensive. However, you can only hope that the preprinted form fits your purpose. Otherwise, you will have to cross out sections, add others, or instruct your customer to skip over this or that. The impression conveyed is not professional.

The number 2 option can be expensive and inconvenient.

The number 3 option can be time consuming and frustrating, and the results can be amateurish looking.

The personal computer, especially coupled with one of the many forms-creation software packages currently available, allows anyone to create custom-designed and professional-looking forms. Once designed, these can be printed on a laser printer, then duplicated either on a photocopier or, if large quantities are required, printed by an inexpensive job printer, who might work with your laser-printed version or who might print the form from a computer diskette you provide.

TIP: Many printers will take your job via modem. You just transmit your form to them electronically. Not only is no laser printout required, you don't even have to send a disk.

If you plan to use your computer to create conventional paper forms, you might do so with any good word-processing software or you may use one of the software packages designed specifically for creating forms. However, another of the great advantages of the personal computer is that you may fill out the forms you create electronically. Instead of putting pencil to paper, you call up the appropriate form on screen and type in the required information. Of course, this may not be possible for a customer to do, unless an employee assists him—in effect, verbally asking the questions, then typing in the responses. However, computer filling forms is ideal in most in-house situations. Sophisticated forms software performs such operations as performing calculations and linking information to databases, thereby saving a great deal of valuable time and reducing the possibility of error. You can even set up on screen forms to accept only certain answers. For example, you can set up the form so that the line "Number of coupons requested (choose 0-5)" will not accept an answer of "6."

The example forms reproduced on the following pages were all created with a personal computer and word-processing or forms software.

3.3. BALANCE SHEETS AND CASH FLOW STATEMENTS

3.3.1. Balance Sheets

This form is the simplest kind of balance sheet, a straightforward statement of assets and liabilities:

Statement of Assets and Liabilities

Date

Assets:

Cash	0.00
Accounts receivable, net	0.00
Inventory	0.00
Prepaid expenses	0.00
Buildings and equipment	0.00
Accumulated depreciation	0.00
Investments in other companies	0.00
	0.00
Total assets	$ 0.00

Liabilities & Equity:

Accounts Payable	0.00
Accrued liabilities	0.00
Common stock	0.00
Retained Earnings	0.00
This entry has a note[1]	0.00
Press the "Endnote" button to create your own notes	0.00
	0.00
	0.00
	0.00
	0.00
	0.00
	0.00
	0.00
	0.00
	0.00
Total liabilities and equity	$ 0.00

[1]Notes:

238

The following is a more traditional balance sheet, which literally weighs assets against liabilities—assets on the left, liabilities on the right. It is followed by a series of forms that provide supporting information for the assets and liabilities *summarized* on the balance sheet:

Balance Sheet

(Company Name)

19

Year Ending   **($000)**

☞ **Assets**   **Liabilities** ☞

Current Assets: **Current Liabilities:**

Cash: ....   Accounts Payable: ....
Accounts Receivable: _____   Short-Term Notes: ....
  Less allowance: _____   Current Portion of Long-Term Notes: _____
  Less doubtful accts.: _____   Interest Payable: ....
Net realizable value: _____   Taxes Payable: ....
Inventory: _____   Accrued Payroll: ....
Temporary Investment: ..... _____   **TOTAL CURRENT LIABILITIES:** _____
Prepaid Expenses: .... _____   Equity: .... _____
TOTAL CURRENT ASSETS: .. _____   Total Owner's Equity-(proprietorship)
Long-Term Investments: .. _____

Fixed Assets: **OR:**

Land: .... _____   (Name's) Equity: ....
Buildings:_____ at cost,   (Name's) Equity: (Partnership) _____
less accum. depreciation of: _____   Total Partner's Equity: .... _____
Net Book Value: .... _____   Shareholders' Equity: (Corporation)
Equipment: _____ at cost,   Capital Stock: .... _____
less accum. depreciation of: _____   Capital paid-in in excess of par:
Net Book Value: .... _____   Retained Earnings: .... _____
Furniture/Fixtures:_____ at cost,   Total Shareholders' Equity: .... _____
less accum. depreciation of: _____
Net Book Value: .... _____
TOTAL NET FIXED ASSETS: ... _____
OTHER ASSETS: .... _____

TOTAL ASSETS: **TOTAL LIABILITIES AND EQUITY:**

Accounts Payable
& Sales Tax Payable

This form covers the month of_____

Accounts Payable

	This Month This Year	This Month Last Year
Balance per Balance Sheet:	$ _____	$ _____

Balance per Detailed Accounts Payable System

	This Month This Year	This Month Last Year
Beginning Balance:	$ _____	_____
Purchases:	_____	_____
Disbursements:	_____	_____
Adjustments:	_____	_____
Ending Balance:	$ _____	_____
Additional Amounts:	_____	_____
Total Accounts Receivable Balance:	$ _____	_____

Detail totals must agree with Accounts Payable on Balance Sheet.

Sales Tax Payable

	This Month This Year	This Month Last Year
Balance per Balance Sheet:	$ _____	$ _____

Balance per Detailed Monthly Sales Tax Schedules

	This Month This Year	This Month Last Year
For Month 1:	$ _____	_____
For Month 2:	_____	_____
For Month 3:	_____	_____
Total Sales Tax Payable for Quarter:	$ _____	_____
Additional Amounts:	_____	_____
Total Sales Tax Payable:	$ _____	_____

Detail totals must agree with Sales Tax Payable on Balance Sheet.

Prepared By _____ Date _____

Reviewed By_____ Date _____

Balance Sheet Support Schedule
Accounts Receivable
& Inventory

This form covers the month of _____

Accounts Receivable

	This Month This Year	This Month Last Year
Balance per Balance Sheet:	$ _____	$ _____

Balance per Accounts Receivable Detail System

	This Month This Year	This Month Last Year
Current:	$ _____	_____
Over 30 Days:	_____	_____
Over 60 Days:	_____	_____
Over 90 Days:	_____	_____
Total Accounts Receivable Balance:	$ _____	_____

Detail totals must agree with Accounts Receivables on Balance Sheet.

Inventory

	This Month This Year	This Month Last Year
Balance per Balance Sheet:	$ _____	$ _____

Balance per Inventory Detailed Listing Subsystem

	This Month This Year	This Month Last Year
Raw Materials:	$ _____	_____
Work in Process:	_____	_____
Finished Goods:	_____	_____
Other:	_____	_____
Total Inventory Balance:	$ _____	_____

Detail totals must agree with Inventory on Balance Sheet.

Prepared By _____ Date _____

Reviewed By _____ Date _____

Balance Sheet Support Schedule
Deposits

This form covers the month of_____

Deposits	This Month This Year	This Month Last Year
Balance per Balance Sheet:	$ _____	$ _____

Balance per Deposits Listing	This Month This Year	This Month Last Year
Rent:	$ _____	_____
Utility:	_____	_____
Other:	_____	_____
Total Deposits Balance:	$ _____	_____

Detail totals must agree with Deposits Balance on Balance Sheet.

Prepared By _____ Date _____

Reviewed By_____ Date _____

Balance Sheet Support Schedule
Income Taxes Payable
& Accrued Liabilities

This form covers the month of _____

Income Taxes Payable

	This Month This Year	This Month Last Year
Balance per Balance Sheet:	$ _____	$ _____

Balance per State & Federal Income Tax Schedules

	This Month This Year	This Month Last Year
Federal Tax Liability Estimate - 1st Quarter:	$ _____	_____
Federal Tax Liability Estimate - 2nd Quarter:	_____	_____
Federal Tax Liability Estimate - 3rd Quarter:	_____	_____
Federal Tax Liability Estimate - 4th Quarter:	_____	_____
Other Federal Tax Carryover:	_____	_____
Total Federal Income Tax Liability:	_____	_____
State Tax Liability Estimate - 1st Quarter:	_____	_____
State Tax Liability Estimate - 2nd Quarter:	_____	_____
State Tax Liability Estimate - 3rd Quarter:	_____	_____
State Tax Liability Estimate - 4th Quarter:	_____	_____
Other State Tax Carryover:	_____	_____
Total Federal Income Tax Liability:	_____	_____
Total State & Federal Income Tax Liability:	$ _____	_____

Detail totals must agree with Taxes Payable on Balance Sheet.

Accrued Liabilities

	This Month This Year	This Month Last Year
Balance per Balance Sheet:	$ _____	$ _____

Balance per Detailed Listing

	This Month This Year	This Month Last Year
Accrual #1:	$ _____	_____
Accrual #2:	_____	_____
Accrual #3:	_____	_____
Accrual Unmatched Payables:	_____	_____
Reasonableness Accrual:	_____	_____
Total Accruals:	$ _____	_____

Detail totals must agree with Accrued Liability on Balance Sheet.

Prepared By _____ Date _____

Reviewed By _____ Date _____

Balance Sheet Support Schedule
Notes Payable

This form covers the month of_____

Notes Payable

	This Month This Year	This Month Last Year
Balance per Balance Sheet:	$ _____	$ _____

Balance per Notes Payable Amortization Schedule

		This Month This Year	This Month Last Year
Note 1 -	Beginning Balance:	$ _____	_____
	Principal Payments:	_____	_____
	Adjustments:	_____	_____
Note 1 Balance:		$ _____	_____
Note 2 -	Beginning Balance:	$ _____	_____
	Principal Payments:	_____	_____
	Adjustments:	_____	_____
Note 2 Balance:		$ _____	_____
Note 3 -	Beginning Balance:	$ _____	_____
	Principal Payments:	_____	_____
	Adjustments:	_____	_____
Note 3 Balance:		$ _____	_____
Note 4 -	Beginning Balance:	$ _____	_____
	Principal Payments:	_____	_____
	Adjustments:	_____	_____
Note 4 Balance:		$ _____	_____
Total Notes Payable Balance:		$ _____	_____

Detail totals must agree with Notes Payable on Balance Sheet.

Prepared By _____ Date _____

Reviewed By_____ Date _____

Balance Sheet Support Schedule
Prepaid Expenses

This form covers the month of _____

═══ Prepaid Expenses ═══

	This Month This Year	This Month Last Year
Balance per Balance Sheet:	$ _____	$ _____

═══ Balance per Prepaid Expenses Amorization Schedules ═══

Prepaid Insurance for the Period _____ to _____

	This Month This Year	This Month Last Year
Total of Payments:	$ _____	_____
Months in Period:	_____	_____
Monthly Amortized Amount:	= $ _____	_____
Remaining Periods:	_____	_____
Total Prepaid Expense Balance:	= $ _____	_____

Prepaid Worker's Comp for the Period _____ to _____

Total of Payments:	$ _____	_____
Months in Period:	_____	_____
Monthly Amortized Amount:	= $ _____	_____
Remaining Periods:	_____	_____
Total Prepaid Expense Balance:	= $ _____	_____

Prepaid Other for the Period _____ to _____

Total of Payments:	$ _____	_____
Months in Period:	_____	_____
Monthly Amortized Amount:	= $ _____	_____
Remaining Periods:	_____	_____
Total Other Balance:	= $ _____	_____
Total of All Prepaid Expense Balances:	= $ _____	_____

Prepared By _____ Date _____

Reviewed By_____ Date _____

Balance Sheet Support Schedule
Payroll Payable
& Payroll Taxes Payable

This form covers the month of_____

=== Payroll Payable ===

	This Month This Year	This Month Last Year
Balance per Balance Sheet:	$ _____	$ _____

=== Balance per Detailed Wage Register ===

	This Month This Year	This Month Last Year
For the week of _____	$ _____	_____
Adjustments: _____	_____	_____
Total Wages Payable per Register:	_____	_____
Total Payroll Payable:	$ _____	_____

Detail totals must agree with Accounts Receivables on Balance Sheet.

*Most companies pay their employees one to two weeks later than when the work is done. This is a liability to the company and must be presented on financials as such. This schedule supports the amount on the balance sheet or in the general ledger.

=== Payroll Taxes Payable ===

	This Month This Year	This Month Last Year
Balance per Balance Sheet:	$ _____	$ _____

=== Balance per State & Federal Payroll Tax Schedules ===

	This Month This Year	This Month Last Year
Federal W/H Liability:	$ _____	_____
FICA Liability:	_____	_____
FICA W/H Liabilty:	_____	_____
FUTA Liability:	_____	_____
Total Federal Payroll Tax Liability:	_____	_____
State W/H Liability:	_____	_____
State Unemployment Tax Liability:	_____	_____
State Disability Tax Liability:	_____	_____
Other State Payroll Tax Liability (list):	_____	_____
Total State Payroll Tax Liability:	_____	_____
Total State & Federal Payroll Tax Liability:	$ _____	_____

Detail totals must agree with Payroll Taxes Payable on Balance Sheet.

Prepared By _____ Date _____

Reviewed By_____ Date _____

Another kind of balance sheet is the statement of daily cash balance. This is essential to calculating cash flow:

DAILY CASH BALANCE

DATE OF... _____

Cash on Hand:	$ _____
Cash Sales-Counter	$ _____
Cash Sales-C.O.D.	$ _____
Collections:	$ _____
Less Deposits:	$ _____
_____ :	$ _____
Balance:	$ _____

Cash:	$ _____
Checks:	$ _____
Cash Payouts:	$ _____
Out Tickets:	$ _____
_____	$ _____
Balance:	$ _____

Remarks

_____

_____

_____

_____

_____

3.3.2. Cash Flow Statement

Cash Flow is the fuel that keeps a business going. Just as you need an instrument gauge to keep you informed of how much gasoline you've got in the tank of your car, cash flow statements, prepared at regular intervals, keep you apprised of your ongoing cash situation. Here is a straightforward form:

<Organization>
<Address>
<City, State, Zip>

Cash Flow Statement

For the [Period (Quarter, Month, etc.)] Ended [Date When Period Ends]

Inflows:		
Cash Receipts		0.00
		0.00
		0.00
		0.00
Total inflows	$	0.00
Outflows:		
Advertising		0.00
Employee salaries		0.00
Legal services		0.00
Materials		0.00
Item		0.00
Item		0.00
Item		0.00
Item		0.00
Item		0.00
Item		0.00
Item		0.00
Total outflows	$	0.00
Overall Total:	$	0.00

Notes:

3.3.3. Cash and Check Control Forms

Managing money is not just about making the right investments, acquiring the right merchandise, and paying the right employees the appropriate salaries. It also involves controlling and tracking checks and cash that come into and go out of the business. Effective cash/check-control forms create a valuable paper trail.

Check requisitions and check control logs provide a means of centralizing check writing and disbursement:

Check Requisition

Check Amount _____ Date _____

Make check payable to: Expense Breakdown:

_____   Account   Amount

_____   _____   _____

_____   _____   _____

Description: _____   _____

_____   _____   _____

_____   _____   _____

_____   _____   _____

_____   _____   _____

Requested by _____ Authorized by _____

Check Requisition

Check Amount _____ Date _____

Make check payable to: Expense Breakdown:

_____   Account   Amount

_____   _____   _____

_____   _____   _____

Description: _____   _____

_____   _____   _____

_____   _____   _____

_____   _____   _____

Requested by _____ Authorized by _____

CHECK CONTROL LOG

Period _____

Account _____

Date Reconciled to Trial
Balance _____

Date	Beginning Balance	Batch Number	Batch Total	Credit	Check #'s Used/Voided	Deposit Amount	Ending Balance

Most businesses find it cumbersome and awkward to fill out a lengthy requisition for funds to purchase small, day-to-day office supplies or services. A petty cash fund is designed to meet these casual expenses. But there should be nothing casual about the way the money is disbursed. Vouchers and requests for replenishment of petty cash will help keep track of these funds:

PETTY CASH VOUCHER		Date:	
Account	Description	Amount	
Received by _____ Authorized by _____		Total	

(Cut Here)

PETTY CASH VOUCHER		Date:	
Account	Description	Amount	
Received by _____ Authorized by _____		Total	

Request for Replenishment of Petty Cash

Date of Request:	Location:

Requested By:	Profit Center Number:

Date of Expenditure	Supplier	Description	Amount
		Total Funds Expended:	
		Cash Unexpended	
		Cash (over) Short	
		Total Petty Cash Fund Authorized	

Above Expenditures Totalling _____

Made on behalf of the company and requested for replenishment is in order.

Manager:	Approved By:

Another means of cash control is continually synchronizing your ledger with your bank statements. A simple worksheet will help:

Bank Reconciliation Worksheet

	Beginning Balance	Debit	Credit	Ending Balance
Bank Balance as of				
Outstanding Checks:				
Outstanding Deposits:				
Adjustments:				
Totals				

Adjusted Bank Balance $ _____

	Beginning Balance	Debit	Credit	Ending Balance
Ledger Balance as of				
Outstanding Checks:				
Outstanding Deposits:				
Adjustments:				
Totals				

Adjusted General Ledger Balance must agree with Adjusted Bank Balance $ _____

Prepared by _____ Date _____

Reviewed by _____ Date _____

3.4. FINANCIAL PROJECTIONS FORMS

3.4.1. The "Black Art"

Financial projection is the "black art" of cost and allocation planning. Even with the best information processed by the most experienced analyst, a financial projection is a guess—an educated and informed guess, perhaps, but a guess nevertheless. No set of forms will change that. However, a well-designed format for figuring and presenting projections will allow you and others to see the figures more clearly and in perspective. Three types of forms will be helpful in making most projections:

- Project outline
- Break-even analysis
- Project cost summary

3.4.2. Project Outline

This can be little more than a blank sheet, specifying the name of the project, a brief description of it, and what you intend to do to complete the project. A sample form is printed on page 255.

3.4.3. Break-even Analysis

Break-even analyses are sometimes called profit-and-loss projections (P&Ls) or "ultimates." There are many ways to work up and represent break-evens. Page 256 shows a very straightforward format, which may be adapted and modified to suit most projects.

3.4.4. Project Cost Summary

In most organizations, a summary of project cost is required before a project is funded. Page 257 shows a typical form.

PROJECT OUTLINE

Title:

Subject:

Description:

Plan of Action:

Breakeven Analysis Worksheet
For Month of....

Total Expenses = Total Revenues
Fixed Overhead Expenses + Variable Expenses (cost of sales) = Total Revenues
Fixed Overhead Expenses = Contribution Margin
Total Revenues = Volume X Price per Unit
Variable Expenses = Volume X Variable Cost per Unit

☞ Example

Total Revenues = 4000 units X $3.00 per unit	=	$ 12,000
Variable Expenses (cost of sales) = 4000 units X $.50 per unit	-	$ 2,000
Contribution Margin	=	$ 10,000
Fixed Overhead Expenses	-	$ 10,000
Income	=	$0
Fixed Overhead Expenses		$10,000
Contribution Margin (per unit)	<	$2.50
Breakeven Units = $10,000 < $2.50	=	$4,000 units

Total Revenues = Volume X Price per Unit
Total Revenues =   units   X $ = $

Variable Expenses = Volume X Variable Cost per Unit (cost of sales)
Variable Expenses =   units   X $ - $

Contribution Margin   = $
Fixed Overhead Expenses   - $
Income   = $

Contribution Margin (per Unit) = Contribution Margin> Volume (number of units)
Contribution Margin (per Unit) =
                                           /   / $

Breakeven Volume (units) = Fixed Overhead < Contribution Margin (per unit)
Breakeven Volume (units) =
                                           /   = $

Project Cost Summary

Appropriation Detail

Project Title _____
Project Number _____
Date of Request _____

Plant/Mgr. _____
Responsibility Center No. _____
Product Lines _____

Purpose of Request _____
Cost Distribution _____
Completion Date _____

Project Description

_____
_____
_____

Project Justification

_____
_____
_____

Investment Summary	Start-up	1st Full Year	5 Year Total	10 Year Total	Project Total	Start-up	1st Full Year	5 Year Total
Capital Investment								
Working Capital								
Total Investment								
Sales								
Net Income								
Cash Flow								
Discounted ROI								
Payback in years								

Appovals

Requestor _____
V.P. Responsible _____
Date _____

(for request to $20,000)
V.P. Finance _____
President _____
Date _____

(for request over $20,000)
Board of Directors
By _____
Date _____

3.5. Credit and Collection Forms

3.5.1. Bad Check Notice

A Bad Check Notice form is an efficient means of dealing with checks returned for insufficient funds or other reason. A sample form is printed on page 259.

3.5.2. Credit Application and Approval Forms

The credit process requires forms for the applicant, an authorization to release credit information pursuant top the application, credit inquiry forms (for soliciting information from credit references), and a credit approval form. The forms on pages 260–263 are basic examples.

Additionally, you may want to send a new customer a credit terms reminder form. A sample form is printed on page 264.

NOTICE OF RETURNED CHECK

To: _____

_____

_____

_____

From:_____

_____

_____

_____

Re: Invoice # _____

Please be advised that your check #_____
in the amount of $_____
was returned for

> [] Insufficient funds
> [] No signature
> [] Other

We have charged your account an additional $_____
returned check fee.

Please send a new

> [] check
> [] cashier's check

in the total amount of $_____ without delay.

Credit Application

From: _____   **Date** _____

_____

_____

Thank you for your interest in our company's products and services. We appreciate your business and look forward to a long and prosperous business relationship. Please complete the credit application and return to the above address, attention credit department. Please note our credit terms. You will be advised shortly of your credit status with our company. Thank you.

All payments are due per our terms. Our terms are 2% 10 days. Net 30 days.

Your Company Name _____

Address _____

_____

Contact Name _____   **Phone** _____

Bank References:

Bank Name _____

Phone Number _____

Bank Address _____   **Account #** _____

Bank Name _____

Phone Number _____

Bank Address _____   **Account #** _____

Credit References:

Company Name _____

Credit Address _____

Phone _____

Company Name _____

Credit Address _____

Phone _____

Company Name _____

Credit Address _____

Phone _____

Authorization to Release Credit Information

From: _____

_____

_____

To: _____

_____

_____

Date: _____

Dear _____

Thank you for your recent interest in establishing credit with our company. Please sign the authorization to release information agreement below and complete the enclosed form. Then send them to us with your most recent financial statements. We will contact your credit and bank references. Then we will contact you regarding your credit terms with our company.

Thank you,

_____
CREDIT MANAGER

We have recently applied for credit with _____
We have been requested to provide information for their use in reviewing credit worthiness. Therefore, I authorize the investigation of my firm

_____ and its related credit information.
FIRM NAME

The release in any manner of all information by you is authorized whether such information is of record or not. I do hereby release all persons, agencies, firms, companies, and so forth from any damages resulting from providing such information.

This authorization is valid for 30 days from the date of my signature below. Please keep a copy of my release request for your files. Thank you .

Signature _____ Date _____

Credit Inquiry

Date: _____

On: _____

Address: _____ Apt.# _____

City, State, Zip: _____

Contact: _____

Phone No.:_____

In order that we might process a credit application that we have received on the above account, we would appreciate it if you would provide us with the information requested below. Please know we will treat your response with confidentiality.

Dollar Sales From _____ To _____ Totaled _____

Total Dollar Sales in Year _____ = _____ in Year _____ = _____

Terms _____ Special Terms _____

Largest Amount Owed _____ When _____ Current? ☐ Yes ☐ No

Total Amount Now Owed _____ Current? ☐ Yes ☐ No   Amt. Past Due

Recent Trends: ☐ Promptness   ☐ Full Term   ☐ Slightly Slow   ☐ Very Slow

Makes Unjust Claims _____

_____

_____

Credit   ☐ Honored   ☐ Refused   Explain: _____

_____

👉 **Check Manner of Payment** 👈

☐ Prompt & Takes Discounts   ☐ Slow, but Collectable   ☐ An Excellent Account- Best Recommendation

☐ Prompt and Satisfactory   ☐ Slow & Unsatisfactory

☐ Prompt to _____ Days Slow   ☐ Accepts C.O.D.'s Promptly   ☐ We do not recommend extending credit to this account.

☐ Makes Partial Payments   ☐ Collected by an Attorney

☐ Asks for Additional Time   ☐ In Hands of an attorney

Special Comments:

We will be pleased to share any information we have that will assist in your credit decisions. Thank you for your assistance.

_____
Name

_____
Title

Credit Approval Form

To be completed by the Credit Department

Company Name [   ]

Company Address [   ]

[   ]

[   ]

Contact Name [   ]

Phone Number [   ]

Bank References [   ]

[   ]

[   ]

Credit References [   ]

[   ]

[   ]

Approximate monthly sales per sales manager $ [   ]

Credit Terms [   ]

Credit Limit [   ]

Any Special Instructions [   ]

[   ]

Prepared by [   ]

Approvals:

Credit Manager [   ]   **Date** [   ]

Sales Manager [   ]   **Date** [   ]

Controller [   ]   **Date** [   ]

General Manager [   ]   **Date** [   ]

Credit Terms Reminder Letter

From: _____

_____

_____

To: _____

_____

_____

Date: _____

Dear New Customer,

Thank you for your recent order with our company. As a reminder to your Purchasing and Accounts payable departments, our credit terms are as follows

Thank you for adhering to our credit policy. We hope our business relationship is a long and prosperous one.
Thank You again.

Sincerely, _____

3.6. PAYMENT REQUESTS

3.6.1. Reminders

If you decide that you do not have time to create and send full-scale collection letters to stir past-due and delinquent accounts, you may want to try the following forms, beginning with a simple past-due reminder:

Past Due Reminder Letter

Date: _____

To: _____

_____

_____

_____

From: _____

_____

_____

Dear Customer,

Your Account # _____ is

currently _____ days past due.

Our terms are

Please send payment in full as soon as possible.

If the account is delinquent, a more urgent reminder is in order:

REQUEST FOR PAYMENT

From: _____
_____
_____

To: _____
_____
_____

Date: _____

Dear Customer,
We received your order and promptly processed the order according to specifications desired. Please send the amount listed below **IMMEDIATELY**. Payment is expected in the form of check, money order, VISA or Mastercard. Please place the reference number on your payment. We appreciate your interest in our product/service and your prompt attention to this matter.
Thank You.

Accounting Department

Amount Due: $ _____

Reference # _____

From: _____

Check Payment $ _____

Check # _____

VISA acct. # _____

Mastercard # _____

3.6.2. Series

This series of reminders escalates in intensity as time passes:

PLEASE . . .

WE'D APPRECIATE YOUR ATTENTION!

Our records do not reflect payment of your account. Kindly review your records and please remit. Thank You.

Amount $ _____

Date(s) _____

Invoice No. (s) _____

To

☐ Customer Use Only
Payment Enclosed

☐ Remittance previously
(Copy of check enclosed)

PAST DUE

This bill is now overdue. Please remit promptly to maintain your credit standing. Thank You.

Amount $ _____

Date(s) _____

Invoice No. (s) _____

To

☐ Customer Use Only
Payment Enclosed

☐ Remittance previously
(Copy of check enclosed)

FINAL NOTICE

This bill is now Long Past due. Please remit today or contact us to avoid Final Action.

Amount $ _____

Date(s) _____

Invoice No. (s) _____

To

☐ Customer Use Only
Payment Enclosed

☐ Remittance previously
(Copy of check enclosed)

3.6.3. Final Demand

When all else fails, send the customer a copy of an "action order," which announces your intention to put the delinquent account into a collection status:

```
ACTION COPY          Please institute collection procedures for this account.


                                                         Amount $_____

        ┌                              ┐        Date(s)_____

  To                                            Invoice No. (s) _____

                                                ☐ Customer Use Only
        └                              ┘           Payment Enclosed
                                                ☐ Remittance previously
                                                   (Copy of check enclosed)
```

3.6.4. Record Keeping

Not only is it important to communicate with the delinquent customer, it is equally important to keep track internally of overdue accounts and bad debts. An overdue account form will aid in collection efforts by keeping an accurate history of the account, while a bad debt write-off sheet will serve to reconcile your books while preventing your making further mistakes with this customer:

Overdue Account File

Account Number: _____

Name: _____
Telephone #: _____
Address: _____

Employer: _____
Telephone #: _____
Address: _____

Guarantor: _____
Telephone #: _____
Address: _____

Spouse's Name: _____

Date account Opened: _____
Date Delin. File Started: _____
Original Balance Due: _____

Date:	Amount Paid:	Balance Due:	Date:	Amount Paid:	Balance Due:

Dates:	History of Collection Efforts:

Bad Debt Write-off Sheet

Customer Name: _____ **I.D.#:** _____

Customer Address: _____

Total Balance Due: _____

Date of Last Purchase: _____

Date of Last Payment: _____

Comments:

```
┌──────────────────────────────────────┐
│                                      │
│                                      │
│                                      │
│                                      │
│                                      │
│                                      │
│                                      │
│                                      │
└──────────────────────────────────────┘
```

Write-Off Requested By: _____

Date: _____

Approval Signatures:

Credit Manager: _____ **Date:** _____

Controller: _____ **Date:** _____

Sale Manager: _____ **Date:** _____

3.7. PROMISSORY NOTE

3.7.1. The Simplest Credit Form

A great many business transactions are enabled not through the use of complicated credit agreements, but a simple and straightforward promissory note. This form can be used in a wide variety of situations:

Thank You!   WE APPRECIATE YOUR BUSINESS

PROMISSORY NOTE

$ _____ Date _____ 19 _____

For Value Received, _____

_____

Promise to pay to the order of_____

_____

the sum of _____

to be paid as follows:_____

_____

_____

with interest to be paid, at the rate of _____
per centum per annum, from date payment is
due.

_____ L. S.
(FOR SIGNATURE OF CUSTOMER)

_____ L. S.
(ADDITIONAL SIGNATURE IF AVAILABLE)

SIGNED AND SEALED IN PRESENCE OF:

_____
(WITNESS)

271

3.8. EMPLOYMENT FORMS

3.8.1. Job Announcements

In addition to ads and the like, strategic postings of job announcements are effective means of recruiting employees, especially when used within an organization. All three of the following forms include space for the essential information:

NEW JOB POSTING

Open Position

Job Title: _____

Department: _____

Pay Grade: _____ ☐ Exempt ☐ Non Exempt

Reports to: _____

Location: _____

Job Summary

_____
_____
_____

Duties and Responsibilities:

_____
_____
_____
_____
_____
_____
_____
_____
_____
_____
_____
_____

Minimum Requirements:

_____
_____
_____

Job Posting Date: _____

All bids must be received by the Personnel Department within ten days of the job posting.

JOB ANNOUNCEMENT

Job Title		
Department		
Salary		
Supervisor	☐ Exempt	☐ Non

Job Summary

Required Qualifications (special skills, education, etc.)

Interested candidates should contact the Personnel Department by

Posted Date

To be eligible for consideration for the above position you must have been in your current position a minimum of _____ months.

POSITION DESCRIPTION

Position Title

Department

Location

Grade Level

Exempt ☐   Non-Exempt ☐

Position Summary

Major Responsibilities

Required skills/education

Approvals

Supervisor   Date

Manager   Date

Human Resources   Date

3.8.2. Application Form and Supporting Documents

If you wish to use a job application form, tailor it precisely to the needs of your organization. The example that follows on page 276 is generic. The emphasis is on gathering information concerning education and experience, as well as learning about any criminal record. An application should also require the applicant to affirm and certify that all statements made are true. Making a false statement on an employment application provides prima facie grounds for dismissal.

> **TIP:** Application forms should include an "equal opportunity employer statement," such as: "We are an equal opportunity employer. We abide by all local, state, and federal laws prohibiting discrimination in employment. No question in this application is intended to elicit information in violation of those laws."

> **PITFALL:** Beware of asking discriminatory questions. You may not ask questions concerning sex, race, religion, or national origin. You may not ask questions concerning marital status or whether or not the applicant has or is planning to have children. However, you may ask the applicant to verify his or her right to work in the United States. You may not ask the applicant's age, except to ask for proof that he or she is not below the legal age for employment. Care must also be taken not to violate the Americans with Disabilities Act.

In addition to the application, you may ask applicants to authorize the release of information from persons and organizations the applicant provides as references. The forms should be provided to the applicant, who is responsible for securing the necessary releases. A sample form is printed on page 277.

You can use a form to save time when you check the applicant's references. A form also makes it easy for the reference to provide the information you seek. See page 278 for a sample form.

EMPLOYMENT APPLICATION

Last Name_____
First Name_____ M.I._____
SSN:_____
Address: _____
_____
_____

Phone: (Day)_____(Home)_____

Position desired:_____

Education	School	Major Yrs Completed	Grad?	Degree
High School			Y/N	
Trade School			Y/N	
College			Y/N	
Graduate School			Y/N	

Experience (Describe Fully. Use Back of Sheet If Necessary)
_____
_____
_____
_____
_____

May We Contact Previous Employers? Y/N
If yes, please list:

Name   Company   Telephone
_____
_____
_____
_____

Have you been convicted of a crime in the past 10 years, excluding misdemeanors and summary offenses, which has not been annulled, expunged, or sealed by a court? (A conviction record will not necessarily bar employment.) Y/N

If "yes," describe in full: _____
_____
_____
_____

Can you verify your legal right to work in the U.S. by providing a birth certificate or other proof of U.S. citizenship or resident alien status? Y/N

CERTIFICATION

I certify that, to the best of my knowledge and belief, the answers given by me to the foregoing questions and the statements made by me on this application are correct and complete. I understand that misrepresentation or omission of facts in this application may lead to my dismissal.

SIGNED:_____ DATE:_____

Authorization to Release Information

From:

To:

I have applied for a position with:

I have been requested to provide information for the above-named party's use in reviewing my background and qualifications. Therefore, I authorize the investigation of my past and present work, character, education, military and employment qualifications.

The release in any manner of all information by you is authorized whether such information is of record or not, and I do hereby release all persons, agencies, firms, companies, and so forth, from any damages resulting from providing such information.

This authorization is valid for 90 days from the date of my signature below. Please keep this copy of my release request for your files. Thank you for your cooperation.

Signature: _____ Date: _____

Witness: _____ Date: _____

Medical information is often protected by state and civil codes. Consult your attorney if you wish to seek this information.

Note: Many employers are reluctant to provide information on previous employees. If you ask each prospective employee to distribute this form to his or her references before you contact them, the prior employers may be more willing to release information.

Pre-Employment Reference Check   Via Letter

From: _____   To: _____
_____   Date _____   _____
_____   _____
_____   _____

We would appreciate your assistance in verifying the information listed below regarding an employment application. It is to be understood that all information is confidential and will be treated as such in our company personnel files. Attached, please find an authorization to release information signed by the applicant. A self-addressed, stamped envelope is enclosed for your convenience in replying. We appreciate your assistance in this matter. Thank You.

Sincerely,

Human Resource Manager

The following information was provided to us by the applicant. Please make any appropriate corrections

Name _____   SSN _____

Job Title _____   Final Salary $_____

Dates of Employment _____

Reason for Termination _____

Please review and rate the applicant in these areas:

	OUTSTANDING	GOOD	AVERAGE	POOR	
Attendance	1	2	3	4	
Quality of Work	1	2	3	4	
Quantity of Work	1	2	3	4	
Cooperation	1	2	3	4	
Responsibility	1	2	3	4	

Signed _____   Title _____   Date _____

3.8.3. Applicant Evaluation

No form or formula can substitute for careful thought and good judgment in evaluating job candidates. However, a well-designed form can make it easier to list, lay out, weigh, and compare essential qualifications, skills, and traits a particular position may call for. Sample forms are printed on pages 280–283.

> **Pitfall:** As with application forms, no information relating to applicant rating should concern such matters as race, sex, religion, age, or national origin. Also be wary of violating the Americans with Disabilities Act.

3.8.4. Salary Recommendation

The form on page 284 can serve to recommend the appropriate salary level for a new hire as well as for the promotion of current employees.

3.8.5. Rejection

Ideally, turning down a candidate should be done with a personal letter. The volume of candidates and limitations of time do not always permit this. In this case, a form letter is better than no response at all. A sample form is printed on page 285.

> **Tip:** If possible, reply to all job applicants. It is absolutely necessary that you inform interviewees of the status of their application. Don't leave them languishing in limbo.

3.8.6. New Employee Notice

Once a new employee is hired, it is customary and highly desirable to announce the hire via a memo. Again, if possible, a personalized memo message is best. However, a form announcement is preferable to none at all. A sample form is printed on page 286.

APPLICANT RATING

Position _____   Interviewed By _____

Candidate # 1 _____   Date Interviewed _____
Candidate # 2 _____   Date Interviewed _____
Candidate # 3 _____   Date Interviewed _____

Critical Job Requirements	Poor		Average		Excellent
	1	2	3	4	5
	1	2	3	4	5
	1	2	3	4	5
	1	2	3	4	5
	1	2	3	4	5
	1	2	3	4	5
	1	2	3	4	5
	1	2	3	4	5
	1	2	3	4	5
	1	2	3	4	5
	1	2	3	4	5
	1	2	3	4	5

Strengths _____

Weaknesses _____

Other _____

APPLICANT RATING

Applicant Name					Page 1 of 2
Position			Department		
Interviewed By			Interview Date		

Job Experience	Poor		Average		Excellent
Relevance to Position	1	2	3	4	5
Accomplishments	1	2	3	4	5
Analytical/Problem Solving	1	2	3	4	5
Leadership	1	2	3	4	5
Career Goals	1	2	3	4	5
Academics					
Relevance of Studies to Job	1	2	3	4	5
Abilities as a Student	1	2	3	4	5
Characteristics					
Grooming	1	2	3	4	5
Attitude	1	2	3	4	5
Grasp of Ideas	1	2	3	4	5
Stability	1	2	3	4	5
Personality	1	2	3	4	5
Preparation for Interview					
Knowledge of Company	1	2	3	4	5
Relevance of Questions	1	2	3	4	5

Summary of Strengths and Weaknesses

Job Experience: _____

_____

Academics: _____

_____

Characteristics: _____

_____

Interview Prep.: _____

_____

Comments: _____

_____

CLERICAL APPLICANT RATING FORM

Applicant's Name	Position Applied	Department	Interviewed by

OFFICE SKILLS	Excellent	Good	Fair	Poor	N/A
Typing					
10 key calculator					
Short Hand					
Switchboard					
Computer Skills					
Grammar					
Foreign					

JOB EXPERIENCE	Excellent	Good	Fair	Poor	N/A
Record of Job Success					
Compatibility					
Ability to Communicate					
Energy, Ambition, Motivation					
Other:					
Other:					

General Comments and Overall Appraisal: _____

APPLICANT COMPARISON SUMMARY

Position		Interviewed by	
Candidate #1		Date Interviewed	
Candidate #2		Date Interviewed	
Candidate #3		Date Interviewed	

Critical Job Requirements	Candidate No. 1	Candidate No. 2	Candidate No. 3	Comments

LEGEND

= Meets critical job requirements
+ Exceeds critical job requirements
− Does not meet critical job requirements

SALARY RECOMMENDATION

| Employee Name | I.D. No. |
| Department | Location |

	Current	Proposed
Title	_____	_____
Salary Grade	_____	_____
Base Rate	_____	_____
Merit Amount	_____	_____
Promotion Amount	_____	_____
Bonus	_____	_____
Other	_____	_____

Date of last increase: _____   Effective date: _____

Type of last increase: ☐ new hire   Date of proposed increase: ☐ new hire
                        ☐ merit   ☐ merit
                        ☐ promotion   ☐ promotion
                        ☐ other: _____   ☐ other: _____

Explanation for proposed salary increase _____

_____

_____

_____

_____

_____

_____

Approvals	
Supervisor	Date
Manager	Date
Human Resources	Date

APPLICANT LETTER

From: _____
      _____
      _____
      _____

To: _____
      _____
      _____
      _____

Date: _____

Date: _____

Thank you for considering a position with our firm. Your qualifications have been reviewed by our management team. While your background is an interesting one, we have received a number of résumés from people whose qualifications are a closer match with our firm's current needs.

We would like to again thank you for your interest in our firm and wish you continued success in pursuit of your career objectives.

Sincerely,

New Employee Notice

Date:

To: All Employees

From:

Subject: New Employee

I am pleased to announce that

(new employee name)

has joined our staff as

(job title)

in his/her new position,

will report to

Our new employee comes to us from

(last employer)

where he/she was

(job title & respons.)

and prior to that was

(job title & respons.)

phone extension will be:

and Email address
is:

and other information:

Please join me in welcoming our new employee to our staff, and in wishing much success!

3.8.7. Entry Agreements

Full-scale employee agreements and contracts are beyond the scope of this book. However, certain agreements, concluded as a requirement for employment, may be considered standard. It is estimated that, currently, at least 60 percent of employers require drug or alcohol screening as a condition of employment. A release form is required from the employee before such screening can be performed. See sample form below.

Proprietary information and trade secrets are vital to the survival of an organization; therefore, confidentiality is a legitimate condition of employment. An agreement should be concluded at the commencement of employment. A sample form is printed on page 288.

Consent for Drug/Alcohol Screening

If you are offered and accept employment with _____ (company name) you will be working with and around machinery and equipment that can cause injury to yourself and others. In the interest of safety for all concerned, you will be required to take a urine test for alcohol and or drug use.

I, _____ have been fully informed by my potential employer of the reason for this urine test for alcohol and or drugs. I understand what I am being tested for, the procedure involved, and do hereby freely give my consent. I also understand that the results of this test will be sent to my potential employer and become part of my record.

I authorize these test results to be released to_____ (company name)

Signature _____ Date _____

Witness _____ Date _____

Confidentiality Agreement

When you begin employment with this company, you will have access to information that the company considers confidential. This includes proprietary information, trade secrets, marketing strategy and intellectual property to which the company holds rights.

The purpose of this agreement is to inform you of your obligation to keep company information confidential. We also wish to remind you about the types of information that the company considers privileged. The following are types of information that you are bound to keep confidential:

_____
_____
_____
_____
_____
_____

You may already have been advised of your obligations in this matter. This letter is intended to remind you of your obligation to keep privileged information confidential and to restate our seriousness in this matter.

We do not wish to cast doubt regarding your integrity or honesty. All employees are required to read and understand this obligation.

If you have any questions regarding this policy, please contact:
_____

Signed   _____

Date   _____

Thank you for your cooperation

3.9. EMPLOYEE PERFORMANCE AND CONDUCT

3.9.1. Performance Review

Feedback at regular intervals is a key to improving employee performance. In addition to improving performance, regular reviews:

1. Provide a basis for equitable salary increases and promotion

2. Insure that both the employee and employer—or subordinate and supervisor—understand one another's expectations

3. Provide an opportunity for modifying employee performance or employer expectation

4. Provide an opportunity for modifying the job description, if necessary

5. Gauge the employee's aptitude in a given position

6. Provide the basis for disciplinary action, if necessary.

The employee review should be made in writing. However, it can be narrative and essentially free form, or it can consist of a rating form. An example is shown on pages 290–292.

3.9.2. Employee Grievances

Employee grievances must be taken seriously, not only to preserve and enhance the organization's team cohesiveness and ability to produce a maximum effort, but also to avoid costly arbitration or litigation of disputes at some later time. One way to encourage employees to express their needs in a positive way is to create a standard grievance form—and appoint a manager to receive and review such forms. A sample form is printed on page 293.

Employee Performance Review

Employee Name_____ Title _____

Department _____ Supervisor_____

Date Hired _____ Last Review Date _____ Date Hired _____

The following definitions apply to each factor rated below:

Level 6 - Far exceeds job requirements
Level 5 - Consistently exceeds job requirements
Level 4 - Meets and usually exceeds job requirements
Level 3 - Consistently meets job requirements
Level 2 - Inconsistently meets job requirements
Level 1 - Does not meet job requirements
———————— (Circle Appropriate Level) ————————

QUANTITY OF WORK

Volume of work produced regularly by employee and the speed and consistency of output:

Comments: _____

Level 6
Level 5
Level 4
Level 3
Level 2
Level 1

QUALITY OF WORK

Extent to which employee can be relied upon to carry assignments to completion:

Comments:

Level 6
Level 5
Level 4
Level 3
Level 2
Level 1

JOB INVOLVEMENT

Amount of interest and enthusiasm shown in work

Comments: _____

Level 6
Level 5
Level 4
Level 3
Level 2
Level 1

PAGE 1 OF 3

Employee Performance Review (continued)

ABILITY TO WORK WITH OTHERS

Extent to which employee interacts effectively with others in the performance of his/her job

Comments: _____
_____
_____
_____

Level 6
Level 5
Level 4
Level 3
Level 2
Level 1

FLEXIBILITY

Extent to which employee is able to perform a variety of assignments within his/her job duties

Comments: _____
_____
_____
_____

Level 6
Level 5
Level 4
Level 3
Level 2
Level 1

JOB KNOWLEDGE

Extent of information and understanding the employee possesses

Comments: _____
_____
_____
_____

Level 6
Level 5
Level 4
Level 3
Level 2
Level 1

INITIATIVE

Extent to which employee is a self-starter in achieving the objectives of the job

Comments: _____
_____
_____
_____

Level 6
Level 5
Level 4
Level 3
Level 2
Level 1

OVERALL EVALUATION OF EMPLOYEE PERFORMANCE

Comments: _____
_____
_____
_____

Level 6
Level 5
Level 4
Level 3
Level 2
Level 1

Is attendance a problem? ☐ Yes ☐ No   Comments: _____
_____
_____

PAGE 2 OF 3

Employee Performance Review (continued)

CAREER DEVELOPMENT

I. Strengths

_____

_____

_____

II. Developmental Needs

_____

_____

_____

III. Developmental Plan (include long term goals):

_____

_____

_____

EMPLOYEE COMMENTS

General comments regarding the evaluation of your performance: .

_____

_____

_____

_____

I have read and do acknowlege this review of my performance as an employee of this company:

Employee _____   Date _____

This review has been carefully read and approved by:

Supervisor _____   Date _____

Dept. Manager _____   Date _____

Human Resources _____   Date _____

President _____   Date _____

PAGE 3 OF 3

GRIEVANCE FORM

Date [＿＿＿＿＿]   Employee Name [＿＿＿＿＿＿＿＿＿＿＿＿＿＿]   Dept. [＿＿＿＿＿＿＿]

State your grievance in detail, including the date(s) of act(s) or omissions causing it.

[＿＿＿＿＿＿＿＿＿＿＿＿＿＿＿＿＿＿＿＿＿＿＿＿＿＿＿＿＿＿＿]

Identify other employees with personal knowledge of your grievance.

[＿＿＿＿＿＿＿＿＿＿＿＿＿＿＿＿＿＿＿＿＿＿＿＿＿＿＿＿＿＿＿]

State your efforts to resolve this grievance.

[＿＿＿＿＿＿＿＿＿＿＿＿＿＿＿＿＿＿＿＿＿＿＿＿＿＿＿＿＿＿＿]

Describe the solution you would like.

[＿＿＿＿＿＿＿＿＿＿＿＿＿＿＿＿＿＿＿＿＿＿＿＿＿＿＿＿＿＿＿]

Employee's Signature [＿＿＿＿＿＿＿＿＿＿＿＿]   Date [＿＿＿＿＿＿＿＿]

Employee Accepted ☐
Employee Appealed ☐

Date Received [＿＿＿＿＿]   Grievance Team Member- Informal Review

Actions Taken [＿＿＿＿＿＿＿＿＿＿＿＿＿＿＿＿＿＿＿＿＿]

Disposition [＿＿＿＿＿＿＿＿＿＿＿＿＿＿＿＿＿＿＿＿＿]

Assigned Team Member [＿＿＿＿＿＿＿＿＿＿]   Date Communicated [＿＿＿＿]

Employee Accepted ☐
Employee Appealed ☐

Date Received [＿＿＿＿＿]   Grievance Team Member - Formal Review

Actions Taken [＿＿＿＿＿＿＿＿＿＿＿＿＿＿＿＿＿＿＿＿＿]

Disposition [＿＿＿＿＿＿＿＿＿＿＿＿＿＿＿＿＿＿＿＿＿]

Grievance Review Team [＿＿＿＿＿＿＿＿＿＿]   Date Communicated [＿＿＿＿]

Employee Accepted ☐
Employee Appealed ☐

Date Received [＿＿＿＿＿]   Grievance Team & Management - Formal Review

Actions Taken [＿＿＿＿＿＿＿＿＿＿＿＿＿＿＿＿＿＿＿＿＿]

Disposition [＿＿＿＿＿＿＿＿＿＿＿＿＿＿＿＿＿＿＿＿＿]

Management Team [＿＿＿＿＿＿＿＿＿＿]   Date Communicated [＿＿＿＿]

3.9.3. Disciplinary Forms

Ongoing communication with employees is critical to the success of any enterprise. For a variety of reasons, ranging from employee development to the self-preservation of the business, it is critically important to document and correct employee errors and abuses. If possible, this should be done through individualized letters or memos. However, when this is not possible, a well-constructed form is the next best thing.

> **PITFALL:** Using a form to discipline employees always conveys an authoritarian message. This may not be appropriate—or very effective—in some situations. Use disciplinary forms cautiously.

The first form resembles a traffic ticket and is intended to document infractions rather than profound or far-reaching problems:

EMPLOYEE WARNING NOTICE

Name _____ Date _____ 1st Notice ☐
Dept. _____ Clock No._____ 2nd Notice ☐
                                                 3rd Notice ☐

NATURE OF VIOLATION   **REMARKS**

☐ Defective Work
☐ Safety
☐ Conduct
☐ Lateness
☐ Absence
☐ Attitude
☐ Housekeeping
☐ Disobedience
☐ Carelessness

I have read this notice and understand _____ Employee's Signature

_____ Signature of Foreman or Supervisor   _____ Official Signature

The second type of form is for more serious problems and is designed as much to document the situation as it is to provide warning to the employee:

EMPLOYEE
WARNING NOTICE

NAME		DATE OF NOTICE
EMPLOYEE CLOCK NO.	DEPARTMENT	SHIFT

NATURE OF WARNING

☐ Work Quality	☐ Lateness/Early Quit	☐ Disobedience
☐ Safety	☐ Unexcused Absence(s)	☐ Carelessness
☐ Poor Productivity	☐ Excessive Absences	☐ Conduct
☐ Other: _____		

PREVIOUS WARNINGS

☐ 1st Warning   ☐ Oral   ☐ Written   Date _____ By _____
☐ 2nd Warning   ☐ Oral   ☐ Written   Date _____ By _____
☐ 3rd Warning   ☐ Oral

☐ Written   Date _____   By _____

EMPLOYER / SUPERVISOR COMMENTS

_____
_____
_____
_____

EMPLOYEE COMMENTS

☐ I agree with the above statements   ☐ I disagree with the above statements

Why: _____
_____
_____

EMPLOYEE'S SIGNATURE _____ DATE _____

DISCIPLINARY ACTION TAKEN

☐ No ☐ Yes Explain _____
_____

I have read this notice and understand it.

EMPLOYEE'S SIGNATURE _____ DATE _____   ☐ Refused to sign notice

EMPLOYER/SUPERVISOR _____ DATE _____

WITNESS _____ DATE _____

Absenteeism is the most common employee problem. Keep track of absenteeism with a convenient form. Be certain to furnish the employee with a copy:

ABSENTEE REPORT

Date _____

Name of Employee_____

Dept._____ Clock No._____

was ABSENT from work today.

CHECK
☐ No Work
☐ Illness
☐ Vacation
☐ _____
_____
☐ Not Known

Remarks _____

_____

_____

_____

_____

Signed_____

THIS REPORT MUST BE FILLED OUT AND SENT TO OFFICE EACH DAY

3.9.4. Termination

Termination should not be handled through the use of a form. A letter is usually more appropriate. However, forms may be used to make an accurate record of the circumstances of separation. A sample form is printed on page 297.

It is also helpful to furnish employees as well as managers with "separation checklists," in order to insure that the break is a clean one and that no unresolved issues linger. Sample forms are printed on pages 298 and 299.

SEPARATION NOTICE

Name		Effective Date
Department	Shift	Position	Hire Date
		Supervisor	Last Day Worked

TYPE OF SEPARATION

☐ Resignation   ☐ Discharge
☐ Mutual Agreement   ☐ Layoff
☐ Leave of Absence   ☐ Retirement
☐ Other _____

REASON

☐ Personal   ☐ Poor Productivity
☐ Better Position   ☐ Company Rules Violation
☐ Absenteeism/Lateness   ☐ Lack of Work
☐ Other _____

EVALUATION

ITEM	Outstanding	Satisfactory	Unsatisfactory
Quality of Work			
Productivity			
Attitude			
Conduct			
Attendance			

Would you re-employ?

☐ Yes   ☐ No   ☐ With some reservation

Signed:	Date
Approved:	Date

Remarks: _____

EMPLOYEE'S SEPARATION CHECKLIST

Employee Name
Date of Termination

The following items are to have been collected prior to your separation with the company. Please have all these below listed items returned to your manager prior to your separation date. Thank you.

☐ All keys returned.

☐ Company vehicle keys returned.

☐ Company vehicle returned.

☐ Company credit cards returned.

☐ Company phone credit cards returned.

☐ Company equipment returned (e.g.,portable phones,beepers,p.c.'s).

☐ COBRA election forms signed and returned.

☐ 401K election forms signed and returned.

☐ Profit sharing election forms signed and returned.

Your files,desks and work area will be inventoried for all equipment and work utensils given to you by the company.

☐ Desk and working premises inventoried.

MANAGER DISMISSAL CHECKLIST

Employee Name

Date of
Termination

Collect the following items from the employee prior to separation from
the company:

☐ All keys returned

☐ Company vehicle returned

☐ Company vehicle keys returned

☐ Company credit cards returned

☐ Company phone credit cards returned

☐ Company equipment returned (e.g., portable phones, beepers,
computers)

☐ Cobra election forms signed and returned

☐ 401K election forms signed and returned

☐ Profit sharing election forms signed and returned

☐ Company documents and files inventoried

☐ Desk and working premises inventoried

☐ Human resources and Payroll Departments notified of departure

☐ Final expense report received, reviewed and approved, expense check prepared

☐ Final check prepared includes all accrued vacation pay, sick pay, accrued
wages, bonus,etc..)

☐ Exit interview prepared

☐ Exit interview given

☐ Final checks (payroll and expense) given to employee .

All of the above duties have been completed in a satisfactory manner.

Company has no further liability with the terminating employee

Manager _____   **Date** _____

3.10. Expense Forms, Time Management Forms, Memo Forms, and Meeting Agenda Form

3.10.1. Expense Report

A clear, simple, but comprehensive expense report not only provides a full record of expenses, but helps to expedite reimbursement. A sample form is printed on page 301.

3.10.2. Time Management

A step beyond a simple to-do list is a schedule of deadlines. A form such as the one on page 302 will help organize individual or departmental schedules.

3.10.3. Memo Forms

We have already discussed a wide variety of memos and memo styles. Consider creating convenient memo forms for quick, informal intra-office notes. Sample forms are printed on pages 303 and 304.

3.10.4. Meeting Agenda

Meetings seem to be a way of life for American business. Listen to water-cooler conversation, and, judging from the grumbling, you'll most likely conclude that the vast majority of meetings are unsatisfactory. The trouble with many meetings is that they are unfocused. This can be remedied to a large extent with a good agenda. Try the following form as an aid to organizing an agenda. Distribute the agenda as a memo prior to the meeting. You might also include a sheet for attendees to keep their notes. See sample form printed on pages 305 and 306.

Expense Report

<Organization>
<Address>
<City, State, Zip>

EMPLOYEE NAME: _____

DATE OF TRIP: _____

EMPLOYEE TITLE: _____

PURPOSE OF TRIP: _____

Date	Description	Travel	Lodging	Breakfast	Lunch	Dinner	Transport	Entertain	Other	TOTALS
										0.00
										0.00
										0.00
										0.00
										0.00
										0.00
										0.00
										0.00
										0.00
										0.00
										0.00
TOTALS		0.00	0.00	0.00	0.00	0.00	0.00	0.00	0.00	

Advances and Charges to Company 0.00

TOTAL DUE $0.00

EMPLOYEE SIGNATURE: _____

APPROVED BY: _____

This Week's Deadlines   Week of: _____

Check Day Planned										
S	M	T	W	T	F	S	Time Needed	Activity/Deadline	Follow-Up	X

DATE_____ TIME_____

TO_____

OFFICE MEMO

AVOID VERBAL ORDERS

DATE_____

A.M
TIME_____ P.M.

TO_____ SUBJECT_____

WRITE IT!

DATE_____ TIME_____

TO_____

_____

_____

_____

_____

_____

_____

_____

_____

_____

_____ FROM _____

MEETING AGENDA

<Organization>
<Address>
<City, State Zip>

Meeting Description _____

Results Desired _____

Date _____ **Start Time** _____ **Location** _____

Scheduled Time			Actual Time		
Start	Stop	Total Hours	Start	Stop	Total Hours
[Start Time]	[Stop Time]				

Persons Attending	
1	
2	
3	
4	
5	
6	
7	
8	
9	
10	

Items To Be Discussed		✔
1		
2		
3		
4		
5		
6		
7		
8		
9		
10		

Materials Needed	**Person Responsible**

MEETING NOTES

3.11. INDEPENDENT CONTRACTOR FORMS

3.11.1. Bid Form

This form can be used by you, as an independent contractor, or it can be furnished to an independent contractor in order to make bids uniform. It provides space for describing the work to be done, without, however, appearing overwhelmingly legalistic. A sample form is printed on page 308.

3.11.2. Contractor Agreement

A form such as the one on page 309 covers the essential bases without splitting hairs.

3.11.3. Contractor Invoice

Once work is completed, an invoice should be drawn up, itemizing and summarizing the work performed and the charges. A sample form is printed on page 310.

BID PROPOSAL

PROPOSAL SUBMITTED TO:	WORK TO BE PERFORMED AT:
(Name)	(Name)
(Address)	(Address)
(City, State, Zip)	(City, State, Zip)
(Phone) (Fax)	(Phone) (Fax)

We hereby propose to furnish all materials and necessary equipment and perform
all labor necessary to complete the following work:

_____
_____
_____
_____
_____
_____
_____
_____
_____
_____

All material is guaranteed to be specified above and the above work to be performed in accordance with the
drawings and specifications submitted for above work and completed in a substantial workmanlike manner

for the sum of _____ with payments to be made as follows: _____
_____
_____

Respectfully submitted,

Contractor
Name _____   Address _____

                                  City_____ State _____ Zip _____
Contractor
License # _____   Phone _____ Fax _____

ACCEPTANCE OF PROPOSAL

You are hereby authorized to furnish all material, equipment and labor required to complete
the work described in the above proposal, for which the undersigned agrees to pay the
amount stated in said proposal and according to the terms therefore.

_____   _____
(Date)   (Owner/Contractor)

INDEPENDENT CONTRACTOR'S AGREEMENT

Date

Dear

The following will outline our agreement and summarize the terms of the arrangement which we have discussed.

Your have been retained by

as an independent contractor for the project of

You will be responsible for successfully completing the above described project according to specifications and within policy guidelines discussed.

The project is to be completed by

at a cost not to exceed $

You will invoice us for your services rendered at the end of each month.

We will not deduct or withhold any taxes, FICA or other deduction which we are legally required to make from the pay of regular employee. As an independent contractor, you will not be entitled to any fringe benefits, such as unemployment insurance, medical insurance, pension plans, or other such benefits that would be offered to regular employees.

During this project you may be in contact with or directly working with proprietary information which is important to our company and its competitive position. All information must be treated with strict confidence and may not be used at any time or in any manner in work you may do with others in our industry.

If you agree to the above terms, please sign and return one copy of this letter for our records. You may retain the other copy for your files.

Agreed:

Independent Contractor   Date

Company Representative   Date

Contractor's Job Invoice

TO:

Name _____

Address _____

City _____ State ___ Zip _____

Phone:_____ Fax _____

INVOICE # _____

Job ID: _____

Job Location _____

_____

_____

☐Extra ☐Down Payment ☐Progress Payment Terms _____

☐Final Payment ☐Day Work ☐Contract Start/Date: _____ End/Date:_____

DESCRIPTION OF WORK PERFORMED

SUMMARY

Labor

Materials

Change Order #

\# ....

\# ....

\# ....

\# ....

Subtotal:

Less Previous

Other:

Tax:

Grand Total:

3.12. Lease/Rental Forms

3.12.1. Rental Agreement

Frankly, you should think twice before using a simple form to conclude a rental or lease agreement. In some areas, it is very difficult to resolve landlord-tenant disputes, even in what appears to be open-and-shut cases, such as failure to pay rent. In complex situations or hot rental markets, you should seek the advice of a qualified real estate attorney in drawing up a lease agreement. However, in straightforward situations, a simple rental agreement may suffice. Page 312 shows a very basic document.

3.12.2. Lease Termination Notice

For whatever reason, the time may come to terminate a lease agreement. The notice document can be quite basic. However, it is usually necessary to document service of the notice. If improperly served, the tenant can appeal the termination in court, usually with the result that more time is bought. A sample form is printed on page 313.

3.12.3. Late Notice

A timely rent reminder can avert major problems. The notice need not be dire, threatening, or complicated. A sample form is printed on page 314.

RENTAL AGREEMENT

This agreement entered into this_____ day of _____ 19_____ , between

_____ (Lessor) and_____ (Lessee)

In consideration of the rental payments and the performance of all covenants and conditions contained herein, Lessor agrees to rent to Lessee, and Lessee agrees to rent from Lessor, for use as a residence, the premises described as: _____

located at,_____

State of_____ for a month-to-month tenancy commencing on the _____ day of

_____ 19 _____

The monthly rent of _____ dollars ($)

per month will be payable in advance on the _____ day of each month.

   Lessor acknowledges receiving the sum of_____ dollars

as a security deposit, refundable, subject to the agreed upon terms and as provided by law.

APARTMENT INVENTORY

Lessee acknowledges receipt, in good condition, the items listed, and agrees to pay for all loss or damage other than normal wear and tear.

NUMBER	FURNISHINGS	DESCRIPTION
_____	Beds	_____
_____	Carpet	_____
_____	Chairs	_____
_____	Coffee Table	_____
_____	Desk	_____
_____	Dresser	_____
_____	Dresser Bench	_____
_____	End Tables	_____
_____	Lamps	_____
_____	Mattress	_____
_____	Mirror	_____
_____	Pictures	_____
_____	Pillows	_____
_____	Draperies	_____
_____	Other	_____

30-DAY NOTICE TO TERMINATE TENANCY

To: _____ ,Tenant

Name: _____

Address: _____

NOTICE is given that the tenancy under which you occupy the above referenced premises is hereby terminated thirty (30) days from the date of service of this notice upon you. You must vacate the premises on or before the date of termination and must deliver rent for the premises through and including that date.

Dated this _____ day of _____ 19 _____

Owner: _____

By _____

CERTIFICATE OF SERVICE

I, _____ , being at least eighteen (18) years of age, certify under penalty of perjury that I served the THIRTY-DAY NOTICE TO TERMINATE TENANCY, on the above named tenant in following manner:

> (a) I personally delivered a copy of the notice to the tenant. _____

> (b) I mailed a true and correct copy to tenant, by certified mail, to the address indicated above. _____

> Executed on the _____ day of _____ , 19 _____

> Signed _____

_____

_____

_____

A REMINDER . . .

Your rent has not been received and is now
past due. Your immediate payment will
be appreciated. Thank you.

TOTAL NOW DUE	$
Date of This Notice	

3.13. FORMS FOR PURCHASING SERVICES AND GOODS

3.13.1. Work Orders

This work order doubles as a request for a quote. It can be used by an independent contractor or it can be given to an independent contractor in order to aid in bid evaluation by making bids uniform. This form is printed on page 316.

3.13.2. Change Work Orders

Nothing gives rise to more contractor disputes than misunderstandings over changes in original agreements and original work orders. Resist the temptation to issue or accept verbal or informal change orders. Specify changes in writing and obtain all necessary signatures. The first form on page 317 is primarily for changing work; the second form is for additional work (page 318).

3.13.3. Purchase and Production Orders

At minimum, purchase and production orders should include billing and shipping instruction and should specify merchandise ordered, quantity ordered, and amount to be paid. A variety of forms follow on pages 319–323.

Work Order/Request for Quote

Overview: _____

Customer Name: _____

Customer Address: _____

**Contact
Person:** _____

Phone Number: _____

Project Description: _____
_____
_____

Specific Instructions: _____

Materials and Quantities to be Used:

_____
_____
_____
_____

Additional Outside Services Required:

_____
_____
_____
_____

Comments:

_____
_____
_____
_____
_____

Sample of Design or Sketch of Design:

Pricing: _____
_____
_____
_____
_____

Submitted by: _____   **Date:** _____

CHANGE ORDER

Number _____

PHONE	DATE
JOB NAME	
JOB LOCATION	
JOB NUMBER	JOB PHONE
EXISTING CONTRACT NO.	DATE OF EXISTING CONTRACT

To _____

_____

_____

We hereby agree to make the change(s) specified below:

NOTE: This Change Order becomes part of and in conformance with the existing contract.

WE AGREE hereby to make the change(s) specified above at this price	$	
DATE	PREVIOUS CONTRACT AMOUNT	$
AUTHORIZED SIGNATURE (CONTRACTOR)	REVISED CONTRACT TOTAL	$

ACCEPTED- The above prices and specifications of this Change Order are satisfactory and are hereby accepted. All work to be performed under same terms and conditions as specified in original contract unless otherwise stipulated.

DATE OF ACCEPTANCE

SIGNATURE (OWNER)

CONTRACT CHANGE ORDER

PROJECT:

_____
(Name)

_____
(Address)

_____
(City, State, Zip)

_____
(Phone)   (Fax)

TO CONTRACTOR:

_____
(Name)

_____
(Address)

_____
(City, State, Zip)

_____
(Phone)   (Fax)

The contract is hereby modified and amended as follows:

_____

_____

_____

_____

_____

_____

_____

_____

_____

_____

_____

_____

_____

_____

_____

_____

_____

_____

_____

_____

_____

_____

_____

_____

_____

_____

It is mutually agreed that the contract price is increased/decreased by: _____
payable/deductible immediately upon completion of the work called for in this order.

As a result of this change order, the time for completion of the above-mentioned contract is hereby extended by an additional _____ days.

This change order is incorporated into and governed by the above mentioned contract and is incorporated therein.

_____   _____
(Contractor/Owner)   (Owner/Contractor)

ORDER FORM

SALESPERSON		ORDER NO.
FILLED BY		REQUISITION NO.
CHECKED BY		DEPARTMENT
DATE SHIPPED		TIME TAKEN	SHIP WHEN
DATE BILLED		TERMS

DATE _____

SOLD TO _____

ADDRESS _____

SHIP _____

VIA _____

✓	QUANTITY	DESCRIPTION	AMOUNT

Order Card

Please send me:

Quantity	Description	Unit Price	Extended
_____	_____	_____	_____
_____	_____	_____	_____
_____	_____	_____	_____
_____	_____	_____	_____

☐ Payment Enclosed   ☐ Bill Me   Total $ _____

Name _____   Phone _____

Address _____

City _____ State _____ Zip Code _____

Order Card

Please send me:

Quantity	Description	Unit Price	Extended
_____	_____	_____	_____
_____	_____	_____	_____
_____	_____	_____	_____
_____	_____	_____	_____

☐ Payment Enclosed   ☐ Bill Me   Total $ _____

Name _____   Phone _____

Address _____

City _____ State _____ Zip Code _____

Order Card

Please send me:

Quantity	Description	Unit Price	Extended
_____	_____	_____	_____
_____	_____	_____	_____
_____	_____	_____	_____
_____	_____	_____	_____

☐ Payment Enclosed   ☐ Bill Me   Total $ _____

Name _____   Phone _____

Address _____

City _____ State _____ Zip Code _____

PURCHASE ORDER

THIS NUMBER MUST APPEAR ON INVOICE, B/L, BUNDLES, CASES, PACKING LISTS AND CORRESPONDENCE.

SHIP TO

DATE OF ORDER	DATE WANTED	TERMS	F.O.B.	SHIP VIA	

QUANTITY	DESCRIPTION	PRICE	AMOUNT
		Total	

AUTHORIZED SIGNATURE

Production Order

Sales Order #_____ Customer ID _____ Production Order # _____

Description of Finished Product:_____

_____

_____

_____

Inventory:_____

_____

_____

Required Parts & Materials	Product ID #	On Hand	Out of Stock	Lead Time

Scheduled Completion Date: _____ Actual Date: _____

Scheduled Shipping Date: _____ Actual Date: _____

Signed By: _____ Date: _____

PRODUCTION ORDER

TO

FOR

DEPT.

DELIVER TO

SHIP VIA:

OUR NO.

DATE

CUST. NO.

DELIVERY WANTED

QUANTITY WANTED	DESCRIPTION	QUANTITY COMPLETED

PACKING INSTRUCTIONS

DATE COMPLETED

DATE BILLED

BALANCE ON BACK ORDER

No. Date

REMARKS

PRODUCTION AUTHORIZED

BY

3.13.4. Vendor Evaluation and Screening Form

Developing a dependable stable of suppliers is key to serving your own customers successfully. It pays to evaluate and screen potential vendors before entering into commitments with them. The following form suggests the areas of most concern in the evaluation:

Vendor Information Screen

Name of Firm _____ Phone _____

Address _____

_____

_____

Headquarters Office _____

☐ Corporation ☐ Partnership ☐ Individual ☐ Other

Date Business Started _____

Location _____

President _____

Other Officers: _____ _____

_____ _____

_____ _____

_____ _____

Has this company provided products or services to our company   ☐ Yes   ☐ No

If so, when and what type? _____

Current clients with approximate purchase value:

_____ _____

_____ _____

_____ _____

Trade References: _____ _____
Name,   _____ _____
Phone   _____ _____

Bank References: _____ _____
Name,   _____ _____
Branch
Phone   _____ _____

Completed by: _____ Date: _____

Approved by: _____ Date: _____

3.13.5. Receipt for Goods

Creating a paper trail for goods received will forestall any number of disputes. The receipt form should allow space for comments on condition of the goods received. See form below and those on pages 326 and 327.

In an office or plant where numerous shipments are received daily, an accurate log of goods received is essential. A sample form is printed on page 328.

RECEIVING REPORT

Received ☐   Date ————————— 19 ——
Shipped To ☐   _____

Shipped From _____ Weight _____
Delivered By

FREIGHT		EXPRESS		PARCEL POST		DELIVERED		PICK UP	CHARGE PAID	
CHARGE COLLECT AMOUNT			FOR DEPARTMENT				FREIGHT BILL NO.			
PURCHASE ORDER NO.			PARTIAL		COMPLETE		DATE OF INVOICE			
QTY. ORD.	QTY. BK. ORD.	QTY. SHIPPED	DESCRIPTION OF MATERIALS							

Condition or Remarks:

RECEIVING CLERK

DELIVERY RECEIPT

Received ☐   Date_____ 19 _____
Shipped To ☐ _____

Shipped From _____ Weight _____
Delivered By

FREIGHT		EXPRESS		PARCEL POST		DELIVERED		PICK UP		CHARGES PAID	
CHARGES COLLECT AMOUNT				FOR DEPARTMENT				FREIGHT BILL NO.			
PURCHASE ORDER NO.			PARTIAL POST			COMPLETE			DATE OF INVOICE		

QTY. ORD.	QTY. BK. ORD.	QTY. SHIPPED	DESCRIPTION OF MATERIALS

Condition or Remarks:

RECEIVING CLERK

DELIVERY RECEIPT

VIA

DATE	YOUR NO.	OUR NO.

DELIVERED TO.

✔	QUANTITY	NO.	DESCRIPTION
	NO. PACKAGES	WEIGHT	
			RECEIVED IN GOOD ORDER BY
			X

MAKE REPORT IN DUPLICATE
RETAIN ONE FOR REFERENCE

DAILY REPORT OF GOODS RECEIVED

RECEIVING CLERK ____________________ DATE ____________________ SHEET NO. __________

RECEIVED FROM	VIA	NO. PKGS	WEIGHT	QUANTITY	DESCRIPTION OF GOODS	P.O. OR REQ. NO.	CHARGES PAID		DELIVERED TO

REMARKS ____________________

____

3.13.6.   Rejection of Goods

Goods rejected or returned should be accompanied by a clear explanation of the reason for return. Goods returned should be carefully itemized and described, with particular emphasis on their condition:

RETURNED GOODS REPORT

Date_____

Received From_____

Address_____

Via ☐   ☐ Parcel   ☐ _____

Reason Returned: _____

DESCRIPTION			
No.	Quantity	ITEM	Condition

Credit To_____

Remarks_____

_____

Received By: _____ Date _____

3.14. Forms for Selling and Delivering Services and Goods

3.14.1. Quotations

In addition to the forms included in Chapter 3.11, the quotation form on page 331 is useful for making bids and supplying estimates.

The specifics of a bid can be supplied on a backup form. A sample form is printed on page 332.

All oral bids should be memorialized as soon as possible in a written follow-up. A sample form is printed on page 333.

The kind of invoices and order forms offered in Chapter 3.13 can be applied equally to selling as to purchasing goods.

3.14.2. Adjustments

It is important to acknowledge complaints and requests for adjustments as quickly as possible. A form like the one on page 334 will save time.

All too often, a customer will issue short payment for goods or services received without bothering to specify the reason for the short payment. Instead of demanding payment in full, it is a good customer-relations practice to alert the customer to the short pay and to inquire about the reason for it. A sample form is printed on page 335.

All returned goods should be acknowledged and credited appropriately. A sample form is printed on page 336.

QUOTATION

SUBMITTED TO	PHONE	DATE
ADDRESS	DESCRIPTION	
TO BE COMPLETED /		

WE HEREBY SUBMIT OUR QUOTATION, SUBJECT TO ALL TERMS AND CONDITIONS AS SET FORTH BELOW :

LABOR / MATERIALS	TAXABLE	NON-TAXABLE

This quotation may be withdrawn by us if order is not placed within _____ days. Please refer to above Quotation Number when placing order.	SUBTOTALS	
	TAX @ _____	
Authorized Signature	TOTAL TAXABLE ➜	
	TOTAL	

CONTRACTOR'S ESTIMATE DETAIL

DATE	
Est.#:	

(Contractor's Name)	(Owner's Name)
(Contractor's License Number)	(Job Adress)
(Contractor's Address)	(City, State, Zip)
(City, State, Zip)	(Lot) (Block) (Tract)
(Telephone - FAX)	(Telephone - FAX)

DESCRIPTION	EQUIP.	UNIT COST OR MATERIAL PRICE			LABOR PRICE		
	Equipment Cost	Unit	Unit Price	Total Material	Hours	Rate	Total Labor

TOTAL MATERIAL	TOTAL MANHOUR	TOTAL LABOR	TOTAL EQUIP.	GRAND TOTAL

BID CONFIRMATION

FROM: _____
(Name)

_____
(Address)

_____
(City, State, Zip)

_____
(Telephone)

FROM: _____
(Name)

_____
(Address)

_____
(City, State, Zip)

TO: _____
(Name)

_____
(Address)

_____
(City, State, Zip)

This is a written confirmation of the oral bid of _____ . The bid price is $ _____
(Date of bid)

The bid INCLUDES the following: _____

_____

_____

_____

_____

_____

The bid specifically EXCLUDES: _____

_____

_____

_____

_____

If there is any misunderstanding as to the content, terms or conditions of the bid, please contact the undersigned

Date: _____
(Date Confirmation Signed)

FIRM NAME: _____

BY: _____
(Signature of Person Sending Confirmation)

Response to Request for Adjustment of Account

Date: _____

From: _____

_____

_____

_____

To: _____

_____

_____

Dear Customer,

Thank you for writing us regarding your account.

We have received your request and are researching your account and its history. We should complete our research soon and may make any necessary adjustments on your next statement.

Yours truly,

Sincerely,

Reason for Customer Short Pay

Date: _____

From: _____   **To:** _____
_____   _____
_____   _____
_____   _____

Dear Customer,

We recently received payment from you for our invoice # _____
Thank you. However we were unable to determine why there was a short pay. Below please tell us the reason for the short pay so that we may review our records and determine if the short pay is acceptable.

Sincerely, _____

Accounting Department

Amount of short-paid _____   **Reference #** _____

Customer Reply Form Below

From: _____

Reason for short-paid: _____
_____
_____

Check Payment $ _____   **Check #** _____

VISA Account # _____   **Mastercard #** _____

CREDIT MEMO

DATE	REFERENCE NO.
OUR ORDER NO.	YOUR ORDER NO.

TO:

SHIPPED TO:

SALESPERSON	TERMS	DATE RETURNED	RETURNED VIA	F.O.B.		P.P.D. COL.
QUANITY	DESCRIPTION			PRICE	AMOUNT	

WE CREDIT YOUR
ACCOUNT AS SHOWN

AUTHORIZED SIGNATURE

3.14.3. Invoice and Statement Forms

All deliveries and sales should be accompanied by an invoice or a statement. Here is a variety of forms:

Customer Invoice

From:_____   Invoice # _____

Address: _____   Invoice Date: _____

                                          Phone: _____

To: _____   Ship To: _____

Address _____   Address_____

_____   _____

Phone: _____   Phone:_____

Quantity	Unit	Item #	Price	Discount	Extended Price
_____	____	_____	____	_____	_____
_____	____	_____	____	_____	_____
_____	____	_____	____	_____	_____
_____	____	_____	____	_____	_____
_____	____	_____	____	_____	_____
_____	____	_____	____	_____	_____
_____	____	_____	____	_____	_____
_____	____	_____	____	_____	_____
_____	____	_____	____	_____	_____
_____	____	_____	____	_____	_____
_____	____	_____	____	_____	_____
_____	____	_____	____	_____	_____
_____	____	_____	____	_____	_____
_____	____	_____	____	_____	_____
_____	____	_____	____	_____	_____
_____	____	_____	____	_____	_____
_____	____	_____	____	_____	_____
_____	____	_____	____	_____	_____
_____	____	_____	____	_____	_____
_____	____	_____	____	_____	_____

Taxable Sale: _____

Nontaxable Sale: _____

Total Sale: _____

Sales Tax: _____

Balance Due: _____

Thank you for your order!:

JOB INVOICE

BILL TO		PHONE	
ADDRESS		CUSTOMER ORDER NO.	
CITY		ORDER TAKEN BY	
JOB NAME AND LOCATION		DATE ORDERED	
DESCRIPTION OF WORK		DATE PROMISED	☐ A.M. ☐ P.M.
		☐ DAY WORK ☐ CONTRACT ☐ EXTRA	

QUAN.	DESCRIPTION OF MATERIAL USED	PRICE	AMOUNT

HOURS	LABOR	AMOUNT	TOTAL MATERIALS	
	@		TOTAL LABOR	
	@			
	@			
	@		SUB TOTAL	
I hereby acknowledge the satisfactory completion of the above described work.	TOTAL LABOR		TAX	
SIGNATURE	DATE COMPLETED		**TOTAL**	

INVOICE

INVOICE DATE	
OUR ORDER NO.	
YOUR ORDER NO.	
TERMS	F.O.B.
SALESPERSON	
SHIPPED VIA	

TO

PPD. OR COLL.

QUANTITY	DESCRIPTION	PRICE	AMOUNT

Invoice

Invoice Date	
Invoice Number	

Company Name	**Phone**
Address Line 1	**PO #**
Address Line 2	**Order Date**
City/State	**Ordered by:**
Zip Code	**Terms**

Part #	Description	Qty	Price	Total

Thank You!
We appreciate your business.

Subtotal	
Tax Rate	
Tax	
Shipping	
Total Due	

Invoice

Invoice Number:
Date:

<Organization>
<Address>
<City, State, Zip>
<Telephone>
Fax <Fax>

To:

Ship to (if different address):

SALESPERSON	ORDER NO.	DATE SHIPPED	SHIPPED VIA	F.O.B.	TERMS

QTY.	DESCRIPTION	UNIT PRICE	TOTAL
			0.00
			0.00
			0.00
			0.00
			0.00
			0.00
			0.00
		SUBTOTAL	0.00
		SALES TAX RATE %	
		SALES TAX	0.00
		SHIPPING & HANDLING	
		TOTAL DUE	$0.00

THANK YOU FOR YOUR ORDER!

STATEMENT

DETACH AND RETURN THIS STUB WITH YOUR REMITTANCE

DATE	AMOUNT

DATE	REFERENCE	CHARGES	CREDITS	BALANCE

YOUR CHECK IS YOUR RECEIPT ● PAY LAST AMOUNT SHOWN

3.14.4. Customer Update

Customer relations are strengthened in proportion to the accuracy and frequency of communication with the customer. Be prepared to initiate updates on orders:

NOTE

From:

To:

Date:

Dear Customer,

Here's a quick note to let you know about:

Our Order Number:

Your Order Number:

Your P.O. Number:

Job Number:

REMARKS:

3.14.5.   Receipt for Payment

Casual exchanges of cash for goods can be acknowledged with a simple receipt:

DATE _____ 19 ____

RECEIVED
FROM   _____

_____ DOLLARS $_____

FOR _____

AMOUNT OF ACCOUNT		
THIS PAYMENT		
BALANCE DUE		

CASH ☐
CHECK ☐
MONEY OR. ☐
CRED. CD. ☐   BY _____

Thank you

DATE _____ 19 ____

RECEIVED
FROM   _____

_____ DOLLARS $_____

FOR _____

AMOUNT OF ACCOUNT		
THIS PAYMENT		
BALANCE DUE		

CASH ☐
CHECK ☐
MONEY OR. ☐
CRED. CD. ☐   BY _____

Thank you

DATE _____ 19 ____

RECEIVED
FROM   _____

_____ DOLLARS $_____

FOR _____

AMOUNT OF ACCOUNT		
THIS PAYMENT		
BALANCE DUE		

CASH ☐
CHECK ☐
MONEY OR. ☐
CRED. CD. ☐   BY _____

Thank you

3.14.6. Shipping Forms

A shipping order should include precise shipping instructions and should itemize the goods shipped. A sample form is shown below.

If your business ships numerous quantities of goods daily, a shipping log is essential. See a sample form on page 346.

SHIPPING ORDER

DATE	
CUSTOMER ORDER NO.	

TERMS	F.O.B.
SALESPERSON	
SHIP WHEN	
SHIP VIA	
PPD. OR COLL.	

S
H
I
P

T
o

L TO

QUANTITY	DESCRIPTION	PRICE	AMOUNT

DAILY REPORT OF SHIPMENTS

SHEET _____

DATE _____

SHIPPING CLERK _____

ORDER NO.	CUSTOMER	DESTINATION	SHIPPED VIA	DESCRIPTION OF PACKAGE	FOR OFFICE USE ONLY

3.15. SALES AIDS

3.15.1. Prospect Forms

One of the secrets of sales is cultivating prospects. This should not be a scatter-gun affair, but a careful and systematic process. Carefully track each major sales prospect, recording all information relevant to sales potential. A sample form is printed on page 348.

3.15.2. Sales Call Logs

Part of cultivating prospects and building stronger relations with current customers is tracking sales calls. The forms on pages 349 and 350 facilitate this process.

3.15.3. Product Information Sheet

Another essential sales aid is the product information sheet. This should provide the sales person with information at his fingertips, and it can also be used to answer customers' questions. See sample form on page 351.

3.15.4. Telemarketing Forms

To be most effective, telemarketing should be conducted systematically rather than randomly. Accurate record keeping is, therefore, essential. Sample forms can be found on pages 352 and 353.

3.15.5. Sales Order Form

This form is intended to be filled out by the salesperson, not the customer. A sample form is printed on page 354.

Sales Prospect File

▨ New Prospect ▨ Existing Client   Date _____

Company Name_____

Contact_____

Title _____

Address _____
_____

Phone Number :

Source of Initial Contact

▨ Call-In ▨   Direct Mail ▨ Referral-By   _____

Existing Supplier_____

Approximate Monthly Sales Volume _____

Action Taken to Follow-Up:
_____
_____

Sales Calls History

Comments:
_____
_____
_____
_____
_____
_____
_____
_____
_____
_____
_____

Additional Information:
_____
_____
_____
_____
_____
_____
_____
_____
_____
_____
_____

SALES CALL
FROM

DATE

_____ PROSPECT CUSTOMER

FIRM

ADDRESS

CITY	STATE	ZIP

PARTY SEEN

COMMENT

_____

_____

_____

_____

_____

_____

_____

_____

_____

SEND REPORTS TO OFFICE DAILY

SALES CALL LOG

Number: _____   Date: _____

Company Name: _____

Contact: _____   Phone: _____

Type of Call: ☐ Customer   ☐ Prospect

Comments _____
_____
_____

Purpose of call: _____
_____
_____

Opening Conversation: _____
_____
_____

Sales Story: _____
_____
_____
_____

Benefits to Customers: _____
_____
_____

Objections/Resistance Response: _____
_____
_____
_____

Closing Conversation: _____
_____
_____
_____

When to Follow Up: _____
_____

PRODUCT INFORMATION

Reviewed by: _____   **Date:** _____

Product: _____

Brand Name: _____

UPC Code or ID #: _____

Suggested Price: _____

Sales Price: _____

Product Description:

Features:

Applications:

Technical Specs.:

Competitors:

Telemarketer's Information Worksheet

Sales Representative _____

Account Number/Prospect _____

Contact _____

Phone (   ) _____

Mailing Address _____

_____

Shipping Address _____

Shipping Instructions _____

_____

Purpose of This Call _____

_____

_____

Last Purchase Date _____

Description _____

Existing Sales Potential _____

_____

Future Sales Potential _____

_____

Referral Potential _____

_____

Comments _____

_____

_____

_____

_____

_____

_____

_____

_____

Next Follow Up _____

_____

Telemarketing Progress Report

For the Period of:_____

	Number of Calls Completed			Number of Orders Placed		
	To Clients	To Prospects	Goal	From Clients	From Prospects	Goal
Monday	_____	_____	_____	_____	_____	_____
Tuesday	_____	_____	_____	_____	_____	_____
Wednesday	_____	_____	_____	_____	_____	_____
Thursday	_____	_____	_____	_____	_____	_____
Friday	_____	_____	_____	_____	_____	_____
Saturday	_____	_____	_____	_____	_____	_____
Sunday	_____	_____	_____	_____	_____	_____
Weekly Total	_____	_____	_____	_____	_____	_____
Last Week	_____	_____	_____	_____	_____	_____

Comments:_____
_____
_____
_____
_____
_____
_____
_____
_____
_____
_____
_____
_____
_____
_____
_____
_____
_____
_____
_____
_____
_____
_____
_____
_____
_____

SALES ORDER FORM   Date: _____

Customer Name: _____

Phone Number: _____ **P.O. Number:** _____

Fax Number: _____ **P.O. Date** _____

Contact: _____ **Ship To:** _____

Address: _____ **Address:** _____

_____ _____

_____ _____

Special Instructions: _____

Item No.	Description	Quantity	Unit Price	Discount %	Extended Price

Gross Total _____

Tax _____

Order Taken By: _____ **Freight** _____

Labor _____

Balance Due _____

3.16. PRESS RELEASE

3.16.1. Press Release Form

Issuing press releases on a standard-looking, but attention-getting form increases the chances of getting your information publicized:

PRESSRELEASE

<Organization> • <Address> • <City, State Zip> • <Telephone> • Fax: <Fax>

For Immediate Release

Date:
Contact: <Name>
Phone: <Telephone>
Fax: <Fax>

[Title of Press Release]

[City and State of Origin]—

Part Four

---❖---

FAX AND E-MAIL

4.1. OBJECTIVES AND STRATEGIES

4.1.1. How to Keep from Drowning in a Sea of Information

Not very long ago, the world of business was sharply divided between those who had direct access to information and those who had just second hand access. The former was management, the latter labor. Today, virtually everyone has direct access to critical information—oceans of it. The personal computer and modem, linked to such online information services as CompuServe™, America Online™, Genie™, Microsoft Network™, Prodigy™, and the like, as well as the vast network of networks known as the Internet, has dramatically leveled the playing field. Today, labor and management are not defined by who has the keys to the vital information. In fact, information floods us, so that the very overabundance of data threatens to become overwhelming. Nowadays, the difference between the leaders and followers is not access to information, but the ability to stay afloat in a sea of data by knowing what information to gather, cultivate, attend to, and act upon—and what information to let drift on by.

As a user of fax and e-mail, you must recognize that you are casting your vessels of data on this great sea. It is no longer sufficient to supply information. You must be savvy enough to do so in a way that commands attention, that distinguishes your messages from the rest.

4.2. NUTS AND BOLTS

4.2.1. Just the Fax

A remarkably short time ago, sophisticated offices owned telex machines. They were arcane devices, usually secluded in a small room of their own: the Telex Room. They cost a pretty penny, and you needed a special cable connection. Telex was out of reach for many businesses. Being able to put a telex number on your corporate stationery was quite impressive.

It's hard to find an office with a telex machine these days. They've been replaced by a much more flexible device—the fax machine—which is within the financial reach of everyone, businesses and individuals included. You can, if you wish, dedicate a little room to the fax machine. But, then, you can also put it on your kitchen table and work from home.

The fax machine is a tremendous convenience. Much correspondence can now be sent via fax rather than mail. It is a boon to businesses of all sizes. How can there be a downside to something like this?

Well, there is.

The fax machine shares the same downside common to all forms of electronic communication. It's just so easy. Mountains of faxes are spit out by the machines in many offices, making it difficult, sometimes, to get the attention your message requires. Here are some basics:

1. *Invest in a dedicated fax line.* This is not an issue for larger businesses with even modestly deep pockets, but for individuals and some freelancers, a separate fax line may represent a substantial investment. If you cannot afford a dedicated line, you should purchase one of the many "voice-data switches" available on the market. These devices allow you to plug in your voice phone and fax machine (and, often, a computer modem as well) into a single service wall jack. The device recognizes whether an incoming call is a voice call, a fax call, or a computer data call, and it accordingly dispatches the call to your phone, fax, or computer.

PITFALL: The voice-data switch is not perfect. Some older fax machines do not generate the tone ("CNG") required to alert the voice-data switch to route the call to the fax machine. Call-waiting service also plays tricks on voice-data switches, causing them sometimes to transfer voice calls to your fax machine. However, even with its minor flaws, the voice-data switch is far preferable to requiring clients and customers to phone you in advance of sending a fax, so that you can unplug the phone and switch to the fax.

2. *Know how to use the "fax header" feature of your fax machine.* On most machines, this feature can be customized. The fax header, printed at the top of each page your fax machine transmits, functions as a kind of return address, telling the recipient who sent the fax and furnishing such information as your name, your fax number, and your voice number. You might even find that you have room for a friendly message: "Greetings from Joe Blow! Fax: 555-555-5555 Voice: 555-444-4444."

3. *Know what and when to fax.* The fax machine is a powerful communications tool, which provides some of the benefits of a phone call and some of the benefits of a letter. Like any powerful tool, however, the fax can be abused and should be used responsibly.

   a. To the extent that it is possible, keep your messages brief—a single page, preceded by a separate cover sheet. This will avoid tying up a client or customer's fax line.

   b. Avoid sending "junk mail" via fax. A few years ago, when fax machines were first really beginning to proliferate, many businesses saw the machine as an advertising tool and transmitted loads of unsolicited matter. The FCC acted to curb such transmissions—but, really, no law was necessary, because the general ill will generated by fax junk mail soon sent its own message: *Tie up our fax line with garbage, and we will not give you our business—ever.*

TIP: Not all unsolicited faxes are taboo, of course, anymore than unsolicited phone calls. You might announce a new product or service via fax rather than a call to a customer. However, avoid blanketing the business community with electronic "flyers." Also, do not send dozens of pages unsolicited. Provide just enough information to invite interest and inquiry.

4.2.2. Getting the Message into the Right Hands

In most larger offices, fax machines are rather like the hall phone in an old-fashioned boarding house. They are shared resources, usually placed in a more-or-less "public" area. You need to insure that your fax reaches the intended recipient. Hence the cover sheet.

> **PITFALL:** Because fax machines are usually shared, never send confidential or sensitive material by fax without making a confirming voice call first. Get your recipient's permission to send the fax, and alert him to its arrival—just before you transmit.

The cover sheet functions as a shipping and routing label, as well as a kind of manifest. It should include the recipient's name and the name of his/her company, as well as the recipient's fax number. It should also include your own name and company name, as well as your address, fax, and voice phone numbers. Finally, be certain to include the number of pages included in the transmission. Make it clear whether the total listed on the cover sheet does or does not include the cover sheet.

> **TIP:** Why include the *recipient's* fax number on the cover sheet? Have you ever reached a wrong number because you've misdialed the phone? Well, the same can and does happen with fax transmissions. Much of the time, the wrong number will not reach a fax machine—so you will be instantly alerted to the fact that you have misdialed. But, sometimes, the transmission will go out. If you've included the recipient's fax number on the cover sheet, some good Samaritan may be moved to forward the message for you. You may want to include a line on your cover sheet to this effect: "IF THIS FAX REACHES YOU IN ERROR, PLEASE FORWARD IT TO THE NUMBER ABOVE OR CONTACT SENDER. WE APPRECIATE IT!"

Confidentiality Statement

You may want to include a confidentiality statement on your cover sheet. This asserts to any and all who may see your fax message that it is private and confidential, and that, even though you have, in effect, "published" the material electronically by faxing it, you do not intend to make the material public and you do not give permission to do so. The confidentiality statement asserts your ownership of and right to the material. A simple statement such as the following is quite sufficient: "THIS FAX MESSAGE CONTAINS PROPRIETARY

INFORMATION INTENDED FOR THE ADDRESSEE ONLY. IT MUST NOT BE USED FOR ANY OTHER PURPOSE. IF THIS MESSAGE REACHES YOU IN ERROR, PLEASE CONTACT SENDER IMMEDIATELY."

Advertising

Cover sheets are necessary utilitarian items, but they also provide an opportunity for promoting your company's products and services—or, at least, promoting the firm's image. This and other cover sheet issues are treated in 4.4. Fax Cover Sheets.

4.2.3. To Type or Write by Hand?

One of the wonderful things about fax communications is that you are not limited to the transmission of typed text. You can transmit just about any image, including the image of your own handwriting. But is it proper to send handwritten notes in lieu of typed correspondence?

Like so many other issues, it all depends . . .

1. In general, use typewritten (or word-processed) notes.

2. Handwritten notes are acceptable for messages sent to close associates or clients with whom you have an established relationship.

3. Restrict handwritten notes to very brief messages.

4. If your handwriting is poor, avoid handwritten notes.

5. Avoid colored ink.

> TIP: Handwriting can be an asset, adding a personal touch to very brief correspondence. Handwriting can also be used to emphasize important points in an otherwise typewritten fax message.

4.2.4. Technical Limitations of Fax Machines: A Quick Guide

Marvelous as they are, fax machines do have limitations.

1. Most fax machines are sheet fed, which means that if you want to transmit something from a bound book, you will need to photocopy the book page before transmitting it.

2. Because fax machines use analog telephone lines to transmit a digitized image, the image suffers a considerable degree of degradation. Accordingly:

 a. Start with the highest-quality original as possible. Letters printed on a high-quality laser printer transmit very well.

 b. Avoid colored inks.

 c. Line drawings will transmit better than photographs or "halftone" illustrations.

Pitfall: Never try to feed a photograph directly through your fax machine! Make a photocopy first.

Improving Fax Performance

In addition to transmitting high-contrast, high-quality originals, you can also improve fax performance by purchasing the best machine you can and using its "high-resolution" mode. This will make transmission slower, but it will improve the quality of the image.

There is yet another alternative that is becoming increasingly popular.

The fax machine is an example of how the electronic revolution has failed to bring about the so-called "paperless office" that so many pundits have predicted. If anything, this electronic device has served to increase the use of paper in business. However, it is quite possible to send faxes without using paper. These days, most modems used with IBM-compatible PC and Apple Macintosh-compatible machines have fax capability (they are called fax modems). With a fax modem and the appropriate software, you can create and transmit faxes directly from your computer. The advantages of this, in addition to saving paper, include speed and efficiency—you don't have to print out and then transmit the document—and, more importantly, quality. Since the document is transmitted digitally, without any optical intervention, the received image will be considerably sharper. This will impress your clients.

By themselves, a fax modem and computer are not full substitutes for a standalone fax machine. While it easy to generate documents on your computer, then transmit them—usually, this is no more difficult than issuing a "print" command, which "prints" to the fax modem rather than to a printer—you cannot transmit hard copy. However, add a scanner to your computer and fax modem, and you will have the capability of scanning hard copy, which you can them transmit.

TIP: A growing segment of the office-machine industry is the development of so-called "hydra" devices. The Hydra, fans of Greek mythology will remember, was a mythical creature with many heads. The latest generation of office machines features devices that combine the technologically related functions of copier, fax, scanner, and laser printer in a single device. Often, hydras can be used in conjunction with your personal computer. They are an interesting option, especially for small businesses.

4.2.5. The Basics of E-Mail Communication

Many corporations routinely use e-mail—electronic mail—to communicate both within the company and to other users of e-mail outside the company. If your desktop computer is hooked up to a corporate network, you almost certainly have the ability to send and receive e-mail messages. The next section, 4.3. A Matter of Style, includes a complete discussion of how to use e-mail effectively.

You don't need to be part of a corporate giant to take advantage of e-mail. All you need is a computer, modem, telephone line, and two e-mail addresses: your own and that of your correspondent. You can obtain an electronic mailbox (and address) by subscribing to any of the commercial online services, such as CompuServe™, America Online™, Prodigy™, Genie™, Microsoft Network™, and so on. An e-mail address will be assigned to you. The wonderful part is that you are not limited to corresponding with others who happen to use the same commercial provider as you do. A CompuServe user can communicate with an America Online customer and vice versa. Through commercial providers, you can also reach out to anyone who has an e-mail address on the vast network of networks known as the Internet. If, instead of using a commercial service, you subscribe directly to the Internet via a SLIP/PPP connection, you will be able to establish a so-called "domain name" address, the functional equivalent of an e-mail address. Consult any of the large number of books devoted to the Internet. Some of the most useful are listed in Appendix A.

There is no great trick to sending "straight" text messages back and forth via e-mail. Just observe the following rules of thumb:

1. Use ASCII text only: the plain, non-document text, that is free from word-processing formatting codes. ASCII text is the closest thing to a universal language for computers. Using it will enable anyone with any

kind of software to read your message. Note that, in ASCII, you won't be able to use underlining, boldface, or italics. Substitute paired asterisks (*like this*) to indicate italics, and use a lowercase "o" (letter, not numeral) wherever a graphic "bullet" is called for.

2. Set your margins at 0 for the left-hand and 65 for the right. Your monitor may display 80 characters across the screen, and your printer is most likely set to print 80 characters across the width of the paper. But your intended recipient may have set up his equipment differently. A 0 and 65 setting will ensure that none of your lines will be cut off.

4.3. A MATTER OF STYLE

4.3.1. Phone, Letter, or Fax? A Guide to Choosing

The fax machine has made at least one aspect of business life so easy that there is a danger of overusing fax communication.

1. We are often tempted to use it as a substitute for a telephone call—especially when we have less-than-pleasant information to convey.

2. We are often tempted to use it as a substitute for a formal letter, because it is easier to slip a sheet of paper into a machine than it is to address, stamp, and mail a letter.

Use the Telephone

1. Whenever dialogue or discussion is called for

2. Whenever you feel the need to use your voice as part of the message

3. To make the communication as personal as possible without actually meeting face-to-face.

Send a Letter

1. For formal communication and notification

2. For any communication that requires full documentation

3. For communication you want to include your original signature

4. For communication with a personal touch. In these days of fax machines and voice mail, a letter is perceived as something special—evidence that you have taken a little extra time to devote to the correspondent.

5. For relatively non-urgent communication

6. For cover letters to accompany documents, shipments of merchandise, and so forth.

PITFALL: Overnight Overkill—Many of us reflexively reach for the courier envelope rather than use "old-fashioned" first-class mail. Sending correspondence by overnight courier used to be a fairly big deal. Much more expensive than first-class mail, it demonstrated how highly you valued the correspondence and the correspondent. The semi-hysterical markings of the envelope—URGENT! DELIVER IMMEDIATELY! or even EXTREMELY URGENT!—have lost their zing through inflation and overload. Save money by sending only the most critical documents by overnight courier. Your neatly addressed first-class envelope will receive attention, too.

Send a Fax:

1. For routine communication—especially when you can't afford to play telephone tag

2. To convey information quickly—especially information too complex to be digested in a telephone conversation

3. For graphical material—drawings, diagrams, plans, and so forth

4. For draft documents being circulated for comment.

4.3.2. E-Mail—Telegraphic or Conversational? Rules of Style

In many offices, e-mail has replaced paper for routine memos, and it has also taken the place of phone calls and even a stroll down the hall to a colleague's office. Traveling at the speed of light (with some time out for switching and processing), an electronic message takes about the same time to reach the office across the corridor as it does to travel to a client halfway around the world. While e-mail novices may at first be put off by the technology, today's e-mail software has made the process very simple, even prompting you to include the DATE, TO, FROM, SUBJECT memo format information on each and every memo. Most software supplies the "date" and "from" automatically, whereas you can't transmit the message without filling in the "to," and if you try to send without supplying a subject, you'll be prodded with an accusatory question: "Do you really want to send this message without a subject?" Not all users have such e-mail software. Some programs are more free-form, inviting you to write messages that resemble letters more than memos. In either case, the nature and ease of e-mail promotes quick notes rather than deliberately thought-out communication. Sometimes this is a positive feature, but it also has its risks. It is one thing to mumble some hasty words over the phone, but another to commit these to print—even electronic print.

Some rules of thumb:

1. E-mail generally gives you more license than paper communication. Informality is expected and tolerated.

2. Spelling and punctuation errors are not cardinal sins in e-mail.

   PITFALL: However, spelling and punctuation errors are venial sins—more or less minor transgressions that, if you are overly careless, can add up to an impression of sloppiness and even cause some folks to question your literacy. Try to pause long enough to review your message before transmitting it.

3. By its nature, e-mail promotes a conversational style of writing.

4. While e-mail tends to be informal, do remember that it is written speech. Your words may be studied and contemplated.

4.3.3. E-Mail "Emoticons": Guide to a New Shorthand

I have said that electronic communication tends to eliminate distance. It hardly matters to a package of electrons whether they travel a few feet or thousands of miles. However, when you send an e-mail memo to your coworker down the hall, there is a very good chance that you will see him or her later in the day. You may chat, gesture, smile, frown—in short, express emotion. This is not the case with a distant colleague or client, whom you may not see for a long time, if ever. Those who regularly communicate via e-mail have developed a handy visual vocabulary for adding emotional expression to their messages, and it is worth knowing about.

The following set of hieroglyphics are called "emoticons"—a word that combines "emotion" with "icons." They are used to express the emotions that are automatically conveyed in voice communication, but that are often lost in the cold phosphorescent print of the monitor's screen. They use nothing more than the ASCII characters found on your keyboard. The only limitation is that emoticons must be viewed at a 90-degree angle—that is, sideways. Simply tilt your head to the side and start reading:

:-)	Humor (smile face)
:-) :-) :-)	Hah, hah, hah!
:/)	Not funny
'-)	Wink

(@ @)	You're kidding!
:-"	Pursed lips
:-V	Shouting
:-W	Sticking tongue out
:-p	Smirking
<:-O	Eeeeeeek!
:-*	Oops! (covering mouth with hand)
:-T	Keeping a straight face
:-D	Said with a smile
=I :-)=	Uncle Sam
:-#	Censored (or Expletive deleted)
:-x	Kiss, kiss
:-(	Unhappy
:-c	Very unhappy
:-<	Desperately unhappy
(:-(	Even sadder
:-C	Jaw dropped in disbelief
:-I	Disgusted
:-?	Licking your lips
:-J	Tongue in cheek remark
:--8	Speaking out of both sides of your mouth
(:-&	Angry
II*(	Handshake offered . . .
II*)	. . . and accepted
(-_-)	Secretly smiling
@%&$%&	Curses!

4.4. FAX COVER SHEETS

4.4.1. Achieving the "Corporate Look"

First, you should be aware that a variety of preprinted cover-sheet forms are available commercially. You might find it worth your while to purchase a set of these, even if only to check out the range of cover-sheet options available to you. Some personal computer fax software also includes digital versions of prepared cover sheets.

Here are some cover sheet examples. The first is generic and basic:

VIA FAX

To: **Name**
Fax: 555-5550
Name of company
Department/floor

From: **Name**
Name of Company
Fax: 555-5510
Voice: 555-4444

NUMBER OF SHEETS (INCLUDING COVER SHEET): _____

Comments: _____

_____

_____

_____

IF THIS FAX REACHES YOU IN ERROR, PLEASE FORWARD IT TO THE NUMBER ABOVE OR CONTACT SENDER. WE APPRECIATE IT!

Using your word-processing software, some commercially available software fonts, and a laser printer, you might create something fancier:

facsimile
TRANSMITTAL

TO: Name
FAX #:   555–555–3333
RE: Subject
DATE: Date
PAGES: Number, including this cover sheet.

COMMENTS: _____

_____

_____

_____

_____

If this fax reaches you in error, please forward it to the number above or contact sender.
We appreciate it!

From the desk of . . .

Name
Title
Company name
Street address
City, State ZIP

555–555–5555
Fax: 555–555–4444

Here is another:

FAX TRANSMISSION

COMPANY NAME
STREET ADDRESS
CITY, STATE ZIP
555-555-5555
FAX: 555-555-4444

To:	Name	**Date:**	December 4, 1996
Fax #:	555-555-4444	**Pages:**	Number, including this cover sheet.
From:	Name		
Subject:	Subject		

COMMENTS:

Creating Special Attention Getters

You could modify any fax with the addition of a corporate logo. You might also add a touch of self-promotion.

A FAX MESSAGE FROM

Cooper Barrel Corporation
Your traditional container specialist

facsimile transmission

from the

Party Store!
Greatest Name in Fun

Using the wide variety of software fonts available, you can create many attention-getting cover sheets. There are few rules—indeed, perhaps only one worth mentioning: The attention-getting look of your cover sheet projects an image. Be sure it's the image you want.

Dewey, Cheatham & Howe
Attorneys at Law

This is almost certainly *not* the kind of attention a law firm wants for their faxes. But *this* may well be:

DEWEY , CHEATHAM & HOWE
Attorneys at Law

This assumes that the attorneys want to project a dignified, yet somewhat contemporary image. If the firm is more conservative, a different treatment is in order:

Dewey, Cheatham & Howe
Attorneys at Law

Another attention getter is to follow the example of the overnight courier services and use such words as "urgent" or "extremely urgent" on your fax cover sheet.

> **PITFALL:** Remember the story of The Boy Who Cried Wolf? Use the "urgent" tactic inappropriately, and you will, by-and-by, find yourself being ignored.

You can also command attention more quietly, by devoting the same care to selecting your fax cover sheet as you do to choosing stationery. Here are two examples.

To: Name
Fax #: 555-555-4444
Re: Subject
Date: Date
Pages: Number, including this cover sheet.

FACSIMILE

From the desk of . . .

Name
Title
Company name
Street address
City, State ZIP

555-555-5555
Fax: 555-555-4444

C O V E R

FAX

S H E E T

To: Name
Fax #:   555-555-4444
Subject: Subject
Date: Date
Pages: Number, including this cover sheet.

COMMENTS:

Fax Cover Sheet Checklist

1. Include address basics: recipient's name, fax number, company name, room, floor, department, and so forth.

2. Include your name, company, fax number, and voice number.

3. Include a notation of subject.

4. Include the number of pages in the fax transmission. Specify whether or not the total includes the cover sheet.

5. Suit the design of the cover sheet to the image you want to convey.

4.5. The Urgent Request

4.5.1. Surefire Strategies for Securing Prompt Action

I have already mentioned the obvious attention-getter: a strong cover sheet with the word "URGENT" or the phrase "EXTREMELY URGENT" boldly emblazoned on it. I've also observed that this straightforward method of commanding attention is subject to a high degree of inflation. Use it with much frequency, and it will lose its punch. Alternative attention-getting words and phrases include:

FOR IMMEDIATE ACTION
CRITICAL DOCUMENTS
PRIORITY INFORMATION
IMPORTANT ADVISORY
INFORMATION YOU REQUESTED
TIME-SENSITIVE DOCUMENTS

Use any of these as cover-sheet headlines.

Under the Cover

Sending faxes that command attention and prompt action means more than coming up with a good cover sheet. *Sell* your fax with a strong hook in the opening sentence.

> **Tip:** A hook is a *hook* because it grabs the reader. How do you grab a reader? Don't talk about yourself. Don't talk about somebody else. Talk about the reader: what he needs and what concerns him.

Here are some effective hooks:

The following will help you.
You need to know . . .
Want to improve performance?
Want to bolster the bottom line?
There is something you should know about.

You've got a problem.

You've done a great job.

Something good is coming your way.

This is a heads up—for you!

I've got the answer you've been waiting for.

Are you forgetting something?

Beginning a fax with a strong hook will command attention. If you are also looking to bring closure—to prompt a particular action—devote careful thought to how you end your fax. Make it a call to a specific action. As in the classic sales letter, try to end by making it easy for the recipient to act. The most straightforward closing simply tells the reader what to do: "Please complete your projections by 4/5." In more complex situations, or in situations with multiple options, effective closing remarks usually have an "if . . . then" structure: "If you want to increase your department's bottom-line numbers, work with me on coordinating our operations."

> **TIP:** Emotion is generally a stronger pull than logic. But the strongest pull of all is emotion combined with logic—and that is the true power of the "if . . . then" appeal. It is a logical structure that also has a kind of primal, childlike, even baby-simple appeal: "If I do this, I get that."

Urgent Fax Checklist

1. Use a good cover sheet.

2. Find a good hook.

3. Try to address the recipient's needs, problems, and goals—not your own.

4.6. PURCHASE ORDER FAX

4.6.1. What You Must Do to Ensure Clarity

Many companies make purchases using standard purchase order forms. A large variety of these are included in 3.13. Forms for Purchasing Goods and Services. Two important points need to be made about transmitting such forms via fax:

1. Avoid multipart forms, which may jam the fax machine.

2. Insure a high degree of legibility in faxed forms.

    a. Don't fax carbons.

    b. Don't scribble.

    c. Avoid colored inks or pencil.

    d. Use forms with bold lines and printing.

TIP: Design or choose your purchase-order forms with fax transmission in mind. Opt for maximum legibility. Remember, returning unwanted items and reordering needed items consumes time and money. Avoid errors.

Consider using the fax cover sheet to add comments aimed at securing prompt and efficient attention for your order, pointing out special needs or requests, or making other comments. For example:

Our purchase order for **quantity items** follows. Please, if you are unable to fill this order as specified, notify me immediately at 555-5555.

Or:

Our P.O. for **quantity items** follows. Our customers depend on us for fast turnaround. Please help us out by expediting this order!

Or:

A priority purchase order follows. It is vital that you meet the shipment deadline of **date**. This merchandise is time critical.

If you don't use prepared forms for purchase orders, provide the following information on your fax:

1. All necessary vendor address/department information

2. Your name, company name, address

3. Voice and fax numbers

4. Your customer number or account number (if you have one)

5. "Bill to" and "Ship to" instructions

6. A clear description of the merchandise, including all product and/or model numbers, quantity, and price quoted or listed.

7. Include any special instructions or comments you may have. These might include requests for expedited handling of the order, etc.

8. Appropriate signature(s).

> **PITFALL:** Beware of transmitting credit card numbers by fax. If you must transmit a credit card number, try to make a voice call in advance to alert the recipient that your fax is coming. In many businesses, the fax machine is in a relatively public area. Your credit card number will be, in effect, on display.

Purchase Order Fax Checklist

1. Design or choose purchase order forms carefully to insure error-free legibility.

2. Use a cover sheet with purchase order forms—especially if you want to include comments with special instructions or to secure prompt shipment.

3. If you don't use a prepared form, make certain that your order provides complete information.

4. Avoid handwritten orders.

PURCHASE ORDER

TO: **Name of vendor**
ATTN: **Name of contact or department**
From: **Name, Company (include phone number)**
Account Number: **number**

This is our Purchase Order for the following merchandise:

Item	*Quantity*	*Price*
1. item	quantity	$ amount
2. item	quantity	$ amount
3.		
4.		

Ship to: **Name, address (repeat account number)**
Bill to: **Name, address**

We're pleased to place this order with you. Please note that our turnaround time on this project is very tight. It is, therefore, critical that you ship this merchandise NO LATER THAN **DATE.** We appreciate your expediting this order.

_____

Authorized signature

4.7. CONFIRMATIONS

4.7.1. Using the Fax to Double Check Orders and Deliveries

The fax machine is an excellent means of confirming orders and deliveries. You don't waste time playing telephone tag, nor do you risk appearing uncertain or insecure by making a telephone call, yet you provide an opportunity confirm instructions and forestall error.

> TIP: Even if you have sufficient lead time between placement of an order and delivery, it is still more effective to send a confirming fax rather than mail a confirming letter. The fax comes across as a heads up, an alert. It calls for response only if there is a problem.

Send the fax in the form of a brief memo. Ask for response only if there is a problem or error:

> DATE:
> TO:
> FROM:
> SUBJECT: Confirmation of shipping instructions
>
> This is to confirm that we will ship **quantity item(s)** to you at **location** on or before **date.** Expect delivery by **time of day.**
>
> If this is correct, there is no need to reply. If there is an error or if you wish to make any change, please call me immediately at 555-555-5555.

Confirmation Checklist

1. Keep it brief and clear.

2. Give the recipient clear instructions about whom to call if there is a problem or if he wishes to make changes in the order, time of shipment, mode of shipment, and so forth.

4.8. STATUS REPORTS

4.8.1. Using the Fax for a Blow-by-Blow

An informal fax is no substitute for full-scale progress or status reports; however, a brief progress advisory is ideally suited to fax transmission:

1. You avoid annoying your client with a phone call.

2. You convey a high level of service and attention.

3. You reduce the possibility of unpleasant surprises—especially if a project has fallen behind schedule.

4. You demonstrate your responsiveness.

5. You provide an opportunity for client response, if necessary.

A progress or status report, even an informal one, should provide specific information. Avoid such generalities as "the project is coming along," or "work is proceeding as expected." Instead, enumerate a specific milestone or milestones, and plot progress in relation to it or them. For example: "Work on the project has entered the second of five phases. We are now beginning construction of the enclosure."

Next, provide a meaningful context for the progress report. This is usually most effectively done by referring to the original schedule and comparing actual progress to it: "We anticipate completion of Phase 2 by **date,** which puts us **number** days behind our target date of **date.**"

If there is a delay, explain it: "Adverse weather caused the delay. Weather permitting, we hope to gain some time during Phase 3."

The fax can be a simple narrative:

Work on the project has entered the second of five phases. We are now beginning construction of the enclosure. We anticipate completion of Phase 2 by **date,** which puts us **number** days behind our target date of **date.** Adverse weather caused the delay. Weather permitting, we hope to gain some time during Phase 3.

Close by inviting response: "If you have any questions or comments, please call me directly at 555-5555."

An alternative to the narrative style is to present a schedule in tabular form:

Phase 1	Excavation		Completed 5/1
Phase 2*	Enclosure construction	Startup 5/2	Completion 6/3
Phase 3	Roofing	Startup 6/5	Completion 6/25
Phase 4	Interior finishing	Startup 6/30	Completion 8/9

* indicates last phase completed

TIP: Keep the status advisory as positive as possible without concealing problems or fabricating information. Put problems in context. Try to include, along with the statement of the problem, a proposed remedy.

PITFALL: Do not use the status advisory as a vehicle for carrying excuses. State any problems straightforwardly, and, instead of making excuses, offer solutions.

Status Fax Checklist

1. Use the fax only for informal progress updates. It is not a substitute for a full-scale progress report.

2. Place the report in context.

3. Do not disguise problems, but try to provide solutions along with them.

4. Invite the recipient to respond.

Part Five

TELEPHONE

5.1. Objectives and Strategy

5.1.1. PTA

"I hate the telephone."

How many times have you heard that—or said it yourself? No business tool is more used, more necessary, and more hated than the telephone. For every positive function it performs, it presents the potential of a pitfall. If the telephone is essential to making contact with customers and clients, it is also too often the means of putting them off and alienating them. If it makes it easier for you to give clients and customers personal service, it is also a way of treating people like so many numbers.

It.

You should not think about *it*—the phone—but about how you and your subordinates and colleagues use the phone. Concentrate on developing PTA—positive telephone attitude. The ingredients are three in number:

1. A desire to communicate

2. A desire to be helpful

3. A belief that customers are not an intrusion into your day, but the very reason for your day—not an interruption of your business, but the very substance of your business.

> **Pitfall:** Avoid the opposite of PTA. Let's call it BTA—bad telephone attitude. This consists of:
>
> 1. A reluctance to communicate
>
> 2. An unwillingness to help
>
> 3. A feeling that customer's calls are interruptions.

5.1.2. Calls You Make vs. Calls You Take

Making calls requires different strategies from taking calls. Chapters 5.2 through 5.11 deal with the CALLS YOU MAKE. Chapters 5.12 through 5.16 are concerend with the CALLS YOU TAKE.

5.2. NUTS AND BOLTS

5.2.1. A Guide to Voice Mail and Answering Machines

We live in a very annoying world. Some days, you can count on the fingers of one hand the number of phone calls you make that are actually answered by a living, breathing human being instead of voice mail or an ACD.

> **DEFINITION:** ACD—an automatic call distributor, a device that automatically routes incoming calls to the appropriate department. A recorded voice presents the caller with a menu of options, which he or she activates by pressing the appropriate button on the Touch-Tone™ pad.

No wonder you may think that the last thing a caller wants to hear when he phones your business is some sort of recorded voice. But that's not quite the case. Actually, the *last* thing your caller wants to hear is a phone ringing without anyone (or any*thing*) picking it up. True, from the caller's perspective, a human voice responding promptly to the call is the best alternative. But if a human voice is not always available, it is far better for a machine to pick up than for the call to go unanswered.

Make the Automated Response as Personal as Possible

For many, perhaps most, businesses an answering device is necessary. But you should avoid thinking of it as a necessary *evil*. It is a tool—and a useful one, if you take steps to raise its use above the usual level. Do the following:

1. *Use one message during business hours and another after hours.* During the business day, use a message that greets the caller with the name of your firm and your name, followed with something like: "I am away from my desk . . ." or "I am helping other customers . . ." Conclude by asking the caller to leave a message. What's important here is to avoid merely *inviting* a message. *Ask* for one: "Please tell me how I may help you. Just leave a message after the tone, and please include your phone number and the best time to call. I will return your call as soon as possible."

Tip: Take a good look at the second-to-last sentence: *Please tell me how I may help you.* The word "how" is critical. Always ask customers *how* you may help them. Never leave it at "May I help you?" The "how" focuses the customer's response, increasing the odds that the customer will get what he wants—*and* saving you time by making it unnecessary to extract a precise response from the customer.

After-hours, your message should include a greeting, followed by a statement of normal business hours. Do not *ask* the customer to call back during those hours, however. Instead, *ask* for a message: "Please leave a message after the tone, and please include your phone number and the best time to call. We *will* return your call."

Tip: Depending on the nature of your business, you may want to make it possible—even easy—for callers to reach you after hours. If you have an after-hours number you can dependably be reached at, or a beeper, or an answering service, your after-hours message should provide the necessary information.

2. *Change your daytime message daily.* Machines make us complacent. Resist this temptation by going the extra mile. Let your callers know that there is a human being behind the machine. Begin your recorded greeting by including today's date: "Hello, this is Joe Blow of Acme Tool and Die. It's Tuesday, June 23rd, and I'm assisting other customers at the moment. Please tell me how I may help you. Leave a message after the tone, including your phone number and the best time to call back. I *will* return your call. Thank you."

Pitfall: This valuable technique fails miserably if you forget to update the message each day, or if you use this message after business hours. Make provisions to change the message if you know that you will be out of the office on a particular day, or if you are going on vacation. The best messaging systems allow you to call in from a remote location and change your message.

3. *Offer an alternative.* If you use an ACD system, it is a good idea to provide a "safety valve," that is, a means by which the caller can speak to someone else if you are presently unavailable. Generally, the message instructs the caller to press "0" on the Touch-Tone™ pad or to remain on

the line until the (human) operator answers. Of course, you may also provide a similar option using a conventional answering machine. For example: "If your call is urgent, please dial Karen Thompson at 555-555-5555. She will assist you." Or even: "If you call is urgent, please indicate this in your message. I monitor my messages frequently and will get back to you as soon as possible."

5.2.2. Screening Your Calls: The *Dos* and *Don'ts*

Most callers resent the feeling that they are being "screened" by an answering machine. If you are running a small business and are, in fact, a one-person band, you may have to screen calls from time to time in order to get any work done. Be aware, however, that this is a dangerous practice. You risk losing new business (What if the call is a sales inquiry?), and you risk alienating callers and customers.

1. If possible, avoid using the answering machine to screen calls.

2. If you must screen calls, consider purchasing Caller ID™ service from your telephone service provider. This service, combined with an inexpensive display device, will show you the telephone number of the incoming call, giving you an opportunity to decide whether or not to take the call. Newer Caller ID™ devices even display the caller's name along with the number.

   > TIP: Some personal computer modems include a Caller ID™ feature. If you own such a modem, you do not have to purchase a separate display device. However, you still must pay the telephone service provider for Caller ID™ service.

3. If you do use the answering machine to screen calls, don't make it obvious by picking up the phone in the middle of the message and blurting out "Sorry! I was screening my calls!" This won't make the caller feel special. It will make him feel that, next time, he may not be so lucky. It will also make him think that you are undependable. Worse, the next time this caller calls, only to be answered by a recording, he will wonder if *he* is now being screened. If you need to seize the receiver in mid message, say something like: "Hi! I just walked into the office!"

5.2.3. How to Use—Not Abuse—Call Waiting

Larger businesses do everything possible to avoid sending a busy signal. Most install a system that routes multiple calls to an answering device, perhaps even one that offers the caller the option of remaining on the line "on hold." If yours is a small business, you may want to consider installing a "call waiting" option. This means that no caller will ever get a busy signal. However, it also means that your current call will be interrupted by a beep or click signaling the presence of another caller. This causes two potential problems:

1. The interruption can be disconcerting if you are in the middle of a sales pitch, sensitive negotiations, or a complicated explanation.

2. Leaving the current caller—even for a moment—to "take another call" may well irritate the current caller by suggesting that her business is less than your principal focus.

3. If you choose not to pick up the "call waiting" call, that caller will hear not a busy signal, but your phone ringing without an answer. He may assume that you're out, lazy, or even out of business.

5.2.4. "Don't Put Me on Hold!"

Well, sometimes you have to. When you are talking to Customer A, and your other line rings, say to Customer A, "Will you hold, please?" Then switch to Customer B. Say: "Good morning. This is Name of Company. Will you hold, please?" and return to Customer A. "Thank you for holding." That's the way it works.

> **TIP:** Take note of the phrase: "Will you hold, please?" It is a request rather than a command. Avoid saying "Please hold," which, despite the "please," is a command. It offers no choice.

To avoid having to interrupt the current call in order to put an incoming call on hold, consider installing an automated response unit (ARU), which will pick up the other line when you are busy. This unit will answer with a message asking the caller to hold.

TIP: What about a system that plays music while the caller is on hold? You will probably hear some complaints about music-on-hold, but it is generally much better than dead silence. Silence creates doubt and anxiety, leaving the caller to wonder if she's been disconnected or forgotten. If you don't want to use music to break the dead silence, consider a device that plays a recorded message at intervals to let the caller know that you are aware of the call and that you are working as fast as you can to help him.

PITFALL: Avoid using recorded messages that say something like "Your call is important to us." Anyone listening to such a message is bound to think, *If my call is so almighty important, why are you putting me on hold?*

"Hold" is not only for taking multiple calls. At times, you will need to put a caller on hold in order to handle the caller's request; for example, you might have to look up a customer record or recover some other item of information. In this case, explain what you need to do and ask permission before you put the caller on hold. Also: give the caller an estimate of how long he will be on hold: "I need to check the service record on this item. May I put you on hold? It will take about one or two minutes."

TIP: If that minute or two starts to stretch, get back to the caller. Advise him: "I need another couple of minutes. Thanks for your patience."

PITFALL: "Hold" means *hold.* It does not mean just laying the receiver down on your desk, so that the customer is assaulted by a cacophony of ambient noise, which might include somebody saying something like: "Why the heck do *I* have to look for those records? He's not my stinking customer!" Make certain that, once you relinquish control of the phone, you silence it with a genuine *hold* button.

5.2.5. Avoiding Telephone Tag

Everyone is familiar with this game—and it's not much fun: You make a call, leaving a message on voice mail; the caller calls you, leaving a message on *your* voice mail; you call back, leaving a message . . . .

Avoid this game by leaving a specific call-back time: "Hi, Mr. Johnson. I want to talk to you about your order. Please call me back between three and five." Whenever possible, leave a call-back time on your voice mail message: "I will be back in the office at three o'clock and can be reached from three to six."

5.2.6. Foolproof Rules for Leaving a Message

Whether you leave a message on a machine or with a person, provide the following information:

1. Your name

2. Your firm

3. The reason for your call

4. Where and when you can be reached—including the *best* time for reaching you

5. The level of urgency, ranging from very urgent down to "get back to me at your convenience."

> **TIP:** When leaving a message on a machine, don't assume that you'll have unlimited time. You may well get cut off without warning. For this reason, give your name *and* telephone number first. Then launch into the substance of the message.

5.2.7. Foolproof Rules for Taking a Message

When you take a message for an absent colleague, be certain to secure the following information—and write it down:

1. Name of caller

2. Caller's company

3. Time and date of the call

4. Phone number

> **TIP:** The caller may respond with, "She knows my number." Don't surrender. "Well, let's be on the safe side just the same." Or: "She's on the road and may not have your number with her."

5. Best time to reach the caller

6. "May I tell So-and-so the subject of your call?"

7. Assure the caller that you *will* deliver the message.

PITFALL: You have no business assuring the caller that the call will be returned "right away"—unless you know for a certainty that it will be. Only make promises for which you can be responsible.

5.2.8. "He's Not Available"

All callers hate voice mail and answering machines some of the time. And some callers hate these devices all of the time. But even the most resentful caller can at least console himself with the crumb of comforting responsiveness afforded by a recorded voice offering to accept, preserve, and transmit his message. Of course, a caller is happiest when he connects—on the first try—with his intended target. Failing this, it is true, most callers prefer to speak to another human being rather than a machine.

Except when that human being is *less helpful* than a machine.

Worst Case

Caller: "Mr. Wright, please."

Blockhead: "He's not available."

Silence.

Well, maybe this isn't the absolute worst case. It *would* be worse if Blockhead simply hung up on the caller without offering any response at all. That, however, would also be antisocial to the point of psychosis, whereas responding with the minimal truth that so-and-so is not available is merely unhelpful in the extreme.

Basic Rules for Taking a Call

◆ Always offer help.

◆ Never force the *caller* to decide on the next step.

A Better Response

Caller: "Mr. Wright, please."

Responsible Answerer: "I'm sorry, he's unavailable just now. May I take a message?"

An Even Better Response

Caller: "Mr. Wright, please."

Helpful Answerer: "I'm sorry, he's unavailable just now. May I help you?"

The Best Response

Caller: "Mr. Wright, please."

Problem Solver: "I'm sorry, he's in a meeting. He should be available in about an hour. (*Or:* I'm not sure when he'll be available.) May I take a message or is there something *I* can help you with?"

Best Rules for Taking a Call

◆ Offer real information whenever you can.

◆ Head off the caller's frustration by empowering him with a real choice: May I take a message or is there something I can help you with?

◆ Follow through with real help.

TIP: There's an Upside and a Downside. The upside of Problem Solver's response is obvious: greater customer/client satisfaction. Not too long ago, most businesses regarded customer service as a kind of necessary evil wholly subordinate to manufacturing and sales and quite incapable of generating revenue on its own. These days, however, customer service has sprinted from the back office to the front desk and is now seen as essential to survival and prosperity in a competitive business climate. Look at such enterprises as manufacturers of personal computers, for example. Common sense would tell us that the premium product these high-tech companies offer is cutting-edge technology. But the fact is that most consumers perceive few, if any, *technical* differences among the host of personal computers available to them. They care less about ROM, RAM, and MIPS than they do about the availability and efficacy of customer support, maintenance service, and the terms of the warranty. All of these are functions of customer service—*human* technology, rather than *high* technology—and it is these issues that sell computers (and most everything else).

So that's the upside.

But every upside comes at a price, and the price here is time. Your time. What happens when Mr. Caller misses Mr. Wright, gets you instead, you offer to help, and he takes you up on it? You will be obliged to invest time in the call.

That's the downside. Or is it, really?

If you think about customer service the old way—as a necessary evil— then, yes, helping out on a call intended for someone else does eat up your time, even if it *saves* the caller's. But companies that are prospering today have learned that time—*anyone's* time—spent on customer contact is not time "spent" at all. It is, rather, time invested. Remember:

◆ Answering any customer call is an investment of time.

◆ Customer contact time is inherently highly valuable.

◆ Invest in customer contact whenever the opportunity presents itself.

THE GOLDEN RULE: "If you pick up the phone, you own the call."

Michael Ramundo, an Ohio-based marketing and customer service con- sultant, developed a principle he dubbed "call ownership" in order to help customer service reps and others put an end to the he's-not-available tele- phone runaround.

It goes like this: If you pick up the phone, you own the call.

◆ If you can handle the caller's issue, do so, right then and there.

◆ If you cannot handle the issue raised in a call intended for Mr. Wright, you still own the call.

1. Don't pretend that you can handle the issue if you cannot.

2. Don't make the caller tell you a long story to which you can respond only by telling him that he'll have to wait until Mr. Wright returns.

3. Do, to the extent possible, put yourself in Mr. Wright's place and gather the key details that will help him do his job when he can return the call. Obtain from the caller his name, number, callback time, and whatever basics the caller wants to convey to Mr. Wright.

4. Having obtained the key information and having transmitted it to Mr. Wright, make certain to follow up with him to ensure that he has returned the call.

How to "Sell" the Call

It is one thing to take ownership of a call intended for Mr. Wright—a partner, co-worker, or colleague—but what if the call is for another department? You will be sorely tempted just to transfer the call and be rid of it. But, remember, having answered the call, you own it. Now *sell* it to the appropriate department.

If the caller has invested time in explaining the issue to you—and you have invested your time in listening to her—protect your mutual investment by taking the following steps:

1. Get the caller's name.

2. Tell the caller that you must transfer her to another department.

3. Put the caller on hold, *after advising her of approximately how long this will take.*

4. Call ahead to the appropriate department. Brief whoever answers on the situation. Always provide the caller's name.

5. Transfer the call.

What to Do When You Don't Know Where to Turn

What happens when you answer a call only to discover that you do not know who should handle the caller's question, problem, or other issue?

◆ Be honest. Tell the caller what you do know, but also what you do not know.

◆ Assure the caller that you—or someone else—will attempt to obtain the required information.

◆ Assure the caller that you—or someone else—will call back. Set as definite a callback time as possible.

◆ Do your best to find either the information or the person who can supply the information.

◆ You—or someone else—must call back at the promised time, either with the answers, a request for further information, or some kind of progress report.

GUIDELINES: The Art of Breaking the Bad News

The foregoing suggests a strategy for turning a potentially frustrating experience into a positive investment of time in customer contact. Still, the fact remains that the caller's expectation of reaching Mr. Wright has not been fulfilled. How you break this news in the first place does much to aggravate or ameliorate the caller's inevitable annoyance.

Don't say:

◆ I don't know where she's gone off to.

◆ He's never here when you need him.

◆ I've no idea where he's disappeared to.

◆ Well, he should be here.

◆ He's supposed to be here.

◆ She's a hard person to track down.

◆ I'd go and get her, but I can't leave my desk right now.

◆ I don't know. You'll have to call back.

◆ He's at lunch.

◆ She takes very long lunches.

◆ Try again later.

◆ Try back anytime.

Do say:

◆ Mr. Wright is not available at the moment. May I ask him to call you back?

◆ Mr. Wright is in a meeting, and I am not sure when he'll be available. I'll be happy to take a message. Or perhaps there is something I can help you with?

◆ I'm sorry, Mr. Wright is attending a sales conference and will not be back in the office until Wednesday. Perhaps I can help you.

◆ Mr. Wright is on another line. May I take a message?

◆ I expect Mr. Wright to return to the office in about an hour. May I take a message? Or perhaps there is something I can help you with?

5.3. A MATTER OF STYLE

5.3.1. How to Answer Your Phone: A Guide

There are three rules of thumb for answering a telephone call:

1. Answer the call within twenty seconds. Unless they are very highly motivated to get through to you, most customers will hang up after four rings. What next? The customer will likely call one of your competitors.

2. Pick up the phone before you speak. Sounds pretty self-evident, doesn't it? But how many times have you called, say, the firm of Dewey, Cheatham and Howe, only to be greeted with " . . . and Howe"? Avoid such truncated greetings by picking up the phone, putting it to your ear, and *then* issuing your greeting.

3. As to the greeting, make certain that you give one. Don't just answer with "Hello" or "Smith here," but consider that there is at least one thing every caller wants: information. Therefore, greet the caller with information: "Good afternoon. This is Dewey, Cheatham and Howe. George Smith speaking. How may I help you?" This kind of greeting bursts with information:

   ◆ It tells the caller you are civil and civilized, suggesting that your company holds similar values ("Good afternoon").

   ◆ It tells the caller that he or she has reached a specific place. ("Dewey, Cheatham and Howe"), thereby avoiding a waste of time over a misunderstanding if the caller thought he was dialing Pete and Repeat, Inc.

   ◆ It tells the caller that he or she has reached a specific person ("George Smith").

   ◆ Finally, it tells the caller that you are willing to help.

This rich greeting establishes a positive relationship—even before the caller has begun to speak.

5.3.2. About Your Voice

Some people are fortunate enough to have what many consider a "pleasant phone voice." If you're among this select number, congratulations. If not, you can practice in order to cultivate a rhythm and tone of vice that are a pleasure to hear. Work on the following elements of your phone voice:

1. Pace. No mystery here. Just slow down. Almost everybody speaks too quickly, especially on the phone. Concentrate. Deliberately try to speak more slowly that you normally do.

2. Lower your voice in pitch. Unless you are aware that you have a deep voice naturally, concentrate on pitching your voice a little lower than normal. Why? Lower-pitched voices sound more pleasing on the telephone and, even more important, such voices are perceived as conveying more authority. This applies whether the speaker is male or female. Lowering your pitch will also help you to slow you down and enunciate more carefully.

3. Speaking of enunciation, give each word its full value. It is critical that you make certain that you are understood. Whenever you make a call, you risk irritating the callee. If you mumble or slur your words, you can be certain that that risk will turn into reality. Careful enunciation and pronunciation conveys the message that you are an intelligent human being.

5.4. APOLOGIES

5.4.1. How to Make Your Message a Massage

Nobody looks forward to apologizing. But I'd like to change that attitude. I'd like to suggest that we start thinking about accidents, errors, and customer dissatisfaction not as disasters, but as opportunities for building and strengthening customer relationships.

How do you know when you've got a good friend? The real test comes not when you're having fun and things are going great, but when a crisis hits. How friends work with one another, help one another out of a problem—that is the test and the builder of friendship.

The situation between you and your client or customer in times of stress is similar. When it hits the fan, a timely, helpful response can not only repair the damage caused by your company's error or the failure of your product, it can actually improve relations between you and your customer. You can demonstrate that you stand behind your product or service, that you will not abandon your customer, that you will see him through the present problem.

Means and Ends

Common sense tells you that the most important objective in responding to calls concerning problems with a product, service, billing, or delivery is to arrive at an action that resolves the issue. But of nearly equal importance is *how* you arrive at that action:

1. Work at building rapport with the caller. You need to discover the facts of the matter. However, be careful to avoid asking for this information with words that convey command or demand. For example, do not demand "What is your account number?" but inquire: "Do you have your account number handy?" or "Do you happen to have your account number with you?" Be careful to request, rather than demand, information.

2. Structure the conversation so that the words "you" and "I" become "we." You could say something like, "I need to get some information from you." But it is far more effective to say, "Let's fill in some information together." A customer has a problem, you can fix it, so you might be tempted to declare—heroically—"I can fix that for you." Still, it is better to say something like, "We can work that out together without any difficulty at all."

402

TIP: Faced with a problem, few customers call to *complain*. What they really want is help. If you can give them the help they want and need, you become a hero and your company becomes a source of satisfaction rather than failure or irritation.

5.4.2. The Irate Caller

A very small proportion of callers express outright rage. In part, such a reaction may be caused by the failure of company's product. More likely, other factors also enter into the equation: a fight with a spouse, a fight with one's children, a disagreement with a supervisor, a miserable morning commute in bumper-to-bumper traffic—the causes of pent-up rage are legion. While you cannot control all the stressful and enraging factors in your customers' lives, you can recognize that an enraged response from you in return will only fuel the anger. In contrast, a calm, businesslike response will make it that much more difficult for the caller to maintain rage.

If you can't control your customer's lives, you can, to some degree, regulate the stress in your own life. For example:

1. Get more sleep. Fatigue reduces your patience and tolerance, making you susceptible to angry outbursts.

2. Try to handle difficult calls after breakfast or after lunch—not when you are hungry.

3. Moderate your intake of coffee. Caffeine heightens anxiety and rage levels.

4. Turn up the air conditioning. Too much heat makes most people more irritable.

5. Do what you can to make yourself more comfortable. Ditch the buzzing fluorescent tube. Get rid of the clock that ticks too loudly.

So much for controlling what you can. Now: the phone rings, you answer, and a customer lets fly.

1. Begin by doing little or nothing. Let the caller vent. It may be difficult to sit there and take it, but let him bleed off some of that pent-up energy.

   PITFALL: Telling an angry caller to "calm down" is a surefire way to irritate him more. Avoid *telling* the caller to do anything. Above all, avoid telling the caller how he should feel.

2. After the first wave of rage has washed over you and your caller, repeat to the caller—as best you can—the gist of his message. Delete the outrage: "If I understand you correctly . . ." Or: "What I hear you saying is . . ." Or: "Let me make certain that I understand you . . ."

3. If you believe that you have a satisfactory solution to the caller's issue, propose it—quickly.

4. If no immediate solution is available, put the burden on the caller. Politely ask him: "How would you like to resolve the problem?" Bear in mind that rage is frequently the product of a sense of powerlessness. If you ask the caller to tell you what he wants, you give him power and, therefore, reduce his feeling of powerlessness.

   TIP: This isn't just a psychological ploy. Oftentimes, the customer comes up with a very good solution.

5. If you can agree to your caller's solution, take the necessary action. If you are unsure, reply that you need a certain amount of time to think about it. Then tell your caller that you will get back to him *at a specific time.* Before you hang up, agree to that time. However, if the caller's solution is entirely unfeasible, negotiate an alternative. "I can't do that, but here's what I can do."

6. Try to transform "I" *vs.* "You" into "We" *vs.* "The Problem."

   TIP: Some irate callers cross the line into downright abusiveness. Remember your dignity. You are not obliged to take abuse. Do not argue. Do not fight back. Do not trade insults. Instead, issue a warning: "Mr. Johnson, I want to help you so that we can resolve this problem. But if you continue to use this kind of language, I will end the conversation." This alone will usually bring the caller around.

5.4.3. Calls You Originate

Delays

The most common situation that requires a call of apology involves delay—delay in shipping a product, delay in completing a project, and so on. Don't emphasize the apology itself as much as:

1. The reason(s) for the delay

2. The anticipated duration of the delay

3. What you are doing to minimize the delay

Explanation and positive steps are the most effective means of defusing delay situations.

> Hello, **Callee**. This is **Caller** at **Company**. We've experienced a scheduling glitch with one of our suppliers. He has manufacturing delays, which, unfortunately, will mean that we will be unable to ship your order before **date**. That is **number** days later than we had planned.
>
> Some delay is unavoidable, but, by putting extra people on the job at our end, I am confident of meeting the revised date. Maybe I can even better it by a day or two.
>
> In the meantime, is there anything you would like me to do to help you accommodate to the revised ship date?
>
> I appreciate your understanding.

It is always best if you can call in advance of an anticipated problem, when your options and those of your client or customer are likely to be more numerous. A proactive approach is almost always preferable to one that reacts to situations only after they develop. However, only a limited number of problems signal their presence in advance, and the reality is that many of your apology calls will be made after the fact. Here's one way to handle a delayed shipment after the fact.

Caller:	Good morning, **Callee**. This is **Caller** at **Company**. I'm checking on the delivery of your **Merchandise**. My shipping department reports that it should have reached you yesterday. You're up and running now?
Callee:	Yes.
Caller:	I am very happy to hear that. However, I want to apologize to you for the delay you experienced. Parts we were promised didn't show up when they should have. We expedited assembly and shipping, but we didn't quite make the target date. I want to thank you for being so understanding about it. I know how important it is to keep down time to a minimum. It sounds like you're moving along now, but if at any time you have questions about the unit, we're here to help at 555-555-5555.

Shipping Errors

Next to delays, errors is shipping are the most common source of delivery-related complaint. Take the initiative and make the apology:

Caller:	**Callee**, good afternoon. This is **Caller** at **Company**.
	This isn't something I enjoy doing, having to apologize for a mistake. But id did want to apologize personally for having shipped the wrong item to you.
	One of my problems is that I can't think of a good reason for the mistake. That's because it's just that: a mistake. So, instead of offering you an excuse, I'll make you a promise: I won't let this happen to you again.
	Thanks for all of your understanding and patience.

Damaged Shipments

Despite precautions and careful packing, merchandise sometimes arrives damaged. In these cases, your principal objective is to assure your customer that a speedy, totally satisfactory, and absolutely hassle-free adjustment will be made. Most customers are willing to accept the arrival of damaged goods as an accident, pure and simple. They won't necessarily blame you. But you have a chance to be hero—and show your company at its best—by going the extra mile to offer maximum service. It starts with a call:

Caller:	I just heard that your **merchandise** arrived damaged. I'm very sorry to hear that. We want to take care of the problem as quickly as possible and without any hassle for you. So, we've got two good choices: Either return the damaged item to me by **carrier**, and I will immediately trans-ship a replacement and will reimburse you for freight. Or, if you prefer, I will send one of my staff out to your location with a replacement on **Day**. He will pick up the damaged unit. Which would you prefer?

Billing Disputes

Errors and misunderstandings over invoices and statements are also common occurrences. Unresolved, these disputes can be particularly destructive, causing your client or customer to view you as unresponsive or, even worse, a cheat. Nip the problem in the bud with a timely call:

Hi, **Callee**. **Caller** here, from **Company**.

I received your letter dated **date**, and I understand the questions you have concerning the number of hours for which you have been billed. In response, I have thoroughly reviewed the time sheets for the project. First, let me say that I am convinced that we have performed all of the services you requested, and that we completed each phase of the project on time. I think we're agreed on that, correct?

Now, having agreed on that, it seems to me the next step is for you to see, as I have, a full set of our time sheets. What you, as a customer, get are summaries. I'm sending you our internal worksheets, which go into greater detail. May I suggest that you review them for yourself, and, after doing so, if you still have questions, we can go over the time and charges item by item.

You must know that I am eager to resolve these issues. It was very gratifying working on the project, and it is critical to me that you be thoroughly satisfied.

Sometimes the issue is not a dispute, but an out-and-out error:

Good morning, **Callee**. This is **Caller** at **Company**.

No wonder you're upset. I've just reviewed the invoice in question, and you are 100 percent right: We are 100 percent wrong. You've been charged twice for the same item. I apologize for the error and also for putting you through the trouble of chasing up your records. I will immediately forward to you a corrected invoice marked "paid in full."

Thanks for your patience and understanding.

Apology Checklist

1. Change your attitude: Don't look at apologizing as a necessary evil, but as an opportunity to build stronger customer relations.

2. Try to be proactive. If possible, take the initiative in situations where an apology is called for. Don't wait for a complaint.

3. Apologize, but put the emphasis on positive action.

4. Avoid "what I should have done." Stress "this is what I will do."

5. If necessary, empower the customer or client by asking what steps he or she would like you to take.

5.5. COLLECTION CALLS

5.5.1. Mastering the Art of the Gentle Reminder

Ahhhh—the Good Olde Days. Nobody really remembers them, but everybody's always bringing them up. Let me tell you something. I've heard that there used to be a time when business was mostly about "making money." You made something, you sold something, you found somebody to buy something, and you turned it all into cash.

Somewhere, somehow that all changed. As the 1980s gave way to the 1990s, business slipped into a twilight zone in which many of us became mired in the realm of Accounts Receivable. Time was when a business could classify its customers as those who paid on time, those who were delinquent, and those who were deadbeats. Delinquency came after thirty days. Deadbeat-ism was after sixty.

No more. These days, businesses make it a practice to hold payment for sixty days. Ninety days is no longer taboo. In fact, prompt payment has come to be regarded as a violation of nature's law.

Sound grim? Well, it is. Or, at least, it's pretty frustrating. However, there is also good news. Even though your accounts may delay paying you, *they want to pay you.*

Well, let's put this more accurately. Few people like to pay, but nobody enjoys owing. So let's start with that assumption, which then enables us to think about collection calls not as occasions for harassing a customer, but as an opportunity to help him or her.

Here's an example. The account in question has just gone past the thirty-day mark:

> Hello, **Name**. This is **Name** of **Company**. I was just going over some accounts and noticed that yours has passed the thirty-day mark, which means that we're about to send you a new invoice with a **$ amount** service charge tacked on. To tell you the truth, it's easier for me to make this phone call than to process and mail a new invoice. If you can settle your account now—get the check into the mail today—I won't have to do up another invoice and you'll save **$ amount**.

Or you can be even more aggressive about the offer of help:

Hello, **Name**. This is **Name** of **Company**. I'm calling to save you some money. Your account with us has just gone past thirty days, which means that it is subject to a service charge of **$ amount**. Truthfully, I'd much rather have that account paid in full at the present time than collect an additional **$ amount** on it later. If you can get payment to me by **date**, I will waive the service charge.

What happens when your customer tells you that he can't pay at the moment?

Caller:	Hello, **Name**. This is **Name** of **Company**. I noticed that your account has passed the thirty-day mark. Normally, we'd assess a service charge at this point, but, to tell you the truth, I'd rather have the cash at this time, and I'm willing to waive the service charge if you can get a check into the mail.
Callee:	I'd love to, but our cash flow position isn't the greatest just now. I'm going to have to let the bill go for another couple of weeks and pay the service charge.
Caller:	Well, that's not the end of the world, of course. And, obviously, I know what it's like to try to manage cash flow these days. Before we leave the matter, is there anything I can do to help? What I'm thinking is that, if you can send me a check for **percent amount** of the current invoice now and pay the balance by **date**, I'm still willing to waive the service charge. I like to make things as flexible as possible for my customers.

Follow up swiftly if installment payments are missed:

Caller:	Hello, **Name**. I'm **Name**, from **Company**. Your payment of **$ amount**, which was due on **date**, hasn't arrived in our office. When did you send that out?
Callee:	I was planning on sending it out later in the week.
Caller:	It was due on **date**. Can you get it into the mail today?
Callee:	I'm not sure.
Caller:	Well, I'll look for it by the first of the week. Does that sound all right with you?

5.5.2. Mastering the Art of the Not-So-Gentle Reminder

Once an account approaches or exceeds sixty days beyond the due date, it's time for stronger medicine. This does not mean threats, but do convey a sense of urgency:

> *Caller:* Hello. This is **Name** from **Company**. I'm calling to talk to you about your account with us. As you know, the prices we originally quoted you were based on thirty-day net terms. We're approaching sixty days, which means that you will be paying us a **$ amount** carrying charge on this account. Frankly, I'd rather have the account settled now than collect the **$ amount**. Can you get us a check by **date**?
>
> *Callee:* I'll have to talk to my accounting people.
>
> *Caller:* Is there someone in your accounting department that I should be talking to? I'll give him or her an opportunity to save you some money.

Customers can be fairly evasive at this point:

> *Caller:* Hello, **Name**. This is **Name** from **Company**. I'm calling to talk to you about your account with us. The prices we gave you were based on thirty-day net terms, and we're now getting close to the sixty-day point. We're a small company, and, frankly, it's very difficult for us to carry open accounts for any length of time. It would help us a great deal if you could pay the account in full.
>
> *Callee:* I'll look into it.
>
> *Caller:* May I call you at this time tomorrow to get a status report from you and, if necessary, to work out a payment plan together?
>
> *Callee:* Tomorrow is a bad time.
>
> *Caller:* Well, we are running short on time. After **date** the account is subject to a **$ amount** carrying charge, and I'd much rather work with you on a payment strategy that will save you that fee. When is a good time to call?

Your object should be to make certain that your customer is aware of the consequences of neglecting the account, but you should avoid ultimatums. Keep as many positive choices open as possible:

Caller:	Hello, **Name**. This is **Name** from **Company**. I'm calling to talk to you about your account with us. As you know, the prices we originally quoted you were based on thirty-day net terms. We're approaching sixty days, which means that you will be paying us a **$ amount** carrying charge on the account. Frankly, I'd rather have the account settled now than collect the **$ amount**. Can you get us a check by **date**?
Callee:	I'm in a real cash-flow bind just now. You know how it is.
Caller:	Unfortunately, I do. That's why I'd like to work with you on this. To help us both out. We need to come up with a plan that we can both live with. The balance due is **$ amount**. If I can get **$ amount** by **date**, I'd be in a position to waive the carrying charges on the entire balance due—provided the account is completely settled by **date**. How does that sound?
Callee:	I just can't manage it at this time. I'll have to pay you later and just absorb the finance charges.
Caller:	Well, before we give up, can you tell me if I'm in the ballpark?
Callee:	You really want to get some money, don't you?
Caller:	I told you that I know what it's like to have to manage cash flow carefully. Yeah, I can use all the cash I can get. What if we set up **number** payments and spread them out?

Even as an account slips beyond sixty days, do everything you can to keep from conveying a dire message. If the customer feels that all is lost, he'll naturally assume that he has nothing more to lose. Most likely, he'll avoid communicating with you and continue to avoid settling the account. Here is a possible exchange:

Caller:	Hello, **Name**. This is **Name** at **Company**. I was just going over some accounts here, and I noticed that yours is about to go past ninety days. Now that's not disaster, and I'm not calling to dun you, but I did want to alert you to the fact that the account is about to slip through another month unpaid. And what that means to you is a service charge of **$ amount**. If you want to avoid that charge—and pay us only **$ amount**—might I suggest that you send out a check today?
Callee:	I just don't have the cash on hand right now. Can you give me a grace period on that service charge?

Caller: When would you be paying?

Callee: In about two to three weeks.

Caller: Well, that's going to start getting close to 120 days, after which the account is delinquent. I'd like to accommodate you, but, you know, we're a small company, and we can't afford to carry an account that long without a service charge. If you can get me **$ amount** by **date**, we can at least avoid letting the account slip into delinquency. Then we can work out together a schedule for the balance. How does that sound?

TIP: Keep the dialogue going back frequently asking for agreement: "How does that sound?" "Does that seem workable to you?" and so forth.

5.5.3.   You *Can* Wake the Dead

Once an account slips past ninety days, let alone 120, many firms throw in the towel and turn the account over to a collection agency, which will collect a very substantial percentage of the money due—if its efforts succeed in wearing down the debtor. Usually, a better alternative is to refuse to give up—or, at least, make a last-ditch effort to keep the lines open:

Caller: Hello, **Name**. This is **Name** calling from **Company**. I'm calling about your account with us. It's passed 120 days due, and I'm getting pressured here to turn it over to our lawyers. I was hoping that a simple phone call might make that unnecessary. The amount due is **$ amount**. Can you get a check to us today?

Callee: Frankly, no. I've been meaning to call you. We've had some— problems here, and I'm afraid I've had to let some accounts go longer than they should.

Caller: Maybe I can help. The total due, as I said, is **$ amount**. What percentage of this could you manage to pay now? I really want to hold off having to turn this over to Collections—especially if you're in a crunch.

TIP: Instead of threatening collection or legal action, bring it up as a kind of third-party consequence that *both* you and your delinquent account want to avoid. In effect, try to recruit the account for your "team" in opposition to "lawyers" or a "collection agency."

A final example:

Caller: Hello, **Name**. This is **Name** calling from **Company**. I'm calling now to save us both a lot of trouble in the days and weeks to come. Your account with us has been outstanding now for **number** days. We've tried repeatedly to contact you about this, but we've received no reply. I'd like to avoid turning this over to our attorney for collection. Do you think we can work out payment on this account?

Checklist for Collection Calls

1. Control your anger. Offer help instead of rage.

2. Keep the account as part of your team. Don't push him away.

3. Remember: Your account *wants* to pay.

4. Offer as many positive choices as possible.

5. Most creditors give up too soon. Don't abandon your account. Stay with him.

5.6. COMPLAINTS

5.6.1. Who Ya' Gonna' Call?

Finding the right words is important to making any communication effective. However, the right words are only part of what it takes to make an effective complaint. Before you speak the right words, find the right person to speak them to.

Businesses used to have "Complaint Departments"—obviously intended to be the place for complaints. Nowadays, Customer Service handles such issues. But does this mean your best move is to go the Customer Service Department? Not necessarily. Before making a complaint, try to identify the person with the most to gain by making you happy and the most to lose if you are dissatisfied. This may not be very difficult. Just follow the money. In other words, talk to your account executive or the salesperson with whom you most regularly deal. The person most closely associated with *your* business—*your* money—is the person most likely to listen most acutely to your complaint.

5.6.2. Surefire Ways to Make Your Case and Get Your Way

Complaints fail to motivate the desired action for one or both of two reasons:

1. The complaint does not clearly state what is wanted.

2. The complaint addresses personalities rather than issues.

Before you get on the phone to make a complaint, you must *think* about what it is that you want. Do you just want to vent your irritation and rage? Or do you want some specific action to be taken. You may even find it helpful to jot down the desired objectives before you pick up the receiver. Secondly, make certain that you focus on those objectives. Don't get sidetracked into alienating the party on the other end of the line by hurling accusations and criticisms. Your object should not be to make the other person feel miserable and worthless—though you may derive some satisfaction from that—but to correct a problem situation.

Here are some examples:

Caller: We've got a problem. During the past three months, your company has shipped our orders anywhere from five to fifteen days late. Now, I certainly understand that occasional delayed shipments are probably inevitable. But, based on the experience of the last few months, this seems to be developing into a regular—and unacceptable—pattern. I cannot keep disappointing *my* customers this way.

Callee: [apologizes; offers excuses; promises it won't happen again, and so forth]

Caller: What I need are two things from you. First: Please send me a memo or letter of explanation that details the reasons fro the late shipments and that outlines a plan to prevent them from happening again. I expect to receive the letter by September 5.

Second: Can you just work on getting the shipments out on time—beginning with our current order?

I want to stress that I am delighted with your product, and I want to work with you to resolve this problem. But I also need to stress that I can afford to work only with suppliers on whom I can consistently depend.

Another example:

Caller: I'm calling to talk to you about a chain reaction. You know what that is, right? Something happens on one end of a process, and the other end feels it. One reaction sets off another, and that one sets off another, and, pretty soon, you've got one heck of an explosion.

Okay: Well, that's what's happening to us. Your company has consistently shipped me defective merchandise—flawed material that I've had to return. What this has meant is, number one, my time getting wasted, and, two, my customers getting disappointed.

We cannot go on this way. Here's what I need from you: A feasible plan of action to improve your quality control. I need this in place by the next order cycle. I enjoy working with you, and I like what you bring to the table. But I've got to be able to depend on you 100 percent.

Complaint Checklist

1. Avoid clashes of personality.

2. Do not make the complaint until you have a clear idea of what you want to result from the complaint.

3. Focus on objectives, not on shaming the callee.

4. Avoid threats, but do point out the "natural" consequences of failure to correct the subject of the complaint.

5. To whatever degree is possible, stress the positive.

6. Propose as specific a course of action as possible.

5.7. CREDIT

5.7.1. Strategies for Talking to Bankers

Mark Twain put it this way: *A bank will give you a loan, provided that you can prove you don't need the money.*

Well, maybe that's the way you, applying for a loan, feel about it. The fact is that the loan officer is pulled in two opposing directions. On the one hand, she is expected to make loans. That's how the bank survives and prospers. On the other hand, she is expected to keep the bank from making a bad loan or even a risky one. It's a tough position to be in. Most salespeople have but a single objective: to make the sale. For a banker, the objective is to make the sale, but . . .

The loan officer's rock-and-hard-place position presents you with an opportunity: to make her job easier by doing your verbal best to enable her to say yes.

> **PITFALL:** Better take a reality check. A good conversation with a loan officer certainly gives you an edge, but it will not make up for a poor credit history or a balance sheet that strays too far from what the lending institution expects.

The powers that be will base their decision on data that has very little to do with you as a person. However, it is important to enter into the conversation with the assumption that you *will* get the loan—or, rather, it is fatal to enter that conversation assuming that you will fail to get the loan. Enter with high hopes. Project an air of confidence. This is not as difficult as it may at first seem. Begin by purging your vocabulary of the word "if." Instead of saying, "If I secure thee funds . . .," say, "I will use these funds to finance . . ."

If it is true that good words are no magical substitute for good numbers, it is also true that you should enter into the loan negotiation as if good words will make all the difference.

Show, Don't Tell

If the loan officer will, finally, be impressed by numbers more than by words, she will be *least* impressed by adjectives and adverbs. Saying to the loan officer something like "I am a determined, hard-nosed, savvy businessperson" will make far less of a positive impression that declaring how," in 1992, I took seed money of $24,000 and put together a business that now grosses $375,000 a year." Use verbs and nouns. If possible, quantify all statements.

Glitches

Applying for a loan is not the same as the sacrament of Confession. You are not obliged to volunteer all of your failings and peccadilloes. Don't volunteer prejudicial information. However, do respond to any negative issues that the loan officer may raise. Moreover, go into the interview prepared to respond to them.

Banker Talk Checklist

1. Emphasize facts rather than self-generated value judgments.

2. Use nouns, verbs, and numbers. Be sparing with adjectives—they sound like hype.

3. View the lender as a partner, an investor—not a benefactor, to whom you come hat in hand.

4. Project confidence by avoiding conditional statements and, in particular, the word "if."

5.7.2. Tips for Talking to Vendors

In seeking credit from vendors, you may employ a strategy similar to the one you use to secure funds from a bank. After all, your object is to sell the vendor on the notion that he should have confidence and trust in you. In applying to a vendor for credit, you do enjoy two advantages you do not have when dealing with a bank. Whether the loan officer wants to see it this way or not, the decision to loan you money is a decision to enter into partnership with you. In contrast, vendors are accustomed to seeing the credit relationship this way. In order to make it possible for you to do business with him, the vendor understands that he must find a way to extend credit, to make you, in effect, his partner. A second advantage is the fact that vendors are not constrained by anything like the often restrictive regulations that govern banks. A vendor knows that he has to take certain risks to sell his product. The vendor *needs* to let you buy from him. Launch your pitch from the point of that truth.

5.7.3. Getting Around "No"

If you are refused a requested loan or credit, you have two choices: use your feet or use your voice. It may be most expedient simply to walk away and seek another lending institution or vendor. Even if you take this option, however, you should ask the lending institution or vendor what went wrong and, most importantly, what would make a "yes" possible. Do not act on your understandable impulse to vent your anger an frustration. Maintain a cordial relation with the lender or vendor. Conditions change, and it is quite possible that, at some future time, you will be doing business with the firm that spurned you.

In any case, a "no" does not necessarily terminate a relationship. If you choose to use your voice instead of your feet, begin by assuring the lender or vendor that you would like it is important to you to find a way to do business. Investigate with that firm a variety of compromise positions—lesser amounts, different payment terms, and so on. By all means, express your disappointment, but do not cut the cord.

> **Tip:** The most positive response you can make to "no" is "What can I do that will make it possible for you to say 'yes.'"

5.7.4. Making the Offer

You should not rely on the telephone alone to make a credit offer. In fact, you should make a verbal offer only if you are prepared to negotiate it to some degree. If, on the other hand, your figure is firm, you are better off putting it in writing at the outset. A verbal offer, once finalized to your satisfaction, should be immediately backed up in writing.

The tone that should control your call is courtesy and welcome. Remember: You are making it possible for the customer to do business with you. Furthermore, with this important phone call, you are selling the customer on the idea of building a relationship with you.

There is no great challenge to phoning a customer in order to extend the amount of credit he has sought. However, if the terms you are prepared to offer differ from what the customer has requested, your call should accomplish the following:

1. It should *explain* your rationale for extending whatever amount you have decided upon.

2. If at all possible, it should offer realistic hope for a timely reassessment of the customer's credit situation.

This second point is also critical in phone calls made to turn down a request for credit. In addition, of course, you owe your customer an explanation.

Here is a sample telephone message:

> *Caller:*   Hello, **Name**. This is **Name** at **Company**. I have some good news for you. We are delighted to open up a line of credit for you.
>
> At this time, we are prepared to extend to you a **$ amount** line subject to **terms**. I realize this is somewhat less than you asked for, and let me say that your financial statements do indicate a healthy business with a great future. However, this has to be balanced against the fact that you have been in business less than two years. We really want to do business with you—and, once you have crossed the two-year mark, I want to review updated financials with the aim of opening a bigger credit line for you.

5.7.5. What to Say When You Must Say "No"

The cardinal rule is *don't slam the door.* Unless there is absolutely no hope, frame your rejection to avoid alienating the customer:

> *Caller:*   Good morning, **Name**. This is **Name** at **Company**. I am calling to discuss your credit application. As you must be aware, your credit record shows a history of slow payment. Also, given the level and extent of your current obligations, we are going to have to postpone acting on your credit request for 120 days. Our assumption is that this period should give you time to catch up on your open accounts.
>
> *Callee:*   This is very disappointing. We really wanted to do business with you.
>
> *Caller:*   We want to do business with you, too, and, for now, I hope that you will let us serve you on a pay-as-you-go basis. But I want to emphasize that we will look very earnestly at your reapplication in **Month**.

Callee:	I don't see how I can wait that long. There are other vendors, you know.
Caller:	I realize that, and I can't speak for the credit policies of others. I can tell you that no other supplier offers better value than we do, and I ask that, even if you do secure credit from some other supplier now, you check back with us in 120 days.

Credit Offer Checklist

1. Regard the phone call as an adjunct to a letter. Do not rely on verbal offers alone.

2. Create a tone of welcome.

   TIP: Never forget that, in offering credit, you are making it possible for the customer to do business with you.

3. Explain any differences between your offer and what the customer asked for.

4. If possible and appropriate, offer the possibility of reassessment of the credit offer at some specific later time or after some specific condition or conditions have been satisfied.

5. Even if you must turn down a credit request, endeavor to maintain a relationship with the customer.

5.8. FAVORS

5.8.1. How to Get the Help You Need When You Need It

Many people find it downright painful to ask for a favor. They have what is doubtless a laudable aversion to asking to get something for nothing. Yet the fact is, a favor is not something for nothing. In the first place, most people like to be in a position to help others. Only the stiffest, dyed-in-the-wool cynic can deny this truth of human nature. But, if that isn't enough, let's proceed to the second place: In the world of business, what goes around comes around. Securing a favor, it is understood, informally obligates you to perform a favor when asked. It's a kind of good-faith quid-pro-quo system that lubricates so much of the mechanism of business.

> **TIP:** In asking a favor, don't assume that you are seeking something for nothing. The other party probably wants to help. Besides, then you'll owe her one. And she knows that.

Begin the phone call by introducing yourself. If the callee is a friend, fine. If not, be certain to define the basis of your relationship: "We've worked so successfully on the Bascom project, that I feel comfortable asking you for a favor." Next, define the favor clearly.

> **TIP:** Do not qualify (or quantify) the favor: "I've got a *big* favor to ask you." This will create tension and anxiety, and it will set you up for a *no*. Deliver the request without judgment, evaluation, or qualification on your part. Let the callee decide for herself.

Perhaps the most important part of the call is explaining how the favor will help you or benefit you. This is the only significant gauge of the magnitude of the favor and, emotionally, it suggests to the callee the degree of indebtedness *you* will incur.

If the callee complies with your request, thank her enthusiastically, though not effusively. You may also discreetly suggest that you will be pleased to return the favor. Don't trivialize this with an "I owe you one, buddy," and don't build it up with something to the effect of, "If there is ever *anything* I can do for you . . ." Instead, conclude with a statement like this: "I hope that you'll call on me to return the favor."

If the callee declines the request, be graceful and understanding. Chances are, she really is *not* in a position to help you. Be charitable. Express the fact that you *understand* her position.

An example:

Caller: Hello, **Name**. This is **Name** at **Company**. I'm calling to ask a favor.

Callee: Oh?

Caller: **Customer company** has just asked us to bid on **type of project**. As you recall, this is quite similar to the kind of work my company did for you last year. From our point of view, that project was a great success, and I believe you think of it the same way.

Callee: We were very pleased.

Caller: I also believe that you know **Name** at **Customer company**. Is that the case?

Callee: Yes, I know him.

Caller: Well, it seemed to me that you would make an ideal reference. And I'd like to ask you make a quick phone call to **Name** at **Customer company** and tell her something about the kind of job we did for you. Would you be agreeable to that?

Callee: Sure.

Caller: It would be very helpful if you could stress **point** and **point**, which **Customer company** is particularly concerned about. Here's **Name**'s direct number, if you don't happen to have it handy: 555-555-5555.

Callee: I'll call right away.

Caller: I would really appreciate that. This would be a major contract for us. It means a great deal, and I would be very grateful for whatever kind words you could pass along. I hope you'll call on me some time to return the favor.

Favor Checklist

1. Don't think of a favor as something for nothing.

2. Most people enjoy feeling helpful. Asking for a favor gives them an opportunity to experience a positive feeling.

3. Don't editorialize about the favor you're seeking. Let the other person evaluate it and decide whether or not it's asking for too much.

4. Explain the favor clearly, and also explain the benefit you will enjoy because of it.

5. Express gratitude. Indicate a willingness to return the favor.

5.9. GOODWILL

5.9.1. Making the Condolence Call

Odd. At precisely those moments when others need our kind words most, we often feel least able to communicate. Death, serious illness, or other loss erects barriers. We *want* to say the "right thing," but we are fearful of intruding on another's grief, or we fear that what we say will only cause more pain.

The fact is, all other things being equal, a person who has suffered a loss craves comfort and kind words. How do you come up with the right thing to say? Not from looking in a book—though I invite you to read on—but by looking into yourself. Imagine what *you* would like to hear in a situation such as the one the callee finds himself in. Think about your feelings, and try to speak from these. You might approach the call this way:

1. Express your sorrow at hearing of the death or loss.

2. Acknowledge the callee's sorrow.

3. Say something good about the deceased. If possible, share a specific memory about him or her.

    TIP: You may think that bringing up a common memory will only increase the other's pain. This is not the case. Demonstrating that the deceased still lives in memory brings comfort.

4. Acknowledge present pain, but remind the callee of the healing power of time.

    PITFALL: Do not trivialize grief. You may give comfort by suggesting that the passage of time will salve the hurt, but do not imply that the callee will soon forget about the deceased.

5. Offer your help and support.

    Caller: Hello, Fred. It's Carl. I just heard about Sarah. It was a shock to me, and I can only imagine what a blow it must be to you. She was not only your top manager, but a close, close friend.

425

Callee:	Yes. It's terrible.
Caller:	Well, I know it doesn't seem like it at the moment, but you—you and your company—will get through this. Sarah, above all things, would not want the company to falter. That's the kind of person she was. Remember when she broke her leg skiing? She was out of the hospital and behind her desk in record time. The company meant a lot to her—and, if she could, she'd be telling you to get on with it.
Callee:	That was Sarah, all right.
Caller:	You know, she's still there with you—in the company the two of you built. Remember that. And, Fred, if there is anything I can do to help right now, let me know. Don't hesitate to call.

5.9.2. Scoring Points with a Timely Congratulations

Extending congratulations is not just a pleasant exercise in etiquette and an occasion to spread good feelings—though it *is* that—it is also an opportunity to build on existing relationships and to inaugurate new ones. Congratulating a potential customer or client on a new position gives you the perfect excuse for a call.

> **TIP:** It pays to keep abreast of developments within the industry or industries you serve. If you learn that Joe Blow has just been appointed production manager at Apex Publishing, and you happen to be a sales rep for a printer, better call to congratulate Joe. And you had better do it before everyone else does.

Begin your call by introducing yourself and establishing the basis of your relationship: "Hello, Mr. Blow. This is Matt Helms at Repro Printing. I just read in *Press Today* that you've been named production head at Apex." Here the basis of the relationship is a simple news story. But that's sufficient. Now, continue:

> I want to extend my congratulations. Apex does great work, and the position should be both challenging and rewarding. I also wanted to let you know that my firm offers a wide variety of printing services, and I'd like to help you get off to a great start in your new position by getting together with you to explain some of what we have to offer.

There is a thin line separating a blatant sales call from a call that offers the new appointee genuine help and advice. There is nothing wrong with crossing that line. If you are seen as a trusted counselor, you will likely create the basis of an enduring business relationship.

Does every call of congratulations *have* to be a stratagem to capture new business? Of course not. But the basis for new business exists, there is nothing wrong with building on it. You might prefer to do so less directly: "So, again, Mr. Blow, let me congratulate you. I know we can be of help to you. Just give me a call whenever you want to get together."

5.9.3. How to Give Invitations a Personal Touch

Only casual, informal invitations should be handled entirely by phone. However, you might use a follow-up phone call to add an extra personal touch to a mailed invitation. In either case, the key is to be 100 percent positive. Never issue a grudging or hesitant invitation: "I don't suppose you'd want to attend . . ." Instead, express your earnest wish that the callee will attend: "Lois and I are having an informal get-together on the 12th. It certainly would be great to see you there."

If you make a call to reinforce a mailed invitation, use it as an occasion to "sell" the event: "You know, Mary, we'd really love for you to come. There will be a good many important contacts there, and I'd like you to meet them. I mean, we intend to have a good time—but, don't kid yourself, there will be plenty of networking going on."

5.9.4. The Magic of a Thank You Call

The key to an effective thank you call is to be specific, expressing thanks and then explaining how valuable the service, favor, or recommendation is. Make as clear as possible the effect of the callee's action: "You turned around the entire situation. What could have been a real snafu became a very productive transaction." You don't need to exaggerate the good consequences of the act, but do try to be as specific as possible. The result will go far beyond courtesy. It will build a strong relationship.

5.10. INFORMATION

5.10.1. Surefire Ways to Get the News You Need

Getting information should be an easy process. Unfortunately, it is often complicated and frustrating. Preparation will help.

1. Decide exactly what you need to know.

2. Try to determine who can best supply this information to you.

When you make the phone call, identify yourself by name, then state what you need and why you need it. If the information you are seeking is likely to lead to business for the callee, make this clear: "I am in the market from widgets. I need to talk to someone about your credit policy for small-quantity purchases."

> **TIP:** It is axiomatic that work expands to fill the time allotted to it. Therefore, create a sense of urgency about your request for information: "I am authorized at this point to make the purchase. I need to move on this now. What is your credit policy for small-quantity purchases?"

Use the call to get as much and as detailed information as you need. The quality of the information is likely to increase with the more you ask. As you and the callee invest more time in the call, the exchange becomes increasingly valuable. You may have to be persistent. If the callee cannot give you the information you require, ask for referral to someone who can. Always make it clear how the information given to you will ultimately benefit the organization you are calling: "I can't proceed with the purchase until I have this information."

5.11. SALES

5.11.1. Script or no Script?

The telephone can be used in two ways to make sales. You can employ the fully scripted solicitation, in which you or a staff member makes calls and reads a written pitch. This approach is the most practical method for carrying out full-scale campaigns. But there are many other situations where a prepared script is neither practical nor appropriate. For example, when you are offering a new product or service, you might draw up a short list of current customers—always your best prospects—who you are reasonably certain will be interested in the product or service. Go down the list, and give each a "spontaneous"—an unscripted—call.

5.11.2. Preparing for "Spontaneity"

The ability to think on your feet is greatly prized in business. In part, this is a natural-born talent. Either you've got it, or you don't. However, it is also a skill that can be honed and developed—and even entirely acquired. In fact, you can prepare yourself for spontaneity by making it your business to become thoroughly knowledgeable about the products or services you are sell. Add to this knowledge, genuine enthusiasm, and it becomes surprisingly easy to think on your feet.

But why stop here? There is a middle ground between utter spontaneity on the one hand and a fully scripted "spiel" on the other. Approach the "spontaneous" phone solicitation armed with notes—"crib sheets" or "fact sheets" or "cue cards"—listing the most important sales points of the merchandise or services you offer.

> **TIP:** Put your information in a loose-leaf binder, with tabs, arranged alphabetically or with the hottest products up front. Alternatively, use your personal computer and any one of the many database software package available to create "pop-up" screens with product information.

How Much Information?

The material on your prompt cards should be just comprehensive enough to interest, or "hook," your customer. Don't oversell. That is, don't bore him with details he doesn't want to hear. Ask questions like, "Do you want to hear more?" Or offer: "I can recite the whole spec sheet, if you like."

5.11.3. The Essential Steps

Making an effective "spontaneous" sales call involves more than transmitting information. As a rule, you need to move with your potential customer through the following steps:

1. Get your callee's attention.

2. Identify a need your callee has.

3. Show how you can fill this need.

4. Persuade the callee to buy.

5. Prompt the callee to act.

5.11.4. Putting the Steps to Work

Let's walk through some examples of "spontaneous" calls that take the callee through the five steps. But don't expect magic. You know, the people who rely least on magic are professional magicians. They understand the importance of preparation in order to create the illusion of magic. Take a lesson from them. Instead of making calls to a random list of people you don't know—names on pages torn from the telephone book—consider warming the cold calls by selecting names from special-interest lists you purchase or lease, from your own customer lists, or perhaps even from lists based on your own research. Calls made to a list of your established customers have the greatest potential for panning out as productive sales endeavors.

> **TIP:** Most telemarketing experts agree: Do not waste time—your's and the callee's—by making "spontaneous" calls to random strangers. Genuine cold calls, calls made to names in the phone book, should be scripted. The subject is covered in a later section of this chapter.

At minimum, then, have on hand:

1. A short list of potentially interested customers to call concerning **merchandise.**

2. A list of selling points that specifically answer the question: *Why should I be interested in* **merchandise**?

Here's how it might go:

Caller: Hello, **Name**. This is **Name** at **Company**. I'm calling because we had a conversation a short time ago concerning **type of merchandise**. I wanted to let you know that we are now stocking **merchandise**, and I think what we've got will suit your needs just perfectly. Better yet, we're able to offer **merchandise** at a very special introductory price.

                Are you interested?

Callee: Sure.

Caller: Fine! I'll tell you a little about it.

                First, you had mentioned **points callee had previously raised**. Well, let me tell you: **merchandise** can do all of that and more. For example, **list features**.

                Second, installation is much easier than it used to be for products of this type. What we're carrying now has a special feature that **explain**.

                Finally: price. This is a pleasant surprise. The base price is **$ amount**. Now, with the options you'll probably want—**list**—the total comes to **$ amount**. I think that you'll agree we're talking about a very reasonable cost. However, that's our regular price. Our introductory price, with the options package, is only **$ amount**.

                Let me just add one other feature. That's our warranty. You know, the standard is pretty high in this industry. Warranties generally run **number** years. *Ours* goes to **number** years.

                Name, the introductory pricing period will end on **date**. It would be great to be able to demonstrate the unit to you well before then, so that you'll have an opportunity to take advantage of the special price. I can make a call on you at your office, if you like. When would be a good time for you?

TIP: Another great way to warm up cold calls is to gather referrals from established customers. Current customers—provided they are satisfied customers—are your best salespeople. When a current customer furnishes you with a lead to new business, follow it. Begin any "spontaneous" sales calls to referrals by mentioning that So-and-so suggested you make the call.

5.11.5. Random Cold Calls

If you do not "warm" your cold calls with some degree of selectivity and targeting—that is, if you make genuinely random cold calls—your best strategy option is to script the call fully. Spontaneous calls are not effective in pure cold call situations. They pretty much require some preexisting relationship basis. The callee may be a current customer, a referral, or at least someone who, based on your research, you believe will be interested in the product or service you offer. There *are* two alternatives to both a spontaneous call and a fully scripted call. These are discussed in 5.11.6 and 5.11.7.

5.11.6. The Outline

Creating and following an outline, rather than a fully written-out script, allows you or very *experienced* and thoroughly *knowledgeable* sales staff a measure of creativity in making the cold call.

An effective outline consists of at least nine selling steps in addition to as many key selling elements—such as product/service benefits, terms, conditions, etc.—as required to explain the merchandise being offered. The selling steps are as follows:

1. *Verify the prospect's name.* Remember: this is an unsolicited phone call. Getting a name at the outset of the call confers on the call a purpose, telling the caller that you are calling him or her—not just anybody. Equally important, it allows you to use your prospect's name, a gesture that is an effective ice breaker.

2. *Identify yourself and your firm.* Do not attempt to "trick" your prospect into listening to what you have to say by holding back the fact that you are calling from a company that is trying to sell something. Failure to come clean will only create (richly deserved) suspicion and will stir up resistance, impatience, and a desire to slam down the receiver. Give your name and the name of your firm: "This is Joe Blow, calling from ABC, Incorporated."

3. *Say why you are calling.* Cut to the chase on this point, too. Announce the purpose of your call in highly positive terms, using such words as:

alternative	gain	smart
benefit	inform	taste
breakthrough	information	test
choice	money	touch
choose	new	trustworthy
desirable	opportunity	value
distinctive	option	wanted
easy	prove	win
family	see	wise
free		

You want, first and foremost, to *sell* your prospect on the proposition of taking your call and listening to you.

PITFALL: Some words are *poison* in a cold call. Take care to avoid:

buy	cost	decide
cheap	deal	sell
contract		

4. *Ask a "test" question.* Instead of pounding your pitch into the callee's ear, empower him with a test question. This will give him an opportunity to speak. Make sure, however, that the question is likely to produce the answer you want. Start out with an appealing, inviting, intriguing question, framed precisely to highlight the benefits of whatever it is you propose to sell. Focus the question on benefits to the callee, not on benefits to yourself. Do not ask, "Would you be interested in buying such and such?" Instead, try something like "If you're like most savvy consumers, you are always on the lookout for ways to save major money. Is that the case?" A test launches the sales pitch by inviting a yes. However—and this is important—it allows the customer to say no, if he really and truly is not interested. If the response is negative, reply with "Thanks for your time and have a nice day," hang up, and go on to the next prospect. You've wasted relatively little time on a hopeless prospect. If, on the other hand, the response is positive, you have a strong, customer-motivated basis for proceeding.

5. *Make the presentation.* Clearly list all selling points, always emphasizing product *benefits* rather than product *features.* Let me explain the critical difference between features and benefits.

   a. The *features* of a merchandise or a service are what it actually does. "Brand X detergent will clean your dishes very well—in fact, better than any other detergent."

   b. The *benefits* are the good things the product or service will do *for the customer.* Benefits are characteristically linked to emotion. "Brand X detergent enhances your dining experience because you and your guests feel as if you are dining with sparkling-new china."

6. *Overcome objections.* The outline you prepare must anticipate the callee's objections to buying what you have to sell.

   TIP: Veteran telemarketers clip their outline on a clipboard, using a short sheet of paper. Beneath the outline, they clip a longer sheet, labeled at the bottom (which extends beyond the short top sheet, so that the label is clearly visible) with a specific type of objection to anticipate: "COSTS TOO MUCH." Flip the top sheet, and you have an outline strategy for countering the objection that the merchandise is too expensive. Now, clipped beneath this sheet is an even longer one, labeled at the bottom with another common objection: "HARD TO SET UP." Beneath this, yet a longer sheet, labeled "DIFFICULT TO USE," and so on. Thus, responses to a spectrum of objections are handily tabbed and immediately accessible. If you have a personal computer and the appropriate database software, you can create these tabs on series of "pop-up" screens activated by a single keystroke.

7. *Ask for the order.* After you have countered an objection, do not ask your if you have answered the question adequately. Instead, use the counter as a platform from which to leap into asking for the order.

   TIP: One way to "ask" for an order is simply to say, "Would you like to order one?" But that is not a very effective way of asking. It is time to be more aggressive. Leap over that question, right into, "Would you like to charge your order on a major credit card or would you prefer C.O.D.?" Or: "Would you like that in black or white?"

8. *Verify information.* Include in your outline a checklist asking for verification of the customer's name, billing address, shipping address, and credit information. The outline should also prompt the salesperson to read back the order to the customer.

9. *Thank the customer.* Remind yourself or your sales staff to take this step. Include it explicitly in the outline.

Congratulations! You've made a sale. Or haven't you? Let's go back to step #7. If the customer still resists when you ask for the order, it's time to pose the following question: "What have I left unanswered? What will make it possible for you to purchase this product?" At this point in the pitch, it is only by probing the source of the resistance that you have any hope of overcoming it by directly addressing the callee's concerns and doubts.

5.11.7. The ADRMP

Another alternative to spontaneity on the one hand and the fully scripted telephone sales presentation on the other is the Automated Dialing-Recording Message Player (ADRMP). This electronic device—which may be a standalone device, or an add-on circuit board and software for your personal computer—automatically dials preprogrammed telephone numbers and plays a recorded massage to whomever answers the phone.

The advantages of an ADRMP are obvious:

1. The machine is a tireless caller.

2. The machine makes the same, unvarying presentation time after time.

3. The machine will never become frustrated.

4. The machine permits you to record a professional voice, perhaps even the voice of a recognized celebrity.

5. The machine does not demand commissions or an hourly wage.

Of course, many of the disadvantages are also obvious—and some are quite serious:

1. Many, perhaps most, people resent a "computer" calling them and, in consequence, will slam down the receiver without listening to the actual sales presentation.

2. Even customers who listen to the message may resent being randomly targeted in so blatant a way.

3. A callee may ask himself: *If this company uses a machine to call me, how will I be treated if I buy anything?*

4. The machine cannot respond to customer questions or counter customer resistance.

5. ADRMPs are under attack in some states and jurisdictions and are subject to restrictive legislation. In some places, the devices may be illegal.

> **TIP:** ADRMPs are probably most effective for following up orders. For example, a mail-order fulfillment operation might program the numbers of customers who have placed catalog orders, and the ADRMP might call them to confirm that the order arrived, asking the customer to call only if the order has failed to arrive. An ADRMP is also useful for initial collection "reminder" calls. Customers who have neglected to make a payment are less embarrassed by a machine reminder than by a human caller and, therefore, less likely to resent the reminder.

5.11.8.   The Fully Scripted Call

The script takes the outline to the next level, making the same points and achieving the same goals, but with a greater degree of control—and a proportionately reduced degree of freedom and creativity on the part of the salesperson. Keep the script within 300 to 500 words in length—that is, a maximum of ninety seconds of telephone time, without rushing.

The advantages of the full script over the outline are as follows:

1. The script can be used by novices, which means that you can hire low-cost telephone help rather than experienced telemarketers. Theoretically, then, you can put more people on more phones, thereby increasing call volume.

2. Scripts insure adherence to your selling goals and policies.

3. Scripts reduce misunderstanding and miscommunication. In this way, scripts may increase customer satisfaction.

4. Although it takes somewhat longer to write a script than it does to create an outline, scripts reduce training time and expense because they can be used by novice telemarketers.

Despite these advantages, scripts do have their drawbacks:

1. It is quite possible to read a script poorly and tediously, creating frustration in the callee.

2. Working from a script allows little room for creativity and may reduce the telemarketer's individual initiative.

3. Forced to depart from the script—for example, to answer a question—the inexperienced telemarketer may lose his place, stumble, and become confused.

4. Directed to adhere to the script, a telemarketer may find it difficult or even impossible to meet customer objections and counter resistance.

Turning Out a Bulletproof Script

It is possible to minimize the disadvantages of the script by taking the following steps to bulletproof the document:

1. Devote time and thought to preparing a truly effective script.

2. Include the same kind of tabbed responses to objections that you include in an outline.

3. Rehearse your delivery, and develop your voice.

Elements of an Effective Script

In addition to following the steps given for an effective outline, the script should:

1. Use language that talks to rather than at the callee

2. Use the pronoun *you* more often than *I, we,* or the noun *company*

   TIP: If you remember to make frequent use of *you* in preference to the other pronouns, you will inevitably focus the script on the needs of the target customer rather than on what you need.

3. Start with a strong opening statement that gets your target's interest

4. Include questions designed to get and keep your target involved

5. Include only questions that can be answered with a "yes" or that prompt a positive choice among positive alternatives

6. Promote benefits rather than features

7. Employ descriptive language

8. Make use of testimonials and examples of success

9. Conclude with a call to act, prompting the target to act now

Handling Resistance

A good script anticipates potential customer objections and provides responses to them. As with the outline method, use a clipboard with labeled and tabbed responses to specific objections, or put the objection responses into a personal computer database, so that the appropriate response can be "popped up" on your monitor screen as required.

> **TIP:** As you gain experience selling your product or service over the telephone, compile a list of the resistance and objections you actually encounter. Work on creating responses to each of these and add them to your tabbed catalog of resistance responses.

> **PITFALL:** Do not counter an objection with an argument. This will generate hostility, and hostility will definitely not generate a sale. For example, if your target objects that the merchandise is "too expensive," don't deny it, but, instead, put the issue back on the customer. "What do you pay for **merchandise** now?" you might ask. Then go on to work with the answer: "Does that price *include* freight?" Or: "How much do you have to buy to get that price?" Or: "Are you fully satisfied with the quality (the warranty, the color, the variety, the service, and so forth)?"

What happens when your target tells you flat out : "I don't want it"?

Well, it ain't over yet—not as long as you don't hang up. Respond with a question, "Please tell me why you don't want it?" In fact, respond to all *major* resistance with a question. To be sure, this is not slam-dunk save. No doubt about it: the sale is in trouble. However, asking a question is your *best chance* of salvaging the sale. Besides, you might learn something that you can use to improve your sales presentation.

Delivery

While telemarketing does not require the talented and trained voice of a television or radio announcer, it does call for someone who can deliver the presentation pleasingly, smoothly, with clear pronunciation, with conviction, at an even pace, and with enthusiasm.

> **TIP:** The single most important element in the delivery is pace. Most of us speak too fast. Slow down.

Enthusiasm: maybe you've got it, maybe you don't. If you believe in the product you are selling—and you have a personal stake in it—enthusiasm tends to come naturally. Another way to foster this quality is actually to deliver your presentation with a smile. Of course, the callee cannot see you, but the very act of smiling infuses your voice and your delivery with a degree of *audible* enthusiasm.

> **TIP:** Foster enthusiasm with the script itself. Keep the script simple and always positive. One surefire way to translate possible doubt into positive enthusiasm is to convert "I" to "you." Instead of saying *I think that,* say *You will discover that.*

5.11.9. Sample Scripts

Here are some sample scripts that incorporate the points and techniques just discussed:

1

> Good morning/afternoon. My name is **Name**. Could you please give me the name of the person who handles purchasing? Thank you very much.
>
> **Target Name**, this is **Name**, with **Company**. **We manufacture merchandise** for companies like yours, including **list three high-profile customers**.
>
> Do you currently use **type of merchandise**? What brands? What are you accustomed to paying?
>
> Well, then, you will want to hear what I have to offer.
>
> Our **merchandise** is highly cost-effective and represents the best value available today. It provides **list benefits**, and every one of my customers has been enthusiastic about including **list three different high-profile customers**.
>
> [Let me just give you an example]. **Name** at **High-profile company** tells us that **include a brief testimonial**. At **another High-profile company**, net revenues have shot up **percent amount**—mostly as a result of using **merchandise**.
>
> **Callee Name, merchandise** is fully guaranteed for **period**. Let me ask you: What kind of guarantee do you have at present?

You will agree, then, that our guarantee gives you a significant advantage. Also: exclusive next-day service is available—on-site!

We ship in quantities of **quantity**, and the price for each unit is **$ amount**. Most customers order **quantity**. With your approval, I can get that out to you right away. Would you like express delivery—ship date **date** at **$ amount**—or standard at **$ amount**?

[Customer places order.]

Let me make sure that I'm spelling your name correctly. I'll also confirm **quantity, price, shipping mode and date**.

Thank you for your order. Have a great day!

2

Hello. Am I speaking with **Target Name**? Hi. I'm **Name**, calling from **Company**. Would you be interested in hearing about an opportunity to dramatically improve your bottom line in the area of **type of product/service**?

I thought so.

So, I am correct in assuming that you would like to increase your share of this market?

Wonderful! Then I'm speaking with the right person and won't be wasting your time or mine.

Name, do you currently use **service** or do you handle this with in-house staff?

You know, we have discovered that few business professionals can find the time to do a cost-accounting study to determine just how terribly resource-intensive in-house **service** is. Let me share with you the results of our own survey of **number** of businesses similar to yours. Our survey revealed that in-house **service** operations consume **number** hours per week at a cost of **$ amount**. And that, **Name**, is a minimum figure. Our survey revealed that costs *can* run as high as **$ amount**.

I'm sure you agree that such costs are unacceptable. In fact, it was the results of this survey that convinced us to get into the business of providing **service** needs for businesses just like yours—for people unwilling to accept such outrageous in-house burdens.

Let me give it to you straight, right here and right now: We can fulfill all of your **service** needs for **$ amount**. Period. End of story.

Now, you heard me right. For **$ amount** per **time period** you get: **list services**.

What does that mean to your bottom line? It means at least **$ amount** *saved* each and every **time period**.

We do need some lead time to set up your account—**number** days—so it will be to your advantage to place an order with me today. By expediting processing, I will get you on the system no later than **date**.

All I need is some very basic information: list.

You'll be on the system **number** days after we receive your first payment of **$ amount**.

Before I leave you, let me just make sure I'm spelling your name correctly. The title of your position?

We look forward to working with you!

5.12. COLLECTION CALLS

5.12.1. Keys to Keeping Your Cool

The remaining chapters in this part of the book, 5.12 through 5.16, deal not with calls you initiate, but those you answer. Perhaps the most unnerving of these involve collection calls.

Professional collection calls usually come at you in a coolly professional tone. Most of us respond in a way that is anything but cool, however. Usually, the overwhelming impulse is to promise immediate payment—whether you can make good on that promise or not. Of course, if you can settle the account—if, for example, the delinquency is due to an oversight or error, not to cash-flow difficulties—do so quickly. Tell the collector what you are doing: how much you are sending and when. Then be certain that you do it. If, however, finances are a problem, fight the shamefaced impulse to promise a check-in-hand sprint to the mailbox. Instead, make another "purchase." Buy time.

Tell the caller that you are aware of the problem and that you need to review the current status of your accounts. Arrange to call back at a specific time. Obtain the name and number of the person in charge of your account, agree on the call-back time, hang up, then set about calculating just how much you can afford to pay and when. Be certain to call back as promised.

> TIP: A proactive approach can avert this situation. When you become aware of an impending problem—when you are going to be late paying a bill, or if you are unable to pay a bill—take the initiative, and make a call. Inform your creditor of the problem, explain it, and propose an alternative payment plan. Negotiate with your creditor before he calls *you*.

Your Secret Weapon

Owing money—especially when you can't handle the payments at present—makes you feel powerless. And understandably so. However, you have a secret weapon. Creditors know from bitter experience that delinquent accounts regularly turn into wholly "non-productive" accounts—write-offs, bad debts. Unless very large amounts of money are involved, legal action is generally impractical. True, the creditor can see to it that your credit record is besmirched, but that won't get him his money. The creditor knows all this. Therefore, your offer to negotiate payment terms you can live with is likely to meet with a significant degree of acceptance. After all, some payment is better than no payment.

Steps to Take

1. Buy time. Don't be pressured into making an on-the-spot agreement you can't keep. Buy the time you need to work out a viable proposal.

2. Call back.

3. Focus the conversation briefly and concisely on the reasons for the delinquency. Keep it general.

4. Propose a plan.

TIP: Don't be too generous. Start with the lowest numbers and easiest terms you believe you can get away with. Be prepared to work up from there. Make certain that *you* know what your realistic upper limit is.

PITFALL: Do not let yourself be talked into—or threatened into—a plan you cannot live with. Defaulting twice will only make the situation twice as difficult.

Sample Script

Collector: Are you aware that your account is sixty days past due? When are you sending payment to settle this account?

You: Yes, I do understand that it is overdue. I am experiencing financial difficulties. Allow me to review the current state of my accounts and call you back tomorrow. Can I call you at ten? I will give you a firm response at that time.

Here is the callback:

You: This is **Name**. You called me yesterday regarding my account with you.

Collector: Yes.

You: I have gone over my books carefully, and I've come up with a plan that will settle this account as quickly as I am able to. Here is what I suggest . . .

Collections Checklist

1. Buy time. Understand your feelings, and don't let them push you into an unworkable arrangement.

2. Remember your secret weapon: You *are* willing to pay.

3. Negotiate a viable plan.

5.13. COMPLAINTS

5.13.1. Tips for a Constructive Response

Responding to complaints is more than a necessary evil. Something goes wrong with one of your company's products. A customer is irritated and angry with your company. She calls you. Your response is forthcoming, forthright, and helpful. You communicate your commitment to stand behind the product or service and make things right again. The customer may still be upset with the product, but, chances are, she will feel positive emotions about your company.

Responding to complaints is an opportunity to build a positive relationship with your customer. When you pick up the phone and encounter a customer with a problem, you must communicate two ideas:

1. Your forthright promise to help

2. Your complete ability to help.

From this point, go on to the following:

1. Express understanding and concern.

2. If you have an immediate solution, tell the customer what you propose to do. Explain any steps he must take to make the repair, replacement, or adjustment possible (for example, take the product to the nearest authorized repair shop).

3. Provide any information the customer needs (for example, a list of authorized repair facilities in his area).

4. Apologize, but do not run your company down. Emphasize that you are grateful for the customer's patience and understanding.

When There's No Quick Fix

It is not possible to solve all problems over the telephone. In cases where there is no quick fix, attempt to furnish your best advice and the most attractive alternatives.

5.13.2. Disputing Claims

Customers rarely complain without a good reason. Sometimes, however, their complaint is unjustified. In such cases, your job is to refute the complaint without alienating the customer. Here are points to remember:

1. Make a wholehearted effort to understand what your customer wants. Express understanding and concern for his issues.

2. If you conclude that the complaint is unjustified, explain your refutation.

    PITFALL: Avoid such subjective issues as taste or judgment. Never bring up personality. Make certain that you focus the discussion exclusively and narrowly on the product or service issue at hand.

3. Make a strenuous effort to present whatever alternatives are possible: "We cannot make a refund in this case, but we can give you a 10 percent discount on a replacement part . . ."

    PITFALL: Avoid apologizing in this case! After all, you are disputing the claim precisely because you have done *nothing* to apologize for. Indeed, few things are more aggravating to a customer than declaring, in effect, "I'm sorry, I'm right and you're wrong." But please note: You *should* express your regret that the customer experienced a problem or is dissatisfied.

4. Conclude by telling your customer that you hope the alternative you have offered will be of value to him.

5.13.3. Sample Scenarios

Caller: I purchased a **product** from you, and I am not happy with it. [Describes problems].

You: I am sorry to hear that **product** isn't performing to your satisfaction. There are two ways we can work to resolve the problem and get you up and running as quickly and painlessly as possible.

From what you describe, I feel confident that the problem is with a bad **part**. I can either send you a replacement **part**, with full instructions for installing it. Or, if you prefer, you may return the entire unit to us, and we will replace the defective part. The first alternative is the quickest way to resolve the problem—but you may feel more comfortable having us perform the work. It's up to you.

Caller: I'd rather have you guys do the work.

You: I understand. Let me give you a few directions. First, please be careful to pack the unit in its original carton with all of the original shipping material. The carton and the shipping material are specifically designed to prevent damage. Send the unit to **address** and mark on the carton the following return authorization number: **number**. Ship via **carrier**. We will reimburse you for shipping costs.

Caller: What's your turnaround time?

You: Right now, we're averaging **time period**.

Customer name, I apologize for the inconvenience you have been caused, and I thank you for your patience and understanding. We'll resolve the problem as quickly as possible.

Caller: Yes, hello. My name is **Name**, and I'm really steamed about **product**, which I just bought. Your advertisements said that it would do **describes functions**. Well, it doesn't. And what are you going to do about it?

You: I'm sorry to hear that you are disappointed in **product**. Let me tell you up-front that the last thing we want to do is to mislead any of our customers. That's a terrible way to do business, and it certainly is not the way we do business.

Name, based on what you're telling me, I believe that you misread our advertisement. The product functions you are describing apply to our model **number**, a significantly more feature-rich—and, therefore, more expensive—model.

I can offer the following alternatives: If you like, I will authorize a full cash refund. Just repack **product** in its original carton, including all accessories, and take it to the dealer from whom you purchased it. Or, I will be happy to talk with you now about model **number**, which offers the features you describe—and more. There are also some intermediate-range models you might want to know about. If you like, you may exchange your current unit for one of these—and pay the difference. How would you like to proceed?

Caller: This **Name** calling. I bought a **product**, which I'm just not happy with. I want to get a full cash refund.

You: I'm looking your order up on my computer now. It's just coming up onto the screen. **Name**, you purchased the **product** on terms that specify no cash refund.

Caller: I know, but I'm really unhappy, and I won't settle for anything less than a full refund. I don't intend to be a victim of your company's policy.

You: **Name**, these terms are not simply a matter of "company policy." They are part of the reason that we were able to offer **product** to you at such a low cost. The non-refund terms are part of the bargain you made with us when you purchased **product**. Now, that does not mean you are left out in the cold. You have the option of exchanging **product** for something else, or you can return **product** and accept a store credit, which has no time limit whatsoever. You can use it like cash here at the store.

               I think that you'll agree that this option provides you with quite a bit of flexibility—enough to make a purchase decision you will be happy with.

Caller: I am so unhappy with **product** that I intend never to do business with you again!

You: I can understand and appreciate your anger. The fact is that [product] failed you and, what's even worse, it failed you repeatedly. I'm sure that my telling you how rare such a failure is—let alone repeated failure—isn't much help to you. The point is, that our product failed *you.*

               There's no problem with refunding the purchase price to you. If that's what you want, I will authorize it immediately. It will be sent out as soon as we receive your unit. Might I suggest another alternative?

               Try just one more replacement **product**. Don't give up on us just yet. If you like, I will send, without charge, a service representative to your site to supervise installation and to ensure that the unit is operating in an optimal environment.

Caller: I recently purchased a Model 487 widget from you, hooked it up to the power supply on my RevMaster PBY, and the 487 promptly burned out! I want a refund.

You: I'm very sorry this happened. However, my company cannot take responsibility for the damage in this case. The Model 487 is designed for direct current only. By hooking it up to your RevMaster, you ran AC through it. Our spec sheet and warning labels clearly caution against doing this, explaining that alternating current will destroy the coils. I'm afraid that voids the warranty.

          However, **Name**, we won't leave you hanging. I do have some alternatives to offer. Although I cannot make a warranty replacement in this case, I can offer to repair the motor. I assume that the only damage is to the winding coil. Repair will run $85 plus $6.75 for shipping. If you prefer, you can take the unit directly to one of our authorized repair shops. By the way, once the repair is made, your warranty will be reactivated and continue in force.

Caller: What is the matter with your shipping department? I ordered model 12345 and received 34567 instead! I want to make an exchange as quickly as possible.

You: I am calling up your record on my computer right now. It should come up on the monitor in just a second or two. Yes. There we are. **Name**, we clearly have an order here for model 34567.

Caller: Yes. *You* took the order down incorrectly!

You: I can retrieve the paperwork, if you like—get your original purchase order. This will take about a minute and a half. May I put you on hold?

Caller: Yes, go ahead.

You: I have the purchase order here, signed by you, and—I'm afraid—specifying model 34567. If you like, I'll fax you the document . . .

Caller: No. I guess I just blew it.

You: Unfortunately, the model you ordered and received is a custom design, which means that I cannot simply exchange it for 12345. What I *can* offer is **$ amount** credit on your 34567 toward purchase of a 12345. But, of course, there is yet another alternative. You can simply keep and use what you have. The 34567 should deliver satisfaction. How would you like to proceed?

Complaint Response Checklist

1. Learn to *welcome* complaints—as opportunities to build customer satisfaction.

2. Focus on issues, not personalities.

3. Focus on what you *can* do, not on what *cannot* be done.

4. In difficult situations, offer as many alternatives as possible.

5. Remember: choice empowers your customer. A customer who feels empowered is less likely to feel frustrated or dissatisfied.

5.14. FAVORS AND CHARITABLE REQUESTS

5.14.1. How to Say Yes—and How to Say No

It's no secret: saying yes to requests for favors or charitable donations is easier than saying no. The only trick to saying yes is to be certain that both you and the caller are agreed on just what it is you've said "yes" to. Begin by making certain that you understand what is being asked of you, and end by quickly reviewing the arrangement.

But, obviously, you cannot say yes to everything. Funds and time are limited. Moreover, it is certainly possible that you will be approached to do a favor that you either cannot do or are unwilling to do, and it is also likely that, sooner or later, you will be solicited by a charitable cause in which you do not believe.

If possible, structure your response this way—in the case of declining to perform a favor:

1. Express regret

2. Explain why you cannot perform the favor

3. Apologize

4. If possible and appropriate, suggest future circumstances and conditions that will enable you to perform the favor—next time.

In the case of declining charitable solicitations, try the following:

1. Acknowledge that the cause is worthy of support.

2. Enumerate reasons for declining support at the present time.

3. If possible and appropriate, offer a realistic hope for a donation at a future time.

TIP: If you genuinely disagree with the validity of the cause, you may want to make your views known. Remember, however, that nothing is gained by self-righteous posturing or deliberately giving offense.

The following are examples of declining charitable requests:

Your organization's efforts to fund **program** are highly commendable and, certainly, you are addressing a vital community need. I only wish that you had contacted me earlier in the year. Our company's budget for community giving has already been allocated, and I am sure you can appreciate the importance of remaining within the limits of a budget.

Name, we allocate our charitable budget early in **Month**. I would like to invite you to contact us next **Month**, when we will be able to give your program serious consideration. I appreciate your understanding in the *present* situation.

Another:

I am very sorry that we cannot contribute to **Charity** this year. **Company** is committed to several charities, including some that address the same needs as your organization. I know that your work is important and your needs very real, but our funds are limited, and I am forced to make difficult choices. I do not see our being able to accommodate your request any time soon, but I wish you success in your work.

Finally:

I agree that **name of cause** is worthwhile, but, in all candor, I cannot say that I agree with the policies and general approach of your organization. I particularly object to **specify**. For this reason, I believe that it would be hypocritical of me to make the donation you ask for. I trust that you will understand.

5.15.   INFORMATION

5.15.1.   Giving Information Without Wasting Time

Information is the lifeblood of any enterprise. Most telephone calls you handle involve nothing more—or less—than conveying information. Often, the exchange requires little more than a direct and courteous response to a simple question. This, of course, is the most desirable situation. You can help to set up this scenario by answering the phone with the phrase, "How may I help you?" Make certain that you include the *how*. It will tend to focus the caller's request, packaging it, as it were, in a way that you can handle most efficiently. Another useful tactic is to echo back to the caller what she has asked for, perhaps modifying the statement enough to define it more precisely: "You want the *complete* price list, or the price list for the standard models only?"

Once you have a clear understanding of what is being asked, provide the information. If this requires you to put the caller on hold, or to ask a question of a coworker, or to look something up yourself, tell the caller what you are doing, and tell him approximately how long it will take you to do it.

> TIP: Remember, when it is necessary to put a caller on hold, *ask* permission: "May I put you on hold so that I can look up the answer? It will take about thirty seconds."

When you use a computer to recover requested information, be aware that your customer cannot see what you are doing. Give him a blow-by-blow: "I'm going to search for that record right now. I'm typing it into the system . . . and it's searching . . . should be another few seconds. Yes. There. What's come up on my screen is a pair of orders from you, one dated May 3 and the other July 1." You might think of this as "sharing the screen."

> TIP: The caller has called requesting information. Give him information—including information about what you're doing to get him the information he's requested.

Always conclude the call by asking the customer, "Have I answered all of your questions?" If the answer is yes, you may make the exit even more useful and friendly by inviting future calls—directly to yourself: "Mr. Smith, please feel free to call any time. Just ask for me. I'm Herbert Henchman." Another closing option is to ask, "May I help you with anything else today?"

> PITFALL: Is it possible to give *too much* information? Yes, it is. Exercise your judgment in order to give the caller all the additional information he has asked for *plus* all the information you judge necessary. Do not overload the caller with marginally useful or confusing data.

5.16. SALES INQUIRIES

5.16.1. Surefire Ways to Turn Customer Inquiries into Orders

You pick up the phone, and the caller tells you that she's looking for some "information" on the style and prices of widgets you carry. "I just want to get information," she emphasizes, as if to alert you that she has no intention to make a purchase.

Now, think about that. There may well be some people in the world who are so bored with their lives that they fill their empty hours with idle requests for information. It is far more likely, however, that the caller asking for "information" is really doing two things:

1. Shopping

2. Calling for help.

Regardless of what the caller may tell you, don't be deceived into handing out mere information. Address the "hidden" motives of the caller by selling and by helping. If you are offering a worthwhile product or service, the two acts are really one and the same.

> **PITFALL:** The advice to *sell* to every caller does not give license to be obnoxious about it. No, you should not insist, "Ma'am, it's clear to me that what you *really* want to do is *buy* a widget today. I know that's true, because I read it in a book." But you *should* present the information requested in a manner that facilitates a sale.

Begin with the basic telephone answering strategies already discussed:

1. Do not start speaking until you have picked up the receiver and have it to ear and mouth.

2. Greet the caller with your company name and your name.

3. Focus the caller with *How may I help you?*

TIP: Remember—not "May I help you?" or "What can I do for you?" but
"*How* may I help you?" That single word, *how*, will focus the caller, prompting him to tell you what she wants. If all goes well, it will evoke a response
like, "I'm looking for a good, mid-priced widget."

Once you have a response—"I'm looking for a good, mid-priced widget"—it's up to you to develop it into a sale.

1. Make the caller feel that she has come to the right place: "I can help you
   with that."

2. Work with the caller to develop the initial statement into whatever you
   need to make an informed and helpful response that will likely result in
   a sale.

   PITFALL: Failure to close a sale often begins misunderstanding or inade-
   quate understanding, which is a function of insufficient information. Don't
   blame the customer for this. It's your *job* to make certain that the information you receive and supply is adequate.

   TIP: Of course, it takes time to make a sale. Just be aware that most of the
   time must be spent on providing and understanding information.
   Compared with this, the time devoted on your efforts at persuasion is
   slight. Be prepared to invest time in information. Not only is this "okay,"
   it's essential to the sales process.

3. Do not avoid asking questions. This is how you gather the information
   you need to help the caller and to convert an "information-only" call
   into a sale.

   TIP: All too often, sales personnel are trained to *avoid* asking questions.
   Why? There is a belief that, once the customer starts asking questions, he's
   likely to ask himself *Do I really want to buy this?* That *is* a risk. But, the fact
   is, if you don't ask questions, your chances of making a sale are reduced
   and, even more important, your opportunity to create satisfaction in the
   customer is drastically limited. The goal of selling *this* item to *this* customer
   this time is a puny goal. Enduring sales success comes not just by making
   sales, but by creating satisfied customers, who will buy more from you and
   who will tell others to buy more from you.

Here is a call-answering scenario. The phone rings, and you pick it up:

You: **Company**. This is **Name**. How may I help you?

Caller: I am looking for **product**.

You: I can help you with that. We offer a wide variety of products. If I might, I'll ask you a few questions so that we'll find just what you're looking for. [You should have a list of questions prepared relating to the product you sell. Take VCRs, for example. Questions should include: "What's most important to you in a VCR—playback of rented tapes, recording or TV programs, playing tapes you make with your camcorder?" "Do you want stereo hi-fi sound?" "What kind of television do you have?" Having established these parameters, offer what you have and begin to talk about price.]

Caller: [Responds to questions].

You: Based on what you've just told me, I suggest that you consider either **product A** or **product B**. Both will do **functions based on answers to questions.** The significant differences are that **product A** will also **list additional functions**. The price of **product A** is **$ amount**, compared with **$ amount** for **product B**. Now, if you want those additional features, the additional cost is justified. If you're looking for something more basic, which still fits your requirements, you might want to spend less on **product B**.

At this point, you have responded to the caller's request for information—but you have also set up a sale. Why not attempt to close? Ask:

May I take your order for **product A** or **product B**?

Maybe you'll get an order. However, if the customer hesitates or simply says that she is not yet ready to order, ask another question:

Is there any more information I could supply to help you make your choice?

TIP: *Choice* is a word you should always use in preference to *decide* or *decision*. Whereas *decision* suggests compulsion, *choice* connotes empowerment and freedom. It puts the sale in a positive context.

Some sales situations are more complex. Despite your questions, the caller may remain unclear about her needs. Or it is possible that the range of product options you offer is simply to extensive to be covered adequately in a phone conversation. If you depend heavily on the telephone to make sales, you might consider drawing up a "decision tree" or a "flow chart," with the yes and no responses branching from one decision to another, in order to help your sales staff "walk" customers through the options and help them clarify their needs. You might also combine the telephone with the fax machine. Offer to fax—right now, while you're still on the line—a checklist or chart that will aid the customer in making a decision. Finally, you can use the response to a telephone inquiry to obtain a name and address for a catalog mailing. Ten days after mailing the catalog, follow up with a telephone call.

5.16.2.   Some Techniques for Focusing Inquiry Calls

These days, it seems, nobody wants to be called "salesman" or "salesperson." Go into any chain store, and you're likely to see folks with name tags labeled "Sales Associate" or "Sales Counselor." Maybe it seems like a semantics game to you. Maybe it *is*. But it's worth thinking about the phrase *sales counselor*. For, if you think of yourself as a counselor—someone willing to work with the caller to ensure that her needs are met and met optimally—you will create a sales situation in which the customer perceives the selling process not as a pro forma step toward getting merchandise, but as something that actually adds value to the purchase.

1.   Create a set of questions tied to intended use.

2.   Next, turn to cost.

> **Tip:** Preface this phase of the sale with a "helping" remark: "Let's work together a moment to determine just what product will be best for you." Be patient.

> **Pitfall:** It is critically important that you avoid any signs of impatience. If the customer senses your impatience, she, too, will become impatient and anxious—and, likely, you will not close the sale.

> **Tip:** Regarding time—the more of it you and your potential customer invest in the initial phases of the sales process, the more likely it is that the process will be consummated and the sale closed.

5.16.3. Some Techniques for Overcoming Resistance

What is resistance? Most often, it is not a specific objection to closing the sale, but, rather, some variation on "I don't know . . ." When the objection is more specific, it is usually expressed in such phrases as:

"Isn't that terribly expensive?"

"I've heard those things don't work."

"I've heard a new model is going to make that obsolete."

"I've always used Brand X."

"I don't have the staff to operate it."

Human nature often prompts us to avoid confrontation. Characteristically, then, much resistance is expressed in the form of postponement:

"Can you call me about it later?"

"I've been too busy to think about it."

"I'm not ready to buy yet."

Overcome the first type of resistance by educating the caller. Don't argue. Just show the alternatives. For example:

Caller: It's too expensive.

You: I wouldn't deny that **product** requires an investment. But our experience has shown that it *is* precisely that: an *investment*—a cost-effective investment of resources. On average, in installations we've done for firms the size of yours, the initial outlay is amortized within **time period**. Of course, we also offer you a wide range of financing choices for you.

TIP: Resistance is not just something a customer puts up to thwart you. It is an obstacle that both you and the customer confront. Overcome resistance by showing your customer how to get around the obstacle.

The second kind of resistance—postponement—should not be met by coaxing or goading. Instead, shoulder some of the caller's burden of uncertainty:

"What can I do to help you make your choice?"

"What additional information will help you move on to the next step?"

"How can I help you define your options?"

Sales Inquiry Checklist

1. Treat all informational inquiries as opportunities to make a sale.

2. Set a worthwhile goal: not just to make a one-shot sale, but to create a customer.

3. Cast yourself in the role of sales counselor.

4. Learn to view sales as the art of *helping* the customer make choices.

Part Six

INTERVIEWS AND
CONFERENCES

6.1. OBJECTIVES AND STRATEGY

6.1.1. Hints for Honing Your Verbal Edge

There is a disease called Tourette's Syndrome—named after Gilles de la Tourette, the French neurologist who first described it in 1885—that causes sufferers to bark, grunt, or blurt out obscenities. These outbursts are involuntary, and they happen in the course of ordinary conversation. Victims of the disorder point out that these socially inappropriate, bizarre, and downright offensive verbal tics are most likely to emerge at precisely the worst times—a job interview, for example.

Bizarre and sad, Tourette's Syndrome is very rare. So why do I mention it? Because I believe it is an extreme example of the kind of fear that most of us harbor, at some level of consciousness, whenever we find ourselves in a high-stakes interview or conference situation. Think about it—the feelings: your tongue gets stuck to the roof of your mouth, you feel a tightening of the throat, your heart pounds, your stomach churns. What *are* you afraid of? The answer, I submit, is that, like the Tourette victim, you are afraid of saying precisely the *wrong* thing, you are afraid of making yourself look foolish, and of sabotaging a project, a promotion, or even your job.

Are these fears realistic? Well, probably a lot less realistic than you believe. But that does not mean the fear is unreal. The feelings are undeniable, and it is undeniable, too, that negative feelings can and do work against your ability to express yourself effectively and persuasively.

Your first task in high-stakes interview and conference situations is to understand your fear and not so much try to overcome it, as simply to work *around* it. The beauty of these workarounds is that they are precisely the strategies and techniques required to create clear, effective, and persuasive interviews and conferences.

6.2. Nuts and Bolts

6.2.1. Doing Your Homework: How Much Do You Need to Know?

Let's forget the interview/conference situation for a moment. Let's say you've been asked to prepare a major presentation—a speech, a whole dog-and-pony show—on your company's newest computer memory chip. Odds are that you would not attempt to "wing" the presentation—at least not if you had any interest in keeping your job. No, you would prepare by gathering relevant facts and figures, specs, comparatives, and so on. In fact, you would probably go an extra mile or more beyond this and research current trends, cutting-edge indications, and future prospects. A lot is riding in the presentation. Such preparation is only reasonable.

A lot also rides on certain interviews and conferences. Yet people rarely prepare adequately for them. Most folks believe that the interviewer holds all the cards, that the occasion is spontaneous, and that, therefore, preparation is impossible or, at least, fruitless.

This is far from the case. Prepare for a high-stakes interview as thoroughly as you would for a major presentation. Gather relevant facts and figures. Familiarize yourself with the leading issues. Understand and appreciate the important trends. Then formulate your stance on these. Rehearse the facts and your presentation in your mind.

> TIP: People prepare a lifetime for so-called overnight success. Why not prepare overnight for success the next morning? When in doubt, *learn* something.

6.2.2. Setting Up an Interview or Conference: Timing Is the Key

You cannot always control when an interview or conference will take place, but, if you have any say in the matter, try to observe the following:

1. Ask for a raise—or other benefit or promotion—after you have successfully completed a project.

2. Avoid asking for a raise after the failure of a project or in the midst of a disaster.

464

3. Observe the rhythms of your office. Try to synchronize high-stakes interviews/conferences with them.

4. In general, Mondays are bad days to raise issues that can be put off until Tuesday.

5. Many people find it difficult to focus on Friday.

6. The high-energy time for most people comes late in the morning—ideally, between ten and eleven.

7. The low-energy time is late afternoon, between two and four.

6.3.   A MATTER OF STYLE

6.3.1.   Learning to Use Your Feelings

In ancient times, Greek orators developed the art of rhetoric: precise rules and strategies to be used in persuasive speech making. That was then. This is now—and "now" usually doesn't allow time for a full-blown speech to get your point across. Most often, you have a moment or two to be persuasive. We measure our discourse not in minutes, let alone hours, but in sound bites. Under such pressure to perform, clarity and strength of expression are all too often clouded by a haze of emotion and debilitating anxiety.

But if feelings interfere with communication, they are also the very substance of communication. Learn to use your feelings, and you will connect with the feelings of others. Connect with the feelings of others, and you will persuade them.

Feelings: Right and Wrong

Even a first-year psych student will tell you that there is no such thing as "bad" feeling or a "good" feeling. Feelings just *are,* period. But anybody in the business of persuasion—that includes salespeople, lawyers, advertising folk, and ministers of the Gospel—will tell you that there are very definitely "right" feelings and "wrong" feelings. This distinction has absolutely nothing to do with morality. "Right" feelings are those that you want your listener to have. They are the feelings that will prompt him to act the way you want him to. "Wrong" feelings are those that motivate your listener to act in way contrary to what you want. I'm not saying that you should abandon logic and common sense in attempting to persuade your listener, but it is almost always more immediately effective and feasible to pave an emotional road along which you can push your argument. If you bludgeon your listener with a host of logical arguments, chances are he will emerge from the exchange more or less numbed. Begin, however, by cultivating the "right" feelings in him, and it is far more likely that he will move in the desired direction.

6.3.2. Conquering Your Fear

Is the scheme I've just laid out manipulative? Assuredly so. And the most important person you must first manipulate is yourself. Prior to the interview/conference:

1. Recognize the negative feelings that you have.

2. Now, deliberately try to imagine the worst things that can happen to you as a result of the interview/conference. Develop a full scenario. Play it out. Experience the emotions *before* the interview rather than waiting for them to sneak up on you.

3. Finally, having played out the worst that can happen, imagine the best outcome. How will you feel? What will it be like to succeed in this encounter? Play out this scenario, too.

> **TIP:** Will this exercise cure your case of "nerves"? Probably not. But it will make the emotions associated with a high-stakes interview/conference more familiar and, therefore, less threatening. To that extent, it *will* reduce your anxiety and help you perform despite your "wrong" feelings.

There is more to overcoming your fears. It is a mistake to think that, in order to cope with your fear, to keep it from interfering with your ability to communicate, you must change the emotion. The fact is, you probably cannot change the emotion—at least, not right away. That's bad news, I guess. But it hardly matters, because there is better news to come: You don't *have* to change the emotion.

The great American psychologist and philosopher William James once said, "We do not run because we are afraid, we are afraid because we run." Anyone who has been through natural childbirth training—either as a mother or a "coach"—is familiar with the emphasis placed on breathing exercises and routines. It's critical to keep the baby supplied with loads of oxygen, right?

Yes, of course. But the breathing routines have nothing to do with that. There real function is to give the mother (and the "coach") something to concentrate on. If you are breathing in a regular, self-conscious way, you are less apt to cry out and scream. And if you don't hear yourself screaming, well, things can't be all that bad, can they? We don't scream because we are scared, we are scared because we scream.

In a high-stakes interview/conference, the equivalent of a childbirth scream is the tight, high, pinched voice of fear. The problem is that not only does such a thin, scared voice sound unconvincing to your listener, it sounds even worse to yourself. You hear it, and a part of your brain says: *Hey, we're scared!* And the fear mounts, and the voice gets thinner and higher—may even crack—you get more scared, and your listener drifts further and further off into the realm of those "wrong" feelings.

Your task is to head off this vicious cycle. Concentrate not on your fears, but on your voice. Do whatever you can *consciously* and *deliberately* to lower your voice in pitch (this is true whether you are male or female), to make it resonant, to enunciate each syllable of each word, giving everything you say value and conviction.

Will this make the fear go away?

Probably not. But, scared as you may be, what you, and your listener, will hear is the voice of self-confident authority. As you listen, you may well begin actually to feel some of that confidence. Furthermore, the verbal and non-verbal signals you'll be getting from your listener will be signals indicating the "right—rather than the "wrong"—feelings. And that, too, will build your confidence. You will have started a *positive* feedback cycle.

6.3.3.   Don't Beg. But Do Bargain

Just as timing—in the sense of when to set up an interview—is important, so is timing in the sense of the rhythm of the conversation, the give and the take.

How can you establish this rhythm? Don't *ask* for what you want. *Negotiate* for it.

> **TIP:** Asking is taking; negotiating is trading one valuable commodity for another. It is taking *and* giving. Successful interview/conference outcomes are almost always based on negotiation.

Negotiation keeps issues alive. If you simply ask, "Can I get a raise?" and the answer is "No," the conversation grinds to a halt. Dead. In contrast, if you approach this issue as a negotiation, it tends to become a living thing—or at least a request that invites a creative response:

> Since I took over management of Project X, we've seen a 15 percent increase in profit margin, and we've added two new territories. Best of all, the year's not over. You've given me a lot of creative freedom, for which I'm grateful. However, I now feel that it is time for my salary level to catch up to the level of my responsibilities, qualifications, and, most of all, achievements.

6.3.4. Getting Big Results from Small Talk

Not all business communication is contained within formal interviews and conferences. Nor is all business communication focused on specific goals. While you don't go into the office to discuss a promotion or a major new project each and every day, you do *talk* every day.

Ask any old-line, hard-line manager, and he (it's almost invariably a man) will tell you that office "small talk" is one of the great time-wasting plagues of the business world. Yet small talk need not be the equivalent of idle chatter and gossip. At the very least , it can raise office morale and help to build a community of colleagues, a genuine team. Any organization works best when its constituents are accustomed to seeing one another as fully rounded human beings rather than as mere cogs in a great machine.

Small talk should be encouraged. Exploit it to learn about your coworkers and to let them learn about you. Beyond this, there is shop talk—the informal creative, business-focused conversation that is conducted in the corridor, beside the water cooler, or during a casual visit to a colleague's office.

> PITFALL: The danger of small talk is that it may degenerate into gossip. The most destructive kind of gossip consists of rumors, half-truths, and out-and-out fabrications about the status of the organization. ("I hear the merger's going get us all canned.") The most effective way to curb this kind of small talk is not to generate it and not to participate in it. That does not mean that you need to alienate your colleagues by self-righteously declaring that you "don't deal in gossip." Simply and quietly decline to participate in it.

6.3.5. How to Make Your Body Language Say What You Want It to Say

Everybody's heard about body language—the non-verbal "ques" we all broadcast to the world, which "speak" volumes about how we feel concerning ourselves, the people with whom we are communicating, and the issues being discussed. Generally, it does not pay to become overly self-conscious about your body language. That is likely to result in stiffness and artificiality, making you come across as pretentious at best and phony at worst. Having said this, it *is* a good idea to realize a few major points about body language:

1. Practice good posture. As your mother told you, stand straight and do not slouch.

2. Make good use of your hands. Use them to punctuate important points.

3. Do not clasp your hands in front of you. This makes you look insecure.

4. Do not fold your arms across your chest. This makes you appear closed to ideas and suggestions.

5. Do not stand with your hands on your hips. This communicates defiance and impatience.

6. Keep your hands away from your face. Hands to face suggests shame and that you have something to hide.

7. Rubbing your cheek or forehead telegraphs anxiety.

8. Bringing your hand to the back of your neck communicates a desire to leave—to "pull" yourself out of the situation.

9. If you are seated, any leg movement suggests your desire to leave.

> **TIP:** Hands—they are too important to leave to their own devices. Think about how you use them. Make them part of your presentation.

No discussion of body language would be complete without a strong mention of eye contact. Many of us find it difficult to look our conversation partner in the eye. But even if maintaining eye contact takes your deliberate concentration, make the effort. Looking askance suggests evasiveness. Shifting your gaze from side to side—well, we all know the expression "shifty-eyed."

> **TIP:** In cases where you need to underscore your authority, you might fix your gaze slightly *above* your listener's eye level—at about the forehead. This conveys your dominance.

6.3.6. Reading Body Language Cues

You can essentially stand the preceding discussion on its head to generate some pointers for reading body language. Why would you *want* to read body language? There is a great difference between a monologue and a conversation. Conversation thrives on give and take, on feedback. By watching your listener—and not just listening to what he's got to say—you can gauge how well your ideas are being received. You may be able to tailor your presentation accordingly. Watch out for:

1. Hands clasped in front. This suggests that your listener is not comfortable. Either he lacks confidence in himself—or in what you are saying.

2. Arms folded across the chest. This communicates resistance.

3. Hands on hips. This communicates defiance and impatience.

4. When the hands fall to the sides—or, if the listener is seated, are laid naturally on the lap—you can infer that you are getting across.

5. Hands spread out, palms up, in front of the listener, suggest a call for help.

6. If the seated listener leans forward at any point, he is indicating intense engagement in what you are saying.

7. Hands near the face suggest that the listener either has serious doubts about what is being discussed or is uncomfortable with the subject matter. The gesture also suggests that the listener is being less than honest.

8. Rubbing the cheek or forehead telegraphs anxiety.

9. Bringing the hand to the back of the neck communicates a desire to leave—as if your listener wants to "pull" himself out of the situation.

10. If the listener is seated, any leg movement suggests a desire to leave.

6.3.7. Tips for Becoming a Great Listener

To become an effective communicator, you must be an effective listener. This begins with the obvious: a polite attitude that allows your conversation partner to be heard. However, learning to listen goes beyond sitting quietly and nodding your head.

1. Be generous with your verbal and non-verbal ques. During natural pauses in the rhythm of what you are being told, interject "yes" or "I see" or some other relatively neutral form of encouragement. These expressions are the lubricants of conversation. On the nonverbal front, avoid (if you can) the negative body-language cues discussed in 6.3.5. Do nod and smile at intervals. Endeavor to maintain eye contact.

2. Ask questions.

3. Preface questions with positives phrases: "That's really interesting . . .," "I hadn't thought of it this way . . .," "You raise a provocative point . . .," and so on.

4. Synchronize your comments and questions with the natural rhythm of the conversation.

6.3.8.   What—and What Not—to Wear

Fashions change, and that fact means that no one can prescribe absolutely just what you should wear to a business interview or conference. A general rule of thumb is possible, however: wear what satisfies these three criteria:

1. It makes you comfortable.

2. It expresses how you feel about yourself.

3. It is appropriate to your field or industry.

> TIP: Maybe you work in an industry where it is important to *wow* your colleagues and clients with drop-dead clothes. In many fields, however, this is a risky strategy. Better to dress so as to convey the message that you are capable of getting yourself together in a professional and appropriate manner.

Be Sharp. Be Clean.

Here is one other universal rule: Whatever you choose to wear, make certain that it is sharp and clean. Suits—for men and women—should be dry-cleaned, shirts and blouses freshly laundered. You don't have to buy new clothes every other week, but the clothes you wear must be in impeccable repair.

> TIP: Don't neglect personal hygiene, either. Shower or bathe, of course, and be certain to use deodorant. Avoid using too much perfume, cologne, or after-shave. Not only might your conversation partners find these scents objectionable (a sizable number of people are actually mildly allergic to perfumes), but using too much perfume, cologne, or after-shave conveys the subtle psychological message that you are trying to "cover up" something.

Be Safe. Be Dull?

In most industries and in most workplaces, the most effective clothing for the purposes of business communication is essentially conservative and traditional. Does this mean you should look dull? No, but use the conservative look as a base, a norm, on which you build your own personal look.

> TIP: Fashion is communication. As with any other form of communication, start by knowing what you want to say.

Some Unisex "Rules"

1. Dress to convey an impression of reliability and attention to detail.

2. Do not let any single article of attire become distracting.

   Tip: Dress so that the focus of attention is *you,* not your outfit.

3. Dark colors convey authority, and dark blue conveys the greatest degree of authority. (This explains the color of a police officer's uniform.)

   Pitfall: Gentlemen: Black suits can be impressive, but be aware that, to some people, black clothing is associated with clergymen and funeral directors.

4. Wear natural fabrics. Synthetics often have a sheen and texture that makes them look cheap. Also, they tend to "drape" less attractively than clothing made of natural fibers. Synthetic fabrics retain body odors. Finally, why associate yourself with something "synthetic," which implies phoniness or superficiality.

Checklist for Men

1. Dark colors, especially blue, convey authority.

2. Solids and subtle patterns are safest.

3. Muted, narrow pin stripes ("banker stripes"), are associated with conservative finance and politics.

4. For many people, checked patterns suggest images of a cheesy traveling salesman.

5. Choose 100 percent wool for your general-purpose suits.

6. It may be wise to select warm-weather suits made of a summer-weight wool rather than linen or linen-blend, both of which tend to wrinkle badly and quickly.

7. Smart European cuts are fine for "young" industries and *if* you have the slender build such a cut flatters. You may be safer with a more generous—and conservative—American cut.

8. Wear only long-sleeved shirts for business purposes.

9. French cuffs, with *simple* cuff links, are a nice touch and add an extra measure of elegance and attention to detail.

10. Shirt color should be white or very pale blue. Favor solids over patterns, and muted stripes over any other patterns.

   PITFALL: Many perceive shirt monograms as status symbols. Just be aware that other folks see monograms as egotistical and pretentious. If you *do* choose to wear monogrammed shirts, have the monogram placed on one cuff—not above the pocket.

11. Cotton is the best fabric for shirts.

   TIP: Experts disagree as to whether the shoes or the necktie is the first article of clothing noticed when you meet a colleague or client. In either case, the tie is important.

12. Choose 100 percent silk for neckties.

13. The tie should complement the suit, but not match it.

14. The pattern of the tie should not compete with the pattern of the suit.

15. Tie widths vary with changing fashion, but a safe rule of thumb is that the width of the tie should approximate the width of the suit lapels.

16. Fashion seems to cycle between loudish patterns and more staid looks. However, any of the following traditional patterns are always acceptable: solids, foulards, stripes, and muted paisley prints.

17. Avoid polka dots, pictures, and sporting images (golf clubs, polo mallets, horses, hounds) on ties.

   PITFALL: The sight of a designer logo on a tie drives some people crazy. In the eyes of some, it brands you as a slave to superficial fashion. Avoid the look.

18. Tie a careful knot—generally, the smaller the better.

19. The necktie should not extend below your trouser belt.

20. Shoes should be of black or brown leather. Avoid other colors and materials.

21. Shoes should be in impeccable repair and well polished.

22. Heels should be relatively unworn.

23. Managers tend to wear lace-up wing tips, while accountant types seem to favor tasseled slip-on dress shoes. Those in "creative" positions—such as advertising art directors—often wear expensive Italian loafer styles.

24. Socks should be in blue, black, dark gray, or dark brown.

25. Socks should be long enough to permit you to cross your legs without showing hairy bare skin.

26. Suspenders (or "braces") became very popular as tokens of corporate power in the late 1980s and early 1990s. These days, *some* people find them pretentious.

27. Worn by a man, jewelry can send powerful messages—possibly messages you don't wish to convey.

28. Simple cuff links and a wedding band (if you're married) are safe jewelry choices for men.

29. Avoid neck chains, stick pins, bracelets, and pinky rings.

30. In most industries, earrings are taboo.

Checklist for Women

1. Women enjoy a greater range of choices than men, but they are also under greater economic pressure to invest in current fashions.

2. The woman's business suit need not be an imitation of a man's wardrobe.

3. Charcoal gray suit with a white blouse is the single safest combination.

4. Solids, pinstripes, and muted plaids in a variety of colors are all appropriate business attire choices.

5. Natural fabrics are great. But women may also want to consider natural-synthetic blends, which resist wrinkling.

6. Skirt length varies from season to season. However, wear a more conservative length than you might wear on social occasions.

7. Long-sleeve blouses are most desirable.

8. Avoid sleeveless blouses.

9. For blouses, choose natural fabrics, preferably cotton or silk.

10. Almost any attractive color is acceptable for a blouse. However, remember that white and pale blue are the most universally accepted colors in the business world. Pearl gray and the deeper blues are also good color choices.

11. A beautiful scarf can add a dramatic accent.

    PITFALL: Avoid the matching scarf-and-blouse look, which many regard as a bit tacky.

12. Choose pure silk for the scarf.

13. The color and pattern of neckwear should complement your suit.

14. Avoid large polka dots (though small ones are fine).

15. Conservative is the best approach to choosing business shoes: a closed-toe pump with a $1^1/_2$-inch heel is a safe choice.

16. Avoid very high heels.

17. Shoe color should complement your suit and accessories. Good colors are navy, burgundy, black, and brown.

18. In hosiery, favor neutral or skin tones. Black hosiery tones down shorter hemlines and is also appropriate for business wear.

    TIP: Keep an extra pair of pantyhose or stockings in your briefcase or purse.

19. The belt should match or complement the shoes.

    PITFALL: Women may wear belts made of a wider variety of materials than men's belts. However, beware: snake skin, alligator, and lizard belts may be attractive, but some clients and colleagues sensitive to environmental issues may be offended if you wear the skin of endangered or potentially endangered animal species.

20. With jewelry, less is more. Wedding bands or engagement rings are always acceptable, but avoid wearing rings on multiple fingers. Earrings should be small and discreet. Avoid long, dangling earrings that jangle or make noise.

    PITFALL: Pierce your ears, not your nose.

21. Avoid fake pearls or gaudy costume jewelry.

22. Avoid charm bracelets and jewelry with your initials on it.

23. Anklets are not acceptable in general business situations.

24. As with jewelry, less is more. The natural look is usually perceived most positively.

25. If you are comfortable without lipstick, avoid it.

6.4. HOT ISSUES

6.4.1. Communicating in the New Multicultural, Multiethnic World of Business

Cynics and hate mongers alike decry "political correctness" and long for something perceived as the "good old days" when the world of business was more homogeneous. The fact is that the good old days weren't always all that good. Women, African-Americans, Asian-Americans, Jews, Catholics, Irish, Italians, and other racial, ethnic, and religious minorities were often excluded from the upper echelons of the corporate world. Moreover, certain businesses tended to serve certain customers—and to exclude (or, at least, disregard) others. To be sure, today's business world is hardly a level playing field. There are still plenty of prejudices to go around. But conditions have changed and continue to change. Federal and state legislation makes all discrimination based on sex, race, religion, and disability illegal. But, even more importantly, the vast majority of businesses have realized that, in order to compete in an increasingly multi-ethnic and multicultural marketplace, the corporate organization must open itself at all levels to a wide variety of people from a wide variety of backgrounds.

1. Become sensitive to the needs, beliefs, and preferences of your colleagues, supervisors, and subordinates, as well as your customers and clients.

2. Do not make assumptions based on your own particular background or orientation.

3. Welcome diversity as an enhanced business opportunity.

PITFALL: "Humor" based on prejudice or hate of any kind is always obscene and never acceptable, especially in a professional or business context. In some situations, prejudicial remarks constitute harassment and may result in legal action.

6.4.2. What You Must Know About Sexism and Sexual Harassment

Rightly or wrongly, we all make certain assumptions about likes and dislikes, abilities and interests, based on gender. When these assumptions adversely affect the way we communicate with colleagues, supervisors, subordinates, customers, and clients, we may be guilty of sexism. In extreme cases, our words or actions may border on sexual harassment.

> PITFALL: *Sexual harassment* consists of unwanted and offensive sexual advances or derogatory or discriminatory remarks made by an employer to an employee, a supervisor to a subordinate, one employee to another employee, or, in some cases, by an employee to a customer or client. In the workplace, such actions or remarks are said to create a hostile climate.

Speaking or acting in a sexually offensive manner is not only destructive to employee morale, and, therefore, to productivity, it exposes you and your company to legal liability—not only of a civil nature, but possibly to criminal prosecution. Many issues of sexism, sexual discrimination, and sexual harassment are related especially to the employment selection and interview process:

1. Employers are forbidden by law to ask any questions bearing on the applicant's marital status, sexual orientation, age, or ethnic or national origins.

2. Employers should not ask an applicant if she "plans to have children." This is inappropriate and has a discriminatory undertone.

6.4.3. Age-ism: What It Is and How to Avoid It

Many businesses make their appeal to certain age groups. Usually, there is nothing wrong in this. However, be certain that you are not making assumptions that reduce your potential customer base. Communicating—and advertising—in such ways that exclude older customers is often counterproductive. At worst, some potential customers may find it offensive.

Within the workplace, discriminating—through actions or remarks—on the basis of age is illegal. Aside from establishing that a candidate for employment meets minimum age requirements for lawful employment, employers are forbidden by law to ask an applicant questions regarding his or her age.

6.5. Interviewing Prospective Employees

6.5.1. Key Questions to Ask

Too often too many managers think of their company in terms of the products or services it produces and the revenue versus costs that result from the process. Too often they forget that the substance of the process is *people*. A company is its *people* first—*then* its product and balances sheet. Perhaps it is this skewed perception that prompts most managers to regard interviewing as an unwelcome intrusion into daily "business." Managers often do little to prepare for interviewing job applicants. Often, they find themselves at a loss for meaningful questions.

The recruiting-related questions that are meaningful for you, for your department, and for your company depend on the *needs* and *goals* of your company, your department, and yourself. Before calling a candidate in for an interview, be certain that you have a clear understanding of what these are. Write them down. Then structure specific questions, to ask at the interview, aimed at determining how well the applicant is likely to address each of these issues. The following are the most basic questions you should ask—or modify to suit your particular situation and needs:

1. *What can you tell me about yourself that demonstrates your qualifications for this position?* Too many interviewers stop with the first part of the question: *What can you tell me about yourself?* This is vague and likely to elicit an unwanted rambling autobiography. Focus the question by narrowing it to a match between the applicant and the needs and goals of the company, the department, and yourself.

   TIP: Look for answers that reveal an understanding and appreciation of problems, goals, and needs—and that target these: "I am a troubleshooter. I've always been good at analyzing a situation and working with the team to solve the problem."

2. *Why do you want to leave your present company?* Beware of negative answers: "I don't get along with my boss," or "I'm bored." Negative answers indicate attitudes that are not likely to change with a change in employment venue. The top-flight candidate will respond positively: "I want greater challenges, and I believe I will find them at your company."

480

Tip: Some candidates may answer neither positively nor negatively. For example: "We've just relocated into the area, and I had to leave my job" or "I want to work closer to home, so that I can spend more time with my family." You might consider that a truly savvy potential employee—a creative candidate—would endeavor to come up with a response that addresses *your* needs rather than his.

3. *What do you know about us that prompted you to apply with us?* The purpose of this question is *not* to gain an outside perspective on your company—though that may be a side benefit of the question—but to determine whether or not the applicant had the initiative and creativity to learn about your company before the interview. Furthermore, the greater the candidate's understanding of what you do and what you need, the more likely it is that she will be a successful hire.

4. *How much experience do you have in **field**?* If you have done your homework—that is, evaluated the applicant's résumé—you should have a good idea of the answer, at least in general terms. This question gives the candidate an opportunity to elaborate on and demonstrate his familiarity with the field or specific job for which you are considering him.

5. *What do you most like and most dislike about your current job?* The savvy candidate will minimize the negative part of this question, concentrating instead on what aspects her present job she most enjoys. Invite negativity precisely so that you can gauge the candidate's positive energies.

   Pitfall: Look out for the candidate who responds to this question with comments related to personality: "What I hate most about my job is my supervisor."

6. *How many hours a week do you need to get your job done?* This is the only "trick" question you should ask. It will help you gauge:
   a. The candidate's commitment to the job
   b. The candidate's efficiency on the job
   c. The candidate's creativity

   Candidates who reply with a mechanical "forty hours" demonstrate little initiative. Candidates who tell you that (for example) "sixty hours" is the norm demonstrate a willingness to work, but may also suggest that they are unable to accomplish their assigned tasks within a reasonable time frame. The creative, flexible candidate is likely to replay with something like:"I try to plan my time efficiently. But, of course, business has crunch periods, and when that happens, I put in whatever hours are necessary to get the job done."

Pitfall: Don't get hung up on doggedly insisting that the candidate give you a precise response ("48.4 hours, ma'am!"). The question is designed roughly to *gauge* commitment, efficiency, and creativity.

7. *How much are you making now and what kind of salary are looking for?* This question should come late in the interview process. Generally speaking, the first party in the employment"negotiation"who mentions a figure is in the weaker bargaining position. Chances are, of course, that an ad or job description already states a salary range.

Tip: Note that a truly creative and savvy candidate may be reluctant to furnish precise numbers, replying instead with something like:"Given my skills and qualifications—and the nature of the responsibilities you have outlined—what figure did *you* have in mind?"Or: "I expect a salary appropriate to my qualifications and demonstrated abilities." Or even: "What salary range has been authorized for this position?" You may find these "evasions"annoying—but they indicate a thoughtful candidate.

8. *What's the most difficult situation you ever faced on the job and how did you resolve it?* Invite war stories. They tell you a lot about a candidate's creativity, attitude, and ability to act with grace under pressure. Look for positive outcomes. If the applicant hands you a disaster story, better think twice.

9. *What are looking for in this job?* Watch out for narrow responses: money, an office with a window, and so on. The creative employee will not focus exclusively on her needs, but will use words like *contribute, enhance, improve* in her response and will frame the response in terms of contributing to the achievement of the company's goals and the fulfillment of its needs.

10. *In a nutshell: Why should I hire you?* What you are looking for here is something of a menu listing what the candidate brings to the company table. The more specific the response, the better. Look for a recitation of skills, abilities, and qualifications that mesh precisely with what you, your department, and your company need.

Finally, conclude with one more question: *Do you have any questions you'd like me to address?* As revealing as answers are, questions may tell even more. Give the candidate ample opportunity to express his concerns and doubts and to satisfy his curiosity.

6.5.2. Employment Questions to Avoid

Inappropriate Questions—and How to Answer Them

As mentioned in 6.4., federal law has made certain employment-related questions not only inappropriate, but illegal. Do not ask questions bearing on:

1. Marital status

2. Sexual orientation

3. Age

4. Ethnic or national origin

5. Religious beliefs—or lack thereof

Certain fairly innocent-sounding questions should also be avoided. For example, asking a candidate—especially a female candidate—if she has children or plans to have children lays you open for possible charges of sexual discrimination. You may be accused of failing to hire the candidate because you "obviously" felt her family obligations would automatically make her an unreliable employee.

Similarly, you may have genuine concerns about a candidate's age—and how it might affect his ability to do his job. Nevertheless, such questions are inappropriate. If the position is physically demanding, you may point this out and ask the candidate if he feels capable of the demands. The best course is to establish certain objective capability-oriented tests. For example, if the job requires heavy lifting, state as a job requirement that the applicant must be able to lift and carry sixty pounds. Then test this.

Perhaps yours is a family values-oriented company. Great! Just avoid probing into the candidate's family life or lack thereof, as well as her religious beliefs or lack thereof. If such issues are important to you, you may ask such questions as "What do you enjoy doing in your leisure time?" If the candidate is family-centered, her response will reflect this. You might also ask something like: "Our's is a community-oriented company. How are you active in your community?" If the candidate is affiliated with a church or synagogue, this may well emerge.

> **PITFALL:** You should not ask the candidate if he is "active in his church." This is tantamount to asking a question about religious beliefs.

Many of us take great pride in our nation and in a Made-in-the-USA spirit. It's natural to ask something like "Were you born in the United States?" However, you should avoid the question, since it exposes you to a possible charge of discriminating on the basis of national origin. Of course, in order to comply with federal immigration laws, you certainly may require as part of the job application process proof of U.S. citizenship or resident alien ("Green Card") status.

Drugs

Unfortunately—even tragically—about half of the *Fortune* 500 companies include some form of drug testing either during or after the hiring process. While it is inappropriate to ask candidates if they use illegal drugs, it is perfectly legal to require drug testing as a condition of employment, and you may ask the candidate if she is willing to take a drug test.

> **PITFALL:** Do not depend on the candidate's verbal response alone. Applicants should be asked to sign a waiver form, giving you permission to have a drug-screening test administered.

> **TIP:** Savvy candidates will—quite rightly—want assurance that any drug testing will be performed by a qualified laboratory, which will fully explain the test and provide a complete list of food, non-drug, over-the-counter medications, or prescription drug items that may cause *false positive* results. This is important for your firm's protection, too. At least 5 percent of drug tests yield false positives due to the presence of innocuous substances. (Some sources put this figure at 14 percent!) If you make a negative employment decision based on a false positive, you expose your company to possible civil action initiated by the rejected candidate.

6.6. CONFERENCES WITH COLLEAGUES

6.6.1. Effective Conferences

There are four principles for establishing effective communication between you and your colleagues:

1. *Respect your colleagues.* You can think of this as the Corporate Golden Rule: Do unto your colleague as you would have him do unto you. Listen to coworkers. Hear what they have to say. Then demonstrate that you have heard them and that you value what they say.

   TIP: Make clear how you value what your colleagues say by punctuating conversations with such phrases as "That's interesting,""It's worth thinking about,""I never thought of that before,""I see," and so on.

2. *Establish ground rules, define responsibilities, and refine and modify these definitions as necessary.* It is amazing how many companies misuse—and frustrate—their workforce assets by poorly defining responsibilities and areas of authority, even when official job descriptions exist. Openly discuss your responsibilities and "turf" areas. Understand them. Agree to them. Don't be afraid to alter them as the demands of your business may require.

   TIP: Consensus on responsibility is a key to efficient operation and to successful communication.

3. *When necessary, sound your horn.* For those of us accustomed to driving in the cities of the United States, motorists in London, England, seem extraordinarily polite. They almost never sound their horns. The result is terrifying. They would just as soon ram into you as honk you a warning. In the workplace, learn to avoid unpleasant—maybe even hurtful or disastrous—encounters with coworkers by sounding your horn only as necessary. Learn to do so in a calm but firm and unmistakable way—a way that educates and informs rather than scolds or threatens.

4. *Make creative small talk.* Contrary to what many—all too many—managers believe, small talk in the workplace is not necessarily a waste of time. It is the means through which coworkers bond into an effective team by learning to appreciate and respect one another as human beings, not just job titles. Demonstrate an interest in your fellow workers by asking about families, hobbies, interests, and outside activities. Small talk builds morale and improves cohesiveness.

6.6.2.　What to Say When You Need Information or Help

Identify Sources of Information and Aid

Before you ask for information or help, you need to identify the best sources of both. This may be obvious to you, but if it is not, ask yourself the following questions:

1. Who does what job?

2. Who seems to command influence and enjoy respect?

3. Who seems to be "in the loop"—communicating with upper levels of management most frequently and effectively?

4. Who has been climbing the corporate ladder?

5. Who answers questions frequently?

6. Who is frequently quoted?

7. Who makes the key decisions?

8. Who writes the significant memos?

9. Who runs the meetings?

Zero in on the people whose names are the answers to most of these questions.

Show That You Are Interested

Cultivate the people you identify as key by taking an interest in what they do and say. Engage them in conversation about what interests them. If you run across an article or memo concerning a subject of interest to them, copy it or clip it and send it along to them.

Get Them to Talk

Building on the key person's interests is a great way to build an information-sharing and helping relationship. You can accelerate the development of the relationship by asking for a conversation, using such phrases as:

1. "I'd like a chance to speak with you."
2. "What's a good time to talk about something?"
3. "I need to find out _____, and I'd really like to talk to you about it. What's a convenient time for you?"
4. "Mind if I pick your brain?"

> TIP: Most people like to feel useful and valuable. Most people like to help. Don't hesitate to rely on this truth of human nature.

6.6.3. How to Disagree Professionally

Sam Rayburn, the longtime and highly venerated Speaker of the U.S. House of Representatives, counseled the members of the House that "we can disagree without being disagreeable." That is the chief principle that should guide you in disagreeing with your colleagues. Working well with your colleagues is hardly about avoiding disputes. Rather, it is about identifying issues on which you differ and then separating those issues from the personalities behind them. Pit issue against issue, not personality against personality, ego against ego. If you focus opposing points of view on a particular issue or problem, you don't automatically resolve the dispute, but you do go a long way toward forging disparate personalities into a cooperative team whose members may have differing views, but who are nevertheless committed to common goals.

> TIP: The key to disagreeing with a colleague is to shift the focus from the disagreement to some alternative or set of alternatives—that is, to shift from a negative to a positive.

6.6.4.   How to Complain and Criticize Without Alienating Your Colleagues

Criticism can be positive—it can build relationships, foster a team spirit, and improve performance and productivity—when the following is true:

1. Your colleagues are not functioning well.

2. A situation is threatening your working relationship with a colleague.

3. You have a sincere desire to upgrade a colleague's performance for the good of the organization.

Despite the fact that criticism in these cases can be positive, you may meet with negative responses:

1. You may be confronted with hostility.

2. You may be confronted with defensiveness.

3. You may be told that you have misunderstood the situation.

On the other hand, the criticism may actually be welcomed:

1. "I didn't realize I was doing that." Or: "I didn't think there was a better way." Or: "I was totally unaware of that."

2. "You're right. I could be doing a better job if I approached the problem your way."

You can maximize the chances for a positive reaction—and a positive outcome—by observing the following guidelines:

1. *Make certain the situation really does call for criticism.* You *should* be hesitant to offer criticism. Make certain that your criticism is motivated by a genuine problem or issue, not by your personal dislikes or frustrations. Make certain, too, that the problem or issue is serious enough to warrant criticism. After all, you are risking the creation of bad feelings. Make certain that the "cure" is not apt to be worse than the "disease."

2. *Don't go blundering into the criticism.* Practice a certain amount of finesse. Instead of opening up with your big guns, ask your colleague if she would like to hear how you feel about what she's doing. That is, ask her

permission to offer criticism. This will help translate "criticism" into "feedback"—which is far more neutral and apt to trigger less defensiveness than criticism.

3. *Choose the right place and time.* Never criticize a colleague in front of others. Instead, find—or create—an appropriate time: "George, there's something I need to discuss with you. When would be a good time for us to have a few uninterrupted moments together?"

   PITFALL: Avoid delivering criticism first thing in the morning—especially Monday morning. Avoid delivering it right before quitting time, especially before a weekend. You don't want to send your colleague home to stew about something you've said.

   TIP: Don't deliver criticism in the heat of anger—for example, right after some incident has occurred. Try to cool down and reflect before offering criticism.

4. *Back up your criticism with substance.* The most frustrating and enraging kind of criticism is delivered in vague generalities. Be concrete. Use specific incidents, instances, and events. Also, concentrating on specifics will help to keep the criticism from degenerating into a personal attack.

5. *Offer alternatives.* It's easy to criticize, but much harder to come up with positive alternatives. Generally, you should not offer criticism to a colleague unless you are prepared to offer alternatives that will be helpful to him and to the organization.

6. *Be friendly.* This does not mean that you should approach your colleague in a phony, sickeningly sweet or patronizing manner. However, be considerate and sensitive. Don't tease or taunt. Don't raise your voice. Watch your vocabulary. Avoid such phrases as "you must," "you should," "you have to," "you never," "you always," and the like.

7. *Where possible, combine praise with criticism.* This is not just to soften the blow, but to let your colleague know that you appreciate her value, her qualifications, and abilities.

8. *Criticize only what can be improved or corrected.* Make certain that you don't lay the blame for some essentially uncorrectable problem at the feet of your fellow worker.

9. *One at a time, please.* Don't lay multiple criticism on anyone. Tackle one issue at a time.

10. *Follow up with positive feedback.* If the situation improves or the issue is corrected, offer praise, congratulations, and thanks. Express your admiration.

6.6.5. Guidelines for Generating Great Ideas

Sometimes the best ideas come from informal discussions held in the corridor. Sometimes. But the trouble with spontaneity is that it's so—well—*spontaneous.* You can't control it. You can't summon it up at will. The following are some techniques for putting spontaneity "on tap" and making it more reliable as a generator of ideas and solutions when you really need them:

1. *Problem polling.* Gather an impromptu meeting in a room with a blackboard or the equivalent. Ask the participants to call out the problems and issues of greatest concern to them. Have someone write them on the board. Do not discuss the problems or issues. Do not analyze. Do not interrupt the flow until the flow stops. Then restate each concern in positive terms. For instance: "I'm worried about quality control" becomes "Our objective is to improve quality control in order to reduce returns by 15 percent."

2. *Brainstorming.* This is a tried-and-tested method for generating ideas. It works in small peer groups—usually of eight participants or fewer. Define an issue, then ask for ideas. You objective is quantity rather than quality. Allow no discussion of the ideas. Allow no judgment or criticism or, for that matter, praise. Have someone write each of the ideas on a blackboard. After the flow of ideas peters out, begin to analyze the ideas, focusing on how to establish criteria for judging the value of each idea. In this way, you should be able to winnow the welter of ideas down to a few viable ones.

3. *Small-group discussion.* Break larger groups into small groups (four participants is a good number), each of which is assigned a particular problem or issue to discuss. Appoint a leader of each group, whose job it is to keep the talk focused. Another participant should record the results of the discussion. After a period of time, reconvene the smaller groups into a larger group and ask the recorders to share the results of the individual discussions.

6.7.   CONFERENCES WITH SUBORDINATES

6.7.1.   The Verbal Keys to Win–Win Management

This may sound old-fashioned, but here goes: The keystone to effective management is personal dedication. As a manager, your job is to foster personal dedication not by selling your staff on the company, but by persuading them that their personal goals mesh with those of the company.

> TIP: Personal goals include security, achievement, a sense of accomplishment, financial success, and so on.

Yet even this connection between personal goals and company objectives may be too abstract to guide employee performance on a day-to-day basis. A more direct way to manage employees for optimum performance and close coordination is to nurture in them a sense of personal loyalty to yourself. How do you do this? Communicate the following:

1. That you are accessible

2. That you are willing to hear—and respond to—grievances and complaints

3. Absolute clarity about your expectations

4. Generous positive feedback

5. Helpful and constructive criticism

6. A sense of fun and enjoyment in your directives.

Take a closer look at some of these steps to creating personal loyalty:

A Willingness to Listen to Complaints

This takes strength on your part. It's relatively easy to get your staff to be open with you—once. How you respond to that openness determines whether the productive honesty will continue. Use a what's-bothering-you-let's-talk-about-it approach: "Sarah, I can see that you're steamed about something. I want to hear about it. Don't pull any punches."

But when no punches are pulled, you'd better be willing to roll with them. Learn from negative comments.

> **PITFALL:** The worst thing you can do is ask for honesty, only to react to it with anger.

After the employee gets the gripe off his chest, try to translate the negative into a positive solution. If Issue A upsets Joe Blow, ask him what can be done to resolve Issue A and improve the situation.

Making Your Expectations Clear

Effective management is not magic. It is largely effective communication, and, in turn, effective communication largely consists of clear and precise directions. Begin with these.

1. The most certain way to be clear is to write out your instructions in the form of a memo.

2. Use plain English. Quantify instructions wherever possible: how many, when, where, how much time, and so on.

3. Always invite questions.

Motivate with Feedback

1. Feedback—even critical feedback—should reassure your subordinate that you have confidence in his skills and abilities.

2. Suggest that achieving the desired goal is clearly possible.

> **PITFALL:** Avoid demoralizing the employee by heaping criticism and threats upon him without suggesting ways in which he might achieve what you want.

Be specific in your feedback. To the degree that it is possible to do so, stress the positive. Practice delivering feedback in a sincere tone. When you criticize, always suggest alternatives. Never simply demean an employee or reject his work.

Infuse Your Directives with a Sense of Fun

The best managers enjoy what they do. Don't turn your directives into jokes, but feel free to use imagination when you give directions, discuss ideas, or deliver feedback.

6.7.2. Delegating Effectively

Learning to delegate responsibility is essential to effective management. In large part, the task depends on giving clear directions and making your expectations clear, as discussed in 6.7.1. Beyond this, the manager should set herself in the position of coach by giving subordinates the opportunity to solve their own problems. You want to cultivate a high degree of independence. However, do not abdicate your responsibilities, and do not give your subordinates that they have been cast adrift and are on their own.

1. Establish clear directions.

2. Instruct subordinates to come to you if they have a problem they cannot solve.

3. Encourage subordinates to bring difficult or interesting issues to your attention—not so that you can resolve them, but so that the two of you can work together to resolve them.

6.7.3. Motivating Your Staff

If you follow the communication suggestions just discussed, chances are your staff will be well motivated. However, various circumstances—including economic problems, business disappointments, and the like—can severely affect morale, even if you strive to manage effectively.

6.7.4. When and How to Criticize

The guidelines for communicating criticism to subordinates are similar to criticizing your colleagues, except that you are in a more powerful position with subordinates. This has its advantages as well as its liabilities. For while your subordinates are more likely to accept criticism—and to expect it—there is a greater potential for anxiety and, with anxiety, resentment of you. Avoid these negative consequences by communicating criticism in the manner of a tutor or a coach. Make it clear that you are committed not just to your department's or company's bottom line, but to the development of the employee as a long-term member of the team.

As with criticizing colleagues, the first thing to do is to *be certain of your need to criticize.* Be certain that your criticism is not simply an expression of frustration, anger, or irritation. If your remarks will not address and improve the situation—but merely attack the person—hold your peace.

Other points to remember:

1. *Ask permission to criticize.* This may seem to undercut your authority, but, actually, it will enhance the effectiveness of your words. Instead of starting out with something like, "You're not doing an effective job with so-and-so," begin with "We have a problem with so-and-so, which I would like to discuss with you."

2. *Be certain that the cure will not be worse than the disease.* Even skillfully delivered, criticism can be damaging to a fragile ego. Use judgment to decide whether the problem or issue is worth the risk that critical words entail.

3. *Do not criticize subordinates in front of others.* "Tom," you might say, "I need to speak to you about an important matter. When is a good time for us to get together for a few minutes of uninterrupted time?"

4. *Avoid criticism first thing in the morning or at quitting time.* Neither of these is a good time for accepting or acting on criticism. Of the two, the end of the day is worse. You don't want your subordinate brooding at home about a problem at work.

5. *Be specific.* Do not issue blanket criticism or criticism in general terms. Always cite specific issues and incidents. To the extent that it is possible to do so, quantify your criticism: "Turnaround time in your area is a good 15 percent more than we need it to be."

6. *Remember that you are both on the same team.* Approach the subordinate not just as an employee, but as a member of *your* team. Be friendly.

7. *Address issues, not personalities.* Don't tell an employee what you think of him. Focus on the issue. It is certainly acceptable, too, if appropriate, to focus on a particular negative or harmful behavior—just be certain that it is a behavior in a certain circumstance or set of circumstances. Be sure that you can be specific.

8. *Combine praise with criticism.* Point out that, generally, you are pleased with the subordinate's work, but that, as regards issue X, an improvement needs to be made.

   Pitfall: Failure to temper criticism with praise may result in an attack on the employee's self-worth and therefore produce a demoralized employee, whose performance will deteriorate rather than improve.

9. *Be certain that what you criticize can be changed.* It does no good to criticize a subordinate for something over which she has little or no control.

10. *Address one issue at a time.* Do not overwhelm a subordinate with a laundry list of faults and problems.

6.7.5. The Vocabulary of Authority

By virtue of your position in the organization, you already have authority over your subordinates. Your vocabulary does not need to stress your dominance so much as your willingness to work with the subordinate to help him be the best that he can be. Use words like:

advice	counsel	glitch	manage
advise	determine	help	navigate
analyze	discuss	invest	plan
assist	evaluate	lead	reconsider
consider	expedite	learn	rethink
control	formulate	lesson	revise
cope	future		

And avoid such words as:

blame	disaster	hopeless	mess
catastrophe	exploded	idiotic	misguided
crisis	fault	impossible	snafu
destroyed	foul-up		

In addition, try to eliminate:

demand	must	you'd better
force	no choice	

6.7.6. Reading the Non-Verbal Cues

How do you know that you are getting through? Because your subordinate *tells* you she understands? Because he *promises* to do better "next time"?

In part, yes. Ask for feedback: "Is this helping you?" However, in a criticism situation, you should expect instances of verbal compliance combined with the nonverbal signals of resistance. Look out for:

1. Avoidance of eye contact, which suggests that you are simply not getting through.

2. Hands to face or mouth, which suggests that the employee is not being fully honest with you.

3. Arms folded across the chest or hands on hips, which suggests resistance, even defiance.

4. Rubbing the back of the neck or, if the employee is seated, nervous leg movement, which suggests a desire to leave—*now*.

If you pick up any of these nonverbal cues, try to bring the issue of communication out into the open. Verbalize it: "I get the feeling that I'm not communicating as effectively as I would like. Do you agree with such-and-such?" Or: "Does what I say disturb you? Does what I say seem inaccurate to you?"

> **PITFALL:** Avoid accusing the subordinate of *failing* to listen or *failing* to understand. In reacting to non-verbal cues, put the burden on yourself rather than the subordinate.

Subordinate Conferences Checklist

1. Focus on issues, situations, and, if necessary, specific instances of behavior rather than on personalities.

2. To the extent that it is possible to do so, cast yourself in the role of coach or mentor or guide. It is to your advantage to cultivate as much responsible independence in the subordinate as possible.

3. In all directives, praise, and criticism, be as specific as possible. Don't *worry* about choosing words to express yourself well. You will express yourself effectively if you focus on specific issues, problems, goals, and accomplishments.

4. Avoid threats.

5. Avoid the laundry-list approach to criticism.

6. It is to your advantage to build your subordinate up, not tear him down.

6.8. CONFERENCES WITH YOUR BOSS

6.8.1. Keys to Getting Respect

Bosses and supervisors come in many varieties, but few of them are deliberately tyrannical or irrational or demanding of mindless obedience. Most are interested in a department or firm that runs productively and profitably, and that means working with a staff capable of creative, independent action, a commitment to the team, and personal loyalty. Communicating effectively with your supervisors requires many of the same strategies as communicating with colleagues and even subordinates:

1. *Respect.* This is not synonymous with reverence, awe, or fear. Think of the supervisor as the team leader. Listen to her, then demonstrate that you have heard her and that you value what she says. Don't hesitate to ask questions in order to ensure that the both of you are "singing from the same songsheet."

2. *Establish ground rules, define responsibilities, and refine and modify these definitions as necessary.* Make certain that your responsibilities and areas of authority are clearly defined for each and every project you are assigned.

3. *Be supportively critical.* Provide ample feedback. Do not complain, but demonstrate a commitment to refine and improve procedures.

4. *Discuss operations and issues frequently.* Make the company the chief subject of small talk with your boss. Live and breathe your work—but make it fun.

6.8.2. How to Negotiate a Raise

Why do you want a raise? To buy a new car? A new house? Send a kid—or kids—through college? How about just to make ends meet for a change? Your boss may or may not care about your needs outside of the workplace. Even if he does, you can't count on that influencing his decision to give you more money. In fact, if he's doing his job, he will recognize that outside needs are largely irrelevant to deciding whether to give you a raise. There are, after all, dozens of people in the company who want a new car, a new house, and have kids to send through college. What you say to negotiate a raise should relate exclusively to your work and your performance on the job.

> TIP: Focusing on your job actually makes the negotiation easier. You are obliged to do no more than make an argument based on your performance at work. You are not required to justify your entire life, bringing up issues relating to how you spend or invest your resources.

Enter the discussion armed with three sets of facts:

1. A verbal résumé highlighting the year's accomplishments and reminding your boss of your duties, skills, qualifications, and responsibilities

2. Performance results—what your contributions have meant to the firm, particularly over the preceding year or six months. To the degree that it is possible to do so, quantify this information: "My work on the revised order forms has saved us at least $35,000 this quarter."

3. Facts about what others, in similar positions, get paid—assuming that, on average, they get paid more than you do

> TIP: To determine your relative worth in the job market, look for salary surveys that are frequently published by organizations in various fields. You should also attempt to gain a sense of whether your particular skills and qualifications are in short supply, great demand—or, relatively speaking, a glut on the market.

Of course, you should also be familiar with the facts of your firm's overall performance, as well as the performance and trends of the industry generally. This will ensure your ability to provide a context for your personal facts and figures.

Perhaps the key point to bear in mind is that you are not *asking* for a raise at all. You are *negotiating* for one. That is, you are not seeking something for nothing. You have valuable skills and experience to offer, for which you have the right to get the best compensation.

> TIP: Avoid being the first actually to mention a figure. It is a general rule of negotiation that the first person who states a figure is in the weaker bargaining position. The problem is not so much that the figure you might propose will be too high, but that it will be too low—and therefore limiting.

Anticipating Resistance

You should be prepared for resistance. Expect the following:

◆ If it were up to me, you'd get a raise in heartbeat. I'll make the recommendation, but I am really powerless to make the final decision.

Reply: Is there someone else I should talk to, then? And can I count on your recommendation to him or her?

◆ You know, a lot of folks here are doing a great job—and they're not asking for the kind of raise you are.

Reply: I'm talking only about myself, of course, and what's appropriate in my case.

◆ I can't possibly offer you 10 percent; 5, maybe.

Reply: [Say nothing—but don't leave. Let the silence hang in the air. It will be awkward—but more uncomfortable for your boss than for you. Perhaps the silence will produce a better offer.]

◆ [After the silence, your boss still says that the 5 percent figure is final.]

Reply: I see. I will work at that salary, provided that we have a firm understanding that, next quarter, we will review what I've accomplished. I am committed to this firm, and I intend to accomplish a great deal in those three months.

◆ I just can't do it.

Reply: Tell me what would make it possible for you to say yes—for me to get a level of compensation more appropriate to my skills and accomplishments?

6.8.3.   How to Negotiate a Promotion

Depending how you want to look at it, getting a promotion is either more daunting than getting a raise—or easier. A pessimist will tell you that negotiating for a promotion is harder than angling for a raise, because you are really going after two objectives: position and money. The optimist will tell you that it is easier, because you are trading increased responsibility for increased wages—not just asking for more money to keep on doing the same job. The debate between the forces of optimism and pessimism is endless. The most effective decision is this:

If you have a choice, go for the promotion. Not only does it reinforce and build relations with your employer, it offers the greatest possibilities for future growth, and it provides you with a fallback position. If you are turned down for the promotion, you can always negotiate for a raise within your present position. There is very little to fall back on when you are asking for a raise only.

The strategy for negotiating a promotion is similar to that for negotiating a raise, except that you need to stress how your excellent performance in Position A is an accurate predictor of your performance in Position B. If you have excelled operating with limited responsibilities, your argument should run, you will do even better if you are operating within a larger sphere.

Anticipating Resistance

Common resistance replies include:

♦ I'm not sure that you're ready yet.

Reply: What will it take to convince you that I am?

♦ This is not the time to talk about it.

Reply: When would be a better time? I'd like to set something up now.

♦ You're doing a great job where you are. I really don't want to move you at this time.

Reply: It's great to be appreciated, but I am confident that I can use my skills to even greater advantage in a more responsible position. I want to make the maximum contribution possible to our department.

♦ Give me another year.

Reply: I'd like to set up a review before that time. Can we plan that now? I don't want it to go beyond a year.

♦ We are planning to fill the position with somebody from the outside.

Reply: Is that final? What would it take to change your thinking on that?

6.8.4. Promoting an Idea or Project

How many times has this happened to you?

You're in a meeting. Suddenly, an idea occurs to you. You think: *I should say something.* But then inertia takes over. You worry about getting shot down.

That phrase—"shot down,"'"shot down in flames"—runs through your mind, and you stay your tongue. In the meantime, Joe Blow at the other end of the table pipes up with precisely the idea that had been running through your head. The boss loves the idea. *Everybody* loves the idea.

Don't fall victim to metaphors like *he shot me down*. The consequences of broaching a new idea are dual: you may incur rejection, or you may incur praise and ultimate promotion. The consequences of silence are singular—or, at least, seem to be: nothing will happen. But, in business, personally maintaining the status quo often is an illusion. You are actually slipping backwards—back and out.

> **Tip:** If you work in an environment that habitually discourages innovation and the sharing of ideas, perhaps you should consider moving to a company that encourages and nurtures new directions. This is not just for your personal growth. A company that resists change is not likely to prosper.

The introduction of new ideas can range from a fully developed written proposal prepared in accordance with company policy, to a spur-of-the-moment brainstorm. The fact is, that you can pave the way for acceptance of either.

1. If you are presenting a formal proposal, take the time to highlight—verbally—points requiring special attention.

2. Send off the proposal with an enthusiastic word or two: "It's been very exciting to work on this."

3. Invite feedback. Underscore that you value your supervisor's opinion. Do not say, "I hope you like this," but: "I'd appreciate all the feedback I can get on this." Prompt your boss to *invest* her time in the project.

In introducing spontaneous, spur-of-the-moment ideas, don't be too modest, but resist the urge to burst out with a *Eureka!* Use phrases such as:

This just occurred to me . . .

Let me try this out on you . . .

I just had a thought that might warrant working up into something . . .

Help me out with this one . . .

What do you think about . . . ?

Anticipating Resistance

◆ This looks like an awfully tough sell to me. I just don't know . . .

Reply: We both know that they're all tough sells. What I ask is that you look over the proposal and examine the figures—then let me know just how tough you think it is. I trust your feedback on this.

◆ I can't get to this for while.

Reply: I know things are crazy right now. But I am confident that you'll be as excited about this as I am. It's worth making time for.

◆ All new projects are on hold.

Reply: Even if that's the case, I'm so excited about this one that I'd really like to get you take on it so that we can hit the ground running with it when the time is right.

◆ We've got to move slowly and cautiously.

Reply: I agree—and that's why I've taken plenty of time with this proposal. I do not want to rush it past you. Take your time with it. The more you can tell me, the better. Then I will devote the necessary hours to revision and rethinking.

6.8.5. Buying Time: How to Extend a Deadline

Nothing creates more pressure than working under deadline. Nothing generates more excuses than missing a deadline. Sure, you might be able to get your boss to *accept* your excuse, but you will never get her to *like* it. For that reason, it's best not to make excuses. Instead, recognize that buying time is subject to negotiation, like anything else. You are asking for time and understanding in exchange for—what?—a better product, a more successful result.

> **TIP:** It is always better to move proactively here. As soon as it becomes apparent to you that you will slip a deadline, negotiate for an extension. Do not wait for the problem to occur, then make excuses after the fact. Proactive negotiation does not mean starting a conversation with "I'm going to need more time." Your boss is not going to be terribly interested in what *you* need. Instead, focus on the result: "In order to do the best possible work on this project, we will need to schedule an additional week."

Move proactively. This demonstrates that you are in control of events rather than yielding to them. Avoid creating an atmosphere of crisis. Avoid using words such as—

cannot	impossible	slipped
crisis	late	trouble
delay	neglected	unaware
due	no	unreasonable
forgot	problem	

Instead, frame your negotiation in terms such as:

alter	caution	modify
aware	expedite	possible
better	if	priorities
can	investigate	reschedule
care	manage	resources
careful	methodical	will

Anticipating Resistance

You might encounter such responses as:

◆ This is a very serious deadline. You'd better move heaven and earth to meet it.

Reply: I am deadly serious about the deadline. That's why I'm talking to you about it now. I can give you a job you'll be 75 percent happy with if I deliver on deadline. Give me another week, and I can promise 100—no, 110—percent. If the deadline's serious, so is the project.

◆ What are you guys doing down there?

Reply: One thing we're doing is evaluating the project in terms of how best to use our resources. If we try cutting corners now, it will cost us time later. That's why I want to modify the schedule—to build a better foundation at this early point, so that we'll avoid time-eating trouble later. That's my judgment in the matter.

◆ You can't move any faster than this?

Reply: I suppose we could—but I wouldn't be comfortable with the results, and if I'm not comfortable, I don't expect you to be confident.

◆ Can you guarantee this will be the only delay?

Reply: I can guarantee that I will do everything possible to make certain that the schedule won't have to be altered again. I am building in some time to handle the unexpected, so we have a cushion. But, if we get into a situation where we get nothing but the unexpected, well, I'd be lying to you if I said that I could guarantee absolutely no further changes. I am confident of the schedule. I am confident that we will meet the modified deadline—and, most important, meet it with a product that works.

6.8.6. Tips for Accepting an Assignment with Grace and Enthusiasm

My dad gave me advice that fathers have been giving sons for generations (and now, I'm sure, daughters as well): When you shake hands with someone you meet, do so firmly and warmly. It's valuable advice. A handshake is a powerful initial gesture of communication—an opportunity to convey strength, warmth, eagerness, loyalty, a willingness to do the job and do it right. Grip *too* firmly, and you convey overbearing dominance. Offer the hand limply, and you convey weakness and hesitation.

The manner in which you accept an assignment presents similar opportunities and similar potential hazards. Like the handshake, it is an inaugural act of communication. It can set the tone for an entire relationship.

1. If you are genuinely excited by the assignment, go ahead and express your feelings.

2. If you are less than thrilled, you have four choices:

   a. Decline the assignment. This is covered in 6.8.7. Of course, it may not be an option in a particular case.

   b. You can accept the job grudgingly. This will ensure that you *and* your boss are unhappy, and that any work you do will be judged harshly. Maybe you'll get fired. (This is not the option of choice.)

   c. You can feign enthusiasm. If you are a good actor, this is a viable option. But it is a strain to maintain insincerity.

d. You can accept the assignment and convey the message that you will work enthusiastically and professionally to get the job done well.

PITFALL: What if you are compelled to accept an assignment you know will be a disaster? Resist the urge to explode. Instead, respond positively, but mention that you will be back with some important questions. This will buy you time to evaluate all the pros and cons coolly and responsibly. You may discover that the assignment is not as bad as you first thought. Or, if, on further consideration, it remains a dog, you can work up a calm, reasoned, well-argued analysis and return to your boss with that. Maybe—just maybe—you can convince her to rethink the assignment. You will have benefited yourself, your boss, and your organization.

The key is to be as positive as possible without being phony. Use positive language, lacing your remarks with words like:

able	equipped	pleased
agree	exciting	prepared
approve	experience	studied
confidence	gratifying	thrilled
confident	great	viable
delighted	learning	willing
enthusiastic	opportunity	workable

Resist the temptation to burst out with such terms as:

can't	frightened	stupid
disaster	nervous	unqualified
doubt	refuse	unworkable
fail	reject	waste

Potential Responses to Anticipate

◆ Now, don't get too carried away.

Reply: Are you kidding? I live on enthusiasm. It's what drives me.

◆ I'm relying on you.

Reply: I understand, and I will not let you down.

♦ Are you absolutely sure you can do this?

Reply: You've made the right choice. I've prepared for this kind of assignment, and I am thrilled to get it. I'll make it work.

♦ You seem doubtful about something.

Reply: I do have some questions. Give me a day to review the assignment, and I'll run my questions by you at that time.

♦ You don't seem too thrilled.

Reply: Rest assured that I will do a great job. I'm a careful sort. I always study an assignment carefully before I let myself get too carried away. I'll be back with some questions for you.

6.8.7. Tips for Declining an Assignment Graciously and Firmly

Maybe you can decline an assignment. Maybe you cannot. If you are uncertain about how enthusiastic you are over an assignment, at least try to buy time before accepting or rejecting it. As discussed in 6.8.6., ask for time to review the assignment, and say that you will return with any questions.

If you decide to decline an assignment, you have three choices:

1. You may attack the assignment itself, demonstrating that the project is unworkable or unnecessary.

2. You may argue that you are not the best person for the project.

3. You may say that you prefer not to work on the project, providing whatever reasons you may have.

Each of these approaches has advantages and disadvantages. Perhaps the strongest position you can take is the first, asserting that the project is not worth undertaking. The problem here is that you should be certain of your judgment. Also—and this is important—if the project is valuable to someone in command (your boss, for instance), it is probably not to your advantage to expend energy looking for a way to shoot it down.

The second option carries with it the danger of making you look *generally* incapable. If you're not the right person for *this* assignment, what *are* you right for? If you employ this strategy, you must express yourself precisely, so that there can be no mistake that, although you are generally brilliant, this particular project is not your forte. As usual, the best approach is to be as positive as possible. Instead of saying that you are *not* the right person for the job, offer a positive alternative. "I have reviewed the project, and I have concluded that we would be better off with somebody from Special Sales managing this one." Note the pronouns: I, I, and we. You have positioned yourself expressly, deliberately, and consciously to *delegate* the project—not just shrink from it or pass the buck.

Even if your work situation gives you the leeway to decline a project more or less at will—the third alternative—it is best to have a compelling reason for your decision.

> **TIP:** The best way to keep from going wrong is to frame your response in terms of what is best for the organization.

Possible Responses

Quite possibly, your boss will respond with something like "I really want you to take this on." If so, you might be wise to take the cue and accept the project. However, if you are dead set against it, try the following:

> Reply: *I would be glad to take it on, if I didn't believe that we have personnel who are better positioned to do a more effective job on this particular project. I strongly feel that my taking on the assignment is not the best use of our resources.*

6.8.8. How to Take a Compliment

This is not the venue to psychoanalyze why so many of us have a tough time taking a compliment. If you are uncomfortable in this situation, just be assured that you are not alone. However, learning how to take a compliment graciously is as important as learning how to accept and profit from criticism. Responding well to praise not only lets you feel good about accepting your just deserts, it also lets your boss feel good by giving him the pleasure of having bestowed recognition where it is deserved.

> **TIP:** Take a compliment with grace, and your boss will feel that she has acted wisely in placing confidence in you.

How to do it? The simplest method is to say "thank you ." Nothing at all wrong with that. But why not make this a *real* occasion? Try: "Thanks. Coming from you, that really means something!"

> **TIP:** The secret of accepting a compliment? Offer one in return.

If appropriate, share the praise with others who deserve it. This act always makes you look even better. However, avoid:

◆ Confessing your unworthiness

◆ Denigrating the accomplishment

◆ Delivering a lengthy "acceptance" speech

6.8.9. How to Take—and Profit from—Criticism

If some folks have trouble taking compliments, even more of us have a hard time accepting criticism without either panicking and feeling worthless or getting our backs up and feeling defensive.

> **TIP:** The Golden Rule of accepting criticism: Taking your lumps is an opportunity to learn and improve.

The benefits of criticism include:

1. Learning how to do something better.

2. Learning how others perceive what you do. Even if you disagree with the criticism, it is valuable to learn how *others* see your actions or creations.

3. Criticism gives you an opportunity to communicate in a way that can strengthen your relationship with your boss.

Tough as it may be, you have to begin by *listening* to criticism—and, furthermore, by demonstrating that you are listening.

1. Make and maintain eye contact.

2. Do not fold your arms across your chest. Doing so suggests that you are closed to the critical message.

3. Do not stand with your hands on your hips. This is a posture that suggests defiance.

4. Be generous with verbal cues that you are listening, hearing, and considering: "I see," "I understand," "I didn't think of it that way," "I'll have to consider this," and so on.

Critical Phrases to Anticipate

Criticism may be constructive or it may be insensitive, even brutal. Be prepared to hear the likes of—

◆ You'd better start shaping up.

Reply: I've heard your observations, and I need to review and study the problems you've pointed out. I'll come back with a plan that addresses these issues.

◆ You know, I'm generally pleased with what you've been doing, but I hope that you can show some improvement in the areas we discussed.

Reply: What you've said has been very helpful. I am confident that the shortcomings you've pointed out can be improved very significantly.

◆ I need to see real improvement. And I need to see it pretty damn soon!

Reply: I want to see it, too. I do need to reflect on what we've discussed. However, my initial response is that you are overestimating the magnitude of the problem. I do agree that my department can perform at a higher level. I am committed to making that happen. I appreciate your input. We will do better.

6.8.10.   What to Say When You Goof

Let's face some facts. There are accidents and errors that cost you or your company money. There are some that can cost you your job. There are others whose effects are measured in lives. However, the great majority of accidents and errors are not nearly as bad as you think they are, and they even offer certain positive opportunities:

1. To learn and improve

2. To demonstrate your willingness to accept responsibility

3. To demonstrate your ability to handle a crisis

4. To seek forgiveness.

Admittedly, the last item does not sound like much of a boon for you. But the fact is that, as the saying goes, "to err is human, to forgive, divine," and by giving your boss the opportunity to forgive you, you are giving her the opportunity to be a better person than she thinks she is.

In communicating after any accident or error, let your boss know three things:

1. That she is justified in becoming angry

2. That you thank her for her understanding and patience

3. That you have suggestions for solutions.

When It *Is* Your Fault

The cardinal rule here is to own up—and to own up as soon as possible. The bad news is far better coming from you than from a third party or if the boss discovers it for herself.

> **PITFALL:** Do not panic. Do not run wailing into your boss's office. Take control. Demonstrate that you are in control.

1. You should delay reporting the problem only long enough to assess it. Generally, this is preferable to rushing to your boss with half-truths and erroneous information. *Usually,* the situation is not as bad as it may at first seem.

2. Formulate possible solutions.

3. Armed with accurate information and possible remedies, report the problem.

4. Avoid punishing yourself.

5. Avoid telling your boss how she should feel about you; however, acknowledge her right to feel angry, but thank her for her patience and understanding.

The general strategy is to proceed as quickly as possible from *what happened* to *what can be done.* In other words, move the communication from negative to positive territory as quickly as possible.

6.8.11.   When It's Not Your Fault—But It's Still Your Problem

Subordinates and others for whom you take a degree of responsibility—sub-contractors and suppliers, for example—make mistakes. These are not your fault, but they remain, nevertheless, your problem. Usually, the best way of dealing with these is to handle the problem immediately, efficiently, and on your own authority. However, if you must make a report, take a lesson from President Harry S. Truman. Demonstrate your acceptance of his dictum: *The buck stops here.*

1. You may assess fault, explaining that your subordinate failed to do such-and-such.

2. Demonstrate your willingness to shoulder ultimate responsibility—not just for the error, but for creating a solution.

   TIP: What's the *positive* payoff in this situation? You have the opportunity to communicate that you are a problem solver.

6.8.12.   When a Project Fails

Everything said up to this point is of certain—but limited—value. The limitation is that not all glitches and disasters are directly traceable to blunders and misjudgments. There are times when you are given responsibility for a certain project, and, for any of a number of reasons, it fails to pan out. No one in particular is to blame. It just fizzles.

   In a situation like this, you may or may not be on the line. One thing is for certain, however, you usually do not feel good about yourself when the bubble bursts. Yet it is crucial to salvage whatever you can from the wreckage. The very least that you can recover is knowledge. At the very least, turn the event into a learning experience. Don't just ruin away from it.

   TIP: Thomas Edison, weary from having failed after literally thousands of attempts to find a workable filament for the incandescent electric lamp, was offered condolences by a well-meaning reporter. He brushed the remark aside, declaring that he hadn't failed. He now knew of the existence of thousands of substances that will not work as filaments.

It is from failure and disappointment that the future is created. Don't try to snow your boss with false optimism, but do avoid such words and phrases as the following when you discuss a disappointing project:

beyond repair	catastrophe	huge problem
big mistake	crisis	I told you so
blame	destroyed	mess
blew it	disaster	not my fault
bombed out	don't blame me	not my problem
burned out	fault	screw up
can't be fixed	foul-up	struck out
can't do anything about it	hopeless	unavoidable error

Instead, communicate what you and your organization have gained from the project. Stress the future.

6.8.13. The Raise: How Do You Handle "No"?

There is a school of psychotherapy known as Transactional Analysis. Essentially, these psychologists believe that each person carries within himself three aspects of personality: a parent, an adult, and a child. Each relationship or exchange with another human being is a "transaction" between at least two—possibly more—of these aspects of personality. If we accept the tenets of Transactional Analysis for at least a moment, we can gain insight into what happens when you ask for a raise, and your boss says no. Your "child" hears the boss's "parent." Now, in a mature relationship—or a productive exchange—your "adult" should be in communication with the "adult" aspect of your boss's personality. If, however, as in this case, the relationship tends to become one of parent to child, the effect on you and your ability to communicate is negative:

1. You may become as inarticulate as a child confronted with overwhelming authority.

2. You may be tempted to throw some sort of tantrum.

Neither child-like response is conducive to building a relationship with your boss that is likely—even if it is at some future date—to result in a raise or other advancement. What is the alternative?

1. Self-control? Well, that answer has the virtue of brevity. But it is not very helpful. The problem is that the phrase simply suggests that you deny your feelings. That is a strategy unlikely to work.

2. *Verbal management of the situation.* This is the more feasible alternative. Instead of trying to suppress your "child" feelings, recognize that you must use words to manage the situation *regardless* of what you may feel at the time.

How you handle *no* reveals whatever you want it to reveal about your character, your feelings toward your boss, and your commitment to your job. How you handle *no* will teach your boss a great deal about you. It is up to you to create the lesson that will do you the most good. That brings us to another set of feelings—those of your boss. Remember, your boss probably does not feel good about saying no to you. Does he feel "just as bad" as you do? Almost certainly not. And I am not suggesting that you should feel sorry for him ("The poor man. He had to turn me down!"). But it is to your advantage to recognize that neither you *nor* your boss is likely to *feel* satisfied when he says no. This situation gives you a foundation for building the conditions that will, at some later point, permit a *yes:*

1. Demonstrate that *no* has not reduced your commitment to the company or your loyalty to the boss, but, on the contrary, has strengthened your resolve to make the company better, so that, next time, the answer will be yes.

2. Minimize your boss's bad feelings. You want to be associated with positive emotions, which are of value to your boss.

3. Take the *no* with grace, but do not communicate acquiescence. You deserve the raise. Keep the negotiation open.

6.9. EMPLOYMENT INTERVIEW

6.9.1. How to Talk Yourself into a Great Job

Are you terrified by the prospect of a job interview? Go ahead, admit it. Because you are not alone. However, you do have a secret weapon—a weapon so secret that you probably don't even realize you have it. Here it is: Employers hate interviewing.

And it's a powerful weapon.

Perhaps you think the interviewer enjoys playing God with the fate of you, the interviewee. Not likely. Most managers and executives regard interviewing job candidates as a highly unwelcome intrusion into their daily routine. Beyond this, most are uncomfortable with the whole interview process. These facts put you in an excellent position to score interview points. Go into the interview prepared with questions, comments, and issues *you* can raise. This will relieve the interviewer of much of his work. Now, the easier you make it on the interviewer, the bigger the hit you will make. Want to talk yourself into a great job? Do the interviewer a favor: Take charge of the interview.

6.9.2. A Surefire Strategy for Taking Charge of the Employment Interview

To take charge of the interview, there is only one strategy that qualifies as "surefire": preparation beforehand. This does *not* mean committing yourself to a sleepless night of unfocused worry and fretting about the interview. Instead, perform the following five actions:

1. Learn as much as possible about the organization to which you are applying.

2. Learn what you can about the role of the position for which you are applying.

3. Discover the organization's special needs, goals, and problems; think about how you can address the needs, help achieve the goals, and solve the problems.

4. Prepare a list of your *relevant* and *specific* accomplishments.

5. Think about your salary requirements.

> **TIP:** Communicating effectively in an interview is important, but in order to communicate at all, you've got get to the interview and get to the interview on time. Make certain that you know the exact time and place of the interview. Do not forget to obtain clear directions to the interview, if you are at all unsure how to get there. Make certain that you know how long it will take to travel to the interview. Allow ample extra time. Finally, take along names and contact numbers—this includes the names and numbers of everyone you may have spoken to on the telephone in connection with the interview.

6.9.3. Doing Your Homework

Pre-interview preparation is the work of getting on the inside from the outside. Ideally, you should gather information on a company before you answer an ad, write an application letter, or make a telephone inquiry. Consult the following sources for information:

1. The target company's annual report

2. The target company's catalogs, brochures, ads, and other published material

3. Material supplied by the target company's Public Relations and/or Customer Service departments

4. Trade journal and professional newsletter articles devoted to the target company and/or the target industry in general

5. Books (available in the public library) that mention the target company or discuss the target industry in general

6. Online, check out the Internet and commercial online providers (such as CompuServe™, America Online™, Prodigy™, the Microsoft Network™, and so on).

The kind of information you should look for includes:

1. The business of the company—what it does or makes

2. The size and range of the company—Where does it do business?

3. The company's competition—and the target company's standing among them.

This is a minimum. Beyond this, try to secure a full "official" job description from the company before you go to the interview.

> **PITFALL:** Surprisingly, relatively few firms prepare official job descriptions. Don't be surprised if you are unable to secure one.

In the absence of an official job description, tactfully pump the employer for information. You are called for an interview. "Is there anything you need?" the potential employer asks you over the phone. You wisely ask for a job description. "Well, there is none."

What to do?

Reply: "I have a pretty fair idea of the scope of responsibilities **job title** customarily encompasses, but is there anything special and specific I should know about the position at **target company?** I'd like to be able to prepare for you some specific and specifically useful answers when I see you next week."

You might also contact people who are currently employed in a position similar to the target position. Call friends and friends of friends. You will find that most people are quite willing to help you.

> **PITFALL:** Do *not* contact anyone who works for the target company. They may feel threatened by you and your questions.

6.9.4.   More Homework: What Does the Target Organization Need?

Part of your pre-interview homework assignment is to determine and decide just what it is you need. Far more important to the target employer—and, therefore, more crucial to getting the job—is a knowledge of what the organization needs.

> Fantasy: You walk into the interview with an insider's knowledge of the needs, goals, and problems of this organization.
>
> Reality: You walk into the interview with an insider's knowledge of the needs, goals, and problems of this organization.

That's right. Gaining an insider's knowledge is possible, even from the outside.

1. If you happen to have a reliable source of information within the target company, use it. Ask him or her to identify for you just what the organization requires.

2. Obtain the organization's annual report, brochures, and other published material.

3. Talk to folks in the industry. More than likely, the needs, goals, and problems of one company in a given industry will be shared by others in the same industry.

4. Skim the journals and newsletters devoted to the industry. Look over the last three months of such published material.

5. Get relevant books from the public library.

Focus on the following:

1. Themes or issues critical to the firm

2. Themes or issues critical to the industry as a whole

3. Relevant current events that bear on the company or the industry

6.9.5. Preparing to Play to Your Strengths

Don't forget to review your own accomplishments and qualifications before the interview. Mentally underscore the ones most relevant to the target position.
Review your own résumé. Then perform the following exercise:

1. Think of a job-related problem you had to face within the past two or three years. Jot it down.

2. Describe, step-by-step, your solution to the problem.

3. Assess the results of your solution.

Tip: If at all possible, state these results in terms of *money earned or saved* for the company.

6.9.6. Formulate Your Salary Requirements

Do not go into an interview without a firm salary floor and ideal salary target in mind. However, you should try not to be maneuvered into being the first one to mention a salary figure. He who mentions a figure first, loses at the last.

Just how do you determine these figures?

1. *Study your present situation.* Are you meeting your monthly expenses *and* putting a bit aside? If not, how much more do you need each month?

   TIP: Consider the following areas: housing, food, clothing, automobile and transportation expenses, insurance, medical expenses, support for other family members, charity, education, pet care, bills and debts, taxes, amusements, and gifts. Add 30 percent to this total. That is a reasonable target salary.

2. *Think of the target salary in relation to your present salary.* If you are changing jobs principally to secure a salary increase, you should expect a minimum jump of 10 percent over your present salary.

   TIP: But, yes, there are other great reasons to change jobs besides salary. For example: personal interest and self-fulfillment. Don't be trapped by the 10 percent "rule."

   PITFALL: Watch out for any expenses associated with a new job, which may eat away your net income. What if you have to relocate to a more expensive geographical area? (For instance: Living expenses in the New York City metro area are about 40 percent higher than in the Atlanta, Georgia, metro area.) Will you have a costlier commute? Will you have to buy a new car? Will you need to invest in tools? Purchase a whole new wardrobe?

6.9.7. Anticipating Questions You Will Be Asked

Make certain that you read 6.5.1 Key Questions to Ask in 6.5. Interviewing Prospective Employees. Here you will find a list of questions commonly asked at interviews.

6.9.8. Preparing Questions to Ask

Remember: Most interviewers are not interviewers by choice. They are thrust into the role. They don't like interviewing job candidates. They are uncomfortable with the job and ill-prepared for it. Anything you can do to make their job easier will be greatly appreciated and will count in your favor. Therefore, do not fail to formulate before the interview questions *you* want to ask at the interview.

PITFALL: The interview has wound down. There is an awkward silence. The interviewer asks: "Do *you* have any questions you'd like to ask me?" The awkward silence continues. Finally, you throw in the towel: "No, I don't." Result: You will still be looking for employment tomorrow.

In addition to specific questions you may formulate, here are some general ones to consider asking:

1. Have you had an opportunity to review my résumé?

You would be shocked by the number of interviewers who fail to read your résumé before the interview—or who, at best, take a quick glance at it while you are sitting on the other side of the desk. It is not likely that the interviewer will come out and say, "No, I haven't even looked at your résumé!" Probably, you will get a response like, "I haven't had a chance to review it as thoroughly as I want." Mentally translate this as "No, I haven't even looked at your résumé!" You should respond by offering help: "Perhaps you'll find it helpful for me to summarize the highlights of my qualifications."

2. Is there anything else I can tell you about my background and qualifications?

The more time you prompt the interviewer to invest in you, the better.

TIP: Wherever possible, use the word *qualifications* instead of *experience.* There is an important difference between the two terms. "Qualifications" conveys achievement and positive action, whereas "experience" is more neutral, suggesting events that just happened to happen.

3. How would you describe the duties and responsibilities of this job?

The operative word, addressed to the interviewer, is *you.* His or her take on the what the job "really" entails may be a far cry from what's in the official job description. In any event, the question may give you a handle on which duties are seen as most important.

4. What are the most crucial problems you face right now?

The answer will give you an opportunity to present yourself as a problem solver. A bonus benefit of the question is that it will help you uncover any dire situations that might make you think twice before accepting an offer.

5. What results would you like to see me produce?

The question demonstrates that you intend to perform—to *do* a job rather than *take* a job.

6. What do *you* consider the ideal qualifications for this position?

You want the interviewer to respond by drawing a profile into which you can neatly step. Reply to the interviewer's list of qualifications point by point. Try to achieve a perfect match.

> **PITFALL:** What if the interviewer's idea of idea qualifications is light-years from what you have to offer? You might reconsider this job prospect. After all, it sounds like expectations and performance may differ sharply.

7. Can you give me a "weather report" about this company? Is it stormy? Hot? Cool? Breezy? Calm? Brisk? Or what?

Ideally, this will catch the interviewer off-guard, prompting her to tell you what the organization is *really* like. The question also gives you an opportunity to demonstrate that you are perfectly suited not just to the job, but to the *environment* within the company. "I thrive on intensity. 'Stormy' sounds just fine to me!"

8. Was the person who held this job before me promoted?

The optimist will translate this as "What are my chances for advancement?" The pessimist: "Will I come out of this thing alive?"

9. Is it possible for me to talk with the person who held this job before me?

If a conversation can be arranged, great! If not, ask why not.

10. So, based on what I've told you about myself, don't you think I can give you everything you want in this position?

This is a closing question—a question to conclude the interview and to close the sale. It invites a positive response.

6.9.9.   Prep Props

Prepare a set of props for the interview. This may be a sort of scrapbook, containing such items as at least three copies of your résumé and an "executive briefing"that summarizes your résumé in a single paragraph. Also include letters of commendation, awards, copies of business presentations you have made, photos of equipment you have worked with, and so on.

> **PITFALL:** Make certain that any business documents you bring are non-classified and non-proprietary. Don't show a prospective employer your present company's secrets!

> **TIP:** You maintain control of the scrapbook and related material. You may give the interviewer one of the copies of your résumé, but the other material should stay in your hands. Let the interviewer look all he wants, but don't relinquish the material. You want to convey the concept that this material is yours, that it is of value, and that it is not a giveaway.

6.9.10. How to Get 'Em to Gotta' Have You

An job interview is a sales situation. The product you are selling is yourself—or, rather, the features and benefits you offer to the target employer. As in any sales situation, your object is to move the target from a position of skeptical interest to "gotta have": *We gotta have this person.* Try to think of this process as consisting of five distinct steps:

1. *Use Your Ears.* Listen to what the interviewer says about the company's needs, goals, problems. Listen very carefully to what the interviewer says he or she needs. Respond as directly and specifically as possible to what you hear.

    > **TIP:** Demonstrate that you are listening by occasionally repeating and rephrasing the interviewer's most important points with such phrases as: "What I hear you saying is . . ." or "If I'm understanding you correctly . . . ."

2. *Get Attention.* It is possible for a jaded interviewer to sleep sitting up, eyes open. Prevent this from happening by reminding the interviewer—at the very outset—why *he* or *she* called *you* in for an interview: "Good morning. Ms. Smith. I'm excited to be here, since it seemed to me that my qualifications are such a perfect match for this company."

3. *Move from Attention to Interest.* The interviewer is a human being whom you have just met. Unless you have lived alone on a mountaintop for most of your life, you are already quite accustomed to developing anoth-

er human being's interest in you. In the case of a job interview, you need to focus this process by demonstrating your potential value as a member of the employer's team. Try to translate everything you say into an expression of accomplishment, achievement, or qualification.

> **Tip:** The more specific you are, the better. Don't rely on adjectives: "I'm a terrific salesman." Instead, address what the employer needs:"I have a full understanding of the widget business. I'm effective at selling because I understand the business from the perspective of the seller as well as the buyer."

4. *Move from Interest into Involvement.* This step is accomplished by listening for "buy signals." These include the obvious—remarks like "That interests me," or "I like that," or"Great!" Some are less obvious:"Tell me more about . . ." or "Can you be more specific about . . ." Once you trigger a buy signal of any sort, zoom in on the point that pressed the right button by elaborating on the issue you raised. This is the phase of the interview in which you need to be most specific.

5. *Get Action.* As the interview comes to a conclusion, look for an opportunity to bring it to *positive* closure."I've really enjoyed this. Let me ask you frankly: What can I tell you that would prompt you to make an offer?"

6.9.11.   How to Negotiate Salary

As previously mentioned, do not go into an interview without a clear idea of your salary requirements. However, as also previously noted, try not to be the first to bring up the subject of salary. Certainly, you should not raise the issue—at least, not until the very end of the interview. If, however, you are asked for a figure early in the interview, avoid being pinned to a specific figure:"I'm looking for a salary appropriate to my skills and accomplishments." If pressed, offer a *broad* salary range.

> **Tip:** You can calculate a range this way. Let's say you've decided that you need a minimum of $35,000. As part of your pre-interview homework, you've determined that customary salary range for the target position is $32,000 to $40,000. Therefore, you should"bracket"the range you ask for so that it *interlocks* with what you think is the upper range of the industry standard, on the one hand, and exceeds your own minimum requirement, on the other. Here, for example, you might state a range of $37,000 to $42,000.

Critical Timing

It is important to avoid the subject of salary until:

1. You are in the *final* interview—if there is more than one

2. You believe the interviewer has gotten to know you and has reached the "gotta have" stage

3. You believe that you fully understand the nature and scope of the job.

> **TIP:** Look for a "gotta have" buy signal. It will be something like this: "I think we are on the same wavelength about what the job involves. Now, what salary were you looking for?"

Once a salary range is squarely on the table, you have four options:

1. Accept the range with the comment that "the upper figure is close to what I had in mind."

2. Continue negotiating by responding with your own range, which overlaps the top end of the target employer's.

3. Buy time. Thank the interviewer and ask for twenty-four or forty-eight hours to consider the figure.

4. You can tell the interviewer that you are very far apart on salary.

Each of these alternatives has pluses and minuses. If you are really satisfied with the offer, take the first alternative. Just be aware that *most* employers do not lead off with their top figure. Usually, there is some upward range to latch onto; therefore, consider the second option, in order to stake out a new, somewhat higher range.

> **TIP:** When trying to push the offer higher, don't expect the employer to yield just because you top his top range. At this point, stress the *value* you are offering by reiterating your qualifications.

The final option is hardball, telling the interviewer that the two of you are very far apart.

PITFALL: This is a high-risk alternative! Play hardball, and you might just get kicked out of the game. Unless you are fully prepared to walk away from this particular opportunity, don't play hardball. Instead, ask for time to think the offer over. Then use the time to evaluate all the pros and cons of the job. This serves two purposes:

a. You are less likely to make snap decision—one way or the other—that you will regret.

b. The employer will think, and he may just come up with some more money.

6.9.12. Overcoming Obstacles and Objections

Consultants who make their money as professional negotiators will tell you that "everything is negotiable." Unfortunately, the truth is closer to *many* things are negotiable. Before looking at how to maneuver around your target employer's objections to giving you the salary you want, let's look at reality:

1. At the lower, entry-level salary ranges, compensation levels tend to be fairly firm. As you rise in compensation level, salary ranges increase in flexibility. Beyond about $60,000, there is often substantial room for negotiation.

2. In the middle salary ranges (say, between $20,000 and $60,000), you can reasonably expect to negotiate a salary as much as 15 percent above the initial offer. But that's all.

Now, as to what *can* be negotiated: You will find that objections to your salary requirements almost always center on one of four themes:

1. Your figure exceeds the "authorized" range.

2. "We just can't afford that kind of salary."

3. "Others, similarly qualified, who are already working here don't make that kind of money."

4. Your salary history doesn't seem to warrant what you are asking for.

Objection #1: If you are applying at an entry level, the first objection might be quite real. There may be little you *can* do to overcome the objection.

Objection #2: Refocus the target's concerns from *cost* to *value*—what he will gain from employing you: essentially, an investment in greater profitability.

Objection #3: Remember, *you*—not others—are the issue here. Gently but firmly remind the target of this: "I certainly understand your concern, but I understand that my salary will be based on my performance and my qualifications. I did not understand that it would be capped by what others in the organization earn."

Objection #4: Just as you want to separate consideration of your value from what others are paid, so you want to separate the *record* of what you earned in the past from what you are asking for *now.* "I'm not sure I understand what bearing my past salary has on the work I will do for you. I am asking for a salary suited to the level of performance I offer you. We've discussed this, and I believe that we're both agreed that I offer great value to the company."

6.9.13. More Alternatives

Cash is not the be-all, end-all of compensation. If you reach a dead end on the cash front, don't overlook negotiating for other, non-cash benefits. These might include:

1. Performance-based bonuses

2. Additional paid vacation time

3. Flexible hours

4. Profit sharing

5. Day care services

6. Perks, such as professional membership dues, company car, travel allowances, and so on

7. Relocation expenses (including such items as moving, temporary housing, guaranteed purchase of your former residence).

Part Seven

SPEECHES
AND MEDIA

7.1. OBJECTIVES AND STRATEGY

7.1.1. All Speech Is Persuasion

You will find in this section many guidelines for creating and delivering speeches, either in person or on radio or television. You will also find tactics for specific situations and kinds of speeches. But, within all this variety, one principle remains constant and a single strategy is paramount: Every speech you make is an attempt to persuade. In effect, every speech you make is a kind of sales presentation: you are "selling" a point of view, a course of action, or both. Bear this truth in mind:

1. When you begin to plan the speech

2. When you sit down to write the speech

3. When you deliver the speech.

The result should be an active, living presentation rather than the dull, timid, and perfunctory recitations all too many business speeches are.

7.1.2. What Is My Topic?

I'm not going to answer this right here—although, if you read on, you will find discussions of a series of topic areas. In fact, I haven't the slightest idea what *your* topic is. How could I? But, please look at that question: *What is my topic?* You would think that absolutely no speech could be written without answering the question. It's obvious, right?

The fact is that all too many speeches drift on and on—to the anxiety and boredom of speaker as well as audience—without being propelled by any clearly defined topic at all. Yes, unfortunately, it is perfectly possible to write a speech without a topic.

It's also *possible* to build a replica of Notre Dame Cathedral using toothpicks. The question is *Why do it?* My advice is, *Don't.*

Always ask yourself, *What is my topic?* Define that topic clearly and succinctly before you begin to write your speech.

Tip: Writing is, of course, a creative process. It is perfectly possible to start out with one topic, only to discover, in the course of creation, that you are really more interested in another. Don't panic. It may be a good idea to follow—or, at least, explore—your instinct. However, just make certain that the speech you finally do write is focused on a clearly defined topic or a manageable set of related topics.

7.1.3. Who Is My Audience?

As important as defining your topic is knowing who your audience is. There is nothing mysterious about this requirement. Each and every day you identify different audiences for the things you say. You speak in one way to your boss, another way to Client A, yet another to Client B, and in still other ways to your spouse, cousin, son, daughter, cat, dog, parakeet.

Who your audience is should:

1. Influence your choice of topic

2. Influence your language and tone

3. Influence the level and length of your speech.

If you are asked to speak to a group of toy marketers, you probably shouldn't talk about how to sell groceries.

Avoid guesswork in scoping out your audience. Ask the following questions of whomever it was who invited you to speak:

1. Who will be attending the speech?

2. What will they expect?

3. Is there something they *want* to hear?

4. Do they share certain interests or concerns?

5. What do they *really* care about?

6. Is there anything I should avoid?

7. What would *you* talk about if you were speaking to this group?

8. Why, exactly, did you ask *me* to speak?

Beyond this, you might also ask what the audience knows about you and/or the organization you represent. What are their preconceived notions in this regard?

7.2. NUTS AND BOLTS

7.2.1. Blueprint for a Great Speech

Here are two rules that are a good starting point from which to build any speech:

1. Make it simple.

2. Make it short.

   And here is the simplest possible plan for constructing the speech itself:

1. Tell the audience what you're going to tell them.

2. Tell the audience.

3. Tell the audience what you've told them.

   Some authorities will tell you that this, really, is all you need to know. Maybe. But, the chances are pretty good that a speech written in strict adherence to these rules will turn out pretty dull. Use them as a springboard only. Yes, you *should* keep the speech as short and as simple *as your subject matter will let it be.* Don't complicate a simple subject. And don't flog a dead horse. But don't oversimplify, and don't give an ample subject short shrift.

   Now, we've started very simply. Let's continue simply. The blueprint for the perfect speech follows:

   1. Beginning   2. Middle   3. End

Read on for details.

7.2.2. Beginning

As with any other form of communication, your first task is to overcome the psychological inertia of your audience. An extra effort is required at the outset in order to get both you and your audience "into" the speech. Here are some suggestions:

1. *Declare your subject.* "Tonight I will speak to you about . . ."

2. *Make an offer.* "What I have to say will make your life better."

3. *Entertain with an anecdote.* Most listeners like a good story, and most are highly grateful for whatever entertainment you can give them.

4. *Confess.* "You've come here expecting to learn everything there is to know about X. Well, I have to admit, I don't know everything there is to know about X, but . . ."

5. *Challenge a cherished belief.* "Your family physician makes mistakes. In fact, you should expect him to be wrong XX percent of the time."

6. *Embrace your audience.* "Let me begin by telling you how proud I am to be speaking to a group of X—and the greatest group of X in the world!"

7. *Start with a laugh.* Just make sure that the humor is *very* relevant to the subject of your talk. Do not begin with irrelevant jokes.

8. *Play with your title.* This works if your title is provocative. "I'm calling my talk 'How to Find the Right Mate.' Now, what do I mean by 'right'?"

9. *Promise to be brief.* This will win attention and gratitude. Just make sure you deliver on your promise.

7.2.3. Middle

The best ways to put order into the body of your speech are the ways that come most naturally. There are a half-dozen such approaches:

1. *Chronological structure*—narrating a series of events from first to last

2. *Cause and effect structure*—"before" vs. "after"

3. *Problem and solution order*—or question and answer

4. *Emotional order*—move from a position your audience will find most acceptable to one that will challenge their beliefs

5. *Dramatic order*—a crescendo, building from least intense to most.

6. *Size progression*—from smallest/least to biggest/most

Any one of these basic structures should serve well to give shape to the body of a speech. If you are adventurous, you might add a seventh method: metaphor. This is useful if you have to speak about a particularly complex or unfamiliar subject. The futurist philosopher R. Buckminster Fuller, for example, built an entire ecological vision around the metaphor of the earth as a spaceship. The media theorist Marshal McLuhan explained how television was transforming our world by showing us that the world had been transformed into a "global village."

> **Pitfall:** The effective use of metaphors—especially extended metaphors, metaphors big enough to control an entire speech—requires skill and judgment. Your audience can get lost in the metaphor and lose sight of your point. Or the metaphor can lead you astray into all manner of pseudologic. Be careful out there!

7.2.4. End

Why do so many speeches end so lamely—usually just sort of trailing off into irrelevance? Well, sometimes the speaker runs out of steam as well as time. More often, however, the body of the speech is faulty or the topic is poorly defined. After all, the end of the speech is nothing more or less than the sum of what came before. It is what the speech "adds up to." If the principal content of the speech is worth little, it will add up to even less.

This said, there is still much that an effective conclusion can do for *any* speech. Here are some tried and tested tactics:

1. *Refer to the beginning.* "I started by saying X. Let me conclude by saying Y."

2. *Review and summarize your main points.*

3. *Tell an anecdote that illustrates your main points.*

4. *Conclude with an inspiring quotation.*

5. *Ask a rhetorical question.* "Is this the future we want for our children?"

6. *Put it all in perspective.* "What I've been talking about is theory. It's up to each of us, each and every day, to put test this theory against hard reality."

7. *Make a statement of optimism and hope.*

8. *Ask for cooperation and unity.*

9. *Make a call to action.*

> **Tip:** End when it is time to end. Once you announce that you are reaching the end of your speech, end your speech—briskly.

TIP: Now is the time for eloquence. Pour it on at the end. This is the time to raise what you say to its highest level.

7.2.5. How to Develop Habits of Good Diction

Diction is the choice and use of words in speech. There are no absolute rules for "proper" diction, but there are some useful guidelines for avoiding ineffective diction:

1. Speak in the language of your audience. If you are addressing a group of philosophy professors, don't use words appropriate to the factory floor. If you are speaking to the union rank and file, don't try to impress them with words borrowed from your philosophy professor speech.

2. In general, avoid slang—especially if an adequate term exists in "standard" English.

3. Take time to find the *right* words—those that most accurately and vividly convey what you want to say.

4. Concentrate on nouns and verbs. Do not rely on adjectives and adverbs. "We won a great victory" is okay, but fairly dull. "We triumphed" is shorter and more powerful. The difference is in the verbs. If you can find a verb or noun that requires no help from adverbs and adjectives, use that verb or noun.

7.2.6. Pronunciation and Mispronunciation

If you are in doubt about the pronunciation of any word in your speech, look it up in a good dictionary. If you have any doubts about how to pronounce the names of people you mention in your speech, check out the pronunciation with the person or persons involved. ("Mr. Hjyouitp, I'm mentioning you in my speech. How, exactly, do you prefer that I pronounce your name?")

English offers a wide range of regional as well as socioeconomic variations in pronunciation. Our democracy makes a great show of fostering diversity, yet we speak of America as a great "melting pot," in which differences tend to blend. I believe that it is a mistake to attempt to obliterate the traits of speech that reveal your geographical, ethnic, or social origins. However, look out for the following habits of pronunciation—some of which are regional or ethnic—which most listeners will interpret negatively:

ax for "ask"

d or *t* for "th" (as in "dis ting don't work")

heigth for "height"

-in instead of "-ing" ("I've been workin'...")

pixture instead of "picture"

warsh or *wersh* for "wash"

Also: beware of failing to pronounce the entire word: *'n* for "and," *woulda* for "would have," and so on.

TIP: In informal speaking situations, contractions—such as *don't, can't,* and so on—are perfectly acceptable. In a more formal situations—or when you want particularly to emphasize a point—avoid them. Instead, use "do not," "cannot," and so on.

7.2.7. The Rules of Grammar You Need to Know

If you are uncertain about the rules of grammar, get help. A time-tested source is *The Elements of Style* by William Strunk, Jr., and E. B. White, published in paperback by Collier Books. There are more detailed works on the subject, but this little book is your best stop for quick answers.

PITFALL: For personal computer users, spell-checking software has been a great boon. Also available is a variety of grammar-checking software. Whereas spell checkers are generally extremely reliable, grammar checkers are far less so. Use them with caution. You may find them helpful, but you should not rely on them. Grammar tends to be too complex and, sometimes, too subjective for software solutions to work infallibly.

7.2.8. How to Type a Speech

Yes, *type* it. That's the first point to make. We've all suffered through some poor soul struggling to decipher his notes at the rostrum. You don't know whether to pity the fellow or throttle him.

Type. If you are part of the vanishing breed who still uses a typewriter, make certain the ribbon is new and fresh. At minimum, double space. You may even prefer triple spacing. If you use a personal computer and have a choice of typefaces, select a 14-point sans-serif font. Double or triple space, and always use upper- and lower-case letters.

PITFALL: Perhaps you think typing all capitals makes the speech bolder. Reading all caps is much harder than reading caps and lowercase.

Some other pointers:

1. End each line with a complete word. Avoid hyphenation.

2. Keep numbers together on a single line: *Five hundred dollars* is better than *five
hundred dollars.*

3. Spell out large numbers. *Three billion* is better than 3,000,000,000.

PITFALL: Avoid Roman numerals.

4. Number each page clearly.

5. Spell out difficult words phonetically.

6. Underline words you want to emphasize.

7. Prepare a spare copy of the typescript.

7.2.9.   To Read, to Memorize, or to Ad Lib?

A lot of people think that *reading* a speech is inevitably a deadly experience for the speaker and audience alike. There's no substitute for spontaneity, they argue.

The trouble is, there's a whole wide range of "spontaneity." Very few of us are sufficiently gifted to be able to speak *effectively* off the cuff for an extended period. Maybe even fewer of us have the facility and the time to memorize a speech.

This leaves reading.

And, the good news is, reading is not a bad alternative—provided that:

1. You take the time and effort to write an entertaining and informative speech—keeping your audience in mind as you write.

2. You rehearse the speech beforehand.

3. You type the speech clearly, so that you won't stumble through it.

4. You remember to bring your reading glasses, if you require them.

5. You make certain that the podium is adequately lighted.

6. You are sufficiently familiar with and comfortable with the speech that you don't have to keep your nose glued to it in order to read it.

7.2.10   How to Use Facts and Figures Effectively

Statistics—Ugh! Boring! Boring! Boring!
Wrong! Wrong! Wrong!
Your audience is *hungry* for facts and figures. Rightly or wrongly, people equate facts and figures with truth, whereas mere "words" are nothing more than opinion and interpretation. However, you must use your facts and figures selectively, always placing them in a vivid context where they will drive home your key points.

> PITFALL: Avoid laundry-list recitations of numbers!

The main thing to remember is to make the facts and figures as immediate, tangible, and real as possible. Television commentator Garrick Utley reported from Nicaragua in 1988 that "inflation . . . has been 10,000 percent." Now, that's a pretty staggering figure. Putting something like that in a speech is quite effective. But then Utley made it even more real: "If America had inflation at the same rate as Nicaragua this past year, this pineapple that costs fifty cents would instead cost fifty dollars."
Put life into the numbers you use. Also:

1. If the facts and figures you cite are controversial, mention their source.

2. If you cannot provide up-to-date figures—or can furnish estimates only—explain why.

3. Quote expert testimony to interpret statistics. ("What does this 10 percent decrease mean? Let me quote Dr. So-and-so . . . ")

7.2.11.   To Quote or Not to Quote?

Most neophyte speech makers quote the words of others far too much. Don't let others speak for you. Your audience wants to hear *you*, not somebody who isn't even present—maybe isn't even among the living anymore. When you do quote, observe the following guidelines:

1. Be brief

2. Be selective

3. Work the quotation smoothly into your speech. You can even integrate the syntax of the quotation into your own sentence:

   > President Kennedy called on us to ask not what our country could do for us, but what we could do for our country.

   This is preferable to:

   > President Kennedy said (and I quote), "Ask not what your country can do for you, but what you can do for your country."

4. Spread the wealth. Do not quote too often or too heavily from a single source or person. Your audience will:

   a. Assume you've read only one book within the past ten years.

   b. Wish that the person quoted were speaking instead of you.

5. Be careful of context. Quoting out of context or in the wrong context can change the meaning of the quotation.

6. Don't rely on second-hand sources of quotations. Use them sparingly.

7. Make certain that you can pronounce all the material in the quotation, especially any foreign names (Goethe, anyone?).

7.2.12.   A Guide to Making Effective Use of Visuals

Until recently, the visual aids a business speech maker was most likely to use included:

◆ Flip charts

◆ Overhead transparencies

◆ Slides

◆ Printed handouts

Now more and more presentations are likely to include a video segment and computer-generated graphics.

Flip Charts

It doesn't get simpler than these. Just be sure of the following:

1. You've got a tripod stand to support the flip chart. Propping it up against a stack of books or boxes is not only unprofessional, it probably won't work.

2. Do not crowd graphics on a single page. Use one graphic per page.

3. Arrange the graphics precisely in the order that you will use them in the speech. Include reminder cues in your typescript.

4. Leave a blank page between graphics. Never flip to the graphic until you discuss it. When you are finished discussing that graphic, flip down the blank page. You do not want your audience musing over the graphics instead of listening to you.

5. Stand to the side of the chart while speaking. Do not speak to the chart. Speak to the audience.

6. If your chart contains key terms, make certain that your speech uses exactly the same terms.

Overhead Transparencies

1. You are dependent on a functioning projector. Make certain you have extra bulbs.

2. Number the transparencies clearly and boldly. Otherwise, they can easily fall out of sequence.

3. Dim the room lights only as much as is necessary to see the graphics comfortably. An overhead projector should not require a fully darkened room.

    PITFALL: Darkening a room during a speech may produce two unwanted results:

    a. It makes it difficult or impossible for your audience to take notes.

    b. It may prompt audience members to sleep.

4. Show the graphic only when you are ready to discuss it. After you have finished discussing it, remove it and dim the projector.

Slides

1. Edit slides carefully. Avoid the temptation to use more than necessary.

2. Number each slide, even if they are arranged in a "carousel."

3. You *will* probably have to darken the room significantly. Remember: this keeps people from taking notes, and it risks inducing sleep.

4. Do not keep the room darkened if there is a significant stretch of time between slides.

Certain speeches use 3-D props—such as new products, models, and so forth. These can make a great impact. However:

1. Hide the prop until you are ready to use it.

2. If the thing has working parts, test the operation of everything *before* you make the presentation.

7.2.13. How to Publicize and Publish Your Speech

Aside from employing your in-house or freelance publicist to "broadcast" your speech beyond the confines of a single hall, use the following to get the maximum mileage from your speech:

1. Use a provocative title. The title should offer something of value: "Talking Yourself into a Great Job."

2. Distribute copies of your speech to the audience.

   PITFALL: Do this *after* you have concluded the speech. You do not want your audience reading along with you.

3. Identify specialist publications—trade and professional journals, and so forth—that should be interested in the topic of your talk. Send them copies of your speech.

4. Prepare a press release in advance of the speech.

5. Send copies to such publications as *Vital Speeches of the Day* (City News Publishing Company, P.O. Box 1247, Mount Pleasant, SC 29465), which reprints speeches on a wide variety of topics. Make certain you send a clean, double-spaced, typewritten, proofread copy.

7.3. A MATTER OF STYLE

7.3.1. How to Use Body Language at the Podium

Speech=words. Obvious? Self-evident? Not quite. A 1971 study by psychologist Albert Mehrabian concluded that listeners evaluate the "emotional content" of a speech *primarily* on the basis of facial expressions and body movement. In fact, whereas these visual cues accounted for 55 percent of the "weight" listeners put in the evaluative balance, the actual words counted only 7 percent, while such vocal qualities as tone and pitch of voice made up 38 percent.

> TIP: Put your politics aside for a moment and consider. The famous televised debates between John F. Kennedy and Richard M. Nixon during the 1960 presidential campaign produced no clear winner. Most people who heard the debates on the radio thought Nixon was the more effective of the two. However, most people who watched the debates on television, awarded the plum to Kennedy. Nixon *looked* nervous, shifty, evasive. On radio and television, the *words* were identical.

Work on the following:

1. *Maintain eye contact.* This is not always easy when you have to look down at your typescript. Rehearse the speech. Practice looking up frequently. Each time you look up, try to make contact with a specific person in the audience. Don't stare out blankly. Vary the targets of your gaze, but do pick a specific target each time.

2. *Smile as often as possible*—unless the content of the speech makes this clearly inappropriate.

3. *Use hand gestures to underscore key points.* Avoid fist pounding, but don't be afraid to choreograph useful, expressive gestures as required.

4. *Learn to recognize and overcome your tics and nervous habits.* Avoid continuous hand motions, rubbing your face, putting your hands anywhere near your mouth, shoulder shrugging, shifting your weight from side to side.

5. *Adopt a firm, upright, but comfortable stance at the podium.*

TIP: Soldiers required to stand at attention for extended periods quickly learn to appear rigid without actually standing rigidly. Do not lock your knees, but, instead, flex them slightly. This will have the effect of relaxing you without leading to a slouch position.

7.3.2. What to Wear?

Dress appropriately to the occasion. Most business occasions call for acceptable business wear. Formal dinners may require dinner jackets for men and formal dresses for women. Aside from this, it is wise to practice some common sense:

1. Aim to dress just slightly "better" than your audience—no more, no less.

2. Err on the side of conservatism.

3. Avoid loud patterns and jarring combinations. Your listeners will find these things distracting.

4. For television, wear a light blue, light gray, or light tan shirt. Stark white shirts tend to create glare on the television image. Also avoid zig-zag, checked, and houndstooth patterns. These tend to "strobe" on television—that is, they appear to vibrate, an effect that is irritating as well as distracting.

5. Avoid elaborate jewelry. This is not only a visual distraction, but pendulous jewelry jingles and clacks with every movement, especially if it gets near a microphone.

6. Wear what makes you feel good—as long as it is appropriate to the occasion. This is not time to be uncomfortable.

7.3.3. Slang: It Ain't Always Cool

You need really concern yourself with only one guideline here: If you can find effective "standard English" language for what you want to say, steer clear of slang.

> **PITFALL:** By lacing your speech with slang, you risk alienating listeners, cheapening your message, and compromising your credibility. Since slang changes more rapidly than "standard" English, you also risk revealing yourself as hopelessly "dated."

If you feel that slang is warranted in some aspect of your presentation, observe the following:

1. If you are fully comfortable with the word, your audience will probably feel the same way. If the term makes you uncomfortable, avoid it.

2. Avoid ethnically or racially based slang.

3. Avoid sexually oriented slang.

7.3.4. How Loud? How Fast?

Oratory is louder than normal speech, period. Even if you use a microphone, speak up. Project your voice. You should not have to shout or strain.

> **Tip:** How loud is loud enough? You should enjoy the full, resonant sound of your own voice. It should strike you as almost musical. When you have reached that point, you are probably speaking loudly enough.

Just as you must speak up, you must also slow down. You should not exceed 150 words per minute. That is, it should take you a full two minutes to read a normal, double-spaced, typewritten page of text. This is slower than conversation, which usually proceeds at about 200 words per minute.

> **Tip:** Try writing at the upper lefthand corner of each page of your type-script the words "SLOW DOWN."

7.3.5. Mastering Pitch and Tone

Pitch and tone—the musical qualities of your voice—go together. One piece of advice generally holds true for most speakers: Lower the pitch of your voice.

1. Anxiety tends to raise the pitch of your voice. Consciously lowering pitch will not only disguise your nervousness, it may actually help relieve your nervousness—because you won't sound scared *to yourself.*

2. A lower-pitched voice is generally perceived as more authoritative than a higher-pitched voice. This holds true whether you are a man or a woman.

3. Pitching your voice lower tends to achieve a more pleasing tone. It also has the effect of slowing you down and of encouraging the more precise articulation of each word.

Here are some other tune-up tips:

1. Avoid ending declarative sentences on a rising note. This is a verbal tic more common to women than men. It makes the statement sound tentative, even doubtful—as if the speaker is continually seeking approval.

2. Minimize any nasal quality in your voice by consciously lowering the pitch of your voice. If you have persistent allergies or chronic breathing problems, you would do well to consult a physician.

7.4. HOT ISSUES

7.4.1. Off-Color Stories and Naughty Words: How Far Should I go?

Off-color language and humor are inappropriate in business-speaking occasions. The courts, regulators, and advocates of freedom of speech have spent many years debating just what constitutes obscenity. For the purposes of public speaking, subject what you propose to say to the following questions:

1. Does it make *me* uncomfortable?

2. Would I want my family to hear me saying it?

3. Does it reflect negatively on race, ethnicity, religion, gender, age?

4. Is it hurtful?

5. Does it suggest private matters?

6. Will I feel proud saying it?

7.4.2. Handling Hecklers

Unless you become a nightclub comic, you will probably live out your entire speaking life without ever encountering a heckler. Moreover, most heckling that does occur is innocuous—irritating, rather than malicious. In the unlikely event that you are beset by a heckler, ignore him. Generally, the irritating or disruptive behavior will cease. If, however, the heckler persists, take the following steps:

1. Stop speaking.

2. Look the heckler in the eye. Pause for a beat. Then ask him to hold his question or comment until after the speech.

If these tactics fail, assert yourself more insistently: "As I said, I will be happy to take your questions *after* I have concluded my remarks." If this does not solve the problem, remind the heckler—and the audience—why you are here: "I have been asked to speak here. *My* name is **Name.** What is yours?"

If even this tactic fails, stop. Calmly step back from the podium. Look toward the person who invited you to speak. It is her job now to deal with the heckler. She is your host. If you cannot look toward this person, then look silently out at the audience. Let them apply the necessary collective pressure.

If the situation is truly out of control, leave quietly. Do not subject yourself to rudeness or abuse.

7.5. Gaffes, Goofs, and Mishaps

7.5.1. A Survivor's Tip Sheet

What you've got going for you is the milk of human kindness. The fact is that your audience does not want to see you fail. They are not leaning forward anxiously, hoping to catch you in a mistake. If you deliver a worthwhile product overall, you will be forgiven an error or two. In this context, develop a two-pronged general strategy with regard to errors:

1. Try to prepare sufficiently so that they do not occur.

2. When an error does occur, acknowledge it, and get on with the show.

Barring natural disasters—fire, flood, earthquake—there are three kinds of mishaps to which a speaker is subject:

1. *A slip of the tongue.* If you make a verbal stumble, do not try to cover it up. Usually, this only compounds the error. Instead, pause, smile, and start the entire sentence over again. If the slip was humorous, enjoy the unintended joke *with* your audience.

2. *"Technical difficulties"*—a faulty microphone, a stubborn slide projector, a tardy guest speaker. Do not try to cover up. *Explain* to your listeners what has happened and what you are doing about it.

    PITFALL: Do not blame anyone for the problem, including yourself. Just explain, fix, and get on with the show.

    TIP: The best solution to technical difficulties is proactive. Check out audio-visual equipment beforehand. Have extra projector bulbs on hand. If you've got a guest speaker scheduled for 8 P.M., tell her to arrive by 7:30.

3. *You may make an error of fact.* If the error is detected at all, it will most likely be brought to your attention in a question-and-answer session. If challenged on fact, do not react defensively. Nor should you automatically admit the error. Instead, hear the questioner out. If you are not persuaded that you are in error, respond that your sources indicate a different conclusion. If you like, you may indicate your interest in discussing

the matter with the questioner after the conclusion of the program. Another valid response is to disagree, but to promise to investigate the issue further. Now, if you *are* persuaded that an error has been detected, admit the possibility of a mistake. Thank the questioner and promise to pursue the matter further. Finally, it is possible that you yourself may detect the error even as you speak it. When this happens, stop at a convenient point and correct yourself. Do not try to cover up the mistake. It will haunt you throughout the rest of your presentation, making you prone to yet more errors.

7.6. ACCEPTANCE SPEECHES

7.6.1. How to Communicate Gratitude and Grace

One of the first demonstrations of "good manners" we learn as children is how to say thank you. Somehow, unfortunately, most of us fail to build on this foundation when it comes to "saying a few words" on public and professional occasions that requires us to express gratitude. When you are presented with something—an award, an honor, an appointment—it is critically important to honor the occasion and to honor those who have invested their praise, confidence, and trust in you.

Awards and Honors

Accepting an award or honor gracefully is not as easy as one would think. Most of us have been taught to be—or, at least, to appear—modest, and such childhood lessons come back to haunt us when it's time to acknowledge the plaudits of friends and colleagues. While it is, in fact, true that a certain amount of genuine modesty is a becoming virtue, too much makes those who give the award or recognition uncomfortable. If you gracelessly protest that you are unworthy of the honor—or, worse, if you belittle the honor itself—you will give those who honor you highly unpleasant second thoughts. The object of the acceptance speech is not for you to show off. But it is to give pleasure to those who have bestowed recognition on you. Your remarks should make them feel that they have acted wisely—have made the right choice.

You might try structuring your speech in this way:

1. Begin with an expression of pleasure.

2. If the award is unexpected—*genuinely* unexpected—express your surprise and delight.

3. Share credit with others who deserve it. Name names.

> TIP: Name names, but avoid the laundry list approach that makes so many acceptance speeches excruciating exercises in tedium. Associate a specific role with each name: "I couldn't have written the book without the help and encouragement of Joe Blow, who wielded an editorial pencil at once merciful and merciless."

4. Acknowledge any competitors graciously, praising their ability and hard work.

5. Acknowledge your colleagues and coworkers.

6. Use gentle humor to convey your modesty, but never belittle the honor itself.

Appointments

Accepting an appointment or post of responsibility requires a somewhat different speech than what is appropriate for accepting an award or honor. Your principal object here is twofold:

1. To thank your listeners for showing confidence in you by having given you the position.

2. To assure them that they have made the right choice.

> **TIP:** Think of this kind of speech as a form of congratulations. You are not congratulating yourself, however, but, rather, your listeners—for having wisely placed their confidence in you.

Expunge from your speech any self-doubt you may feel. This is not the appropriate occasion for confessions of inadequacy. Instead:

1. Announce pleasure and gratitude.

2. Acknowledge your own hard work. You see the appointment as the fruition of your efforts.

3. If you had an opponent, acknowledge him or her graciously.

4. Acknowledge your predecessor graciously.

5. Survey the traditions and responsibilities of the position. Make certain that your audience is aware that *you* are aware of the scope and dimension of the responsibilities you are undertaking.

6. Optionally—discuss problems to be resolved or goals to be achieved. Look to the future. Keep these remarks positive.

7. Ask for assistance, cooperation, and good faith.

7.7. After-Dinner Speaking

7.7.1. Tested Strategies for Keeping Your Audience Awake

After-dinner speeches can address just about any subject. There are no set rules or magic formulas. So what sets the after-dinner speech apart from any other speech? The answer is simple: the dinner.

Your audience has just eaten and, more than likely, has also just consumed a "certain amount" of alcoholic refreshment. While it is reasonable to assume that your audience will be in a good mood, their degree of alertness is in question. Of course, all good speeches should be stimulating, but the after-dinner speech needs to be especially so:

1. Choose a subject of special and significant interest to this particular audience.

2. Start off with a surprising statement—a kind of verbal appetizer.

3. Avoid weighty or complex issues requiring great concentration. Favor light and humorous subjects.

4. Favor positive subjects. The after-dinner speech is *not* the time for a speech dealing with crisis.

5. Use vivid language, stressing nouns and verbs rather than abstract concepts.

6. Be brief—especially if the hour is late.

7. Make use of anecdote. Stories go well after dinner.

8. Play to the room. Relate as directly as possible to your audience. Usually, the after-dinner speech is made during an occasion of fellowship and camaraderie.

9. Make liberal use of *relevant* humor.

TIP: Think of yourself as part of the dessert course—not the meat-and-potatoes.

7.8. Anniversaries and Commemorations

7.8.1. How to Celebrate Without the Clichés

Where there's an anniversary, there is certain to be a speech—or two or three or more. If anniversaries are guaranteed to spawn a speech, they are also, unfortunately, likely to produce more than their fair share of dull-witted and half-hearted speeches. Fight this dreary trend by latching on to two key features of effective anniversary speeches:

1. Most people enjoy reminiscing. Nostalgia is pleasurable and fascinating. Bear in mind that an anniversary is an occasion for such reminiscence, a comparison of yesterday with today—an opportunity to reawaken pleasing memories.

2. Do not leave your audience living in the past. The second component of any effective anniversary speech is a look to the future—an anticipation of even better things to come.

Given these two principles, it is quite simple to structure a memorable anniversary talk. Just begin with reminiscences and conclude with a look toward the future. Here are some strategies for successful reminiscing:

1. Travel back through time. Really set the stage. What was the world like when Corporation X was founded? How much did a bottle of Coke cost? What was most popular on the black-and-white TV? What songs were played on the Rockola jukebox? Use plenty of familiar and nostalgic place names and brand names.

2. Create a miniature biography of the founder or other early leading light.

3. Measure change: The businesses began in a garage and now occupies a ten-acre corporate campus.

4. Counterpoint dramatic change to those enduring qualities that have remained constant: loyalty, dedication, commitment to innovation, dedication to quality, etc.

After indulging in the pleasures of recollection, encourage your listeners to celebrate and perpetuate what has always been good about the past, but also to look ahead to even more exciting and rewarding days to come.

> **PITFALL:** Statistics can be valuable for dramatizing differences between today and yesterday. Don't get carried away, however, with laundry lists of facts and figures.

7.9 Charity Events and Community Meetings

7.9.1. Guidelines for Establishing a Good Neighbor Policy

The very heart of oratory is the community, the community and the common good. The art of rhetoric developed in classical times as a vital instrument of creating, shaping, and guiding the community. The Greek and Roman states were, in large part, created through speech. Perhaps you have something less than an empire to deal with. Perhaps you've been asked to make a speech to organize a fund drive for a new playground in your community. No matter. An effective speech can help create the sense of community required to fund that playground.

> **Tip:** Your principal objective is to create a sense of community—a pool of common interests—and to show how you and your company are united with the community in that common interest.

Let cooperation, common cause, and community be the themes that inform your talk from beginning to end:

1. Create images—word pictures—that suggest your participation in a common purpose.

2. State and outline the issues clearly.

3. Demonstrate fairness. Consider all sides of an issue. Only by taking all points of view into consideration can you create a sense of cohesive community.

4. Weigh the pluses and minuses of any solutions or proposals you offer.

5. Invite others to speak.

If you are promoting a particular project or charitable undertaking, use the five-part formula familiar from good sales letters:

1. Begin by getting the attention of your audience. Use a provocative question. Make a bold statement. Make a promise. Present a vivid picture of a critical situation.

2. Identify—clearly, sharply, unmistakably—a community need.

3. Explain how you propose to respond to that need.

4. Compare and contrast your proposal to other available options.

5. Make a call to action. Tell your audience what the next step is. Tell them what they *should* do. Give precise instructions for action.

7.10. CLUB MEETINGS AND TRADE CONVENTIONS

7.10.1. Principles of Working the Network

Speeches delivered to commercial clubs and at trade conventions often concern the organization's programs and activities, the planning of future programs and activities, proposing new members, and nominating new officers. In addition to performing these more or less utilitarian functions, speeches to commercial clubs should reflect the underlying values of the organizations, which, characteristically, include fellowship and service to the industry and/or community.

Reporting

Speeches summarizing programs and activities have an almost unlimited potential for inducing mass coma. Fortunately, this condition can be avoided by observing the following rules of structure:

1. Begin with a *capsule* overview of the nature and purpose of the project or activity. This provides context and meaning for what otherwise might be without context and void of meaning. Be certain to list the principal goals of the project.

2. Assess the progress of the program or activity. What goals have been achieved? Exceeded? Missed?

3. Underscore the benefits of the activity or program.

4. Share entertaining or illustrative anecdotes related to the program.

5. Thank those who participated in the program or activity.

> **TIP:** And if the program has failed? This is the place to put the effort in its best possible light. Thank those who worked tirelessly and uncomplainingly to *try* to make the program a success.

Proposing Programs or Activities

You will likely recognize this speech as a species of sales presentation. Your task is to *sell* your audience on a program. Therefore, your first task is to:

1. Establish a need. This may be a need within the organization, the industry, or the community.

2. Propose ways of addressing this need.

3. Highlight the benefits of your program.

4. Outline a course of action: the next step. This should be as specific as possible; however, the "next step" need not be immediately enacting the proposal, but might be an agreement to discuss and evaluate your proposal, as well as others.

Proposing Candidates for Membership

As the sponsor of a candidate, it is your responsibility to show how this person represents the qualities and attributes members value.

1. Talk about the candidate's position in the community, industry, or profession.

2. Talk about your relationship to the candidate: your friendship and your professional association.
   a. How long have you known him/her?
   b. What makes him/her a good friend and associate?

3. Enumerate the candidate's chief qualities.

   Tip: These should clearly reflect the organization's values. Emphasize the connection between the candidate's qualities and the organization's values and ideals.

4. Conclude with emphasis on the candidate's enthusiasm and eagerness to become a member.

Nominating Officers

The key here is to create a context and then demonstrate that your candidate is the perfect fit for that context.

1. List the requirements of office—not just the technical, official requirements, but the requirements of skill, ability, and character.

2. Name your candidate, asserting that he/she perfectly satisfies the requirements outlined.

3. Elaborate on the match between your candidate's skills, character, and ability and the requirements of the office. Provide evidence—perhaps an effective anecdote.

7.11. CRISIS MANAGEMENT

7.11.1. What to Say at a Scary Time

In most organizations, a crisis usually has at least two dimensions. There is the problem or set of problems: a client fails to come through with the expected contract, the new line of merchandise falls flat, a key employee quits—whatever. But there is also the emotional dimension of the crisis—the impact on morale and attitude. This second dimension is not merely a side effect of the crisis, it is also the fuel that drives the crisis, and that can convert a crisis into an out-and-out full-scale disaster.

The right words said at the right time can do much, first and foremost, to address the morale dimension of the crisis. An effective speech is effective damage control. Beyond this, of course, a timely speech can lay out a plan for coping with the causes of the crisis. Ideally, then, the effective crisis-management speech not only reinforces and nurtures positive morale, it also presents a rational plan for coping with the underlying problems.

In most cases, it is a good strategy to *begin* by addressing the causes of a crisis and presenting a plan for coping with the problems. In the presence of a reasoned, clearly presented, feasible plan, many of the issues of negative morale will simply dissolve. However, after presenting the plan, it is usually a good idea to address directly issues of morale and attitude.

1. Begin by providing information.

    TIP: In a crisis, the enemy is fear. Your enemy's ally is ignorance. Inform your audience. How do you know what to say? Put yourself in the place of your audience? What will they *want* to hear? What will help them act most effectively? Provide information accordingly.

2. Define the extent of the crisis. What happened when? What is likely to happen next? How long it will it all last?

3. Outline an approach to coping with the crisis. Be as specific as possible. Stress order and orderly procedure.

4. Address feelings. Create a sense of community, of team, of getting-through-this-thing-together.

Pitfall: Do not minimize feelings. Do not tell your audience not to worry or to cheer up. You will not be believed.

5. Create a context that puts the crisis in perspective. If at all possible, compare the present problem to crises that have occurred before and that have been successfully overcome.

6. Ask for help and cooperation. Ask for this explicitly.

7. End by reiterating the need for team action.

In a crisis, what you *avoid* saying is as important as what you say. Sometimes it's even *more* important. Avoid the following:

1. Avoid pronouncements of doom and hopelessness.

2. Avoid blame and finger-pointing. This is definitely not the time to divide the organization. And blame does nothing but divide.

3. Avoid expressing personal fears. Keep these to yourself.

4. Avoid wild speculation—either pessimistic or optimistic. Make no predictions lacking a solid basis.

5. Avoid unwarranted humor. Do not assume the demeanor of an undertaker, but don't try to laugh off a genuine crisis either. Take it seriously. Mindless humor will be (quite rightly) perceived as denial.

7.12. EULOGIES

7.12.1. Words That Remember and That Heal

The world of business is a community, and, as in any community, there comes a time to acknowledge loss and to help the members of the community cope with loss. Delivering a eulogy can present an intimidating prospect. Not only is the occasion of the speech bound to be emotionally intense, it is also, by its very nature, a short-notice occasion. There is little time to prepare. Finally, there is the pressure, both perceived and actual, to say something adequate to the memory of the deceased, even while you provide condolence and inspiration to the survivors. In view of these formidable challenges, you should give yourself a break by also taking into account the following:

1. No one expects your speech to work miracles. No one expects your speech to relieve all the pain.

2. No one expects your speech to be the last and final word on the deceased—the sum total of all his or her accomplishments.

3. Your listeners recognize that your task is emotionally difficult. They will be sympathetic and receptive to you, as well as respectful of whatever you say.

4. Whereas in most speaking situations, you face the important challenge of "hooking" your listeners—selling them on the subject of your speech—in the case of the eulogy, the audience is already focused on the subject.

5. Generally, your role as eulogist establishes a bond with the audience from the outset.

True enough, the task of speaking a eulogy is still emotionally demanding, but these factors tend to make the creation of the speech itself easier. Beyond this, what you say should be guided by four principles:

1. Know your audience. Are they mainly business associates of the deceased? Are they mainly family members? Are they employees paying tribute to their CEO? Are they members of the general community, paying their respects to a civic leader? Shape your remarks accordingly.

2. Speak what you feel. Put into words your best, most positive feelings about the deceased.

3. Share memories of events and experiences that you believe reveal the deceased at his best, his most characteristic, and his most human.

   TIP: Reviving memories is important because it is healing. That the deceased lives on in memory helps to put the loss in perspective.

4. As the saying goes, speak no ill of the dead. Do not judge him. Say nothing negative. Your sole task is to evoke admiration, respect, and affection.

   TIP: The English word *eulogy* is derived from the Greek *eulogia* and the Latin *eulogium,* both of which signify *praise.*

Although the eulogy is quite properly driven by your *personal* feelings, most effective eulogies have at least some of the following elements in common:

1. They speak on behalf of the mourners.

2. They admit feelings of grief and pain.

3. They emphasize the great value of the deceased—to the company, the family, the community.

4. They incorporate the speaker's personal experience—his relation to the deceased.

5. They emphasize the special qualities of the deceased.

6. They quote from the deceased.

7. They admit personal sadness and acknowledge a sense of loss.

8. They celebrate memory and the legacy of memory left by the deceased.

   TIP: Humor: inappropriate on this occasion? Not if the deceased was known for her sense of humor, or if sharing a humorous anecdote will reveal something positive about the personality of deceased. Just be certain that the humor does not diminish or belittle the memory of the deceased.

There are some verbal tactics to avoid in delivering a eulogy. In the main, these include anything that falls short of being genuine. Avoid:

1. Clichés, high-flown rhetoric, and canned sentiment.

2. *Dwelling* on tragedy and grief.

3. Casting doubt on any aspect of the life of the deceased.

7.13. INTRODUCTIONS

7.13.1. The Very Fine Art of Saying Just Enough

Introducing a speaker is in itself a common and frequent speaking occasion, yet introductions are all too often prepared in haste and with little thought. The result is a perfunctory or stumbling performance, which fails to perform the chief function of an introduction: to enhance the audience's reception of the featured speaker.

The irony is that preparing to make an adequate introduction is actually quite simple. You need do very little of the work. Pick up the phone, dial the featured speaker, and request from her a résumé or curriculum vitae. There's your research, period. Or you can make it even easier on yourself by calling the speaker and asking *her* to write a paragraph of introduction. Now, of course, there's no guarantee that the introduction your featured speaker writes for herself will be adequate. You should modify the introduction, adding to it, condensing it, embellishing it. Usually, the speaker will be too modest about herself. The result may be a paragraph that says relatively little. In this case, make another phone call: "Dr. Smith, you've been far too modest in the introductory remarks you sent me. Can you give me a few more details concerning your work in combating infectious disease?"

However you obtain the material for the introduction, observe the following guidelines:

1. Keep it brief, but not curt. Two minutes—or thereabouts—should suffice in most cases.

2. Repeat the name of the speaker more than once.

   PITFALL: The cardinal sin of introduction-making is mispronouncing the speaker's name. It is not only rude, it telegraphs to your audience the message that you really don't care about the speaker—so why should they? Check out the pronunciation beforehand. If necessary, write it out phonetically.

3. Make a connection between the speaker and the audience. What does the speaker mean to this particular audience?

PITFALL: This is the place to announce the title of the speaker's talk or, at least, its subject. Be certain that you have consulted with the speaker, know what the title of the talk is, and know what the subject is. Do not mislead the audience and put the speaker into the awkward situation of having to correct you.

4. Conclude the introduction definitively. "No one is better qualified to speak about such-and-such than Joe Blow, the evening's featured guest."

   TIP: Throughout the introduction—and especially at the conclusion—face the *audience,* not the *speaker.* You are, after all, addressing the audience.

People who make introductions all too often make one or more of the following mistakes:

1. They mispronounce the speaker's name.

2. They trot out tissue-thin stock phrases: "This man needs no introduction," and the like.

3. They upstage the speaker by anticipating his conclusions. Don't let the cat out of the bag.

4. They make an introduction that is impossible to live up to: "You are about to hear the most brilliant speech you have ever heard or will ever hear."

5. They make unfair comparisons: "Well, nobody can possibly be as entertaining as Mary Howard was, but let's listen to Ron Stillman give it a try."

6. They recite the speaker's résumé.

7.14. RETIREMENTS

7.14.1. Commemorating Achievement and Saying Goodbye

Retirement speeches come in two varieties, depending on the role of speaker. Are you the retiree or the person charged with honoring the retiree?

You Are the Retiree

If you are the object of the commemoration, your speech need not be lengthy, but it should be generous. Rest assured that the audience *wants* to hear what you have to say. They want to feel a connection with you. They want to acknowledge association and friendship.

1. Begin with thanks:
   a. To those who organized the celebration
   b. To your colleagues and coworkers—for their affection, dedication, and fellowship

   TIP: Try saying something specific when you address point 1b: the time everybody pitched in with extra overtime to meet a big deadline, the blizzard that made for a memorable office overnighter when no one could get home, and so on.

2. Deliver unstinting praise.

3. Honor your mentors and/or those who brought you into the company.

4. Honor and thank your family.

5. Reminisce. Share the past. Emphasize specific anecdotes.

6. Speak—dramatically—about the growth of the company during your years with it.

7. End by looking toward the future. Tell your colleagues what you plan to do next—especially if you *do* plan to do something productive and exciting.

If you feel so inclined, you may add some words of inspiration and advice. Try to emphasize the genuine and strong connection between any such words and your actual experience. Share what you have learned.

Honoring the Retiree

If your role as speaker is to honor the retiree, always begin by making certain that your listeners know who is retiring. This will avoid catastrophic embarrassment that will leave *everyone* feeling bad. Once this is taken care of, proceed to:

1. Honor the retiree's achievements

    TIP: As usual, it is best—most effective and most interesting—to be most specific. Cite specific accomplishments.

    PITFALL: Avoid a laundry-list recitation of qualifications and accomplishments. Be selective. Choose those achievements that are typical and speak volumes about the honoree.

2. Deliver unstinting praise

3. Express your affection for the honoree

4. Share anecdotes. This is the place for good-natured humor liberally laced with affection and fondness.

Often, the honoree is presented with some commemorative gift. If it is part of your assignment to present the gift, share it with the audience. They want to participate in its value and in the act of giving it.

    PITFALL: Never belittle the gift—even if it is a mere token.

Whether you are the retiree or are charged with honoring him, it is important to avoid the following mistakes:

1. Do not turn the occasion into a "downer" by expressing your feelings that So-and-so's departure heralds the end of the world. If you are the retiree, do not imply that your life is now over.

2. Do not fail to be flat-out generous in praise and affection.

3. Do not dwell on the past—the "good old days." Reminisce. Don't wallow.

7.15. Sales Presentations

7.15.1. First the Pitch, *Then* the Windup

The sales presentation is a particularly demanding kind of speech because it is intended to produce a more or less (usually *more* rather than less) direct and immediate result. It is a speech coiled up and aimed at provoking action: a purchase. Yet, in a significant way, the sales speech is no different from any other speech. For all speeches are attempts to persuade, to sell—even if your "product" is nothing more (or less) than a thought or a point of view.

The most thoroughly tried and tested approach to the sales presentation is the so-called "AIDA" approach. It's an acronym:

Attention

Interest

Desire

Action

1. Your first step is to get your listener's *attention.* This is most easily done by making the audience aware of a special opportunity, a need (that they have, but may not even know that they have), a problem.

   TIP: The way to get attention is to focus on what interests your audience. Make heavy use of the pronoun *you.* Focus your remarks on the audience, not yourself or your company.

2. Once you have your listeners' attention, develop, their *interest.* Discuss their need, their opportunity, their problem.

3. Next, create *desire.* This is where you present your product or service as the source of the opportunity, the fulfillment of the need, or the solution to the problem you have just discussed.

4. Finally, urge your listeners to take *action.* Always specify what this action is and how to take it. Make it simple for your listeners to do whatever you want them to do—for example, place an order and write out a check.

Even before you prepare the sale presentation, learn everything you can about your audience. Remember, they are your potential customers. Find out what they want. Tailor your presentation to address their needs, problems, and desires. Conversely, you must know your product or service thoroughly. You need to know what it does and how it performs. You need sufficient knowledge to enable you to present this merchandise as an opportunity or a solution.

It is very likely that you will, in the course of your presentation, encounter resistance. Audience/customer objections are usually best addressed by asking questions about the resistance. For example, if a member of the audience objects that your product is too expensive, ask him what he would be willing to pay. Once you have that figure, bridge the gap between it and your price by talking about value.

> **TIP:** Most objections can be overcome—or, at least, put in a minimizing perspective—by asking questions about them.

One of the most effective methods of overcoming resistance is to prevent it in the first place. This can be done by selling not only the product or service, but yourself. Use body language in a positive manner to communicate honesty and integrity:

1. Maintain eye contact. Choose one person in the audience to look at for a few minutes, then shift to another—but always address your remarks to some individual.

2. Avoid touching your mouth, brow, or face. Such gestures communicate a sense of shame or that you have something to hide.

3. Avoid crossing your arms—a gesture that suggests resistance.

In addition to body language, speak slowly and deliberately. This will combat the stereotype of the fast-talking salesman. Be certain to open your mouth and give each word full value.

Sales Killers

The following is a list of problems that all too often plague sales presentations. Avoid these pitfalls:

1. *A poorly structured, rambling presentation.* Usually, your best bet is to follow the AIDA structure.

2. *The temptation to play devil's advocate.* Overly anxious to block resistance and objections, some sales people present a catalog of reasons *not* to by their product or service. Then, of course, they follow up with arguments intended to knock down the self-raised objections. The trouble is, your audience may be more convinced by the *con* than by the *pro.* Don't give your listeners ammunition to use against you.

3. *Pleading, arguing, bullying.* In the end, the sale will be made because the audience member /customer feels that he has made up his *own* mind. Arm twisting builds up resentment and increases resistance.

4. *Lies and exaggeration.* Aside from the moral issues involved, lying or creating unrealistic expectations is simply bad business. You may trick a customer into making a single purchase, but then you will have lost that customer to future sales.

    TIP: Stop thinking about "making the sale." Instead, set *making a customer* as your goal. You want repeat sales, and you want to motivate positive word-of-mouth advertising.

5. *Evasion.* If you are confronted with a question to which you do not have an answer, reply that you do not know the answer off hand, but that you will look into the issue and try to find an answer.

6. *Half-baked demonstrations.* A real-time, real-life product demonstration is a terrific selling tool—provided that the product really does work. Before you embark on a demonstration, ensure that the product functions as advertised and that you are an expert in its use.

7.16. How to Handle . . .

7.16.1. Newspaper Interviews

The chief point to remember about "what they print in the newspapers" is that none of it is The Truth. If the reporter, the editor, and the publisher are ethical and well-intentioned, the most you can hope for is A Truth, a point of view. With rare exceptions, newspapers do not print full transcripts of an interview. Instead, the interviewee's remarks are worked into a story *created* (the newspaper likes to say "reported") by a writer, who listens selectively and who chooses the quotations to be included based (often) on his questions and (always) on his perceptions. It is critically important, therefore, that you:

1. Make yourself crystal clear.

2. Avoid ambiguity and half-hearted statements.

3. Avoid emphasis on side issues or minor points.

4. Avoid unwanted negativity.

Subtlety of thought and nuances of argument will be lost in a newspaper interview. There simply isn't the space for them. If you give a half-hour interview, expect only a sentence or two or three to actually appear in print.
The following guidelines should be helpful:

1. If at all possible, prepare in advance. Often, the timetable of breaking news does not allow for preparation. But if you know in advance that you will be interviewed, get ready. Make a list of key points that you want to make. Keep it to a half dozen items. Try to anticipate the questions you will be asked. Arm yourself with solid answers.

2. Listen to the interviewer. Don't concentrate on your own anxiety to the exclusion of what the interviewer is asking you.

   TIP: From time to time, show that you are listening intently by repeating the question. ("You want to know why I am in favor of X . . .") This is also a useful tactic for buying you the precious few seconds you may need to sort out your answer in your head.

3. Respond to questions as simply and directly as possible. Get to the point quickly.

Whether intentionally or not, an interviewer may try to put you on a highly uncomfortable spot. Watch out for the following interviewer tactics:

1. Tactic: *Poisoning the well.* The classic example of this is the question, "Tell me, when did you stop beating your wife?" An aggressive interviewer might well frame a question negatively, in order to put you on the defensive. "Does your organization discriminate against minorities?" may become "Why does your organization discriminate against minorities?"

   Response: Avoid an answer that repeats any part of the question. There is a danger that the repetition will get quoted. Instead, transform the question into something positive. "What can we do to fight discrimination? I will run down a list of some of the programs we have put in place."

2. Tactic: *The hypothetical question.* Questions beginning with "what if" are potentially dangerous, because they involve you in world of the interviewer's making. "What if the project fails?"

   Response: "Every indication is that the project will be a success. We have carefully and thoroughly researched all contingencies." The correct response is to reject the hypothesis. Bring the interviewer back to reality— *your* reality.

3. Tactic: *You are offered a straitjacket.* Interviewers sometimes seek to limit your options for an answer. "Who are the three most important men in your organization?"

   Response: Ignore the limits set by the interviewer. "At Acme, we have a team. Each man and woman on that team is vital to the success of our enterprise."

4. Tactic: *You are offered an either/or proposition.* Another means by which some interviewers attempt to limit the range of your response is to back you into an either/or response. "Will you support the amendment or not?"

   Response: An interview is not a court of law, and you are not bound to give one-word, either/or answers. Reject the either/or proposition by pointing out that the "issues involved are too complex for a simple yes or no." Then go on to explain your position.

5. Tactic: *You are asked to speak for another.* "Why does your associate take such an extreme position on X?"

    Response: "Well, that's one you will have to ask him. My own view on X is that . . ."

6. Tactic: *Tell me all about yourself.* Lazy interviewers sometimes throw the ball in your court—and insist that you keep it there—by asking impossibly broad questions.

    Response: The only adequate response strategy is to be prepared for such unfocused questions—then provide the focus yourself. "The most important points are . . ."

7. Tactic: *You are "asked" a declaration.* An interviewer should ask you questions—sentences that an end with a question mark. Some, however, use the interview to make statements they wish to print. "I don't see how your proposal can work, because of X, Y, and Z."

    Response: Turn the statement into a question—a question that you want to answer. "What you are asking is very important. How will we cope with X, Y, and Z?"

7.16.2. Radio Interviews

Just about everything that holds true for a print interview is also true for radio. With the popularity of talk radio, you may actually get an extended segment of time to discuss and develop your points. On the other hand, the "interview" may be limited to a few minutes, or you may be edited down to one or two "sound bites"—brief, fragmentary statements.

What can you expect on a radio interview? Generally—and this is the good news—you can expect a friendly host. It's not that the host wants to avoid controversy, but he doesn't want to create confusion and "dead air"— long silences. The host, therefore, is generally interested in facilitating the conversation and will probably not deliberately challenge you.

> **TIP:** While the host may be friendly and forthcoming, you can be certain that he will appreciate you more if you are a "self starter"—a guest who quickly finds the groove, gets on a roll, and keeps on going. The best way to make yourself into a self-starter is to come to the interview fully prepared. Arm yourself with anecdotes and astounding statistics. Make them brief and to the point.

Many radio interviews are held over the telephone. You never even get inside the studio. This has one disadvantage and a number of advantages.

The disadvantage is that you miss the body language cues your host may give you, and she will miss those you give her. This makes a genuine exchange a bit more difficult.

The advantages include:

1. The calming influence of familiar surroundings—your office, your home.

2. An opportunity to "fake" spontaneity. You might prepare miniature cue cards for yourself on 5 × 7 index cards. Use these with skill, and it will seem as if you have the answers at your fingertips.

PITFALL: Telephone interviews are subject to unwanted interruptions. If you are at work in your office, be certain to hang out a sign: LIVE RADIO INTERVIEW IN PROGRESS! PLEASE DO NOT DISTURB! If you can get a secretary to hold your calls, do so. If you are at home, be certain that your family understands that you must not be disturbed for the next half-hour or so. Also, if you have "call-waiting" service, be certain that you know how to disable it temporarily. In most areas, this is done simply by dialing *70 (less frequently #70).

7.16.3. Television Interviews

As with radio interviews, consult 7.16.1., "Newspaper Interviews," since most of the principles of give and take discussed there apply in the case of television as well. However, television also brings the dimension of physical appearance and body language into unmercifully sharp focus.

1. Most of the time you will be seen tightly framed, from the shoulders up. This tends to magnify any tics or gestural habits you might have. At the same time, many hand gestures will occur outside of the frame and will be lost on your audience.

PITFALL: Be aware of gestures near your face. A hand to the brow or close to the mouth suggests evasion. On television, the effect is amplified. Biting or licking your lips strongly suggests anxiety—another effect magnified by the small screen.

2. Dress appropriately for television. Avoid complex patterns, especially small checks and houndstooth patterns. These create a "strobe" effect on screen, seeming to vibrate. The effect is distracting. It is also best to avoid stark white shirts or blouses. These tend to glare on television. Favor light blue, light gray, even khaki. The same holds true for glittery jewelry. These may create a video "burn" on screen—another distraction. Also, pendulous jewelry tends to clatter and jingle annoyingly, especially in the presence of a microphone.

3. Be conversational in tone, not oratorical. Television is too intimate a medium for speech making.

4. Broadcast television is a more expensive medium than radio. Any TV exposure you get is likely to be comparatively brief. Deliver your message with an awareness that it will almost certainly be compressed into a sound bite or two.

7.16.4. Press Conferences

What is "news"? Ask a dozen people, and you will probably get a dozen answers. But, more than likely, most of those answers will focus on *events*— things that just "happen," and that news personnel respond to and report about. Of course, much news does occur just that way: reporters responding to events or even discovering events. But a great deal of news does not just "happen." An "event" is created and then "sold" to news organizations by profession media-relations staff. The event is not *literally* sold for money, but it is *sold* as a news "product" worth investing in by including in a commercial newspaper, magazine, radio program, or television news show. In most cases, the press conference is one of these manufactured events—a news product that requires selling.

> **Tip:** Anyone can call a press conference. This does not mean that anyone will be interested enough to attend it. Media practices and contact personnel vary from place to place. If you need to call a major press conference, you would do well to obtain the services of an experienced press-relations consultant. Be certain that the consultant is familiar with *local* media and has a full list of solid contacts.

The complex part of a press conference is setting it up. The conference itself is rather simple:

1. You begin with a statement. This is your account of the "event" that is the subject of the press conference. It also presents your stand on the relevant issues. The statement should be brief—perhaps five or ten minutes, in most cases.

   TIP: The most you can hope for in terms of media reportage of your press conference is a summary, a quotation or two, and, on television and radio, a sound bite of perhaps ten seconds. For that reason, make your statement crystal clear and lace it with sentences that are self- contained and that cry out to be quoted. Such sentences are often called "focus statements." Using them will help keep your ideas from being distorted when they are quoted out of context. And they *will* be quoted out of context.

2. The second part of the press conference is the question-and-answer period. Whereas you control the statement portion of the press conference, you have only limited control over the question-and-answer portion. You can set certain ground rules, including, for example, restricting questions to such-and-such a topic. Just be aware that too many rules and restrictions will generate either suspicion, resentment, or indifference on the part of the press.

The guidelines that apply to interviews (see 7.16.1 through 7.16.3) apply equally to presenting yourself effectively at a press conference. In addition, observe the following:

1. While listening to a question, avoid reacting. Keep a—pleasant—poker face. Just as experienced card players learn not to telegraph their hand through frowns, grimaces, nods, or smiles, you should remain relatively impassive until you actually give the answer to the question.

2. Begin your response by making unmistakable eye contact with the questioner. However, as you develop your response, you may want to look around the room, making eye contact with others as well.

3. Keep answers as brief and as simple as the subject allows. Avoid indirection and side issues. Get to the point quickly.

4. Make an effort to take questions from all parts of the room.

5. Don't editorialize on the questions: "Great question!" Just answer.

6. It is generally a good practice for you to repeat the question by way of beginning your response. This is especially important if the question will lead to a strong, positive response.

In section 7.16.1 I included a list of the potential problems and hazards of a newspaper interview. Those apply here as well, with the following additions:

1. *A questioner will try to take over your forum.* Instead of asking a question, he'll make a long statement that is virtually a miniature speech. Remember, this is *your* press conference. You have the right and obligation to suppress the attempted usurpation. Maintaining a civil and polite tone, ask the questioner to as his *question.* "We have a very limited amount of time, Sir. So, I'm going to interrupt you and ask you to ask your question, please."

2. *A questioner may ask you something that you have already amply covered in your opening statement.* When this happens, the safest course is to assume that your message did not get through. Maybe the questioner is none too bright—but, then again, maybe you were none too clear. Answer the question.

3. *A questioner may repeat a question you have already answered.* In this case, you must assume that the questioner simply was not listening. Reply: "That question has already been asked and answered, and I've said all that I can on the subject." Then just move on.

   TIP: If the repeat question can be answered in a word or two, don't be stubborn, Just repeat the answer.

4. *A questioner may ask an off-the-wall question—one that is meaningless and irrelevant.* This can be a tough situation. Be aware that your audience is probably on your side: They don't want to hear a stupid answer to a stupid question any more than you want to give one. However, you will lose audience sympathy if you yield to the temptation to step on the errant questioner. If you can come up with a quick and brief answer, do so. Then move on. If not, reply with "I can't even begin to take that one on" or something in a similar vein. If the problem is that the question is irrelevant, you might reply, "That is not what we are all here to discuss." (Note the plural pronoun—*we.* Include the audience on your side.)

5. *A questioner may launch a personal attack.* Although few professional journalists will indulge themselves in this way, it may happen. Stay calm. As
   in any argument, the principal task is to turn away from a focus on personality and refocus the discourse on the issues. Try to ignore the attack
   by highlighting the issues involved.

6. *No one may ask you what you want to be asked.* The best insurance against
   this is to include all the essential and vital information in your opening
   statement. If, however, you need to emphasize something that remains
   unaddressed as the press conference winds up, go ahead and ask *yourself*
   the question:"I'm surprised that none of you has challenged me on . . ."

> **TIP:** You control when the press conference ends. It is wise to announce
> a time limit at the outset. However, beware of announcing, "This will be
> the last question." What if that "last question" then turns out to be nega-
> tive, hostile, or simply a dud? Then you are left with a sour note at the end
> of your concerto. Instead of using the phrase "this will be the last ques-
> tion," signal the end of the press conference by allowing yourself more
> leeway:"We have only a few moments left. Are there more questions?"

The Ultimate Disaster

Let's get to the core of the nightmare. You are asked a question. And—
and: You draw a blank. Stumped.

What do you do?

Although at the moment it may seem that the sun, moon, and stars are
falling on you, try not to panic. Your best response is the simplest:"I really do
not have an answer to that question at this time. I will investigate the matter,
and I'll comment on it at a later time, after I've studied the problem." Then
move on.

7.16.5. Talking to Kids

Business and community leaders are occasionally asked to speak to children's
groups. Depending on your personality and interests, such a request may be
the source of delight or of abject horror. The following rules of thumb will help
guide you through the task:

1. Most important of all: Never make a speech to children. Instead, put on
   a show-and-tell. Now, in truth, most effective speeches delivered to

adult audiences are really show-and-tell sessions, filled not with empty, abstract adjectives and adverbs, but with living, breathing nouns and verbs that paint a picture of a real, active, intense world. An effective speech appeals to the senses as well as to the mind. It is stocked with words that can be touched, felt, heard, seen, and smelled. With children, just take this approach to the next step. Don't just use words to describe sights, smells, and sounds. Bring those sights, smells, and sounds with you—or, at least, as many of them as you can. Show and tell. Bring props. Bring the tools of your trade—a stethoscope, a laptop computer, whatever.

TIP: You are an insurance broker. You topic is fire prevention. Bring a smoke detector and demonstrate it. Bring a fire extinguisher and demonstrate it. Bring a charred and melted toy—to show what happens if you don't take the steps necessary to prevent fires.

2. Choose a topic that lends itself to a show-and-tell approach. Avoid abstraction. If you cannot find an array of props to suit your chosen topic, think seriously about choosing a different topic.

3. Don't talk down to kids. Don't tell them that "Such-and-such may be difficult for you to understand." Don't try to talk kid talk, either. You are an adult. The children understand that you are an adult. They understand, accept, and appreciate that adults speak differently form children.

4. Involve your audience as much as possible. If you are a parent, you have doubtless seen your child or children sit blankly in front of a television for hours. It is a frightening sight. Yet the passive reception of information is difficult for most children—at least when a live speaker is present. They want to be involved. Ask questions—not to test the kids' knowledge, but to move *your* talk along.

5. The trouble with involvement is that kids can rapidly get *too* involved. If the scene gets rowdy, do not try to speak above the din. Instead, stop speaking. Often, your sudden silence will be enough to quiet your audience. If this tactic fails, tell the children that it is now your turn to talk and that they will be given *their* turn in just a few minutes.

TIP: Experienced teachers learn to speak softly. Children—or any audience, for that matter—will usually quiet down in order to hear the soft-spoken information.

6. When you speak to kids, try to avoid speaking from a desk or lectern. Arrange your listeners in a circle, if possible. You should position yourself as part of the circumference of the circle rather than the center of it. If you are speaking in classroom that does not allow for the circular arrangement, try walking around the room as you speak, circulating among the rows of desks.

7. Children fidget. Get used to it. When they start fidgeting a lot, you might consider taking this as a signal to wrap up your talk.

APPENDICES

SOURCES AND RESOURCES

A. THE BUSINESS COMMUNICATOR'S BOOKSHELF:
A BASIC SELECTION

This appendix and those that follow list sources and resources for the business communicator. We begin with the most basic items:

Any standard hardcover dictionary. Webster's is the old standby. Also excellent is the *American Heritage College Dictionary,* now in its third edition (Houghton-Mifflin, 1993).

Most people find a good thesaurus handy as an aid to finding just the right word for a given situation. The name Roget is to the thesaurus what Webster is to the dictionary:

Roget's Thesaurus (expanded edition, Houghton Mifflin, 1988).

In addition, you should have a reliable grammar and usage guide. Business users will find

Lillian Davis and Bessie M. Miller's *Complete Secretary's Guide* (5th ed., Prentice-Hall, 1986)

particularly valuable. You should also have a copy of the best concise authority on grammar and the style,

William Strunk and E.B. White's *The Elements of Style* (Macmillan, 1979).

If you want to pursue matters of style and usage more thoroughly, get a copy of

The Chicago Manual of Style: The Essential Guide for Authors, Editors, and Publishers (14th ed., University of Chicago Press, 1993),

which is considered the final arbiter on questions of usage and form.
A concise one-volume encyclopedia is also a good investment:

The Columbia Encyclopedia (5th revised ed., Columbia University Press, 1993).

An inexpensive paperback almanac or "fact book" is a valuable quick source of current statistics and general facts of current interest:

World Almanac and Book of Facts (World Almanac, published annually)

Information Please Almanac (Houghton Mifflin, published annually).

For all-round quick reference on a dazzling array of common topics, consult

The New York Public Library Desk Reference (Webster's New World, 1989).

This volume is particularly valuable for the many resources it lists under "Additional Sources of Information."

> **TIP:** Many of the traditional general reference books are now available on personal computer and Macintosh diskette format as well as on CD-ROM. If you prefer electronic formats, check out the software titles at your local retailer.

B. USING THE INTERNET AND OTHER ON-LINE COMPUTER DATABASES

The Internet is without question one of the hot-button topics of the close of the twentieth century. Indeed, it is a dazzling resource: A network of some 32,400 computer networks in 135 countries, it potentially links together more than 25 million computers in what information specialists tout as an electronic "community." The Internet gives you access to a huge amount of information—maybe *too* much, or, at least, an overwhelming volume of data that is not always easy to find. Better approach the Internet by accepting two basic facts:

1. It is *not* a company, an institution, an organization, or a system. It is a network of computers linked together with virtually no supervision.

2. The Internet is drawn by two powerful—and opposing—forces: A passion to gather, organize, and make accessible everything known to humankind versus a passion to maintain a state of anarchy.

Before you can even get connected to the Internet, let alone actually find something of use on it, you must own—and know how to use—a personal computer and a modem. Information on these can be found in:

Sherry Kinkoph, *The Complete Idiot's Guide to Modems and Online Services* (Macmillan/Alpha, 1994).

For those who want a more comprehensive guide to communications and the personal computer, look for the latest edition of:

John Dvorak and Nick Anis's *Dvorak's Guide to PC Telecommunications* (McGraw-Hill, frequent revisions).

The Dvorak volume includes an extensive discussion of the Internet and a listing of other online services. There are many excellent references devoted specifically to the Internet, including

Harley Hahn and Rick Stout's *The Internet Complete Reference* (Osborne-McGraw-Hill, 1994).

Hahn and Stout have also published

The Internet Yellow Pages (2nd ed., Osborne McGraw-Hill, 1995).

With the wealth of published material available on the Internet, this is not the place to launch into an extended discussion of the "information superhighway." However, it is helpful to be aware of the scope of Internet services available to the business communicator. These include:

1. Wide World Web (WWW): This is the most "mainstream" feature of the Internet. Whereas many other aspects of the Internet often require the use of mystifying commands from the world of UNIX computers (rather than the more familiar DOS/Windows and Mac operating systems), the Wide World Web transforms your computer screen into a highly graphic electronic magazine page. WWW software (such as SPRY's MOSAIC program) offers a variety of tools—called "web browsers"—for searching specific WWW sites. Type in a keyword or phrase, and the software will do its best to generate a list relevant online "sites" for you to explore. The Web also features hypertext links. Each WWW site has a "homepage," a kind of interactive table of contents for that site. Certain words and phrases are highlighted. Click on these with your mouse, and you will be transported to a related site.

2. E-mail: Many regard this as the most important feature of the Internet. It enables you to communicate electronically with any individual who has access to the Internet. You need two things: the electronic address of your correspondent and your own e-mail address.

   TIP: Many of the commercial online services (Compuserve™, America Online™, Prodigy™, Microsoft Network™, etc.) provide you with an e-mail address. Unless your place of business supplies you with an e-mail address, this is the simplest way to acquire an electronic mailbox.

3. Newsgroups: Some Internet users say that the newsgroups are the heart of the Net. Newsgroups are sites offering "articles" on specific subjects. Despite the name "newsgroups," the articles electronically "posted" are not really news, but, rather, notes and comments from people interested in the particular topic of the newsgroup. Any of the Internet "Yellow Pages" guides lists a quantity of newsgroups. However, the groups change frequently. You can FTP to **ftp.uu.net** and follow the path: **/usenet/news.answers/alt-hierarchies/** and also **/usenet/news.answers/active-newsgroups/** for the latest listings.

   TIP: But what is "FTP"? Read #4.

4. FTP stands for "file-transfer protocol," and it is an Internet *service* rather than *site.* FTP is a means of downloading (transferring) files from the Internet to your computer. Many sites allow you to access files via "anonymous FTP." No password is required; you just type in the user id "anonymous." Consult one of the "Yellow Pages" books for the electronic addresses of many important FTP-accessible sites. Some commercial online services (for example, Compuserve) provide an FTP "gateway" to the Internet, which makes it particularly easy to jump to any FTP-accessible site.

5. Mailing lists: There is no mystery about this term. It is just what the name implies. If you add your name to one of these lists, messages relevant to the interest area of the list will appear in your electronic mailbox—automatically. Mailing lists are a wonderful way to "get into the loop" and stay there. The trick is knowing which lists are relevant to the topics that concern you. Fortunately, two handy *lists of mailing lists* are available: The SRI List can be had by sending an e- mail request to **mail-server@sri.com.** Publicly Accessible Mailing Lists (PAML) is posted on the Net at **news.lists** and at **news.answers.**

6. Telnet: Some Internet sites are accessible directly through the Telnet program. How do you know which ones? The electronic addresses that are accessible in this way are usually identified by an instruction telling you to "telnet to" such-and-such a site.

7. Gophers: Computers are equipped with mice. Faulty software is plagued by bugs. Wicked "hackers" attempt to infect programs with viruses. The Internet has gophers. A "gopher" is, of course, a furry little animal that burrows. Applied to a human being, "gopher" (go-fer) is a menial type who "goes for" things—coffee, a bagel, whatever. The Internet gophers are a little of both. Since many Internet sites confront the cyber explorer with a bewildering array of files cryptically labeled, it is often more useful to access a Gopher site, type in a keyword or keywords describing what you are after, and let the little critter find what he/she can.

> TIP: While the colorful Wide World Web is the easiest Internet feature to use, be aware that WWW sites represent only a fraction of what is available on the Internet. Moreover, their intensive use of graphics slows down even very fast computers. Often, seeking information through the Web involves a lot of thumb twiddling. If you have an older, slower computer, much of the world can pass you by before the information you want appears on your screen.

Getting Connected

Before you can get to any of these Internet goodies, you need to "get connected." Many businesses are already connected. If yours isn't, the easiest way to gain access to the Internet these days is through one of the major commercial online services, most of which provide no-hassle gateways into the Internet.

> TIP: Another simple on-ramp is via "web browser" software such as that included with Daniel A. Tauber and Brenda Kienan's *Mosaic Access to the Internet* (Sybex, 1995). Currently, the OS/2 Warp operating system from IBM and the Windows 95 operating systems for PCs include software to get you connected. The same is true for a number of the major communication software packages (such as ProComm and WinComm) now on the market. Ask your software retailer.

Alternatives to the Internet

Although much popular attention has been focused of late on the Internet, it is not the only source of useful information for the business communicator. At latest count, there are more than 5,000 electronic databases available on more than 800 systems *outside* of the Internet. Some of these sources are free of charge, but many do involve a subscription premium. The major business-related databases are found on such services as:

Dialog

Nexis

Dow Jones News/Retrieval

Newsnet

> TIP: If online information is important to you, you may want to consider hiring an information broker. These are professional consultants who will find and deliver whatever information you specify. They can save you a lot of time you might otherwise waste floundering in a sea of data. For a directory of reputable information brokers (the best hold Master of Library Science—MLS—degrees or the equivalent), see *The Burwell Directory of Information Brokers* (Houston: Burwell Enterprises, updated frequently), which may be available in your local library or by calling 713-537-8344.

C. WHERE TO FIND ASSOCIATIONS AND ORGANIZATIONS

By far the most useful source of information on associations and organizations is

Encyclopedia of Associations (Gale Research, published annually).

You can purchase the encyclopedia or you can consult it at almost any public library. In addition to the *Encyclopedia,* a select list of highly useful addresses will be found in:

The New York Public Library Desk Reference (Webster's New World, 1989).

D. WHERE TO FIND GENERAL FACTS, FIGURES, AND STATISTICS

There is no substitute for your own research into specific topics. Usually, the most up-to-date information is available in the journals and newsletters that cover your specific field. In addition to these specific sources, consult the general works listed in section A of this appendix, as well as the following:

Congressional Quarterly Almanac (Congressional Quarterly, published annually).

Facts on File World News Digest with Index (Facts on File, updated weekly).

Frederick Martin, *Statesman's Year-Book: Statistical and Historical Annual of the States of the World for the Year* (St. Martin's Press, published annually).

Reader's Digest Almanac (Reader's Digest, published annually).

The famous Guinness series is a stimulating source of surprising facts and figures. Most of the series, which includes such fields as money and sports, in addition to general world records, is available from Facts on File, Inc.

Finally, your local public library has an amazing resource called *The Reader's Guide to Periodical Literature.* This monumental series, continuously updated, allows you to look up a subject (say "Automobile safety") and find the location of recent magazine articles devoted to it. Also consult *The New York Times Index,* updated quarterly, for newspaper articles on particular subjects.

E. Where to Find Government Information

The government publishes a staggering wealth of information. If you are looking for general statistics, consult:

U.S. Bureau of the Census, *County and City Data Book* (Government Printing Office, series).

U.S. Bureau of the Census, *State and Metropolitan Area Data Book* (Government Printing Office, series).

U.S. Bureau of the Census, *Statistical Abstract of the United States* (Government Printing Office, series).

An indispensable guide to and through the federal bureaucracy is

United States Government Manual (Federal Register, published annually).

It includes contact persons, addresses, telephone, numbers, and sources of additional information.

In addition to printed resources, the federal government maintains an extensive online presence. Your best first stop via the Internet is to FTP to **ftp. fedworld.gov** or take the Web to **http://www.fedworld.gov.** You don't need access to the Internet to dial up the FedWorld BBS (electronic Bulletin Board System) directly at 703-321-8020. Set your communications software to 9600 bps, 8/N/1.

F. Where to Find Media Outlets

The standard media directories include:

Bacon's Publicity Checkers (Bacon's, published annually).

Broadcasting/Cablecasting Yearbook (Broadcasting Publications, Inc./A Times-Mirror Company, published annually).

Canadian Advertising Rates and Data (Maclean Hunter, published annually with intermediate updates).

Standard Rate and Data Service (Standard Rate and Data Service, published annually with intermediate updates).

A good primer on using the media is

Dell Dennison and Linda Tobey's *The Advertising Handbook: Make a Big Impact with a Small Business Budget* (Self-Counsel Press, 1991).

G. Where to Find Quotations

The standard book in this field is

John Bartlett's *Bartlett's Familiar Quotations* (Little, Brown, 1980),

but many more specialized quotation references are also useful:

A. J. Augarde, ed., *The Oxford Dictionary of Modern Quotations* (Oxford University press, 1991).

Otto Bettmann, ed., *The Delights of Reading* (Godine, 1987).

Wesley D. Camp, ed., *What a Piece of Work Is Man!* (Prentice-Hall, 1990); this one focuses on *unfamiliar* quotations that are not found in the more standard works.

James Charlton, ed., *The Executive's Quotation Book* (St. Martin's Press, 1983).

Mike Edelhart and James Tinen, eds., *America the Quotable* (Facts on File, 1983).

Lewis Eigen and Jonathan Siegel, eds., *The Manager's Book of Quotations* (AMACOM, 1989).

Elizabeth Frost, ed., *The Bully Pulpit* (Facts on File, 1988); this is a collection of presidential quotations.

C. R. S. Marsden, ed., *Dictionary of Outrageous Quotations* (Salem House, 1988).

H. L. Mencken, ed. *A New Dictionary of Quotations* (Knopf, 1987); this is a reissue of a work by one of the nation's most celebrated curmudgeons.

Elaine Partnow, ed., *The Quotable Woman* (Facts on File, 1985).

Angela Patington, *Oxford Dictionary of Quotations* (Oxford University Press, 1992).

William Safire and Leonard Safire, eds., *Words of Wisdom* (Simon and Schuster, 1990).

James B. Simpson and Daniel J. Boorstin, eds. *Simpson's Contemporary Quotations* (Houghton Mifflin, 1988).

Joseph Telushkin, ed., *Uncommon Sense* (Shapolsky Publishers, 1987); a book of religious and philosophical quotations.

Michael C. Thomsett, *A Treasury of Business Quotations* (Ballantine, 1990).

H. How-To Books: Desktop Publishing

The techniques of desktop publishing can bring professional-looking publications within reach of almost anyone with a personal computer, Mac, or Mac clone. The computer won't do *all* the work, however. A good design sense is essential, and these books will help:

Joe Grossman with David Doty, *Newsletters from the Desktop* (2nd ed., Ventana, 1992).

Anne Fischer Lent, *The Ultimate Desktop Publishing Starter Kit* (Addison-Wesley, 1995).

Roger C. Parker, *Looking Good in Print* (3rd ed., Ventana, 1993).

I. How-To Books: Forms and Legal Documents

With the personal computer, forms have never been easier to design and customize. A wide range of software packages are available, most notably *Formtool* from IMSI and *PerForm for Windows* from Delrina. Consult your software retailer to find the package that's right for your needs. You can also find a wealth of forms—both ready-to-use and models for you to modify—in printed format. In addition to the large section on form in this book, you might want to check out:

J. W. Dicks, *The Small Business Legal Kit* (Adams, 1995).

Ted Nicholas, *The Business Agreements Kit* (Upstart, 1995).

Ted Nicholas, *The Corporate Forms Kit* (Upstart, 1995).

J. HOW-TO BOOKS: LETTERS

A wide range of business letter books is available. Some of the most useful include:

L. E. Frailey, *Handbook of Business Letters* (3rd ed., Prentice-Hall, 1989).

Karen Gilleland and Margaret Coel, *450 Best Sales Letters for Every Selling Situation* (Prentice-Hall, 1991).

Jack Griffin, *The New Handbook of Business Letters* (Prentice-Hall, 1993).

Rosalie Maggio, *How to Say It: Choice Words, Phrases, Sentences, and Paragraphs for Every Situation* (Prentice-Hall, 1990).

Harold E. Meyer, *Lifetime Encyclopedia of Letters* (Prentice-Hall, 1983).

Harold E. Meyer and Scott A. Sievert, *Complete Credit and Collection Model Letter Book* (Prentice-Hall, 1990).

Nate Rosenblatt, *Sales LetterWorks* (Round Lake, 1990).

Linda Braxton Sturgeon and Anne Russell Haggler, *Personal Letters That Mean Business* (Prentice-Hall, 1991).

Ron Tapper, *The Only 250 Letters and Memos Managers Will Ever Need* (Wiley, 1990).

K. How-To Books: Speech Writing

Books that are especially relevant to the business communicator include:

Jeff Scott Cook, *The Elements of Speech Writing and Public Speaking* (Collier, 1989).

Joan Detz, *How to Write and Give a Speech* (St. Martin's, 1984).

Joan Detz, *Can You Say a Few Words?* (St. Martin's, 1991).

Henry Ehrlich, *Writing Effective Speeches* (Paragon House, 1992).

Leon Fletcher, *How to Design and Deliver a Speech* (4th ed., HarperCollins, 1990).

Jack Griffin, *How to Say It Best: Choice Words, Phrases, and Model Speeches for Every Occasion* (Prentice-Hall, 1994).

Ronn Hoff, *"I Can See You Naked": A Fearless Guide to Making Great Presentations* (Andrews and McMeel, 1988).

James C. Humes, *Standing Ovation: How to Be an Effective Speaker and Communicator* (Harper & Row, 1988).

Jerry Tarver, *The Corporate Speech Writer's Handbook: A Guide for Professionals in Business, Agencies, and the Public Sector* (Greenwood, 1987).

You may also find useful the following collection of contemporary business speeches:

Jack Griffin and Alice Marks, eds., *The Business Speaker's Almanac* (Prentice-Hall, 1994).